1991

John Dewey

The Later Works, 1925–1953

Volume 13: 1938–1939

EDITED BY JO ANN BOYDSTON

TEXTUAL EDITOR, BARBARA LEVINE

With an Introduction by Steven M. Cahn

Southern Illinois University Press

Carbondale and Edwardsville

The text of this reprinting is a photo-offset reproduction of the original cloth
edition that contains the full apparatus for the volume awarded the seal of the
Committee on Scholarly Editions of the Modern Language Association.
Editorial expenses were met in part by a grant from the Editions Program of the
National Endowment for the Humanities, an independent Federal agency.

The paperbound edition has been made possible by a special subvention from
the John Dewey Foundation.

The Library of Congress catalogued the first printing of this work (in cloth) as
follows:

Dewey, John, 1859–1952.
  The later works, 1925–1953.

  Vol. 13 has introd. by Steven M. Cahn.
  Continues The middle works, 1899–1924.
  Includes bibliographies and indexes.

  CONTENTS: v. 1. 1925—[etc.]—v. 13. 1938–1939.
  1. Philosophy—Collected works. I. Boydston, Jo Ann, 1924–. II. Title.
B945.D41 1981   191   80-27285
ISBN 0-8093-1425-8 (V. 13)

ISBN 0-8093-1679-X (paperback)

Contents

Introduction
By Steven M. Cahn

In 1939 John Dewey reached his eightieth birthday, an anniversary that occasioned tributes in newspapers and periodicals throughout the country. The American Philosophical Association named Dewey its honorary president and requested that he retain this title for the duration of his life. Also timed to coincide with the celebration was the publication of the initial volume of Paul Arthur Schilpp's The Library of Living Philosophers. This book provided a critical analysis and evaluation of Dewey's philosophy by such contemporaries as Bertrand Russell, George Santayana, Hans Reichenbach, and Alfred North Whitehead. Schilpp's choice of Dewey as the first honoree is clearly justified by one of Whitehead's remarks in the volume: "We are living in the midst of the period subject to Dewey's influence."[1] Whitehead went on to stress the significance of Dewey's philosophical thought for the development of American civilization, and he classed Dewey with philosophers whom he viewed as having performed an analogous role in their own societies— Augustine, Aquinas, Descartes, and Locke.

Most remarkably, while his friends and admirers were planning ways of honoring him for a lifetime of achievements, Dewey not only continued to publish articles at an extraordinary rate but also produced three longer works that are among his finest writings: Theory of Valuation, Experience and Education, and Freedom and Culture. Such an accomplishment at so advanced an age is, I believe, unparalleled in the history of philosophy.

The shorter pieces collected in this volume exhibit Dewey's wide-ranging philosophical interests, including metaphysics, epistemology and philosophy of science, ethics, social and politi-

1. The Philosophy of John Dewey, Library of Living Philosophers, ed. Paul Arthur Schlipp (New York: Tudor Publishing Co., 1951), p. 477.

cal philosophy, aesthetics, and philosophy of education. In our own day, when many admired philosophers rarely venture outside their chosen subspecialties, it is well to remember that most members of the philosophical pantheon assumed that their systems of thought had explanatory power in all fields of philosophical inquiry, and they did not hesitate to test the adequacy of their principal ideas by applying them in one field after another. Dewey followed this tradition and thereby made significant contributions to virtually every area of philosophy.

He consistently maintained that the most reliable method of reaching the truth about any subject matter is the pattern of inquiry exemplified in science: the evaluation of hypotheses by drawing their implications and subjecting them to empirical testing under controlled conditions. In short, Dewey stressed that ideas are to be judged not by their origins but by their consequences.

The most common objection to his view comes from those who grant the scientific method's effectiveness in acquiring factual knowledge but question its usefulness in determining matters of value. Dewey explicitly replied to this familiar challenge in his *Theory of Valuation,* a monograph he contributed to the *Foundations of the Unity of Science,* a two-volume work edited by Otto Neurath, the Austrian philosopher who was a leading member of the Vienna Circle, that group of logical positivists centered in Vienna University during the 1920s and 1930s.

As is evident from the monograph, Dewey had his differences with the logical positivists, but he liked Neurath personally and was persuaded by him to contribute to the project. The charming story of how Neurath succeeded in enlisting Dewey's participation was told by Ernest Nagel:

> I accompanied Neurath and Sidney Hook when they called on Dewey at his home; and Neurath was having obvious difficulty in obtaining Dewey's participation in the *Encyclopedia* venture. Dewey had one objection—there may have been others, but this is the only one I recall—to Neurath's invitation. The objection was that since the Logical Positivists subscribed to the belief in atomic facts or atomic propositions, and since Dewey did not think there are such things, he could not readily contribute to the *Encyclopedia.*

Now at that time Neurath spoke only broken English, and his attempts at explaining his version of Logical Positivism were not very successful. Those of us who knew Neurath will remember his elephantine sort of physique. When he realized that his efforts at explanation were getting him nowhere, he got up, raised his right hand as if he were taking an oath in a court of law (thereby almost filling Dewey's living room), and solemnly declared, "I *swear* we don't believe in atomic propositions." This pronouncement won the day for Neurath. Dewey agreed to write the monograph, and ended by saying, "Well, we ought to celebrate," and brought out the liquor and mixed a drink.[2]

Thus did Dewey come to write *Theory of Valuation.*

The essence of his view about the nature of ethical judgments is that they are neither mere expressions of emotion nor revelations of a transcendent order but rather statements of human ideals, emerging from and testable in experience. What is desired, therefore, may not prove desirable, once consideration is given both to the means needed to achieve the ends and the consequences of the ends themselves.

Dewey's stress on the continuity of means and ends has led some critics to suppose that he denied the concept of an end-in-itself. Brand Blanshard, for example, asked, "What is it that has led Dewey to this strange theory that we can attach no value to ends in themselves?"[3] Dewey, however, proposed no such theory. As he wrote in *Democracy and Education:* "All that we can be sure of educationally is that science should be taught so as to be an end in itself in the lives of students—something worthwhile on account of its own unique intrinsic contribution to the experience of life."[4] And he continued on to make the general point: "Some goods are not good *for* anything; they are just goods. Any other notion leads to an absurdity. For we cannot stop asking the question about an instrumental good, one whose value

2. *Dialogue on John Dewey,* ed. Corliss Lamont (New York: Horizon Press, 1959), pp. 11–12.
3. Blanshard, *Reason and Goodness* (London: George Allen and Unwin, 1961), p. 180.
4. Dewey, *Democracy and Education* (New York: Macmillan Co., 1916), p. 282 [*The Middle Works of John Dewey, 1899–1924,* ed. Jo Ann Boydston (Carbondale and Edwardsville: Southern Illinois University Press, 1980), 9:249].

lies in its being good *for* something, unless there is at some point something intrinsically good, good for itself."[5]

Dewey stressed, however, that intelligent choices need to be made among goods and that doing so depends on empirical considerations. "For example, an end suggests itself. But, when things are weighed as means toward that end, it is found that it will take too much time or too great an expenditure of energy to achieve it, or that, if it were attained, it would bring with it certain accompanying inconveniences and the promise of future troubles. It is then appraised and rejected as a 'bad' end."[6] In this way the experimental method can inform valuation.

Just as Dewey's ethical theory steered between the Scylla and Charybdis of emotivism and intuitionism, so his educational theory also avoided two hazardous alternatives. Already in 1902 in *The Child and the Curriculum*, Dewey had identified the weaknesses in what he then termed "old education" and "new education."

Proponents of the former view considered the curriculum to be the keystone of the educational process. As Dewey stated their position, "Subject-matter furnishes the end, and it determines method. The child is simply the immature being who is to be matured; he is the superficial being who is to be deepened; his is narrow experience which is to be widened. It is his to receive, to accept. His part is fulfilled when he is ductile and docile."[7] The emphasis here is on order and discipline; the teacher is supposed to command, the student to obey.

On the other hand proponents of "new education" disregarded the curriculum and focused attention exclusively on the child. Dewey characterized their outlook as follows: "Literally, we must take our stand with the child and our departure from him. It is he and not the subject-matter which determines both quality and quantity of learning. . . . The source of whatever is dead, mechanical, and formal in schools is found precisely in the subordination of the life and experience of the child to the curricu-

5. Ibid., p. 283 [*Middle Works* 9 : 250].
6. Dewey, *Theory of Valuation* (Chicago: University of Chicago Press, 1939), p. 24 [*The Later Works of John Dewey, 1925–1953*, ed. Jo Ann Boydston (Carbondale and Edwardsville: Southern Illinois University Press, 1988), 13 : 212].
7. Dewey, *The Child and the Curriculum* (Chicago: University of Chicago Press, 1902), p. 8 [*Middle Works* 2 : 276].

lum."[8] The emphasis here is on spontaneity and freedom. And if the student is to display initiative, the teacher must not interfere in the learning process.

In short, "old education" subordinated the child to the curriculum; "new education" subordinated the curriculum to the child. "Old education" required the teacher to be active and the student to be passive. "New education" required the student to be active and the teacher to be passive.

Perhaps the most pervasive misunderstanding in twentieth-century educational thought is the supposition that Dewey advocated "new education." In fact, he was as opposed to "new education" as to "old education." Here is Dewey commenting on "new education":

> The child is expected to "develop" this or that fact or truth out of his own mind. He is told to think things out, or work things out for himself, without being supplied any of the environing conditions which are requisite to start and guide thought. Nothing can be developed from nothing; nothing but the crude can be developed out of the crude—and this is what surely happens when we throw the child back upon his achieved self as a finality, and invite him to spin new truths of nature or of conduct out of that.[9]

But what precisely did Dewey propose in place of both "old education" and "new education"? In his view the teacher's responsibility is to direct the learning process so that the child's immature powers find fulfillment in that systematized outcome of human inquiry we call "the curriculum." The aim of instruction is to discover a path from the child's own experience to the maturity of human experience reflected in art, science, and industry. A teacher who disregards the child and focuses exclusively on the curriculum is like a tour guide who reaches the proper destination but has left the party far behind. A teacher who disregards the curriculum and focuses exclusively on the child is akin to the guide who remains with the party but does not lead them anywhere. Dewey insisted that we cannot afford to neglect either the child or the curriculum; sacrificing one for the other amounts to educational failure.

8. Ibid., p. 9 [*Middle Works* 2:276–77].
9. Ibid., p. 18 [*Middle Works* 2:282].

Proponents of "old education" and "new education" continued their battle throughout the early decades of the twentieth century. All that changed were the labels by which their respective positions were known. In 1938, when Dewey published *Experience and Education*, a series of lectures delivered to the honorary society Kappa Delta Pi, he no longer referred to "old education" and "new education" but instead spoke of "traditional education" and "progressive education."

The latter term requires special comment, since Dewey is himself so often identified as the leading proponent of progressive education. In fact, however, "progressive education" was a term he rarely used. He preferred to talk of education for a "progressive society," by which he simply meant a society that progresses, that improves from generation to generation. Dewey viewed progressive education as nothing more or less than an education that imbues individuals with intelligence, the power of scientific method, and thus enables their society to better itself, to progress.

The term "progressive education" became a shibboleth used by those who in Dewey's name argued for a position identical with that previously called "new education," a position, as we have seen, Dewey opposed. In *Experience and Education* Dewey explicitly states his opposition to progressive education, misunderstood as the rejection of pedagogical authority and the glorification of student caprice. It cannot be overemphasized that Dewey never fell into the trap of supposing that to recognize the dignity of each student requires the teacher to abandon the role of leader of group activities. Indeed, Dewey quoted with admiration Ralph Waldo Emerson's dictum: "Respect the child, respect him to the end, but also respect yourself." [10]

Dewey made clear that the teacher is properly held responsible for what is going on in the classroom, and with responsibility goes authority. To recognize such authority, however, is not to suggest that the teacher should act in an authoritarian manner, exercising complete control over the will of the students. The appropriate relationship is that of guide, not god. *Experience and Education* analyzes and illustrates the appropriate scope and limits of this guiding role.

While educational controversies of the late 1930s were remark-

---

10. *Democracy and Education*, p. 62 [*Middle Works* 9:57].

ably similar to disputes about schooling that had occurred three decades before, the social, political, and economic situation in the United States on the eve of World War II was hardly like that of the early 1900s and was soon to be subject to unprecedented changes occurring at an ever-accelerating rate. It is remarkable, therefore, that when Dewey at the age of eighty published *Freedom and Culture,* a study of the elements of culture that contribute to the maintenance of political freedom, he did not merely propose old solutions to new problems but provided a prophetic analysis of conditions, both internal and external, that in the years to come would seriously threaten the welfare of our democracy.

He emphasized, for instance, that the racial and religious prejudice prevalent in the United States during the 1930s corroded decency and undermined trust in human nature. At a time when discrimination against Catholics, Jews, and Blacks was the rule rather than the exception, Dewey recognized the evil inherent in such hatred and warned of its dangerous potential for crippling the democratic way of life.

He also recognized how similar were dictatorships of the right and the left. He noted that whether a government is Fascist or Communist, it inevitably suppresses basic freedoms, persecutes dissenters, and glorifies the Leader. While others at the time were sympathetic to the policies of the Russian government, Dewey opposed every form of totalitarianism, including the Soviet version, and he insisted on the importance of open discussion, voluntary associations, and free elections.

Nor did Dewey fall prey to isolationism. After the German offensives of 1939, he strongly supported American efforts to stem the Fascist tide. And he fully appreciated, as many of his contemporaries did not, the interlocking of national and international affairs. Even before the nuclear age, he wrote of the ways in which, due to remote influences, "We are at the mercy of events acting upon us in unexpected, abrupt, and violent ways." [11]

One of the central themes of *Freedom and Culture* is that individuals in the modern world increasingly find themselves in the grip of immense forces they can neither control nor under-

11. Dewey, *Freedom and Culture* (New York: G. P. Putnam's Sons, 1939), p. 45; this volume, p. 94.

stand. Dewey realized how new technologies were leading to the concentration of capital in enormous corporations, the interdependence of government and industry, and, perhaps most importantly, the enormous power of what we now refer to as "the media."

He provided an especially incisive description of this latter phenomenon, emphasizing how modern forms of communication can distract the public with trivia, sensationalize events and arouse confused emotions, promulgate partisan views under the guise of serving the public interest, and, in short, create what he termed "pseudo-public opinion." [12] It is particularly noteworthy that Dewey delineated these problems years before the era of television.

What steps did he propose in the face of the weakening of the effects of individual action? He refused to subscribe to what he considered the oversimplified programs of Marxism or laissez-faire capitalism but, instead, urged unwavering commitment to democratic procedures of government, the enhancement of community life, and significant steps toward the equalization of those economic conditions he viewed as essential to equal rights.

Most importantly, Dewey believed that our control over events can be greatly enhanced by the spread of the scientific attitude in our schools and reliance on it in the resolution of public problems and the creation of cultural values. He emphasized that a democratic society is especially well-suited to promote the scientific method, for both democracy and science depend on "freedom of inquiry, toleration of diverse views, freedom of communication, the distribution of what is found out to every individual as the ultimate intellectual consumer." [13]

Dewey concluded *Freedom and Culture* not by proposing a specific political platform but by calling for "collective intelligence operating in cooperative action." [14] This characteristic phrase highlights the essence of his philosophical position: a commitment to a free society, critical intelligence, and the education required for their advance.

It may seem coincidental that this volume of Dewey's works

12. Ibid., p. 148; this volume, p. 168.
13. Ibid., p. 102; this volume, p. 135.
14. Ibid., p. 176; this volume, p. 188.

concentrates so heavily on his views about education, but from his perspective philosophy of education was the most significant phase of philosophy. Charles Frankel once noted that for Dewey "all philosophy was at bottom social philosophy implicitly or explicitly." [15] I would extend this insight and suggest that for Dewey all social philosophy was at bottom philosophy of education implicitly or explicitly. As he put it, "it would be difficult to find a single important problem of general philosophic inquiry that does not come to a burning focus in matters of the determination of the proper subject matter of studies, the choice of methods of teaching, and the problem of the social organization and administration of the schools." [16]

Other philosophers, of course, have recognized the importance of education. Kant, for example, wrote that "the greatest and most difficult problem to which man can devote himself is the problem of education." [17] But I know of only two major philosophers who exemplified this principle in their philosophical work: one was Dewey, the other was Plato. He too found it difficult to discuss any important philosophical problem without reference to the appropriateness of various subjects of study, methods of teaching, or strategies of learning.

But while Dewey's philosophy of education rested on his belief in democracy and the power of scientific method, Plato's philosophy of education rested on his belief in aristocracy and the power of pure reason. Plato proposed a planned society, Dewey a society engaged in continuous planning. Plato considered dialectical speculation to be the means toward the attainment of truth; Dewey maintained that knowledge is only acquired through intelligent action. And whereas Plato divided the members of his ideal society into three classes, Dewey countered that what Plato had overlooked is that "each individual constitutes his own class." [18]

15. *New Studies in the Philosophy of John Dewey,* ed. Steven M. Cahn (Hanover, N.H.: University Press of New England, 1977), p. 5.
16. Dewey, "The Determination of Ultimate Values or Aims through Antecedent or A Priori Speculation or through Pragmatic or Empirical Inquiry," this volume, p. 260.
17. Immanuel Kant, *Education* (Ann Arbor: University of Michigan Press, 1960), p. 11.
18. *Democracy and Education,* p. 104 [*Middle Works* 9:96].

Suffice it to say that John Dewey is the only thinker ever to construct a philosophy of education comparable in scope and depth to that of Plato. And this present volume exhibits Dewey's thought in all its subtlety and power, reflecting almost eighty years of experience and a lifelong commitment to rendering all experience rational.

Experience and Education

Preface

All social movements involve conflicts which are reflected intellectually in controversies. It would not be a sign of
health if such an important social interest as education were not
also an arena of struggles, practical and theoretical. But for theory, at least for the theory that forms a philosophy of education,
the practical conflicts and the controversies that are conducted
upon the level of these conflicts, only set a problem. It is the business of an intelligent theory of education to ascertain the causes
for the conflicts that exist and then, instead of taking one side or
the other, to indicate a plan of operations proceeding from a level
deeper and more inclusive than is represented by the practices
and ideas of the contending parties.

This formulation of the business of the philosophy of education does not mean that the latter should attempt to bring about
a compromise between opposed schools of thought, to find a *via
media*, nor yet make an eclectic combination of points picked out
hither and yon from all schools. It means the necessity of the introduction of a new order of conceptions leading to new modes
of practice. It is for this reason that it is so difficult to develop a
philosophy of education, the moment tradition and custom are
departed from. It is for this reason that the conduct of schools,
based upon a new order of conceptions, is so much more difficult
than is the management of schools which walk in beaten paths.
Hence, every movement in the direction of a new order of ideas
and of activities directed by them calls out, sooner or later, a return to what appear to be simpler and more fundamental ideas
and practices of the past—as is exemplified at present in education in the attempt to revive the principles of ancient Greece and
of the middle ages.

It is in this context that I have suggested at the close of this
little volume that those who are looking ahead to a new move-

ment in education, adapted to the existing need for a new social order, should think in terms of Education itself rather than in terms of some 'ism about education, even such an 'ism as "progressivism." For in spite of itself any movement that thinks and acts in terms of an 'ism becomes so involved in reaction against other 'isms that it is unwittingly controlled by them. For it then forms its principles by reaction against them instead of by a comprehensive constructive survey of actual needs, problems, and possibilities. Whatever value is possessed by the essay presented in this little volume resides in its attempt to call attention to the larger and deeper issues of Education so as to suggest their proper frame of reference.

1.   Traditional *vs.* Progressive Education

Mankind likes to think in terms of extreme opposites. It is given to formulating its beliefs in terms of *Either-Ors,* between which it recognizes no intermediate possibilities. When forced to recognize that the extremes cannot be acted upon, it is still inclined to hold that they are all right in theory but that when it comes to practical matters circumstances compel us to compromise. Educational philosophy is no exception. The history of educational theory is marked by opposition between the idea that education is development from within and that it is formation from without; that it is based upon natural endowments and that education is a process of overcoming natural inclination and substituting in its place habits acquired under external pressure.

At present, the opposition, so far as practical affairs of the school are concerned, tends to take the form of contrast between traditional and progressive education. If the underlying ideas of the former are formulated broadly, without the qualifications required for accurate statement, they are found to be about as follows: The subject-matter of education consists of bodies of information and of skills that have been worked out in the past; therefore, the chief business of the school is to transmit them to the new generation. In the past, there have also been developed standards and rules of conduct; moral training consists in forming habits of action in conformity with these rules and standards. Finally, the general pattern of school organization (by which I mean the relations of pupils to one another and to the teachers) constitutes the school a kind of institution sharply marked off from other social institutions. Call up in imagination the ordinary schoolroom, its time-schedules, schemes of classification, of examination and promotion, of rules of order, and I think you will grasp what is meant by "pattern of organization." If then you contrast this scene with what goes on in the family, for example, you will appreciate what is meant by the school being a kind of institution sharply marked off from any other form of social organization.

The three characteristics just mentioned fix the aims and methods of instruction and discipline. The main purpose or objective is to prepare the young for future responsibilities and for success in life, by means of acquisition of the organized bodies of information and prepared forms of skill which comprehend the material of instruction. Since the subject-matter as well as standards of proper conduct are handed down from the past, the attitude of pupils must, upon the whole, be one of docility, receptivity, and obedience. Books, especially textbooks, are the chief representatives of the lore and wisdom of the past, while teachers are the organs through which pupils are brought into effective connection with the material. Teachers are the agents through which knowledge and skills are communicated and rules of conduct enforced.

I have not made this brief summary for the purpose of criticizing the underlying philosophy. The rise of what is called new education and progressive schools is of itself a product of discontent with traditional education. In effect it is a criticism of the latter. When the implied criticism is made explicit it reads somewhat as follows: The traditional scheme is, in essence, one of imposition from above and from outside. It imposes adult standards, subject-matter, and methods upon those who are only growing slowly toward maturity. The gap is so great that the required subject-matter, the methods of learning and of behaving are foreign to the existing capacities of the young. They are beyond the reach of the experience the young learners already possess. Consequently, they must be imposed; even though good teachers will use devices of art to cover up the imposition so as to relieve it of obviously brutal features.

But the gulf between the mature or adult products and the experience and abilities of the young is so wide that the very situation forbids much active participation by pupils in the development of what is taught. Theirs is to do—and learn, as it was the part of the six hundred to do and die. Learning here means acquisition of what already is incorporated in books and in the heads of the elders. Moreover, that which is taught is thought of as essentially static. It is taught as a finished product, with little regard either to the ways in which it was originally built up or to changes that will surely occur in the future. It is to a large extent the cultural product of societies that assumed the future would be much like the past, and yet it is used as educational food in a society where change is the rule, not the exception.

If one attempts to formulate the philosophy of education implicit in the practices of the newer education, we may, I think, discover certain common principles amid the variety of progressive schools now existing. To imposition from above is opposed expression and cultivation of individuality; to external discipline is opposed free activity; to learning from texts and teachers, learning through experience; to acquisition of isolated skills and techniques by drill, is opposed acquisition of them as means of attaining ends which make direct vital appeal; to preparation for a more or less remote future is opposed making the most of the opportunities of present life; to static aims and materials is opposed acquaintance with a changing world.

Now, all principles by themselves are abstract. They become concrete only in the consequences which result from their application. Just because the principles set forth are so fundamental and far-reaching, everything depends upon the interpretation given them as they are put into practice in the school and the home. It is at this point that the reference made earlier to *Either-Or* philosophies becomes peculiarly pertinent. The general philosophy of the new education may be sound, and yet the difference in abstract principles will not decide the way in which the moral and intellectual preference involved shall be worked out in practice. There is always the danger in a new movement that in rejecting the aims and methods of that which it would supplant, it may develop its principles negatively rather than positively and constructively. Then it takes its clew in practice from that which is rejected instead of from the constructive development of its own philosophy.

I take it that the fundamental unity of the newer philosophy is found in the idea that there is an intimate and necessary relation between the processes of actual experience and education. If this be true, then a positive and constructive development of its own basic idea depends upon having a correct idea of experience. Take, for example, the question of organized subject-matter—

which will be discussed in some detail later. The problem for progressive education is: What is the place and meaning of subject-matter and of organization *within* experience? How does subject-matter function? Is there anything inherent in experience which tends towards progressive organization of its contents? What results follow when the materials of experience are not progressively organized? A philosophy which proceeds on the basis of rejection, of sheer opposition, will neglect these questions. It will tend to suppose that because the old education was based on ready-made organization, therefore it suffices to reject the principle of organization *in toto,* instead of striving to discover what it means and how it is to be attained on the basis of experience. We might go through all the points of difference between the new and the old education and reach similar conclusions. When external control is rejected, the problem becomes that of finding the factors of control that are inherent within experience. When external authority is rejected, it does not follow that all authority should be rejected, but rather that there is need to search for a more effective source of authority. Because the older education imposed the knowledge, methods, and the rules of conduct of the mature person upon the young, it does not follow, except upon the basis of the extreme *Either-Or* philosophy, that the knowledge and skill of the mature person has no directive value for the experience of the immature. On the contrary, basing education upon personal experience may mean more multiplied and more intimate contacts between the mature and the immature than ever existed in the traditional school, and consequently more, rather than less, guidance by others. The problem, then, is: how these contacts can be established without violating the principle of learning through personal experience. The solution of this problem requires a well thought-out philosophy of the social factors that operate in the constitution of individual experience.

What is indicated in the foregoing remarks is that the general principles of the new education do not of themselves solve any of the problems of the actual or practical conduct and management of progressive schools. Rather, they set new problems which have to be worked out on the basis of a new philosophy of experience. The problems are not even recognized, to say nothing of being solved, when it is assumed that it suffices to reject the ideas and practices of the old education and then go to the opposite extreme. Yet I am sure that you will appreciate what is meant when I say that many of the newer schools tend to make little or nothing of organized subject-matter of study; to proceed as if any form of direction and guidance by adults were an invasion of individual freedom, and as if the idea that education should be concerned with the present and future meant that acquaintance with the past has little or no role to play in education. Without pressing these defects to the point of exaggeration, they at least illustrate what is meant by a theory and practice of education which proceeds negatively or by reaction against what has been current in education rather than by a positive and constructive development of purposes, methods, and subject-matter on the foundation of a theory of experience and its educational potentialities.

It is not too much to say that an educational philosophy which professes to be based on the idea of freedom may become as dogmatic as ever was the traditional education which is reacted against. For any theory and set of practices is dogmatic which is not based upon critical examination of its own underlying principles. Let us say that the new education emphasizes the freedom of the learner. Very well. A problem is now set. What does freedom mean and what are the conditions under which it is capable of realization? Let us say that the kind of external imposition which was so common in the traditional school limited rather than promoted the intellectual and moral development of the young. Again, very well. Recognition of this serious defect sets a problem. Just what is the role of the teacher and of books in promoting the educational development of the immature? Admit that traditional education employed as the subject-matter for study facts and ideas so bound up with the past as to give little help in dealing with the issues of the present and future. Very well. Now we have the problem of discovering the connection which actually exists *within* experience between the achievements of the past and the issues of the present. We have the problem of ascertaining how acquaintance with the past may be translated into a potent instrumentality for dealing effectively with the future. We may reject knowledge of the past as the *end* of education and thereby only emphasize its importance as a *means*. When we do that we have a problem that is new in the story of education: How shall the young become acquainted with the past in such a way that the acquaintance is a potent agent in appreciation of the living present?

2. The Need of a Theory of Experience

In short, the point I am making is that rejection of the philosophy and practice of traditional education sets a new type of difficult educational problem for those who believe in the new type of education. We shall operate blindly and in confusion until we recognize this fact; until we thoroughly appreciate that departure from the old solves no problems. What is said in the following pages is, accordingly, intended to indicate some of the main problems with which the newer education is confronted and to suggest the main lines along which their solution is to be sought. I assume that amid all uncertainties there is one permanent frame of reference: namely, the organic connection between education and personal experience; or, that the new philosophy of education is committed to some kind of empirical and experimental philosophy. But experience and experiment are not self-explanatory ideas. Rather, their meaning is part of the problem to be explored. To know the meaning of empiricism we need to understand what experience is.

The belief that all genuine education comes about through experience does not mean that all experiences are genuinely or equally educative. Experience and education cannot be directly equated to each other. For some experiences are mis-educative. Any experience is mis-educative that has the effect of arresting or distorting the growth of further experience. An experience may be such as to engender callousness; it may produce lack of sensitivity and of responsiveness. Then the possibilities of having richer experience in the future are restricted. Again, a given experience may increase a person's automatic skill in a particular direction and yet tend to land him in a groove or rut; the effect again is to narrow the field of further experience. An experience may be immediately enjoyable and yet promote the formation of a slack and careless attitude; this attitude then operates to modify the quality of subsequent experiences so as to prevent a person from getting out of them what they have to give. Again, experiences may be so disconnected from one another that, while each is agreeable or even exciting in itself, they are not linked cumulatively to one another. Energy is then dissipated and a person becomes scatter-brained. Each experience may be lively, vivid, and "interesting," and yet their disconnectedness may artificially generate dispersive, disintegrated, centrifugal habits. The consequence of formation of such habits is inability to control future experiences. They are then taken, either by way of enjoyment or of discontent and revolt, just as they come. Under such circumstances, it is idle to talk of self-control.

Traditional education offers a plethora of examples of experiences of the kinds just mentioned. It is a great mistake to suppose, even tacitly, that the traditional schoolroom was not a place in which pupils had experiences. Yet this is tacitly assumed when progressive education as a plan of learning by experience is placed in sharp opposition to the old. The proper line of attack is that the experiences which were had, by pupils and teachers alike, were largely of a wrong kind. How many students, for example, were rendered callous to ideas, and how many lost the impetus to learn because of the way in which learning was experienced by them? How many acquired special skills by means of automatic drill so that their power of judgment and capacity to act intelligently in new situations was limited? How many came to associate the learning process with ennui and boredom? How many found what they did learn so foreign to the situations of life outside the school as to give them no power of control over the latter? How many came to associate books with dull drudgery, so that they were "conditioned" to all but flashy reading matter?

If I ask these questions, it is not for the sake of wholesale condemnation of the old education. It is for quite another purpose. It is to emphasize the fact, first, that young people in traditional schools do have experiences; and, secondly, that the trouble is not the absence of experiences, but their defective and wrong character—wrong and defective from the standpoint of connection with further experience. The positive side of this point is even more important in connection with progressive education. It is not enough to insist upon the necessity of experience, nor even of activity in experience. Everything depends upon the *quality* of the experience which is had. The quality of any experience has two aspects. There is an immediate aspect of agreeableness or disagreeableness, and there is its influence upon later experiences. The first is obvious and easy to judge. The *effect* of an experience is not borne on its face. It sets a problem to the educator. It is his business to arrange for the kind of experiences which, while they do not repel the student, but rather engage his activities are, nevertheless, more than immediately enjoyable since they promote having desirable future experiences. Just as no man lives or dies to himself, so no experience lives and dies to itself. Wholly independent of desire or intent, every experience lives on in further experiences. Hence the central problem of an education based upon experience is to select the kind of present experiences that live fruitfully and creatively in subsequent experiences.

Later, I shall discuss in more detail the principle of the continuity of experience or what may be called the experiential continuum. Here I wish simply to emphasize the importance of this principle for the philosophy of educative experience. A philosophy of education, like any theory, has to be stated in words, in symbols. But so far as it is more than verbal it is a plan for conducting education. Like any plan, it must be framed with reference to what is to be done and how it is to be done. The more definitely and sincerely it is held that education is a development within, by, and for experience, the more important it is that there shall be clear conceptions of what experience is. Unless experience is so conceived that the result is a plan for deciding upon subject-matter, upon methods of instruction and discipline, and upon material equipment and social organization of the school, it is wholly in the air. It is reduced to a form of words which may be emotionally stirring but for which any other set of words might equally well be substituted unless they indicate operations to be initiated and executed. Just because traditional education was a matter of routine in which the plans and programs were handed down from the past, it does not follow that progressive education is a matter of planless improvisation.

The traditional school could get along without any consistently developed philosophy of education. About all it required in that line was a set of abstract words like culture, discipline, our great cultural heritage, etc., actual guidance being derived not from them but from custom and established routines. Just because progressive schools cannot rely upon established traditions and institutional habits, they must either proceed more or less haphazardly or be directed by ideas which, when they are made articulate and coherent, form a philosophy of education. Revolt against the kind of organization characteristic of the traditional school constitutes a demand for a kind of organization based upon ideas. I think that only slight acquaintance with the history of education is needed to prove that educational reformers and innovators alone have felt the need for a philosophy of education. Those who adhered to the established system needed merely a few fine-sounding words to justify existing practices. The real work was done by habits which were so fixed as to be institutional. The lesson for progressive education is that it requires in an urgent degree, a degree more pressing than was incumbent upon former innovators, a philosophy of education based upon a philosophy of experience.

I remarked incidentally that the philosophy in question is, to paraphrase the saying of Lincoln about democracy, one of education of, by, and for experience. No one of these words, *of*, *by*, or *for*, names anything which is self-evident. Each of them is a challenge to discover and put into operation a principle of order and organization which follows from understanding what educative experience signifies.

It is, accordingly, a much more difficult task to work out the kinds of materials, of methods, and of social relationships that are appropriate to the new education than is the case with traditional education. I think many of the difficulties experienced in the conduct of progressive schools and many of the criticisms leveled against them arise from this source. The difficulties are aggravated and the criticisms are increased when it is supposed that the new education is somehow easier than the old. This belief is, I imagine, more or less current. Perhaps it illustrates again the *Either-Or* philosophy, springing from the idea that about all which is required is *not* to do what is done in traditional schools.

I admit gladly that the new education is *simpler* in principle than the old. It is in harmony with principles of growth, while there is very much which is artificial in the old selection and arrangement of subjects and methods, and artificiality always leads to unnecessary complexity. But the easy and the simple are not identical. To discover what is really simple and to act upon the discovery is an exceedingly difficult task. After the artificial and complex is once institutionally established and ingrained in custom and routine, it is easier to walk in the paths that have been beaten than it is, after taking a new point of view, to work out what is practically involved in the new point of view. The old Ptolemaic astronomical system was more complicated with its cycles and epicycles than the Copernican system. But until organization of actual astronomical phenomena on the ground of the latter principle had been effected the easiest course was to follow the line of least resistance provided by the old intellectual habit. So we come back to the idea that a coherent *theory* of experience, affording positive direction to selection and organization of appropriate educational methods and materials, is required by the attempt to give new direction to the work of the schools. The process is a slow and arduous one. It is a matter of growth, and there are many obstacles which tend to obstruct growth and to deflect it into wrong lines.

I shall have something to say later about organization. All that is needed, perhaps, at this point is to say that we must escape from the tendency to think of organization in terms of the *kind* of organization, whether of content (or subject-matter), or of methods and social relations, that mark traditional education. I think that a good deal of the current opposition to the idea of organization is due to the fact that it is so hard to get away from the picture of the studies of the old school. The moment "organization" is mentioned imagination goes almost automatically to the kind of organization that is familiar, and in revolting against that we are led to shrink from the very idea of any organization. On the other hand, educational reactionaries, who are now gathering force, use the absence of adequate intellectual and moral organization in the newer type of school as proof not only of the need of organization, but to identify any and every kind of organization with that instituted before the rise of experimental science. Failure to develop a conception of organization upon the empirical and experimental basis gives reactionaries a too easy victory. But the fact that the empirical sciences now offer the best type of intellectual organization which can be found in any field shows that there is no reason why we, who call ourselves empiricists, should be "pushovers" in the matter of order and organization.

3. Criteria of Experience

If there is any truth in what has been said about the need of forming a theory of experience in order that education may be intelligently conducted upon the basis of experience, it is clear that the next thing in order in this discussion is to present the principles that are most significant in framing this theory. I shall not, therefore, apologize for engaging in a certain amount of philosophical analysis, which otherwise might be out of place. I may, however, reassure you to some degree by saying that this analysis is not an end in itself but is engaged in for the sake of obtaining criteria to be applied later in discussion of a number of concrete and, to most persons, more interesting issues.

I have already mentioned what I called the category of continuity, or the experiential continuum. This principle is involved, as I pointed out, in every attempt to discriminate between experiences that are worth while educationally and those that are not. It may seem superfluous to argue that this discrimination is necessary not only in criticizing the traditional type of education but also in initiating and conducting a different type. Nevertheless, it is advisable to pursue for a little while the idea that it is necessary. One may safely assume, I suppose, that one thing which has recommended the progressive movement is that it seems more in accord with the democratic ideal to which our people is committed than do the procedures of the traditional school, since the latter have so much of the autocratic about them. Another thing which has contributed to its favorable reception is that its methods are humane in comparison with the harshness so often attending the policies of the traditional school.

The question I would raise concerns why we prefer democratic and humane arrangements to those which are autocratic and harsh. And by "why," I mean the *reason* for preferring them, not just the *causes* which lead us to the preference. One *cause* may be that we have been taught not only in the schools but by the press, the pulpit, the platform, and our laws and law-making bodies that democracy is the best of all social institutions. We may have so assimilated this idea from our surroundings that it has become an habitual part of our mental and moral make-up. But similar causes have led other persons in different surroundings to widely varying conclusions—to prefer fascism, for example. The cause for our preference is not the same thing as the reason why we *should* prefer it.

It is not my purpose here to go in detail into the reason. But I would ask a single question: Can we find any reason that does not ultimately come down to the belief that democratic social arrangements promote a better quality of human experience, one which is more widely accessible and enjoyed, than do non-democratic and anti-democratic forms of social life? Does not the principle of regard for individual freedom and for decency and kindliness of human relations come back in the end to the conviction that these things are tributary to a higher quality of experience on the part of a greater number than are methods of repression and coercion or force? Is it not the reason for our preference that we believe that mutual consultation and convictions reached through persuasion, make possible a better quality of experience than can otherwise be provided on any wide scale?

If the answer to these questions is in the affirmative (and personally I do not see how we can justify our preference for democracy and humanity on any other ground), the ultimate reason for hospitality to progressive education, because of its reliance upon and use of humane methods and its kinship to democracy, goes back to the fact that discrimination is made between the inherent values of different experiences. So I come back to the principle of continuity of experience as a criterion of discrimination.

At bottom, this principle rests upon the fact of habit, when *habit* is interpreted biologically. The basic characteristic of habit is that every experience enacted and undergone modifies the one who acts and undergoes, while this modification affects, whether we wish it or not, the quality of subsequent experiences. For it is a somewhat different person who enters into them. The principle of habit so understood obviously goes deeper than the ordinary conception of *a* habit as a more or less fixed way of doing things, although it includes the latter as one of its special cases. It covers the formation of attitudes, attitudes that are emotional and intellectual; it covers our basic sensitivities and ways of meeting and responding to all the conditions which we meet in living. From this point of view, the principle of continuity of experience means that every experience both takes up something from those which have gone before and modifies in some way the quality of those which come after. As the poet states it,

> . . . all experience is an arch wherethro'
> Gleams that untravell'd world, whose margin fades
> Forever and forever when I move.

So far, however, we have no ground for discrimination among experiences. For the principle is of universal application. There is *some* kind of continuity in every case. It is when we note the different forms in which continuity of experience operates that we get the basis of discriminating among experiences. I may illustrate what is meant by an objection which has been brought against an idea which I once put forth—namely, that the educative process can be identified with growth when that is understood in terms of the active participle, *growing*.

Growth, or growing as developing, not only physically but intellectually and morally, is one exemplification of the principle of continuity. The objection made is that growth might take many different directions: a man, for example, who starts out on a career of burglary may grow in that direction, and by practice may grow into a highly expert burglar. Hence it is argued that "growth" is not enough; we must also specify the direction in which growth takes place, the end towards which it tends. Before, however, we decide that the objection is conclusive we must analyze the case a little further.

That a man may grow in efficiency as a burglar, as a gangster, or as a corrupt politician, cannot be doubted. But from the standpoint of growth as education and education as growth the question is whether growth in this direction promotes or retards growth in general. Does this form of growth create conditions for further growth, or does it set up conditions that shut off the person who has grown in this particular direction from the occasions, stimuli, and opportunities for continuing growth in new directions? What is the effect of growth in a special direction upon the attitudes and habits which alone open up avenues for development in other lines? I shall leave you to answer these questions, saying simply that when and *only* when development in a particular line conduces to continuing growth does it answer to the criterion of education as growing. For the conception is one that must find universal and not specialized limited application.

I return now to the question of continuity as a criterion by which to discriminate between experiences which are educative and those which are mis-educative. As we have seen, there is some kind of continuity in any case since every experience affects for better or worse the attitudes which help decide the quality of further experiences, by setting up certain preference and aversion, and making it easier or harder to act for this or that end. Moreover, every experience influences in some degree the objective conditions under which further experiences are had. For example, a child who learns to speak has a new facility and new desire. But he has also widened the external conditions of subsequent learning. When he learns to read, he similarly opens up a new environment. If a person decides to become a teacher, lawyer, physician, or stockbroker, when he executes his intention he thereby necessarily determines to some extent the environment in which he will act in the future. He has rendered himself more sensitive and responsive to certain conditions, and relatively immune to those things about him that would have been stimuli if he had made another choice.

But, while the principle of continuity applies in some way in every case, the quality of the present experience influences the *way* in which the principle applies. We speak of spoiling a child and of the spoilt child. The effect of overindulging a child is a continuing one. It sets up an attitude which operates as an automatic demand that persons and objects cater to his desires and caprices in the future. It makes him seek the kind of situation that will enable him to do what he feels like doing at the time. It renders him averse to and comparatively incompetent in situations which require effort and perseverance in overcoming obstacles. There is no paradox in the fact that the principle of the continuity of experience may operate so as to leave a person arrested on a low plane of development, in a way which limits later capacity for growth.

On the other hand, if an experience arouses curiosity, strengthens initiative, and sets up desires and purposes that are sufficiently intense to carry a person over dead places in the future, continuity works in a very different way. Every experience is a moving force. Its value can be judged only on the ground of what it moves toward and into. The greater maturity of experience which should belong to the adult as educator puts him in a position to evaluate each experience of the young in a way in which the one having the less mature experience cannot do. It is then the business of the educator to see in what direction an experience is heading. There is no point in his being more mature if, instead of using his greater insight to help organize the conditions of the experience of the immature, he throws away his insight. Failure to take the moving force of an experience into account so as to judge and direct it on the ground of what it is moving into means disloyalty to the principle of experience itself. The disloyalty operates in two directions. The educator is false to the understanding that he should have obtained from his own past experience. He is also unfaithful to the fact that all human experience is ultimately social: that it involves contact and communication. The mature person, to put it in moral terms, has no right to withhold from the young on given occasions whatever capacity for sympathetic understanding his own experience has given him.

No sooner, however, are such things said than there is a tendency to react to the other extreme and take what has been said as a plea for some sort of disguised imposition from outside. It is worth while, accordingly, to say something about the way in which the adult can exercise the wisdom his own wider experience gives him without imposing a merely external control. On one side, it is his business to be on the alert to see what attitudes and habitual tendencies are being created. In this direction he must, if he is an educator, be able to judge what attitudes are actually conducive to continued growth and what are detrimental. He must, in addition, have that sympathetic understanding of individuals as individuals which gives him an idea of what is actually going on in the minds of those who are learning. It is, among other things, the need for these abilities on the part of the parent and teacher which makes a system of education based upon living experience a more difficult affair to conduct successfully than it is to follow the patterns of traditional education.

But there is another aspect of the matter. Experience does not go on simply inside a person. It does go on there, for it influences the formation of attitudes of desire and purpose. But this is not the whole of the story. Every genuine experience has an active side which changes in some degree the objective conditions under which experiences are had. The difference between civilization and savagery, to take an example on a large scale, is found in the degree in which previous experiences have changed the objective conditions under which subsequent experiences take place. The existence of roads, of means of rapid movement and transportation, tools, implements, furniture, electric light and power, are illustrations. Destroy the external conditions of present civilized experience, and for a time our experience would relapse into that of barbaric peoples.

In a word, we live from birth to death in a world of persons and things which in large measure is what it is because of what has been done and transmitted from previous human activities. When this fact is ignored, experience is treated as if it were something which goes on exclusively inside an individual's body and mind. It ought not to be necessary to say that experience does not occur in a vacuum. There are sources outside an individual which give rise to experience. It is constantly fed from these springs. No one would question that a child in a slum tenement has a different experience from that of a child in a cultured home; that the country lad has a different kind of experience from the city boy, or a boy on the seashore one different from the lad who is brought up on inland prairies. Ordinarily we take such facts for granted as too commonplace to record. But when their educational import is recognized, they indicate the second way in which the educator can direct the experience of the young without engaging in imposition. A primary responsibility of educators is that they not only be aware of the general principle of the shaping of actual experience by environing conditions, but that they also recognize in the concrete what surroundings are conducive to having experiences that lead to growth. Above all, they should know how to utilize the surroundings, physical and social, that exist so as to extract from them all that they have to contribute to building up experiences that are worth while.

Traditional education did not have to face this problem; it could systematically dodge this responsibility. The school environment of desks, blackboards, a small school yard, was supposed to suffice. There was no demand that the teacher should become intimately acquainted with the conditions of the local community, physical, historical, economic, occupational, etc., in order to utilize them as educational resources. A system of education based upon the necessary connection of education with experience must, on the contrary, if faithful to its principle, take these things constantly into account. This tax upon the educator is another reason why progressive education is more difficult to carry on than was ever the traditional system.

It is possible to frame schemes of education that pretty systematically subordinate objective conditions to those which reside in the individuals being educated. This happens whenever the place and function of the teacher, of books, of apparatus and equipment, of everything which represents the products of the more mature experience of elders, is systematically subordinated to the immediate inclinations and feelings of the young. Every theory which assumes that importance can be attached to these objective factors only at the expense of imposing external control and of limiting the freedom of individuals rests finally upon the notion that experience is truly experience only when objective conditions are subordinated to what goes on within the individuals having the experience.

I do not mean that it is supposed that objective conditions can be shut out. It is recognized that they must enter in: so much concession is made to the inescapable fact that we live in a world of things and persons. But I think that observation of what goes on in some families and some schools would disclose that some parents and some teachers are acting upon the idea of *subordinating* objective conditions to internal ones. In that case, it is assumed not only that the latter are primary, which in one sense they are, but that just as they temporarily exist they fix the whole educational process.

Let me illustrate from the case of an infant. The needs of a baby for food, rest, and activity are certainly primary and decisive in one respect. Nourishment must be provided; provision must be made for comfortable sleep, and so on. But these facts do not mean that a parent shall feed the baby at any time when the baby is cross or irritable, that there shall not be a program of regular hours of feeding and sleeping, etc. The wise mother takes account of the needs of the infant but not in a way which dispenses with her own responsibility for regulating the objective conditions under which the needs are satisfied. And if she is a wise mother in this respect, she draws upon past experiences of experts as well as her own for the light that these shed upon what experiences are in general most conducive to the normal development of infants. Instead of these conditions being subordinated to the immediate internal condition of the baby, they are definitely ordered so that a particular kind of *interaction* with these immediate internal states may be brought about.

The word "interaction," which has just been used, expresses the second chief principle for interpreting an experience in its educational function and force. It assigns equal rights to both factors in experience—objective and internal conditions. Any normal experience is an interplay of these two sets of conditions. Taken together, or in their interaction, they form what we call a *situation*. The trouble with traditional education was not that it emphasized the external conditions that enter into the control of the experiences but that it paid so little attention to the internal factors which also decide what kind of experience is had. It violated the principle of interaction from one side. But this violation is no reason why the new education should violate the principle from the other side—except upon the basis of the extreme *Either-Or* educational philosophy which has been mentioned.

The illustration drawn from the need for regulation of the objective conditions of a baby's development indicates, first, that the parent has responsibility for arranging the conditions under which an infant's experience of food, sleep, etc., occurs, and, secondly, that the responsibility is fulfilled by utilizing the funded experience of the past, as this is represented, say, by the advice of competent physicians and others who have made a special study of normal physical growth. Does it limit the freedom of the mother when she uses the body of knowledge thus provided to regulate the objective conditions of nourishment and sleep? Or does the enlargement of her intelligence in fulfilling her parental function widen her freedom? Doubtless if a fetish were made of the advice and directions so that they came to be inflexible dictates to be followed under every possible condition, then restriction of freedom of both parent and child would occur. But this restriction would also be a limitation of the intelligence that is exercised in personal judgment.

In what respect does regulation of objective conditions limit the freedom of the baby? Some limitation is certainly placed upon its immediate movements and inclinations when it is put in its crib, at a time when it wants to continue playing, or does not get food at the moment it would like it, or when it isn't picked up and dandled when it cries for attention. Restriction also occurs when mother or nurse snatches a child away from an open fire into which it is about to fall. I shall have more to say later about freedom. Here it is enough to ask whether freedom is to be thought of and adjudged on the basis of relatively momentary incidents or whether its meaning is found in the continuity of developing experience.

The statement that individuals live in a world means, in the concrete, that they live in a series of situations. And when it is said that they live *in* these situations, the meaning of the word "in" is different from its meaning when it is said that pennies are "in" a pocket or paint is "in" a can. It means, once more, that interaction is going on between an individual and objects and other persons. The conceptions of *situation* and of *interaction* are inseparable from each other. An experience is always what it is because of a transaction taking place between an individual and what, at the time, constitutes his environment, whether the latter consists of persons with whom he is talking about some topic or event, the subject talked about being also a part of the situation; or the toys with which he is playing; the book he is reading (in which his environing conditions at the time may be England or ancient Greece or an imaginary region); or the materials of an experiment he is performing. The environment, in other words, is whatever conditions interact with personal needs, desires, purposes, and capacities to create the experience which is had. Even when a person builds a castle in the air he is interacting with the objects which he constructs in fancy.

The two principles of continuity and interaction are not separate from each other. They intercept and unite. They are, so to speak, the longitudinal and lateral aspects of experience. Different situations succeed one another. But because of the principle of continuity something is carried over from the earlier to the later ones. As an individual passes from one situation to another, his world, his environment, expands or contracts. He does not find himself living in another world but in a different part or aspect of one and the same world. What he has learned in the way of knowledge and skill in one situation becomes an instrument of understanding and dealing effectively with the situations which follow. The process goes on as long as life and learning continue. Otherwise the course of experience is disorderly, since the individual factor that enters into making an experience is split. A divided world, a world whose parts and aspects do not hang together, is at once a sign and a cause of a divided personality. When the splitting-up reaches a certain point we call the person insane. A fully integrated personality, on the other hand, exists only when successive experiences are integrated with one another. It can be built up only as a world of related objects is constructed.

Continuity and interaction in their active union with each other provide the measure of the educative significance and value of an experience. The immediate and direct concern of an educator is then with the situations in which interaction takes place. The individual, who enters as a factor into it, is what he is at a given time. It is the other factor, that of objective conditions, which lies to some extent within the possibility of regulation by the educator. As has already been noted, the phrase "objective conditions" covers a wide range. It includes what is done by the educator and the way in which it is done, not only words spoken but the tone of voice in which they are spoken. It includes equipment, books, apparatus, toys, games played. It includes the materials with which an individual interacts, and, most important of all, the total *social* set-up of the situations in which a person is engaged.

When it is said that the objective conditions are those which are within the power of the educator to regulate, it is meant, of course, that his ability to influence directly the experience of others and thereby the education they obtain places upon him the duty of determining that environment which will interact with the existing capacities and needs of those taught to create a worth-while experience. The trouble with traditional education was not that educators took upon themselves the responsibility for providing an environment. The trouble was that they did not consider the other factor in creating an experience; namely, the powers and purposes of those taught. It was assumed that a certain set of conditions was intrinsically desirable, apart from its ability to evoke a certain quality of response in individuals. This lack of mutual adaptation made the process of teaching and learning accidental. Those to whom the provided conditions were suitable managed to learn. Others got on as best they could. Responsibility for selecting objective conditions carries with it, then, the responsibility for understanding the needs and capacities of the individuals who are learning at a given time. It is not enough that certain materials and methods have proved effective with other individuals at other times. There must be a reason for thinking that they will function in generating an experience that has educative quality with particular individuals at a particular time.

It is no reflection upon the nutritive quality of beefsteak that it is not fed to infants. It is not an invidious reflection upon trigonometry that we do not teach it in the first or fifth grade of school. It is not the subject *per se* that is educative or that is conducive to growth. There is no subject that is in and of itself, or without regard to the stage of growth attained by the learner, such that inherent educational value can be attributed to it. Failure to take into account adaptation to the needs and capacities of individuals was the source of the idea that certain subjects and certain methods are intrinsically cultural or intrinsically good for mental discipline. There is no such thing as educational value in the abstract. The notion that some subjects and methods and that acquaintance with certain facts and truths possess educational value in and of themselves is the reason why traditional education reduced the material of education so largely to a diet of predigested materials. According to this notion, it was enough to regulate the quantity and difficulty of the material provided, in a scheme of quantitative grading, from month to month and from year to year. Otherwise a pupil was expected to take it in the doses that were prescribed from without. If the pupil left it instead of taking it, if he engaged in physical truancy, or in the mental truancy of mind-wandering and finally built up an emotional revulsion against the subject, he was held to be at fault. No question was raised as to whether the trouble might not lie in the subject-matter or in the way in which it was offered. The principle of interaction makes it clear that failure of adaptation of material to needs and capacities of individuals may cause an experience to be non-educative quite as much as failure of an individual to adapt himself to the material.

The principle of continuity in its educational application means, nevertheless, that the future has to be taken into account at every stage of the educational process. This idea is easily misunderstood and is badly distorted in traditional education. Its assumption is, that by acquiring certain skills and by learning certain subjects which would be needed later (perhaps in college or perhaps in adult life) pupils are as a matter of course made ready for the needs and circumstances of the future. Now "preparation" is a treacherous idea. In a certain sense every experience should do something to prepare a person for later experiences of a deeper and more expansive quality. That is the very meaning of growth, continuity, reconstruction of experience. But it is a mistake to suppose that the mere acquisition of a certain amount of arithmetic, geography, history, etc., which is taught and studied because it may be useful at some time in the future, has this effect, and it is a mistake to suppose that acquisition of skills in reading and figuring will automatically constitute preparation for their right and effective use under conditions very unlike those in which they were acquired.

Almost everyone has had occasion to look back upon his school days and wonder what has become of the knowledge he was supposed to have amassed during his years of schooling, and why it is that the technical skills he acquired have to be learned over again in changed form in order to stand him in good stead. Indeed, he is lucky who does not find that in order to make progress, in order to go ahead intellectually, he does not have to unlearn much of what he learned in school. These questions cannot be disposed of by saying that the subjects were not actually learned, for they were learned at least sufficiently to enable a pupil to pass examinations in them. One trouble is that the subject-matter in question was learned in isolation; it was put, as it were, in a water-tight compartment. When the question is asked, then, what has become of it, where has it gone to, the right answer is that it is still there in the special compartment in which it was originally stowed away. If exactly the same conditions recurred as those under which it was acquired, it would also recur and be available. But it was segregated when it was acquired and hence is so disconnected from the rest of experience that it is not available under the actual conditions of life. It is contrary to the laws of experience that learning of this kind, no matter how thoroughly engrained at the time, should give genuine preparation.

Nor does failure in preparation end at this point. Perhaps the greatest of all pedagogical fallacies is the notion that a person learns only the particular thing he is studying at the time. Collateral learning in the way of formation of enduring attitudes, of likes and dislikes, may be and often is much more important than the spelling lesson or lesson in geography or history that is learned. For these attitudes are fundamentally what count in the future. The most important attitude that can be formed is that of desire to go on learning. If impetus in this direction is weakened instead of being intensified, something much more than mere lack of preparation takes place. The pupil is actually robbed of native capacities which otherwise would enable him to cope with the circumstances that he meets in the course of his life. We often see persons who have had little schooling and in whose case the absence of set schooling proves to be a positive asset. They have at least retained their native common sense and power of judgment, and its exercise in the actual conditions of living has given them the precious gift of ability to learn from the experiences they have. What avail is it to win prescribed amounts of information about geography and history, to win ability to read and write, if in the process the individual loses his own soul: loses his appreciation of things worth while, of the values to which these things are relative; if he loses desire to apply what he has learned and, above all, loses the ability to extract meaning from his future experiences as they occur?

What, then, is the true meaning of preparation in the educational scheme? In the first place, it means that a person, young or old, gets out of his present experience all that there is in it for him at the time in which he has it. When preparation is made the controlling end, then the potentialities of the present are sacrificed to a supposititious future. When this happens, the actual preparation for the future is missed or distorted. The ideal of using the present simply to get ready for the future contradicts itself. It omits, and even shuts out, the very conditions by which a person can be prepared for his future. We always live at the time we live and not at some other time, and only by extracting at each present time the full meaning of each present experience are we prepared for doing the same thing in the future. This is the only preparation which in the long run amounts to anything.

All this means that attentive care must be devoted to the conditions which give each present experience a worth-while meaning. Instead of inferring that it doesn't make much difference what the present experience is as long as it is enjoyed, the conclusion is the exact opposite. Here is another matter where it is easy to react from one extreme to the other. Because traditional schools tended to sacrifice the present to a remote and more or less unknown future, therefore it comes to be believed that the educator has little responsibility for the kind of present experiences the young undergo. But the relation of the present and the future is not an *Either-Or* affair. The present affects the future anyway. The persons who should have some idea of the connection between the two are those who have achieved maturity. Accordingly, upon them devolves the responsibility for instituting the conditions for the kind of present experience which has a favorable effect upon the future. Education as growth or maturity should be an ever-present process.

4. Social Control

I have said that educational plans and projects, seeing education in terms of life-experience, are thereby committed to framing and adopting an intelligent theory or, if you please, philosophy of experience. Otherwise they are at the mercy of every intellectual breeze that happens to blow. I have tried to illustrate the need for such a theory by calling attention to two principles which are fundamental in the constitution of experience: the principles of interaction and of continuity. If, then, I am asked why I have spent so much time on expounding a rather abstract philosophy, it is because practical attempts to develop schools based upon the idea that education is found in life-experience are bound to exhibit inconsistencies and confusions unless they are guided by some conception of what experience is, and what marks off educative experience from non-educative and mis-educative experience. I now come to a group of actual educational questions the discussion of which will, I hope, provide topics and material that are more concrete than the discussion up to this point.

The two principles of continuity and interaction as criteria of the value of experience are so intimately connected that it is not easy to tell just what special educational problem to take up first. Even the convenient division into problems of subject-matter or studies and of methods of teaching and learning is likely to fail us in selection and organization of topics to discuss. Consequently, the beginning and sequence of topics is somewhat arbitrary. I shall commence, however, with the old question of individual freedom and social control and pass on to the questions that grow naturally out of it.

It is often well in considering educational problems to get a start by temporarily ignoring the school and thinking of other human situations. I take it that no one would deny that the ordinary good citizen is as a matter of fact subject to a great deal of social control and that a considerable part of this control is not felt to involve restriction of personal freedom. Even the theoretical anarchist, whose philosophy commits him to the idea that state or government control is an unmitigated evil, believes that with abolition of the political state other forms of social control would operate: indeed, his opposition to governmental regulation springs from his belief that other and to him more normal modes of control would operate with abolition of the state.

Without taking up this extreme position, let us note some examples of social control that operate in everyday life, and then look for the principle underlying them. Let us begin with the young people themselves. Children at recess or after school play games, from tag and one-old-cat to baseball and football. The games involve rules, and these rules order their conduct. The games do not go on haphazardly or by a succession of improvisations. Without rules there is no game. If disputes arise there is an umpire to appeal to, or discussion and a kind of arbitration are means to a decision; otherwise the game is broken up and comes to an end.

There are certain fairly obvious controlling features of such situations to which I want to call attention. The first is that the rules are a part of the game. They are not outside of it. No rules, then no game; different rules, then a different game. As long as the game goes on with a reasonable smoothness, the players do not feel that they are submitting to external imposition but that they are playing the game. In the second place an individual may at times feel that a decision isn't fair and he may even get angry. But he is not objecting to a rule but to what he claims is a violation of it, to some one-sided and unfair action. In the third place, the rules, and hence the conduct of the game, are fairly standardized. There are recognized ways of counting out, of selection of sides, as well as for positions to be taken, movements to be made, etc. These rules have the sanction of tradition and precedent. Those playing the game have seen, perhaps, professional matches and they want to emulate their elders. An element that is conventional is pretty strong. Usually, a group of youngsters change the rules by which they play only when the adult group to which they look for models have themselves made a change in the rules, while the change made by the elders is at least supposed to conduce to making the game more skillful or more interesting to spectators.

Now, the general conclusion I would draw is that control of individual actions is effected by the whole situation in which individuals are involved, in which they share and of which they are cooperative or interacting parts. For even in a competitive game there is a certain kind of participation, of sharing in a common experience. Stated the other way around, those who take part do not feel that they are bossed by an individual person or are being subjected to the will of some outside superior person. When violent disputes do arise, it is usually on the alleged ground that the umpire or some person on the other side is being unfair; in other words, that in such cases some individual is trying to impose his individual will on someone else.

It may seem to be putting too heavy a load upon a single case to argue that this instance illustrates the general principle of social control of individuals without the violation of freedom. But if the matter were followed out through a number of cases, I think the conclusion that this particular instance does illustrate a general principle would be justified. Games are generally competitive. If we took instances of cooperative activities in which all members of a group take part, as for example in well-ordered family life in which there is mutual confidence, the point would be even clearer. In all such cases it is not the will or desire of any one person which establishes order but the moving spirit of the whole group. The control is social, but individuals are parts of a community, not outside of it.

I do not mean by this that there are no occasions upon which the authority of, say, the parent does not have to intervene and exercise fairly direct control. But I do say that, in the first place, the number of these occasions is slight in comparison with the number of those in which the control is exercised by situations in which all take part. And what is even more important, the authority in question when exercised in a well-regulated household or other community group is not a manifestation of merely personal will; the parent or teacher exercises it as the representative and agent of the interests of the group as a whole. With respect to the first point, in a well-ordered school the main reliance for control of this and that individual is upon the activities carried on and upon the situations in which these activities are maintained. The teacher reduces to a minimum the occasions in which he or she has to exercise authority in a personal way. When it is necessary, in the second place, to speak and act firmly, it is done in behalf of the interest of the group, not as an exhibition of personal power. This makes the difference between action which is arbitrary and that which is just and fair.

Moreover, it is not necessary that the difference should be formulated in words, by either teacher or the young, in order to be felt in experience. The number of children who do not feel the difference (even if they cannot articulate it and reduce it to an intellectual principle) between action that is motivated by personal power and desire to dictate and action that is fair, because in the interest of all, is small. I should even be willing to say that upon the whole children are more sensitive to the signs and symptoms of this difference than are adults. Children learn the difference when playing with one another. They are willing, often too willing if anything, to take suggestions from one child and let him be a leader if his conduct adds to the experienced value of what they are doing, while they resent the attempt at dictation. Then they often withdraw and when asked why, say that it is because so-and-so "is too bossy."

I do not wish to refer to the traditional school in ways which set up a caricature in lieu of a picture. But I think it is fair to say that one reason the personal commands of the teacher so often played an undue role and a reason why the order which existed was so much a matter of sheer obedience to the will of an adult was because the situation almost forced it upon the teacher. The school was not a group or community held together by participation in common activities. Consequently, the normal, proper conditions of control were lacking. Their absence was made up for, and to a considerable extent had to be made up for, by the direct intervention of the teacher, who, as the saying went, "*kept* order." He kept it because order was in the teacher's keeping, instead of residing in the shared work being done.

The conclusion is that in what are called the new schools, the primary source of social control resides in the very nature of the work done as a social enterprise in which all individuals have an opportunity to contribute and to which all feel a responsibility. Most children are naturally "sociable." Isolation is even more irksome to them than to adults. A genuine community life has its ground in this natural sociability. But community life does not organize itself in an enduring way purely spontaneously. It requires thought and planning ahead. The educator is responsible for a knowledge of individuals and for a knowledge of subject-matter that will enable activities to be selected which lend themselves to social organization, an organization in which all individuals have an opportunity to contribute something, and in which the activities in which all participate are the chief carrier of control.

I am not romantic enough about the young to suppose that every pupil will respond or that any child of normally strong impulses will respond on every occasion. There are likely to be some who, when they come to school, are already victims of injurious conditions outside of the school and who have become so passive and unduly docile that they fail to contribute. There will be others who, because of previous experience, are bumptious and unruly and perhaps downright rebellious. But it is certain that the general principle of social control cannot be predicated upon such cases. It is also true that no general rule can be laid down for dealing with such cases. The teacher has to deal with them individually. They fall into general classes, but no two are exactly alike. The educator has to discover as best he or she can the causes for the recalcitrant attitudes. He or she cannot, if the educational process is to go on, make it a question of pitting one will against another in order to see which is strongest, nor yet allow the unruly and non-participating pupils to stand permanently in the way of the educative activities of others. Exclusion perhaps is the only available measure at a given juncture, but it is no solution. For it may strengthen the very causes which have brought about the undesirable anti-social attitude, such as desire for attention or to show off.

Exceptions rarely prove a rule or give a clew to what the rule should be. I would not, therefore, attach too much importance to these exceptional cases, although it is true at present that progressive schools are likely often to have more than their fair share of these cases, since parents may send children to such schools as a last resort. I do not think weakness in control when it is found in progressive schools arises in any event from these exceptional cases. It is much more likely to arise from failure to arrange in advance for the kind of work (by which I mean all kinds of activities engaged in) which will create situations that of themselves tend to exercise control over what this, that, and the other pupil does and how he does it. This failure most often goes back to lack of sufficiently thoughtful planning in advance. The causes for such lack are varied. The one which is peculiarly important to mention in this connection is the idea that such advance planning is unnecessary and even that it is inherently hostile to the legitimate freedom of those being instructed.

Now, of course, it is quite possible to have preparatory planning by the teacher done in such a rigid and intellectually inflexible fashion that it does result in adult imposition, which is none the less external because executed with tact and the semblance of respect for individual freedom. But this kind of planning does not follow inherently from the principle involved. I do not know what the greater maturity of the teacher and the teacher's greater knowledge of the world, of subject-matters and of individuals, is for unless the teacher can arrange conditions that are conducive to community activity and to organization which exercises control over individual impulses by the mere fact that all are engaged in communal projects. Because the kind of advance planning heretofore engaged in has been so routine as to leave little room for the free play of individual thinking or for contributions due to distinctive individual experience, it does not follow that all planning must be rejected. On the contrary, there is incumbent upon the educator the duty of instituting a much more intelligent, and consequently more difficult, kind of planning. He must survey the capacities and needs of the particular set of individuals with whom he is dealing and must at the same time arrange the conditions which provide the subject-matter or content for experiences that satisfy these needs and develop these capacities. The planning must be flexible enough to permit free play for individuality of experience and yet firm enough to give direction towards continuous development of power.

The present occasion is a suitable one to say something about the province and office of the teacher. The principle that development of experience comes about through interaction means that education is essentially a social process. This quality is realized in the degree in which individuals form a community group. It is absurd to exclude the teacher from membership in the group. As the most mature member of the group he has a peculiar responsibility for the conduct of the interactions and intercommunications which are the very life of the group as a community. That children are individuals whose freedom should be respected while the more mature person should have no freedom as an individual is an idea too absurd to require refutation. The tendency to exclude the teacher from a positive and leading share in the direction of the activities of the community of which he is a member is another instance of reaction from one extreme to another. When pupils were a class rather than a social group, the teacher necessarily acted largely from the outside, not as a director of processes of exchange in which all had a share. When education is based upon experience and educative experience is seen to be a social process, the situation changes radically. The teacher loses the position of external boss or dictator but takes on that of leader of group activities.

In discussing the conduct of games as an example of normal social control, reference was made to the presence of a standardized conventional factor. The counterpart of this factor in school life is found in the question of manners, especially of good manners in the manifestations of politeness and courtesy. The more we know about customs in different parts of the world at different times in the history of mankind, the more we learn how much manners differ from place to place and time to time. This fact proves that there is a large conventional factor involved. But there is no group at any time or place which does not have some code of manners as, for example, with respect to proper ways of greeting other persons. The particular form a convention takes has nothing fixed and absolute about it. But the existence of some form of convention is not itself a convention. It is a uniform attendant of all social relationships. At the very least, it is the oil which prevents or reduces friction.

It is possible, of course, for these social forms to become, as we say, "mere formalities." They may become merely outward show with no meaning behind them. But the avoidance of empty ritualistic forms of social intercourse does not mean the rejection of every formal element. It rather indicates the need for development of forms of intercourse that are inherently appropriate to social situations. Visitors to some progressive schools are shocked by the lack of manners they come across. One who knows the situation better is aware that to some extent their absence is due to the eager interest of children to go on with what they are doing. In their eagerness they may, for example, bump into each other and into visitors with no word of apology. One might say that this condition is better than a display of merely external punctilio accompanying intellectual and emotional lack of interest in school work. But it also represents a failure in education, a failure to learn one of the most important lessons of life, that of mutual accommodation and adaptation. Education is going on in a one-sided way, for attitudes and habits are in process of formation that stand in the way of the future learning that springs from easy and ready contact and communication with others.

5. The Nature of Freedom

At the risk of repeating what has been often said by me I want to say something about the other side of the problem of social control, namely, the nature of freedom. The only freedom that is of enduring importance is freedom of intelligence, that is to say, freedom of observation and of judgment exercised in behalf of purposes that are intrinsically worth while. The commonest mistake made about freedom is, I think, to identify it with freedom of movement, or with the external or physical side of activity. Now, this external and physical side of activity cannot be separated from the internal side of activity; from freedom of thought, desire, and purpose. The limitation that was put upon outward action by the fixed arrangements of the typical traditional schoolroom, with its fixed rows of desks and its military regimen of pupils who were permitted to move only at certain fixed signals, put a great restriction upon intellectual and moral freedom. Strait-jacket and chain-gang procedures had to be done away with if there was to be a chance for growth of individuals in the intellectual springs of freedom without which there is no assurance of genuine and continued normal growth.

But the fact still remains that an increased measure of freedom of outer movement is a *means*, not an end. The educational problem is not solved when this aspect of freedom is obtained. Everything then depends, so far as education is concerned, upon what is done with this added liberty. What end does it serve? What consequences flow from it? Let me speak first of the advantages which reside potentially in increase of outward freedom. In the first place, without its existence it is practically impossible for a teacher to gain knowledge of the individuals with whom he is concerned. Enforced quiet and acquiescence prevent pupils from disclosing their real natures. They enforce artificial uniformity. They put seeming before being. They place a premium upon preserving the outward appearance of attention, decorum, and obedience. And everyone who is acquainted with schools in which this system prevailed well knows that thoughts, imaginations, desires, and sly activities ran their own unchecked course behind this façade. They were disclosed to the teacher only when some untoward act led to their detection. One has only to contrast this highly artificial situation with normal human relations outside the schoolroom, say in a well-conducted home, to appreciate how fatal it is to the teacher's acquaintance with and understanding of the individuals who are, supposedly, being educated. Yet without this insight there is only an accidental chance that the material of study and the methods used in instruction will so come home to an individual that his development of mind and character is actually directed. There is a vicious circle. Mechanical uniformity of studies and methods creates a kind of uniform immobility and this reacts to perpetuate uniformity of studies and of recitations, while behind this enforced uniformity individual tendencies operate in irregular and more or less forbidden ways.

The other important advantage of increased outward freedom is found in the very nature of the learning process. That the older methods set a premium upon passivity and receptivity has been pointed out. Physical quiescence puts a tremendous premium upon these traits. The only escape from them in the standardized school is an activity which is irregular and perhaps disobedient. There cannot be complete quietude in a laboratory or workshop. The non-social character of the traditional school is seen in the fact that it erected silence into one of its prime virtues. There is, of course, such a thing as intense intellectual activity without overt bodily activity. But capacity for such intellectual activity marks a comparatively late achievement when it is continued for a long period. There should be brief intervals of time for quiet reflection provided for even the young. But they are periods of genuine reflection only when they follow after times of more overt action and are used to organize what has been gained in periods of activity in which the hands and other parts of the body beside the brain are used. Freedom of movement is also important as a means of maintaining normal physical and mental health. We have still to learn from the example of the Greeks who saw clearly the relation between a sound body and a sound mind. But in all the respects mentioned freedom of outward action is a means to freedom of judgment and of power to carry deliberately chosen ends into execution. The amount of external freedom which is needed varies from individual to individual. It naturally tends to decrease with increasing maturity, though its complete absence prevents even a mature individual from having the contacts which will provide him with new materials upon which his intelligence may exercise itself. The amount and the quality of this kind of free activity as a means of growth is a problem that must engage the thought of the educator at every stage of development.

There can be no greater mistake, however, than to treat such freedom as an end in itself. It then tends to be destructive of the shared cooperative activities which are the normal source of order. But, on the other hand, it turns freedom which should be positive into something negative. For freedom from restriction, the negative side, is to be prized only as a means to a freedom which is power: power to frame purposes, to judge wisely, to evaluate desires by the consequences which will result from acting upon them; power to select and order means to carry chosen ends into operation.

Natural impulses and desires constitute in any case the starting point. But there is no intellectual growth without some reconstruction, some remaking, of impulses and desires in the form in which they first show themselves. This remaking involves inhibition of impulse in its first estate. The alternative to externally imposed inhibition is inhibition through an individual's own reflection and judgment. The old phrase "stop and think" is sound psychology. For thinking is stoppage of the immediate manifestation of impulse until that impulse has been brought into connection with other possible tendencies to action so that a more comprehensive and coherent plan of activity is formed. Some of the other tendencies to action lead to use of eye, ear, and hand to observe objective conditions; others result in recall of what has happened in the past. Thinking is thus a postponement of immediate action, while it effects internal control of impulse through a union of observation and memory, this union being the heart of reflection. What has been said explains the meaning of the well-worn phrase "self-control." The ideal aim of education is creation of power of self-control. But the mere removal of external control is no guarantee for the production of self-control. It is easy to jump out of the frying-pan into the fire. It is easy, in other words, to escape one form of external control only to find oneself in another and more dangerous form of external control. Impulses and desires that are not ordered by intelligence are under the control of accidental circumstances. It may be a loss rather than a gain to escape from the control of another person only to find one's conduct dictated by immediate whim and caprice; that is, at the mercy of impulses into whose formation intelligent judgment has not entered. A person whose conduct is controlled in this way has at most only the illusion of freedom. Actually he is directed by forces over which he has no command.

6. The Meaning of Purpose

It is, then, a sound instinct which identifies freedom with power to frame purposes and to execute or carry into effect purposes so framed. Such freedom is in turn identical with self-control; for the formation of purposes and the organization of means to execute them are the work of intelligence. Plato once defined a slave as the person who executes the purposes of another, and, as has just been said, a person is also a slave who is enslaved to his own blind desires. There is, I think, no point in the philosophy of progressive education which is sounder than its emphasis upon the importance of the participation of the learner in the formation of the purposes which direct his activities in the learning process, just as there is no defect in traditional education greater than its failure to secure the active cooperation of the pupil in construction of the purposes involved in his studying. But the meaning of purposes and ends is not self-evident and self-explanatory. The more their educational importance is emphasized, the more important it is to understand what a purpose is; how it arises and how it functions in experience.

A genuine purpose always starts with an impulse. Obstruction of the immediate execution of an impulse converts it into a desire. Nevertheless neither impulse nor desire is itself a purpose. A purpose is an end-view. That is, it involves foresight of the consequences which will result from acting upon impulse. Foresight of consequences involves the operation of intelligence. It demands, in the first place, observation of objective conditions and circumstances. For impulse and desire produce consequences not by themselves alone but through their interaction or cooperation with surrounding conditions. The impulse for such a simple action as walking is executed only in active conjunction with the ground on which one stands. Under ordinary circumstances, we do not have to pay much attention to the ground. In a ticklish situation we have to observe very carefully just what the conditions are, as in climbing a steep and rough mountain where no trail has been laid out. Exercise of observation is, then, one condition of transformation of impulse into a purpose. As in the sign by a railway crossing, we have to stop, look, listen.

But observation alone is not enough. We have to understand the *significance* of what we see, hear, and touch. This significance consists of the consequences that will result when what is seen is acted upon. A baby may *see* the brightness of a flame and be attracted thereby to reach for it. The significance of the flame is then not its brightness but its power to burn, as the consequence that will result from touching it. We can be aware of consequences only because of previous experiences. In cases that are familiar because of many prior experiences we do not have to stop to remember just what those experiences were. A flame comes to signify light and heat without our having expressly to think of previous experiences of heat and burning. But in unfamiliar cases, we cannot tell just what the consequences of observed conditions will be unless we go over past experiences in our mind, unless we reflect upon them and by seeing what is similar in them to those now present, go on to form a judgment of what may be expected in the present situation.

The formation of purposes is, then, a rather complex intellectual operation. It involves (1) observation of surrounding conditions; (2) knowledge of what has happened in similar situations in the past, a knowledge obtained partly by recollection and partly from the information, advice, and warning of those who have had a wider experience; and (3) judgment which puts together what is observed and what is recalled to see what they signify. A purpose differs from an original impulse and desire through its translation into a plan and method of action based upon foresight of the consequences of acting under given observed conditions in a certain way. "If wishes were horses, beggars would ride." Desire for something may be intense. It may be so strong as to override estimation of the consequences that will follow acting upon it. Such occurrences do not provide the model for education. The crucial educational problem is that of procuring the postponement of immediate action upon desire until observation and judgment have intervened. Unless I am mistaken, this point is definitely relevant to the conduct of progressive schools. Overemphasis upon activity as an end, instead of upon *intelligent* activity, leads to identification of freedom with immediate execution of impulses and desires. This identification is justified by a confusion of impulse with purpose; although, as has just been said, there is no purpose unless overt action is postponed until there is foresight of the consequences of carrying the impulse into execution—a foresight that is impossible without observation, information, and judgment. Mere foresight, even if it takes the form of accurate prediction, is not, of course, enough. The intellectual anticipation, the idea of consequences, must blend with desire and impulse to acquire moving force. It then gives direction to what otherwise is blind, while desire gives ideas impetus and momentum. An idea then becomes a plan in and for an activity to be carried out. Suppose a man has a desire to secure a new home, say by building a house. No matter how strong his desire, it cannot be directly executed. The man must form an idea of what kind of house he wants, including the number and arrangement of rooms, etc. He has to draw a plan, and have blue prints and specifications made. All this might be an idle amusement for spare time unless he also took stock of his resources. He must consider the relation of his funds and available credit to the execution of the plan. He has to investigate available sites, their price, their nearness to his place of business, to a congenial neighborhood, to school facilities, and so on and so on. All of the things reckoned with: his ability to pay, size and needs of family, possible locations, etc., etc., are objective facts. They are no part of the original desire. But they have to be viewed and judged in order that a desire may be converted into a purpose and a purpose into a plan of action.

All of us have desires, all at least who have not become so pathological that they are completely apathetic. These desires are the ultimate moving springs of action. A professional businessman wishes to succeed in his career; a general wishes to win the battle; a parent to have a comfortable home for his family, and to educate his children, and so on indefinitely. The intensity of the desire measures the strength of the efforts that will be put forth. But the wishes are empty castles in the air unless they are translated into the means by which they may be realized. The question of *how soon* or of means takes the place of a projected imaginative end, and, since means are objective, they have to be studied and understood if a genuine purpose is to be formed.

Traditional education tended to ignore the importance of personal impulse and desire as moving springs. But this is no reason why progressive education should identify impulse and desire with purpose and thereby pass lightly over the need for careful observation, for wide range of information, and for judgment if students are to share in the formation of the purposes which activate them. In an *educational* scheme, the occurrence of a desire and impulse is not the final end. It is an occasion and a demand for the formation of a plan and method of activity. Such a plan, to repeat, can be formed only by study of conditions and by securing all relevant information.

The teacher's business is to see that the occasion is taken advantage of. Since freedom resides in the operations of intelligent observation and judgment by which a purpose is developed, guidance given by the teacher to the exercise of the pupils' intelligence is an aid to freedom, not a restriction upon it. Sometimes teachers seem to be afraid even to make suggestions to the members of a group as to what they should do. I have heard of cases in which children are surrounded with objects and materials and then left entirely to themselves, the teacher being loath to suggest even what might be done with the materials lest freedom be infringed upon. Why, then, even supply materials, since they are a source of some suggestion or other? But what is more important is that the suggestion upon which pupils act must in any case come from somewhere. It is impossible to understand why a suggestion from one who has a larger experience and a wider horizon should not be at least as valid as a suggestion arising from some more or less accidental source.

It is possible of course to abuse the office, and to force the activity of the young into channels which express the teacher's purpose rather than that of the pupils. But the way to avoid this danger is not for the adult to withdraw entirely. The way is, first, for the teacher to be intelligently aware of the capacities, needs, and past experiences of those under instruction, and, secondly, to allow the suggestion made to develop into a plan and project by means of the further suggestions contributed and organized into a whole by the members of the group. The plan, in other words, is a cooperative enterprise, not a dictation. The teacher's suggestion is not a mold for a cast-iron result but is a starting point to be developed into a plan through contributions from the experience of all engaged in the learning process. The development occurs through reciprocal give-and-take, the teacher taking but not being afraid also to give. The essential point is that the purpose grow and take shape through the process of social intelligence.

7. Progressive Organization of Subject-Matter

Allusion has been made in passing a number of times to objective conditions involved in experience and to their function in promoting or failing to promote the enriched growth of further experience. By implication, these objective conditions, whether those of observation, of memory, of information procured from others, or of imagination, have been identified with the subject-matter of study and learning; or, speaking more generally, with the stuff of the course of study. Nothing, however, has been said explicitly so far about subject-matter as such. That topic will now be discussed. One consideration stands out clearly when education is conceived in terms of experience. Anything which can be called a study, whether arithmetic, history, geography, or one of the natural sciences, must be derived from materials which at the outset fall within the scope of ordinary life-experience. In this respect the newer education contrasts sharply with procedures which start with facts and truths that are outside the range of the experience of those taught, and which, therefore, have the problem of discovering ways and means of bringing them within experience. Undoubtedly one chief cause for the great success of newer methods in early elementary education has been its observance of the contrary principle.

But finding the material for learning within experience is only the first step. The next step is the progressive development of what is already experienced into a fuller and richer and also more organized form, a form that gradually approximates that in which subject-matter is presented to the skilled, mature person. That this change is possible without departing from the organic connection of education with experience is shown by the fact that this change takes place outside of the school and apart from formal education. The infant, for example, begins with an environment of objects that is very restricted in space and time.

That environment steadily expands by the momentum inherent in experience itself without aid from scholastic instruction. As the infant learns to reach, creep, walk, and talk, the intrinsic subject-matter of its experience widens and deepens. It comes into connection with new objects and events which call out new powers, while the exercise of these powers refines and enlarges the content of its experience. Life-space and life-durations are expanded. The environment, the world of experience, constantly grows larger and, so to speak, thicker. The educator who receives the child at the end of this period has to find ways for doing consciously and deliberately what "nature" accomplishes in the earlier years.

It is hardly necessary to insist upon the first of the two conditions which have been specified. It is a cardinal precept of the newer school of education that the beginning of instruction shall be made with the experience learners already have; that this experience and the capacities that have been developed during its course provide the starting point for all further learning. I am not so sure that the other condition, that of orderly development toward expansion and organization of subject-matter through growth of experience, receives as much attention. Yet the principle of continuity of educative experience requires that equal thought and attention be given to solution of this aspect of the educational problem. Undoubtedly this phase of the problem is more difficult than the other. Those who deal with the pre-school child, with the kindergarten child, and with the boy and girl of the early primary years do not have much difficulty in determining the range of past experience or in finding activities that connect in vital ways with it. With older children both factors of the problem offer increased difficulties to the educator. It is harder to find out the background of the experience of individuals and harder to find out just how the subject-matters already contained in that experience shall be directed so as to lead out to larger and better organized fields.

It is a mistake to suppose that the principle of the leading on of experience to something different is adequately satisfied simply by giving pupils some new experiences any more than it is by seeing to it that they have greater skill and ease in dealing with things with which they are already familiar. It is also essential that the new objects and events be related intellectually to those of earlier experiences, and this means that there be some advance made in conscious articulation of facts and ideas. It thus becomes the office of the educator to select those things within the range of existing experience that have the promise and potentiality of presenting new problems which by stimulating new ways of observation and judgment will expand the area of further experience. He must constantly regard what is already won not as a fixed possession but as an agency and instrumentality for opening new fields which make new demands upon existing powers of observation and of intelligent use of memory. Connectedness in growth must be his constant watchword.

The educator more than the member of any other profession is concerned to have a long look ahead. The physician may feel his job done when he has restored a patient to health. He has undoubtedly the obligation of advising him how to live so as to avoid similar troubles in the future. But, after all, the conduct of his life is his own affair, not the physician's; and what is more important for the present point is that as far as the physician does occupy himself with instruction and advice as to the future of his patient he takes upon himself the function of an educator. The lawyer is occupied with winning a suit for his client or getting the latter out of some complication into which he has got himself. If it goes beyond the case presented to him he too becomes an educator. The educator by the very nature of his work is obliged to see his present work in terms of what it accomplishes, or fails to accomplish, for a future whose objects are linked with those of the present.

Here, again, the problem for the progressive educator is more difficult than for the teacher in the traditional school. The latter had indeed to look ahead. But unless his personality and enthusiasm took him beyond the limits that hedged in the traditional school, he could content himself with thinking of the next examination period or the promotion to the next class. He could envisage the future in terms of factors that lay within the requirements of the school system as that conventionally existed. There is incumbent upon the teacher who links education and actual experience together a more serious and a harder business. He must be aware of the potentialities for leading students into new fields which belong to experiences already had, and must use this knowledge as his criterion for selection and arrangement of the conditions that influence their present experience.

Because the studies of the traditional school consisted of subject-matter that was selected and arranged on the basis of the judgment of adults as to what would be useful for the young sometime in the future, the material to be learned was settled upon outside the present life-experience of the learner. In consequence, it had to do with the past; it was such as had proved useful to men in past ages. By reaction to an opposite extreme, as unfortunate as it was probably natural under the circumstances, the sound idea that education should derive its materials from present experience and should enable the learner to cope with the problems of the present and future has often been converted into the idea that progressive schools can to a very large extent ignore the past. If the present could be cut off from the past, this conclusion would be sound. But the achievements of the past provide the only means at command for understanding the present. Just as the individual has to draw in memory upon his own past to understand the conditions in which he individually finds himself, so the issues and problems of present *social* life are in such intimate and direct connection with the past that students cannot be prepared to understand either these problems or the best way of dealing with them without delving into their roots in the past. In other words, the sound principle that the objectives of learning are in the future and its immediate materials are in present experience can be carried into effect only in the degree that present experience is stretched, as it were, backward. It can expand into the future only as it is also enlarged to take in the past.

If time permitted, discussion of the political and economic issues which the present generation will be compelled to face in the future would render this general statement definite and concrete. The nature of the issues cannot be understood save as we know how they came about. The institutions and customs that exist in the present and that give rise to present social ills and dislocations did not arise overnight. They have a long history behind them. Attempt to deal with them simply on the basis of what is obvious in the present is bound to result in adoption of superficial measures which in the end will only render existing problems more acute and more difficult to solve. Policies framed simply upon the ground of knowledge of the present cut off from the past is the counterpart of heedless carelessness in individual conduct. The way out of scholastic systems that made the past an end in itself is to make acquaintance with the past a *means* of understanding the present. Until this problem is worked out, the present clash of educational ideas and practices will continue. On the one hand, there will be reactionaries that claim that the main, if not the sole, business of education is transmission of the cultural heritage. On the other hand, there will be those who hold that we should ignore the past and deal only with the present and future.

That up to the present time the weakest point in progressive schools is in the matter of selection and organization of intellectual subject-matter is, I think, inevitable under the circumstances. It is as inevitable as it is right and proper that they should break loose from the cut and dried material which formed the staple of the old education. In addition, the field of experience is very wide and it varies in its contents from place to place and from time to time. A single course of studies for all progressive schools is out of the question; it would mean abandoning the fundamental principle of connection with life-experiences. Moreover, progressive schools are new. They have had hardly more than a generation in which to develop. A certain amount of uncertainty and of laxity in choice and organization of subject-matter is, therefore, what was to be expected. It is no ground for fundamental criticism or complaint.

It is a ground for legitimate criticism, however, when the ongoing movement of progressive education fails to recognize that the problem of selection and organization of subject-matter for study and learning is fundamental. Improvisation that takes advantage of special occasions prevents teaching and learning from being stereotyped and dead. But the basic material of study cannot be picked up in a cursory manner. Occasions which are not and cannot be foreseen are bound to arise wherever there is intellectual freedom. They should be utilized. But there is a decided difference between using them in the development of a continuing line of activity and trusting to them to provide the chief material of learning.

Unless a given experience leads out into a field previously unfamiliar no problems arise, while problems are the stimulus to thinking. That the conditions found in present experience should be used as sources of problems is a characteristic which differentiates education based upon experience from traditional education. For in the latter, problems were set from outside. None-theless, growth depends upon the presence of difficulty to be overcome by the exercise of intelligence. Once more, it is part of the educator's responsibility to see equally to two things: First, that the problem grows out of the conditions of the experience being had in the present, and that it is within the range of the capacity of students; and, secondly, that it is such that it arouses in the learner an active quest for information and for production of new ideas. The new facts and new ideas thus obtained become the ground for further experiences in which new problems are presented. The process is a continuous spiral. The inescapable linkage of the present with the past is a principle whose application is not restricted to a study of history. Take natural science, for example. Contemporary social life is what it is in very large measure because of the results of application of physical science. The experience of every child and youth, in the country and the city, is what it is in its present actuality because of appliances which utilize electricity, heat, and chemical processes. A child does not eat a meal that does not involve in its preparation and assimilation chemical and physiological principles. He does not read by artificial light or take a ride in a motor car or on a train without coming into contact with operations and processes which science has engendered.

It is a sound educational principle that students should be in-troduced to scientific subject-matter and be initiated into its facts and laws through acquaintance with everyday social applica-tions. Adherence to this method is not only the most direct ave-nue to understanding of science itself but as the pupils grow more mature it is also the surest road to the understanding of the economic and industrial problems of present society. For they are the products to a very large extent of the application of science in production and distribution of commodities and services, while the latter processes are the most important factor in determining the present relations of human beings and social groups to one another. It is absurd, then, to argue that processes similar to those studied in laboratories and institutes of research are not a part of the daily life-experience of the young and hence do not come within the scope of education based upon experience. That the immature cannot study scientific facts and principles in the way in which mature experts study them goes without saying.

But this fact, instead of exempting the educator from responsibility for using present experiences so that learners may gradually be led, through extraction of facts and laws, to experience of a scientific order, sets one of his main problems.

For if it is true that existing experience in detail and also on a wide scale is what it is because of the application of science, first, to processes of production and distribution of goods and services, and then to the relations which human beings sustain socially to one another, it is impossible to obtain an understanding of present social forces (without which they cannot be mastered and directed) apart from an education which leads learners into knowledge of the very same facts and principles which in their final organization constitute the sciences. Nor does the importance of the principle that learners should be led to acquaintance with scientific subject-matter cease with the insight thereby given into present social issues. The methods of science also point the way to the measures and policies by means of which a better social order can be brought into existence. The applications of science which have produced in large measure the social conditions which now exist do not exhaust the possible field of their application. For so far science has been applied more or less casually and under the influence of ends, such as private advantage and power, which are a heritage from the institutions of a prescientific age.

We are told almost daily and from many sources that it is impossible for human beings to direct their common life intelligently. We are told, on one hand, that the complexity of human relations, domestic and international, and on the other hand, the fact that human beings are so largely creatures of emotion and habit, make impossible large-scale social planning and direction by intelligence. This view would be more credible if any systematic effort, beginning with early education and carried on through the continuous study and learning of the young, had ever been undertaken with a view to making the method of intelligence, exemplified in science, supreme in education. There is nothing in the inherent nature of habit that prevents intelligent method from becoming itself habitual; and there is nothing in the nature of emotion to prevent the development of intense emotional allegiance to the method.

The case of science is here employed as an illustration of progressive selection of subject-matter resident in present experience towards organization: an organization which is free, not externally imposed, because it is in accord with the growth of experience itself. The utilization of subject-matter found in the present life-experience of the learner towards science is perhaps the best illustration that can be found of the basic principle of using existing experience as the means of carrying learners on to a wider, more refined, and better organized environing world, physical and human, than is found in the experiences from which educative growth sets out. Hogben's recent work, *Mathematics for the Million*, shows how mathematics, if it is treated as a mirror of civilization and as a main agency in its progress, can contribute to the desired goal as surely as can the physical sciences. The underlying ideal in any case is that of progressive organization of knowledge. It is with reference to organization of knowledge that we are likely to find *Either-Or* philosophies most acutely active. In practice, if not in so many words, it is often held that since traditional education rested upon a conception of organization of knowledge that was almost completely contemptuous of living present experience, therefore education based upon living experience should be contemptuous of the organization of facts and ideas.

When a moment ago I called this organization an *ideal*, I meant, on the negative side, that the educator cannot start with knowledge already organized and proceed to ladle it out in doses. But as an ideal the active process of organizing facts and ideas is an ever-present educational process. No experience is educative that does not tend both to knowledge of more facts and entertaining of more ideas and to a better, a more orderly, arrangement of them. It is not true that organization is a principle foreign to experience. Otherwise experience would be so dispersive as to be chaotic. The experience of young children centres about persons and the home. Disturbance of the normal order of relationships in the family is now known by psychiatrists to be a fertile source of later mental and emotional troubles—a fact which testifies to the reality of this kind of organization. One of the great advances in early school education, in the kindergarten and early grades, is that it preserves the social and human centre of the organization of experience, instead of the older violent shift of the centre of gravity. But one of the outstanding problems of education, as of music, is modulation. In the case of education, modulation means movement from a social and human centre toward a more objective intellectual scheme of organization, always bearing in mind, however, that intellectual organization is not an end in itself but is the means by which social relations, distinctively human ties and bonds, may be understood and more intelligently ordered.

When education is based in theory and practice upon experience, it goes without saying that the organized subject-matter of the adult and the specialist cannot provide the starting point. Nevertheless, it represents the goal toward which education should continuously move. It is hardly necessary to say that one of the most fundamental principles of the scientific organization of knowledge is the principle of cause-and-effect. The way in which this principle is grasped and formulated by the scientific specialist is certainly very different from the way in which it can be approached in the experience of the young. But neither the relation nor grasp of its meaning is foreign to the experience of even the young child. When a child two or three years of age learns not to approach a flame too closely and yet to draw near enough a stove to get its warmth he is grasping and using the causal relation. There is no intelligent activity that does not conform to the requirements of the relation, and it is intelligent in the degree in which it is not only conformed to but consciously borne in mind.

In the earlier forms of experience the causal relation does not offer itself in the abstract but in the form of the relation of means employed to ends attained; of the relation of means and consequences. Growth in judgment and understanding is essentially growth in ability to form purposes and to select and arrange means for their realization. The most elementary experiences of the young are filled with cases of the means-consequence relation. There is not a meal cooked nor a source of illumination employed that does not exemplify this relation. The trouble with education is not the absence of situations in which the causal relation is exemplified in the relation of means and consequences. Failure to utilize the situations so as to lead the learner on to grasp the relation in the given cases of experience is, however, only too common. The logician gives the names "analysis and synthesis" to the operations by which means are selected and organized in relation to a purpose.

This principle determines the ultimate foundation for the utilization of *activities* in school. Nothing can be more absurd educationally than to make a plea for a variety of active occupations in the school while decrying the need for progressive organization of information and ideas. Intelligent activity is distinguished from aimless ·activity by the fact that it involves selection of means—analysis—out of the variety of conditions that are present, and their arrangement—synthesis—to reach an intended aim or purpose. That the more immature the learner is, the simpler must be the ends held in view and the more rudimentary the means employed, is obvious. But the principle of organization of activity in terms of some perception of the relation of consequences to means applies even with the very young. Otherwise an activity ceases to be educative because it is blind. With increased maturity, the problem of interrelation of means becomes more urgent. In the degree in which intelligent observation is transferred from the relation of means to ends to the more complex question of the relation of means to one another, the idea of cause and effect becomes prominent and explicit. The final justification of shops, kitchens, and so on in the school is not just that they afford opportunity for activity, but that they provide opportunity for the *kind* of activity or for the acquisition of mechanical skills which leads students to attend to the relation of means and ends, and then to consideration of the way things interact with one another to produce definite effects. It is the same in principle as the ground for laboratories in scientific research.

Unless the problem of intellectual organization can be worked out on the ground of experience, reaction is sure to occur toward externally imposed methods of organization. There are signs of this reaction already in evidence. We are told that our schools, old and new, are failing in the main task. They do not develop, it is said, the capacity for critical discrimination and the ability to reason. The ability to think is smothered, we are told, by accumulation of miscellaneous ill-digested information, and by the attempt to acquire forms of skill which will be immediately useful in the business and commercial world. We are told that these evils spring from the influence of science and from the magnification of present requirements at the expense of the tested cultural heritage from the past. It is argued that science and its method must be subordinated; that we must return to the logic of ultimate first principles expressed in the logic of Aristotle and St. Thomas, in order that the young may have sure anchorage in their intellectual and moral life, and not be at the mercy of every passing breeze that blows.

If the method of science had ever been consistently and continuously applied throughout the day-by-day work of the school in all subjects, I should be more impressed by this emotional appeal than I am. I see at bottom but two alternatives between which education must choose if it is not to drift aimlessly. One of them is expressed by the attempt to induce educators to return to the intellectual methods and ideals that arose centuries before scientific method was developed. The appeal may be temporarily successful in a period when general insecurity, emotional and intellectual as well as economic, is rife. For under these conditions the desire to lean on fixed authority is active. Nevertheless, it is so out of touch with all the conditions of modern life that I believe it is folly to seek salvation in this direction. The other alternative is systematic utilization of scientific method as the pattern and ideal of intelligent exploration and exploitation of the potentialities inherent in experience.

The problem involved comes home with peculiar force to progressive schools. Failure to give constant attention to development of the intellectual content of experiences and to obtain ever-increasing organization of facts and ideas may in the end merely strengthen the tendency toward a reactionary return to intellectual and moral authoritarianism. The present is not the time nor place for a disquisition upon scientific method. But certain features of it are so closely connected with any educational scheme based upon experience that they should be noted.

In the first place, the experimental method of science attaches more importance, not less, to ideas as ideas than do other methods. There is no such thing as experiment in the scientific sense unless action is directed by some leading idea. The fact that the ideas employed are hypotheses, not final truths, is the reason why ideas are more jealously guarded and tested in science than anywhere else. The moment they are taken to be first truths in themselves there ceases to be any reason for scrupulous examination of them. As fixed truths they must be accepted and that is the end of the matter. But as hypotheses, they must be continuously tested and revised, a requirement that demands they be accurately formulated.

In the second place, ideas or hypotheses are tested by the consequences which they produce when they are acted upon. This fact means that the consequences of action must be carefully and discriminatingly observed. Activity that is not checked by observation of what follows from it may be temporarily enjoyed. But intellectually it leads nowhere. It does not provide knowledge about the situations in which action occurs nor does it lead to clarification and expansion of ideas.

In the third place, the method of intelligence manifested in the experimental method demands keeping track of ideas, activities, and observed consequences. Keeping track is a matter of reflective review and summarizing, in which there is both discrimination and record of the significant features of a developing experience. To reflect is to look back over what has been done so as to extract the net meanings which are the capital stock for intelligent dealing with further experiences. It is the heart of intellectual organization and of the disciplined mind.

I have been forced to speak in general and often abstract language. But what has been said is organically connected with the requirement that experiences in order to be educative must lead out into an expanding world of subject-matter, a subject-matter of facts or information and of ideas. This condition is satisfied only as the educator views teaching and learning as a continuous process of reconstruction of experience. This condition in turn can be satisfied only as the educator has a long look ahead, and views every present experience as a moving force in influencing what future experiences will be. I am aware that the emphasis I have placed upon scientific method may be misleading, for it may result only in calling up the special technique of laboratory research as that is conducted by specialists. But the meaning of the emphasis placed upon scientific method has little to do with specialized techniques. It means that scientific method is the only authentic means at our command for getting at the significance of our everyday experiences of the world in which we live. It means that scientific method provides a working pattern of the way in which and the conditions under which experiences are used to lead ever onward and outward. Adaptation of the method to individuals of various degrees of maturity is a problem for the educator, and the constant factors in the problem are the formation of ideas, acting upon ideas, observation of the conditions which result, and organization of facts and ideas for future use.

Neither the ideas, nor the activities, nor the observations, nor the organization are the same for a person six years old as they are for one twelve or eighteen years old, to say nothing of the adult scientist. But at every level there is an expanding development of experience if experience is educative in effect. Consequently, whatever the level of experience, we have no choice but either to operate in accord with the pattern it provides or else to neglect the place of intelligence in the development and control of a living and moving experience.

8. Experience—The Means and Goal of Education

In what I have said I have taken for granted the soundness of the principle that education in order to accomplish its ends both for the individual learner and for society must be based upon experience—which is always the actual life-experience of some individual. I have not argued for the acceptance of this principle nor attempted to justify it. Conservatives as well as radicals in education are profoundly discontented with the present educational situation taken as a whole. There is at least this much agreement among intelligent persons of both schools of educational thought. The educational system must move one way or another, either backward to the intellectual and moral standards of a pre-scientific age or forward to ever greater utilization of scientific method in the development of the possibilities of growing, expanding experience. I have but endeavored to point out some of the conditions which must be satisfactorily fulfilled if education takes the latter course.

For I am so confident of the potentialities of education when it is treated as intelligently directed development of the possibilities inherent in ordinary experience that I do not feel it necessary to criticize here the other route nor to advance arguments in favor of taking the route of experience. The only ground for anticipating failure in taking this path resides to my mind in the danger that experience and the experimental method will not be adequately conceived. There is no discipline in the world so severe as the discipline of experience subjected to the tests of intelligent development and direction. Hence the only ground I can see for even a temporary reaction against the standards, aims, and methods of the newer education is the failure of educators who professedly adopt them to be faithful to them in practice. As I have emphasized more than once, the road of the new education is not an easier one to follow than the old road but a more strenuous and difficult one. It will remain so until it has attained its majority and that attainment will require many years of serious cooperative work on the part of its adherents. The greatest danger that attends its future is, I believe, the idea that it is an easy way to follow, so easy that its course may be improvised, if not in an impromptu fashion, at least almost from day to day or from week to week. It is for this reason that instead of extolling its principles, I have confined myself to showing certain conditions which must be fulfilled if it is to have the successful career which by right belongs to it.

I have used frequently in what precedes the words "progressive" and "new" education. I do not wish to close, however, without recording my firm belief that the fundamental issue is not of new versus old education nor of progressive against traditional education but a question of what anything whatever must be to be worthy of the name *education*. I am not, I hope and believe, in favor of any ends or any methods simply because the name progressive may be applied to them. The basic question concerns the nature of education with no qualifying adjectives prefixed. What we want and need is education pure and simple, and we shall make surer and faster progress when we devote ourselves to finding out just what education is and what conditions have to be satisfied in order that education may be a reality and not a name or a slogan. It is for this reason alone that I have emphasized the need for a sound philosophy of experience.

Freedom and Culture

1. The Problem of Freedom

What is freedom and why is it prized? Is desire for freedom inherent in human nature or is it a product of special circumstances? Is it wanted as an end or as a means of getting other things? Does its possession entail responsibilities, and are these responsibilities so onerous that the mass of men will readily surrender liberty for the sake of greater ease? Is the struggle for liberty so arduous that most men are easily distracted from the endeavor to achieve and maintain it? Does freedom in itself and in the things it brings with it seem as important as security of livelihood; as food, shelter, clothing, or even as having a good time? Did man ever care as much for it as we in this country have been taught to believe? Is there any truth in the old notion that the driving force in political history has been the effort of the common man to achieve freedom? Was our own struggle for political independence in any genuine sense animated by desire for freedom, or were there a number of discomforts that our ancestors wanted to get rid of, things having nothing in common save that they were felt to be troublesome?

Is love of liberty ever anything more than a desire to be liberated from some special restriction? And when it is got rid of does the desire for liberty die down until something else feels intolerable? Again, how does the desire for freedom compare in intensity with the desire to feel equal with others, especially with those who have previously been called superiors? How do the fruits of liberty compare with the enjoyments that spring from a feeling of union, of solidarity, with others? Will men surrender their liberties if they believe that by so doing they will obtain the satisfaction that comes from a sense of fusion with others and that respect by others which is the product of the strength furnished by solidarity?

The present state of the world is putting questions like these to citizens of all democratic countries. It is putting them with special force to us in a country where democratic institutions have been bound up with a certain tradition, the "ideology" of which the Declaration of Independence is the classic expression. This tradition has taught us that attainment of freedom is the goal of political history; that self-government is the inherent right of free men and is that which, when it is achieved, men prize above all else. Yet as we look at the world we see supposedly free institutions in many countries not so much overthrown as abandoned willingly, apparently with enthusiasm. We may infer that what has happened is proof they never existed in reality but only in name. Or we may console ourselves with a belief that unusual conditions, such as national frustration and humiliation, have led men to welcome any kind of government that promised to restore national self-respect. But conditions in our country as well as the eclipse of democracy in other countries compel us to ask questions about the career and fate of free societies, even our own.

There perhaps was a time when the questions asked would have seemed to be mainly or exclusively political. Now we know better. For we know that a large part of the causes which have produced the conditions that are expressed in the questions is the dependence of politics upon other forces, notably the economic. The problem of the constitution of human nature is involved, since it is part of our tradition that love of freedom is inherent in its make-up. Is the popular psychology of democracy a myth? The old doctrine about human nature was also tied up with the ethical belief that political democracy is a moral right and that the laws upon which it is based are fundamental moral laws which every form of social organization should obey. If belief in natural rights and natural laws as the foundation of free government is surrendered, does the latter have any other moral basis? For while it would be foolish to believe that the American colonies fought the battles that secured their independence and that they built their government consciously and deliberately upon a foundation of psychological and moral theories, yet the democratic tradition, call it dream or call it penetrating vision, was so closely allied with beliefs about human nature and about the moral ends which political institutions should serve, that a rude shock occurs when these affiliations break down. Is there anything to take their place, anything that will give the kind of support they once gave?

The problems behind the questions asked, the forces which give the questions their urgency, go beyond the particular beliefs which formed the early psychological and moral foundation of democracy. After retiring from public office, Thomas Jefferson in his old age carried on a friendly philosophical correspondence with John Adams. In one of his letters he made a statement about existing American conditions and expressed a hope about their future estate: "The advance of liberalism encourages a hope that the human mind will some day get back to the freedom it enjoyed two thousand years ago. This country, which has given to the world the example of physical liberty, owes to it that of moral emancipation also, for as yet it is but nominal with us. The inquisition of public opinion overwhelms in practice the freedom asserted by the laws in theory." The situation that has developed since his time may well lead us to reverse the ideas he expressed, and inquire whether political freedom can be maintained without that freedom of culture which he expected to be the final result of political freedom. It is no longer easy to entertain the hope that given political freedom as the one thing necessary all other things will in time be added to it—and so to us. For we now know that the relations which exist between persons, outside of political institutions, relations of industry, of communication, of science, art and religion, affect daily associations, and thereby deeply affect the attitudes and habits expressed in government and rules of law. If it is true that the political and legal react to shape the other things, it is even more true that political institutions are an effect, not a cause.

It is this knowledge that sets the theme to be discussed. For this complex of conditions which taxes the terms upon which human beings associate and live together is summed up in the word *Culture*. The problem is to know what kind of culture is so free in itself that it conceives and begets political freedom as its accompaniment and consequence. What about the state of science and knowledge; of the arts, fine and technological; of friendships and family life; of business and finance; of the attitudes and dispositions created in the give and take of ordinary day by day associations? No matter what is the native make-up of human nature, its working activities, those which respond to institutions and rules and which finally shape the pattern of the latter, are created by the whole body of occupations, interests, skills, beliefs that constitute a given culture. As the latter changes, especially as it grows complex and intricate in the way in which American life has changed since our political organization took shape, new problems take the place of those governing the earlier formation and distribution of political powers. The view that love of freedom is so inherent in man that, if it only has a chance given it by abolition of oppressions exercised by church and state, it will produce and maintain free institutions is no longer adequate. The idea naturally arose when settlers in a new country felt that the distance they had put between themselves and the forces that oppressed them effectively symbolized everything that stood between them and permanent achievement of freedom. We are now forced to see that positive conditions, forming the prevailing state of culture, are required. Release from oppressions and repressions which previously existed marked a necessary transition, but transitions are but bridges to something different.

Early republicans were obliged even in their own time to note that general conditions, such as are summed up under the name of culture, had a good deal to do with political institutions. For they held that oppressions of state and church had exercised a corrupting influence upon human nature, so that the original impulse to liberty had either been lost or warped out of shape. This was a virtual admission that surrounding conditions may be stronger than native tendencies. It proved a degree of plasticity in human nature that required exercise of continual solicitude— expressed in the saying that eternal vigilance is the price of liberty. The Founding Fathers were aware that love of power is a trait of human nature, so strong a one that definite barriers had to be erected to keep persons who get into positions of official authority from encroachments that undermine free institutions. Admission that men may be brought by long habit to hug their chains implies a belief that second or acquired nature is stronger than original nature.

Jefferson at least went further than this. For his fear of the growth of manufacturing and trade and his preference for agrarian pursuits amounted to acceptance of the idea that interests bred by certain pursuits may fundamentally alter original human nature and the institutions that are congenial to it. That the development Jefferson dreaded has come about and to a much greater degree than he could have anticipated is an obvious fact. We face today the consequences of the fact that an agricultural and rural people has become an urban industrial population.

Proof is decisive that economic factors are an intrinsic part of the culture that determines the actual turn taken by political measures and rules, no matter what verbal beliefs are held. Although it later became the fashion to blur the connection which exists between economics and politics, and even to reprove those who called attention to it, Madison as well as Jefferson was quite aware of the connection and of its bearing upon democracy. Knowledge that the connection demanded a general distribution of property and the prevention of rise of the extremely poor and the extremely rich, was however different from explicit recognition of a relation between culture and nature so intimate that the former may shape the patterns of thought and action.

Economic relations and habits cannot be set apart in isolation any more than political institutions can be. The state of knowledge of nature, that is, of physical science, is a phase of culture upon which industry and commerce, the production and distribution of goods and the regulation of services directly depend. Unless we take into account the rise of the new science of nature in the seventeenth century and its growth to its present state, our economic agencies of production and distribution and ultimately of consumption cannot be understood. The connection of the events of the industrial revolution with those of the advancing scientific revolution is an incontrovertible witness.

It has not been customary to include the arts, the fine arts, as an important part of the social conditions that bear upon democratic institutions and personal freedom. Even after the influence of the state of industry and of natural science has been admitted, we still tend to draw the line at the idea that literature, music, painting, the drama, architecture, have any intimate connection with the cultural bases of democracy. Even those who call themselves good democrats are often content to look upon the fruits of these arts as adornments of culture rather than as things in whose enjoyment all should partake, if democracy is to be a reality. The state of things in totalitarian countries may induce us to revise this opinion. For it proves that no matter what may be the case with the impulses and powers that lead the creative artist to do his work, works of art once brought into existence are the most compelling of the means of communication by which emotions are stirred and opinions formed. The theater, the movie and music hall, even the picture gallery, eloquence, popular parades, common sports and recreative agencies, have all been brought under regulation as part of the propaganda agencies by which dictatorship is kept in power without being regarded by the masses as oppressive. We are beginning to realize that emotions and imagination are more potent in shaping public sentiment and opinion than information and reason.

Indeed, long before the present crisis came into being there was a saying that if one could control the songs of a nation, one need not care who made its laws. And historical study shows that primitive religions owe their power in determining belief and action to their ability to reach emotions and imagination by rites and ceremonies, by legend and folklore, all clothed with the traits that mark works of art. The Church that has had by far the greatest influence in the modern world took over their agencies of esthetic appeal and incorporated them into its own structure, after adapting them to its own purpose, in winning and holding the allegiance of the masses.

A totalitarian regime is committed to control of the whole life of all its subjects by its hold over feelings, desires, emotions, as well as opinions. This indeed is a mere truism, since a totalitarian state has to be total. But save as we take it into account we shall not appreciate the intensity of the revival of the warfare between state and church that exists in Germany and Russia. The conflict is not the expression of the whim of a leader. It is inherent in any regime that demands the *total* allegiance of all its subjects. It must first of all, and most enduringly of all, if it is to be permanent, command the imagination, with all the impulses and motives we have been accustomed to call *inner*. Religious organizations are those which rule by use of these means, and for that reason are an inherent competitor with any political state that sets out on the totalitarian road. Thus it is that the very things that seem to us in democratic countries the most obnoxious features of the totalitarian state are the very things for which its advocates recommend it. They are the things for whose absence they denounce democratic countries. For they say that failure to enlist the whole make-up of citizens, emotional as well as ideological, condemns democratic states to employ merely external and mechanical devices to hold the loyal support of its citizens. We may regard all this as a symptom of a collective hallucination, such as at times seems to have captured whole populations. But even so, we must recognize the influence of this factor if we are ourselves to escape collective delusion—that totalitarianism rests upon external coercion alone.

Finally, the moral factor is an intrinsic part of the complex of social forces called culture. For no matter whether or not one shares the view, now held on different grounds by different groups, that there is no scientific ground or warrant for moral conviction and judgments—it is certain that human beings hold some things dearer than they do others, and that they struggle for the things they prize, spending time and energy in their behalf: doing so indeed to such an extent that the best measure we have of what is valued is the effort spent in its behalf. Not only so, but for a number of persons to form anything that can be called a community in its pregnant sense there must be values prized in common. Without them, any so-called social group, class, people, nation, tends to fall apart into molecules having but mechanically enforced connections with one another. For the present at least we do not have to ask whether values are moral, having a kind of life and potency of their own, or are but byproducts of the working of other conditions, biological, economic or whatever.

The qualification will indeed seem quite superfluous to most, so habituated have most persons become to believing, at least nominally, that moral forces are the ultimate determinants of the rise and fall of all human societies—while religion has taught many to believe that cosmic as well as social forces are regulated in behalf of moral ends. The qualification is introduced, nevertheless, because of the existence of a school of philosophy holding that opinions about the values which move conduct are lacking in any scientific standing, since (according to them) the only things that can be *known* are physical events. The denial that values have any influence in the long run course of events is also characteristic of the Marxist belief that forces of production ultimately control every human relationship. The idea of the impossibility of intellectual regulation of ideas and judgments about values is shared by a number of intellectuals who have been dazzled by the success of mathematical and physical science. These last remarks suggest that there is at least one other factor in culture which needs some attention:—namely, the existence of schools of social philosophy, of competing ideologies.

The intent of the previous discussion should be obvious. The problem of freedom and of democratic institutions is tied up with the question of what kind of culture exists; with the necessity of free culture for free political institutions. The import of this conclusion extends far beyond its contrast with the simpler faith of those who formulated the democratic tradition. The question of human psychology, of the make-up of human nature in its original state, is involved. It is involved not just in a general way but with respect to its special constituents and their significance in their relations to one another. For every social and political philosophy currently professed will be found upon examination to involve a certain view about the constitution of human nature: in itself and in its relation to physical nature. What is true of this factor is true of every factor in culture, so that they need not here be listed again, although it is necessary to bear them all in mind if we are to appreciate the variety of factors involved in the problem of human freedom.

Running through the problem of the relation of this and that constituent of culture to social institutions in general and political democracy in particular is a question rarely asked. Yet it so underlies any critical consideration of the principles of each of them that some conclusion on the matter ultimately decides the position taken on each special issue. The question is whether any one of the factors is so predominant that it is *the* causal force, so that other factors are secondary and derived effects. Some kind of answer in what philosophers call a *monistic* direction has been usually given. The most obvious present example is the belief that economic conditions are ultimately the controlling forces in human relationships. It is perhaps significant that this view is comparatively recent. At the height of the eighteenth century, Enlightenment, the prevailing view, gave final supremacy to reason, to the advance of science and to education. Even during the last century, a view was held which is expressed in the motto of a certain school of historians: "History is past politics and politics is present history."

Because of the present fashion of economic explanation, this political view may now seem to have been the crotchet of a particular set of historical scholars. But, after all, it only formulated an idea consistently acted upon during the period of the formation of national states. It is possible to regard the present emphasis upon economic factors as a sort of intellectual revenge taken upon its earlier all but total neglect. The very word "political economy" suggests how completely economic considerations were once subordinated to political. The book that was influential in putting an end to this subjection, Adam Smith's *Wealth of Nations,* continued in its title, though not its contents, the older tradition. In the Greek period, we find that Aristotle makes the political factor so controlling that all normal economic activities are relegated to the household, so that all morally justifiable economic practice is literally domestic economy. And in spite of the recent vogue of the Marxist theory, Oppenheimer has produced a considerable body of evidence in support of the thesis that political states are the result of military conquests in which defeated people have become subjects of their conquerors, who, by assuming rule over the conquered, begot the first political states.

The rise of totalitarian states cannot, because of the bare fact of their totalitarianism, be regarded as mere reversions to the earlier theory of supremacy of the political institutional factor. Yet as compared with theories that had subordinated the political to the economic, whether in the Marxist form or in that of the British classical school, it marks reversion to ideas and still more to practices which it was supposed had disappeared forever from the conduct of any modern state. And the practices have been revived and extended with the benefit of scientific technique of control of industry, finance and commerce in ways which show the earlier governmental officials who adopted "mercantile" economics in the interest of government were the veriest bunglers at their professed job.

The idea that morals ought to be, even if it is not, the supreme regulator of social affairs is not so widely entertained as it once was, and there are circumstances which support the conclusion that when moral forces were as influential as they were supposed to be it was because morals were identical with customs which happened in fact to regulate the relations of human beings with one another. However, the idea is still advanced by sermons from the pulpit and editorials from the press that adoption of say the

Golden Rule would speedily do away with all social discord and trouble; and as I write the newspapers report the progress of a campaign for something called "moral re-armament." Upon a deeper level, the point made about the alleged identity of ethics with established customs raises the question whether the effect of the disintegration of customs that for a long time held men together in social groups can be overcome save by development of new generally accepted traditions and customs. This development, upon this view, would be equivalent to the creation of a new ethics.

However, such questions are here brought up for the sake of the emphasis they place upon the question already raised: Is there any one factor or phase of culture which is dominant, or which tends to produce and regulate others, or are economics, morals, art, science, and so on only so many aspects of the interaction of a number of factors, each of which acts upon and is acted upon by the others? In the professional language of philosophy: shall our point of view be monistic or pluralistic? The same question recurs moreover about each one of the factors listed:—about economics, about politics, about science, about art. I shall here illustrate the point by reference not to any of these things but to theories that have at various times been influential about the make-up of human nature. For these psychological theories have been marked by serious attempts to make some one constituent of human nature *the* source of motivation of action; or at least to reduce all conduct to the action of a small number of alleged native "forces." A comparatively recent example was the adoption by the classic school of economic theory of self-interest as the main motivating force of human behavior; an idea linked up on its technical side with the notion that pleasure and pain are the causes and the ends-in-view of all conscious human conduct, in desire to obtain one and avoid the other. Then there was a view that self-interest and sympathy are the two components of human nature, as opposed and balanced centrifugal and centripetal tendencies are the moving forces of celestial nature.

Just now the favorite ideological psychological candidate for control of human activity is love of power. Reasons for its selection are not far to seek. Success of search for economic profit turned out to be largely conditioned in fact upon possession of superior power while success reacted to increase power. Then the rise of national states has been attended by such vast and flagrant organization of military and naval force that politics have become more and more markedly power-politics, leading to the conclusion that there is not any other kind, although in the past the power-element has been more decently and decorously covered up. One interpretation of the Darwinian struggle for existence and survival of the fittest was used as ideological support; and some writers, notably Nietzsche (though not in the crude form often alleged), proposed an ethics of power in opposition to the supposed Christian ethics of sacrifice.

Because human nature is the factor which in one way or another is always interacting with environing conditions in production of culture, the theme receives special attention later. But the shift that has occurred from time to time in theories that have gained currency about the "ruling motive" in human nature suggests a question which is seldom asked. It is the question whether these psychologies have not in fact taken the cart to be the horse. Have they not gathered their notion as to the ruling element in human nature from observation of tendencies that are marked in contemporary collective life, and then bunched these tendencies together in some alleged psychological "force" as their cause? It is significant that human nature was taken to be strongly moved by an inherent love of freedom at the time when there was a struggle for representative government; that the motive of self-interest appeared when conditions in England enlarged the role of money, because of new methods of industrial production; that the growth of organized philanthropic activities brought sympathy into the psychological picture, and that events today are readily converted into love of power as the mainspring of human action.

In any case, the idea of culture that has been made familiar by the work of anthropological students points to the conclusion that whatever are the native constituents of human nature, the culture of a period and group is the determining influence in their arrangement; it is that which determines the patterns of behavior that mark out the activities of any group, family, clan, people, sect, faction, class. It is at least as true that the state of culture determines the order and arrangement of native tendencies as that human nature produces any particular set or system of social phenomena so as to obtain satisfaction for itself. The problem is to find out the way in which the elements of a culture interact with each other and the way in which the elements of human nature are caused to interact with one another under conditions set by their interaction with the existing environment. For example, if our American culture is largely a pecuniary culture, it is not because the original or innate structure of human nature tends of itself to obtaining pecuniary profit. It is rather that a certain complex culture stimulates, promotes and consolidates native tendencies so as to produce a certain pattern of desires and purposes. If we take all the communities, peoples, classes, tribes and nations that ever existed, we may be sure that since human nature in its native constitution is the relative constant, it cannot be appealed to, in isolation, to account for the multitude of diversities presented by different forms of association.

Primitive peoples for reasons that are now pretty evident attribute magical qualities to blood. Popular beliefs about race and inherent race differences have virtually perpetuated the older superstitions. Anthropologists are practically all agreed that the differences we find in different "races" are not due to anything in inherent physiological structure but to the effects exercised upon members of various groups by the cultural conditions under which they are reared; conditions that act upon raw or original human nature unremittingly from the very moment of birth. It has always been known that infants, born without ability in any language, come to speak the language, whatever it may be, of the community in which they were born. Like most uniform phenomena the fact aroused no curiosity and led to no generalization about the influence of cultural conditions. It was taken for granted; as a matter of course it was so "natural" as to appear inevitable. Only since the rise of systematic inquiries carried on by anthropological students has it been noted that the conditions of culture which bring about the common language of a given group produce other traits they have in common;—traits which like the mother tongue differentiate one group or society from others.

Culture as a complex body of customs tends to maintain itself. It can reproduce itself only through effecting certain differential changes in the original or native constitutions of its members.

Each culture has its own pattern, its own characteristic arrangement of its constituent energies. By the mere force of its existence as well as by deliberately adopted methods systematically pursued, it perpetuates itself through transformation of the raw or original human nature of those born immature. These statements do not signify that biological heredity and native individual differences are of no importance. They signify that as they operate within a given social form, they are shaped and take effect *within* that particular form. They are not indigenous traits that mark off one people, one group, one class, from another, but mark differences in every group. Whatever the "white man's burden," it was not imposed by heredity.

We have traveled a seemingly long way from the questions with which we set out, so that it may appear that they had been forgotten on the journey. But the journey was undertaken for the sake of finding out something about the nature of the problem that is expressed in the questions asked. The maintenance of democratic institutions is not such a simple matter as was supposed by some of the Founding Fathers—although the wiser among them realized how immensely the new political experiment was favored by external circumstances—like the ocean that separated settlers from the governments that had an interest in using the colonists for their own purposes; the fact that feudal institutions had been left behind; that so many of the settlers had come here to escape restrictions upon religious beliefs and form of worship; and especially the existence of a vast territory with free land and immense unappropriated natural resources.

The function of culture in determining what elements of human nature are dominant and their pattern or arrangement in connection with one another goes beyond any special point to which attention is called. It affects the very idea of individuality. The idea that human nature is inherently and exclusively individual is itself a product of a cultural individualistic movement. The idea that mind and consciousness are intrinsically individual did not even occur to any one for much the greater part of human history. It would have been rejected as the inevitable source of disorder and chaos if it had occurred to anyone to suggest it:— not that their ideas of human nature on that account were any better than later ones but that they also were functions of culture. All that we can safely say is that human nature, like other forms of life, tends to differentiation, and this moves in the direction of the distinctively individual, and that it also tends toward combination, association. In the lower animals, physical-biological factors determine which tendency is dominant in a given animal or plant species and the ratio existing between the two factors—whether, for example, insects are what students call "solitary" or "social." With human beings, cultural conditions replace strictly physical ones. In the earlier periods of human history they acted almost like physiological conditions as far as deliberate intention was concerned. They were taken to be "natural" and change in them to be unnatural. At a later period the cultural conditions were seen to be subject in some degree to deliberate formation. For a time radicals then identified their policies with the belief that if only artificial social conditions could be got rid of human nature would produce almost automatically a certain kind of social arrangements, those which would give it free scope in its supposed exclusively individual character.

Tendencies toward sociality, such as sympathy, were admitted. But they were taken to be traits of an individual isolated by nature, quite as much as, say, a tendency to combine with others in order to get protection against something threatening one's own private self. Whether complete identification of human nature with individuality would be desirable or undesirable if it existed is an idle academic question. For it does not exist. Some cultural conditions develop the psychological constituents that lead toward differentiation; others stimulate those which lead in the direction of the solidarity of the beehive or anthill. The human problem is that of securing the development of each constituent so that it serves to release and mature the other. Cooperation—called fraternity in the classic French formula—is as much a part of the democratic ideal as is personal initiative. That cultural conditions were allowed to develop (markedly so in the economic phase) which subordinated cooperativeness to liberty and equality serves to explain the decline in the two latter. Indirectly, this decline is responsible for the present tendency to give a bad name to the very word *individualism* and to make *sociality* a term of moral honor beyond criticism. But that association of nullities on even the largest scale would constitute a realization of human nature is as absurd as to suppose that the latter can take place in beings whose only relations to one another are those entered into in behalf of exclusive private advantage.

The problem of freedom of cooperative individualities is then a problem to be viewed in the context of culture. The state of culture is a state of interaction of many factors, the chief of which are law and politics, industry and commerce, science and technology, the arts of expression and communication, and of morals, or the values men prize and the ways in which they evaluate them; and finally, though indirectly, the system of general ideas used by men to justify and to criticize the fundamental conditions under which they live, their social philosophy. We are concerned with the problem of freedom rather than with solutions: in the conviction that solutions are idle until the problem has been placed in the context of the elements that constitute culture as they interact with elements of native human nature. The fundamental postulate of the discussion is that isolation of any one factor, no matter how strong its workings at a given time, is fatal to understanding and to intelligent action. Isolations have abounded, both on the side of taking some one thing in human nature to be a supreme "motive" and in taking some one form of social activity to be supreme. Since the problem is here thought of as that of the ways in which a great number of factors within and without human nature interact, our next task is to ask concerning the reciprocal connections raw human nature and culture bear to one another.

2. Culture and Human Nature

In the American as in the English liberal tradition, the idea of freedom has been connected with the idea of individuality, of *the* individual. The connection has been so close and so often reiterated that it has come to seem inherent. Many persons will be surprised if they hear that freedom has ever been supposed to have another source and foundation than the very nature of individuality. Yet in the continental European tradition the affiliation of the idea of freedom is with the idea of rationality. Those are free who govern themselves by the dictates of reason; those who follow the promptings of appetite and sense are so ruled by them as to be unfree. Thus it was that Hegel at the very time he was glorifying the State wrote a philosophy of history according to which the movement of historical events was from the despotic state of the Oriental World in which only one was free to the era dawning in Germany in the Western World in which *all* are free. The same difference in contexts that give freedom its meaning is found when representatives of totalitarian Germany at the present time claim their regime is giving the subjects of their state a "higher" freedom than can be found in democratic states, individuals in the latter being unfree because their lives are chaotic and undisciplined. The aroma of the continental tradition hangs about the sayings of those who settle so many social problems to their own satisfaction by invoking a distinction between liberty and license, identifying the former with "liberty under law"—for in the classic tradition law and reason are related as child and parent. So far as the saying assigns to law an origin and authority having nothing to do with freedom, so far, that is, as it affirms the impossibility of free conditions determining their own law, it points directly, even if unintentionally, to the totalitarian state.

We do not, however, have to go as far abroad as the European continent to note that freedom has had its practical significance fixed in different ways in different cultural contexts. For in the early nineteenth century there was a great practical difference between the English and the American theories, although both associated freedom with qualities that cause human beings to be *individuals* in the distinctive sense of that word. The contrast is so flat that it would be amusing if it were not so instructive. Jefferson, who was the original and systematic promulgator of the doctrine of free, self-governing institutions, found that the properties of individuals with which these institutions were most closely associated were traits found in the farming class. In his more pessimistic moments he even went so far as to anticipate that the development of manufacturing and commerce would produce a state of affairs in which persons in this country "would eat one another" as they did in Europe. In England, on the other hand, landed proprietors were the great enemy of the new freedom, which was connected in its social and political manifestations with the activities and aims of the manufacturing class.

It is not, of course, the bare fact of contrast which is instructive but the causes for its existence. They are not far to seek. Landed proprietors formed the aristocracy in Great Britain. The hold landed interests had over law-making bodies due to feudalism was hostile to the development of manufacturing and commerce. In the United States traces of feudalism were so faint that laws against primogeniture were about all that was needed to erase them. It was easy in this country to idealize the farmers as the sturdy yeomanry who embodied all the virtues associated with the original Anglo-Saxon love of liberty, the Magna Charta, and the struggle against the despotism of the Stuarts. Farmers were the independent self-supporting class that had no favors to ask from anybody, since they were not dependent for their livelihood nor their ideas upon others, owning and managing their own farms. It is a history that again would be amusing, were it not instructive, to find that as this country changed from an agrarian one to an urban industrial one, the qualities of initiative, invention, vigor and intrinsic contribution to progress which British *laissez-faire* liberalism had associated with manufacturing pursuits were transferred by American Courts and by the politi-

cal representatives of business and finance from Jeffersonian individuals and given to the entrepreneurs who were individuals in
the British sense.

In such considerations as these—which would be reinforced
by an extensive survey of the history of the meaning given to freedom under different conditions—we have one instance and an
important one of the relation of culture to the whole problem of
freedom. The facts fall directly in line with the conclusion of the
previous chapter:—a conclusion summed up in saying that the
idea of Culture, which has become a central idea of anthropology, has such a wide sociological application that it puts a new
face upon the old, old problem of the relation of the individual
and the social. The idea of culture even outlaws the very terms in
which the problem has been conceived, independently of its
effect upon solutions proposed. For most statements of the problem have been posed as if there were some inherent difference
amounting to opposition between what is called the individual
and the social. As a consequence there was a tendency for those
who were interested in theory to line up in two parties, which at
the poles were so far apart that one denied whatever the other
asserted. One party held that social conventions, traditions, institutions, rules are maintained only by some form of coercion,
overt or covert, which encroaches upon the natural freedom of
individuals; while the other school held that individuals are such
by nature that the one standing social problem is the agencies by
which recalcitrant individuals are brought under social control
or "socialized." The term of honor of one school has been that of
reproach of the other. The two extremes serve to define the terms
in which the problem was put. Most persons occupy an intermediate and compromise position, one whose classic expression
is that the basic problem of law and politics is to find the line
which separates legitimate liberty from the proper exercise of law
and political authority, so that each can maintain its own province under its own jurisdiction; law operating only when liberty
oversteps its proper bounds, an operation supposed, during the
heights of *laissez-faire* liberalism, to be legitimate only when police action was required to keep the peace.

Few persons today hold the extreme view of Hobbes, according to which human nature is so inherently anti-social that only
experiences of the evil consequences of the war of all against all,

reigning when human nature has free play, leads men, in connection with the motive of fear, to submit to authority—human nature even then remaining so intractable that the only assurance of safety against its marauding instincts is subjection to sovereignty. But in reading books on sociology it is still not uncommon to find the basic problem stated as if it were to list and analyze agencies by which individuals are tamed or "socialized." The chief difference of these writers from Hobbes consists in the fact that much less emphasis is laid upon merely political pressure, while it is recognized that there are tendencies in original human nature which render it amenable to social rules and regulations. As a result of the successful struggle of the new industrial class in England against the restrictions which existed even after the disappearance of feudalism in its grosser obvious forms, the favorite formula weighted the scales on the side of liberty, holding that each person was free as long as his actions did not restrict the freedom of others. The latter question, moreover, was never decided by going into the concrete consequences produced by the action of one person upon other persons. It was settled by a formal legal principle such as the equal right of every sane individual of a certain age to enter into contractual relations with others—no matter whether actual conditions gave equally free scope of action on both sides or made "free" contract a jughandled affair.

However, the purpose is not to thrash over the old straw of these issues or similar issues on the moral side such as the respective parts of altruistic and egoistic tendencies in human nature. The point concerns the situation in which the problems were envisaged; the context of ideas in which as problems they were placed irrespective of the solution reached. With the intellectual resources now available, we can see that such opinions about the inherent make-up of human nature neglected the fundamental question of how its constituents are stimulated and inhibited, intensified and weakened; how their pattern is determined by interaction with cultural conditions. In consequence of this failure the views held regarding human nature were those appropriate to the purposes and policies a given group wanted to carry through. Those who wished to justify the exercise of authority over others took a pessimistic view of the constitution of human nature; those who wanted relief from something oppressive discovered qualities of great promise in its native makeup. There is here a field which has hardly been entered by intellectual explorers:— the story of the way in which ideas put forth about the makeup of human nature, ideas supposed to be the results of psychological inquiry, have been in fact only reflections of practical measures that different groups, classes, factions wished to see continued in existence or newly adopted, so that what passed as psychology was a branch of political doctrine.

We are thus brought back to the earlier statement of principle. The primary trouble has been that issues have been formulated as if they were matters of the structure of human beings on one side and of the very nature of social rules and authority on the other side, when in reality the underlying issue is that of the relation of the "natural" and the "cultural." Rousseau's attack upon the arts and sciences (as well as upon existing law and government) shocked his eighteenth century contemporaries, since the things he claimed to be operating to corrupt human nature, by creating inequality, were the very things they relied upon to generate unending human progress. Nevertheless, he stated, in a way, the problem of culture versus nature; putting, himself, all emphasis upon and giving all advantage to human nature; since to him, in spite of its raw unrefined condition, it retained its natural goodness as long as loss of original equality had not produced conditions that corrupted it. Kant and his German successors took up the challenge presented in the unpopular paradoxes of Rousseau. They tried to reverse his position; they interpreted all history as the continuing process of culture by which the original animal nature of man becomes refined and is transformed from the animal into the distinctively human.

But Rousseau and his opponents carried over into their discussion of the problem in its new form many of the elements derived from the traditional way of putting it. In German philosophy, the issue was further complicated by the rise of Nationalism which followed the encroachments of Napoleon. Though the Germans were defeated in war, in culture they were to be superior—an idea that still persists in the use of *Kultur* in German nationalistic propaganda, since superiority in culture gives the kind of rightful authority over peoples of less culture that the human has over the animal. The French Revolution, as well as the writings of Rousseau, had the effect, in addition, of identifying in the minds of

German thinkers the cause of culture with that of law and authority. The individual freedom, which was the "natural right" of mankind according to the philosophers of the Revolution, was to the German philosophers of the reaction but the freedom of primitive sensuous animality. A period of subjection to universal law, expressing the higher non-natural essence of humanity, was required to bring about a condition of "higher" and true freedom. Events in Germany, including the rise of totalitarianism, since the time this view was formulated, have borne the stamp of this idea. Anticipation of the existence of some ultimate and a final social state, different from original "natural" freedom and from present subordination, has played a role in all social philosophies—like the Marxist—framed under German intellectual influences. It has had the function once exercised by the idea of the Second Coming.

In no case, however, could the problem have taken its new form without the material made available by anthropological research. For what has been disclosed about the immense variety of cultures shows that the problem of the relation of individuals and their freedom to social convention, custom, tradition and rules has been stated in a wholesale form, and hence not capable of intelligent and scientific attack. Judged by the methods of the natural sciences, the procedure in the social field has been pre-scientific and anti-scientific. For science has developed by analytic observation, and by interpretations of observed facts on the basis of their relations to one another. Social theory has operated on the basis of general "forces," whether those of inherent natural "motives" or those alleged to be social.

Were it not for the inertia of habit (which applies to opinion as well as to overt acts) it would be astonishing to find today writers who are well acquainted with the procedure of physical science and yet appeal to "forces" in explanation of human and social phenomena. For in the former case, they are aware that electricity, heat, light, etc., are names for ways in which definite observable concrete phenomena behave in relation to one another, and that all description and explanation have to be made in terms of verifiable relations of observed singular events. They know that reference to electricity or heat, etc., is but a shorthand reference to relations between events which have been established by investigation of actual occurrences. But in the field of social phenom-

ena they do not hesitate to explain concrete phenomena by reference to motives as forces (such as love of power), although these
so-called forces are but reduplication, in the medium of abstract
words, of the very phenomena to be explained.

Statement in terms of the relations of culture and nature to one
another takes us away from vague abstractions and glittering
generalities. Approach in its terms compels attention to go to the
variety of cultures that exist and to the variety of constituents of
human nature, including native differences between one human
being and another—differences which are not just differences in
quantity. The business of inquiry is with the ways in which specified constituents of human nature, native or already modified, *interact* with specified definite constituents of a given culture; conflicts and agreements between human nature on one side and
social customs and rules on the other being *products* of specifiable modes of interaction. In a given community some individuals are in practical agreement with its existing institutions and
others are in revolt—varying from a condition of moderate irritation and discontent to one of violent rebellion. The resulting
differences when they are sufficiently marked to be labelled
are the sources of the names conservative and radical, forward-
looking or progressive and reactionary, etc. They cut across economic classes. For even revolutionaries have to admit that part of
their problem is to create in an oppressed class consciousness of
their servitude so as to arouse active protest.

This fact, so patent to even superficial observation, is sufficient
disproof of the notion that the problem can be stated as one of
the relation of *the* individual and *the* social, as if these names
stood for any actual existences. It indicates that *ways of interaction* between human nature and cultural conditions are the first
and the fundamental thing to be examined, and that the problem
is to ascertain the effects of interactions between different components of different human beings and different customs, rules,
traditions, institutions—the things called "social." A fallacy has
controlled the traditional statement of the problem. It took results, good or bad—or both—of specific interactions as if they
were original causes, on one side or the other, of what existed or
else of what should exist.

It is just as certain, for example, that slaves have at times been
contented with their estate of servitude as that a slave class has

existed. It is certain that persons who have personally experienced no discomfort—except that commonly called moral—from existing conditions of oppression and injustice have been leaders in campaigns for equality and freedom. It is just as certain that inherent so-called social "instincts" have led men to form criminal gangs marked by certain mutual loyalties as that they have led men to cooperative activities. Now analytic observation of actual interactions to determine the elements operative on each side and their consequences is not easy in any case to execute. But recognition of its necessity is the condition of adequate judgment of actual events. Estimate of the value of any proposed policy is held back by taking the problem as if it were one of individual "forces" on one side and of social forces on the other, the nature of the forces being known in advance. We must start from another set of premises if we are to put the problem of freedom in the context where it belongs.

The questions which are asked at the beginning of the last chapter are genuine questions. But they are not questions in the abstract and cannot be discussed in a wholesale way. They are questions that demand discussion of cultural conditions, conditions of science, art, morals, religion, education and industry, so as to discover which of them in actuality promote and which retard the development of the native constituents of human nature. If we want individuals to be free we must see to it that suitable conditions exist:—a truism which at least indicates the direction in which to look and move.

It tells us among other things to get rid of the ideas that lead us to believe that democratic conditions automatically maintain themselves, or that they can be identified with fulfillment of prescriptions laid down in a constitution. Beliefs of this sort merely divert attention from what is going on, just as the patter of the prestidigitator enables him to do things that are not noticed by those whom he is engaged in fooling. For what is actually going on may be the formation of conditions that are hostile to any kind of democratic liberties. This would be too trite to repeat were it not that so many persons in the high places of business talk as if they believed or could get others to believe that the observance of formulae that have become ritualistic are effective safeguards of our democratic heritage. The same principle warns us to beware of supposing that totalitarian states are brought

about by factors so foreign to us that "It can't happen here";—
to beware especially of the belief that these states rest only upon
unmitigated coercion and intimidation. For in spite of the wide
use of purges, executions, concentration camps, deprivation of
property and of means of livelihood, no regime can endure long
in a country where a scientific spirit has once existed unless it
has the support of so-called idealistic elements in the human constitution. There is a tendency in some quarters to treat remarks
of this sort as if they were a sort of apology or justification of
dictatorships and totalitarian states. This way of reacting to an
attempt to find out what it is that commends, at least for a
time, totalitarian conditions to persons otherwise intelligent and
honorable, is dangerous. It puts hate in place of attempt at understanding; hate once aroused can be directed by skillful manipulation against other objects than those which first aroused it. It
also leads us to think that we are immune from the disease to
which others have given way so long as the evil things we see in
totalitarianism are not known to be developing among us. The
belief that only such things operate to harm democracy keeps us
from being on our guard against the causes that may be at work
undermining the values we nominally prize. It even leads us to
ignore beams in our own eyes such as our own racial prejudices.

It is extremely difficult at a distance to judge just what are the
appeals made to better elements in human nature by, say, such
policies as form the Nazi faith. We may believe that aside from
appeal to fear; from desire to escape responsibilities imposed by
free citizenship; from impulses to submission strengthened by
habits of obedience bred in the past; from desire for compensa-
tion for past humiliations, and from the action of nationalistic
sentiments growing in intensity for over a century (and not in
Germany alone), there is also love for novelty which in this particular case has taken the form of idealistic faith, among the
youth in particular, of being engaged in creating a pattern for
new institutions which the whole world will in time adopt. For
one of the elements of human nature that is often discounted in
both idea and practice is the satisfaction derived from a sense of
sharing in creative activities; the satisfaction increasing in direct
ratio to the scope of the constructive work engaged in.

Other causes may be mentioned, though with the admission
that it is quite possible in good faith to doubt or deny their

operation. There is the satisfaction that comes from a sense of union with others, a feeling capable of being intensified till it becomes a mystical sense of fusion with others and being mistaken for love on a high level of manifestation. The satisfaction obtained by the sentiment of communion with others, of the breaking down of barriers, will be intense in the degree in which it has previously been denied opportunity to manifest itself. The comparative ease with which provincial loyalties, which in Germany had been at least as intense and as influential as state-rights sentiments ever were in this country, were broken down; the similar ease, though less in degree, with which habitual religious beliefs and practices were subordinated to a feeling of racial and social union, would seem to testify that underneath there was yearning for emotional fusion. Something of this kind showed itself in most countries when they were engaged in the World War. For the time being it seemed as if barriers that separated individuals from one another had been swept away. Submission to abolition of political parties and to abolition of labor unions which had had great power, would hardly have come about so readily had there not been some kind of a void which the new regime promised to fill. Just how far the fact of uniformity is accompanied by a sense of equality in a nation where class distinctions had been rigid, one can only guess at. But there is considerable ground for believing that it has been a strong factor in reconciling "humbler" folk to enforced deprivation of material benefits, so that, at least for a time, a sense of honorable equality more than compensates for less to eat, harder and longer hours of work—since it is psychologically true that man does not live by bread alone.

It might seem as if belief in operation of "idealistic" factors was contradicted by the cruel persecutions that have taken place, things indicative of a reign of sadism rather than of desire for union with others irrespective of birth and locale. But history shows that more than once social unity has been promoted by the presence, real or alleged, of some hostile group. It has long been a part of the technique of politicians who wish to maintain themselves in power to foster the idea that the alternative is the danger of being conquered by an enemy. Nor does what has been suggested slur over in any way the effect of powerful and unremitting propaganda. For the intention has been to indicate some of the conditions whose interaction produces the social spectacle. Other powerful factors in the interaction are those technologies produced by modern science which have multiplied the means of modifying the dispositions of the mass of the population; and which, in conjunction with economic centralization, have enabled mass opinion to become like physical goods a matter of mass production. Here also is both a warning and a suggestion to those concerned with cultural conditions which will maintain democratic freedom. The warning is obvious as to the role of propaganda, which now operates with us in channels less direct and less official. The suggestion is that the printing press and radio have made the problem of the intelligent and honest use of means of communication in behalf of openly declared public ends a matter of fundamental concern.

What has been said is stated by way of illustration, and it may, if any one desires, be treated as hypothetical. For even so, the suggestions serve to enforce the point that a social regime can come into enduring existence only as it satisfies some elements of human nature not previously afforded expression. On the other hand getting relief from saturation of elements that have become stale makes almost anything welcome if only it is different. The general principle holds even if the elements that are provided a new outlet are the baser things in human nature: fear, suspicion, jealousy, inferiority complexes; factors that were excited by earlier conditions but that are now given channels of fuller expression. Common observation, especially of the young, shows that nothing is more exasperating and more resented than stirring up certain impulses and tendencies and then checking their manifestation. We should also note that a period of uncertainty and insecurity, accompanied as it is by more or less unsettlement and disturbance, creates a feeling that anything would be better than what exists, together with desire for order and stability upon almost any terms—the latter being a reason why revolutions are so regularly followed by reaction, and explain the fact that Lenin expressed by saying revolutions are authoritative, though not for the reason he gave.

Just which of these factors are involved in our own maintenance of democratic conditions or whether any of them are so involved is, at this juncture, not so pertinent as is the principle they illustrate. Negatively speaking, we have to get away from the influence of belief in bald single forces, whether they are thought of as intrinsically psychological or sociological. This includes getting away from mere hatred of abominable things, and it also means refusing to fall back on such a generalized statement as that Fascist institutions are expressions of the sort of thing to be expected in a stage of contracting capitalism, since they are a kind of final spasm of protest against approaching dissolution. We cannot reject out of hand any cause assigned; it may have some truth. But the primary need is to escape from wholesale reasons, as totalitarian as are the states ruled by dictators. We have to analyze conditions by observations, which are as discriminating as they are extensive, until we discover specific interactions that are taking place, and learn to think in terms of interactions instead of force. We are led to search even for the conditions which have given the interacting factors the power they possess.

The lesson is far from being entirely new. The founders of American political democracy were not so naively devoted to pure theory that they were unaware of the necessity of cultural conditions for the successful working of democratic forms. I could easily fill pages from Thomas Jefferson in which he insists upon the necessity of a free press, general schooling and local neighborhood groups carrying on, through intimate meetings and discussions, the management of their own affairs, if political democracy was to be made secure. These sayings could be backed up by almost equally numerous expressions of his fears for the success of republican institutions in South American countries that had thrown off the Spanish yoke.

He expressly set forth his fear that their traditions were such that domestic military despotisms would be substituted for foreign subjugations. A background of "ignorance, bigotry and superstition" was not a good omen. On one occasion he even went so far as to suggest that the best thing that could happen would be for the South American states to remain under the nominal supremacy of Spain, under the collective guarantee of France, Russia, Holland and the United States, until experience in self-government prepared them for complete independence.

The real source of the weakness that has developed later in the position of our democratic progenitors is not that they isolated the problem of freedom from the positive conditions that would nourish it, but that they did not—and in their time could not—

carry their analysis far enough. The outstanding examples of this inability are their faith in the public press and in schooling. They certainly were not wrong in emphasizing the need of a free press and of common public schools to provide conditions favorable to democracy. But to them the enemy of freedom of the press was official governmental censorship and control; they did not foresee the non-political causes that might restrict its freedom, nor the economic factors that would put a heavy premium on centralization. And they failed to see how education in literacy could become a weapon in the hands of an oppressive government, nor that the chief cause for promotion of elementary education in Europe would be increase of military power.

The inefficacy of education in general, that is, apart from constant attention to all the elements of its constitution, is illustrated in Germany itself. Its schools were so efficient that the country had the lowest rate of illiteracy in the world, the scholarship and scientific researches of its universities were known throughout the civilized globe. In fact it was not so many years ago that a distinguished American educator held them up as models to be followed in this country if the weaknesses of our higher institutions were to be remedied. Nevertheless German lower schools furnished the intellectual fodder for totalitarian propaganda, and the higher schools were the centres of reaction against the German Republic.

The illustrations are simple, and perhaps too familiar to carry much force. Nevertheless they proclaim that while free institutions over a wide territory are not possible without a mechanism, like the press, for quick and extensive communication of ideas and information, and without general literacy to take advantage of the mechanism, yet these very factors create a problem for a democracy instead of providing a final solution. Aside from the fact that the press may distract with trivialities or be an agent of a faction, or be an instrument of inculcating ideas in support of the hidden interest of a group or class (all in the name of public interest), the wide-world present scene is such that individuals are overwhelmed and emotionally confused by publicized reverberation of isolated events. And after a century of belief that the Common School system was bound by the very nature of its work to be what its earlier apostles called a "pillar of the republic," we are learning that everything about the public schools, its official agencies of control, organization and administration, the status of teachers, the subjects taught and methods of teaching them, the prevailing modes of discipline, set *problems;* and that the problems have been largely ignored as far as the relation of schools to democratic institutions is concerned. In fact the attention these things have received from various technical standpoints has been one reason why the central question has been obscured.

After many centuries of struggle and following of false gods, the natural sciences now possess methods by which particular facts and general ideas are brought into effective cooperation with one another. But with respect to means for understanding social events, we are still living in the pre-scientific epoch, although the events to be understood are the consequences of application of scientific knowledge to a degree unprecedented in history. With respect to information and understanding of social events, our state is that on one side of an immense number of undigested and unrelated facts, reported in isolation (and hence easily colored by some twist of interest) and large untested generalizations on the other side.

The generalizations are so general in the sense of remoteness from the events to which they are supposed to apply that they are matters of opinion, and frequently the rallying cries and slogans of factions and classes. They are often expressions of partisan desire clothed in the language of intellect. As matters of opinion, they are batted hither and yon in controversy and are subject to changes of popular fashion. They differ at practically every point from scientific generalizations, since the latter express the relations of facts to one another and, as they are employed to bring together more facts, are tested by the material to which they are applied.

If a glance at an editorial page of a newspaper shows what is meant by untested opinions put forth in the garb of the general principles of sound judgment, the items of the news columns illustrate what is meant by a multitude of diverse unrelated facts. The popular idea of "sensational," as it is derived from the daily press, is more instructive as to meaning of *sensations* than is the treatment accorded that subject in books on psychology. Events are sensational in the degree in which they make a strong impact in isolation from the relations to other events that give them their significance. They appeal to those who like things raw. Ordinary reports of murders, love nests, etc., are of this sort, with an artificial intensity supplied by unusual size or color of type. To say that a response is intellectual, not sensational, in the degree in which its significance is supplied by relations to other things is to state a truism. They are two sets of words used to describe the same thing.

One effect of literacy under existing conditions has been to create in a large number of persons an appetite for the momentary "thrills" caused by impacts that stimulate nerve endings but whose connections with cerebral functions are broken. Then stimulation and excitation are not so ordered that intelligence is produced. At the same time the habit of using judgment is weakened by the habit of depending on external stimuli. Upon the whole it is probably a tribute to the powers of endurance of human nature that the consequences are not more serious than they are.

The new mechanisms resulting from application of scientific discoveries have, of course, immensely extended the range and variety of particular events, or "news items" which are brought to bear upon the senses and the emotions connected with them. The telegraph, telephone, and radio report events going on over the whole face of the globe. They are for the most part events about which the individuals who are told of them can do nothing, except to react with a passing emotional excitation. For, because of lack of relation and organization in reference to one another, no imaginative reproduction of the situation is possible, such as might make up for the absence of personal response. Before we engage in too much pity for the inhabitants of our rural regions before the days of invention of modern devices for circulation of information, we should recall that they knew more about the things that affected their own lives than the city dweller of today is likely to know about the causes of his affairs. They did not possess nearly as many separate items of information, but they were compelled to know, in the sense of *understanding*, the conditions that bore upon the conduct of their own affairs. Today the influences that affect the actions performed by individuals are so remote as to be unknown. We are at the mercy of events acting upon us in unexpected, abrupt, and violent ways.

The bearing of these considerations upon the cultural conditions involved in maintenance of freedom is not far to seek. It is very directly connected with what now seems to us the oversimplification of the democratic idea indulged in by the authors of our republican government. They had in mind persons whose daily occupations stimulated initiative and vigor, and who possessed information which even if narrow in scope, bore pretty directly upon what they had to do, while its sources were pretty much within their control. Their judgment was exercised upon things within the range of their activities and their contacts. The press, the telegraph, the telephone and radio have broadened indefinitely the range of information at the disposal of the average person. It would be foolish to deny that a certain quickening of sluggish minds has resulted. But quite aside from having opened avenues through which organized propaganda may operate continuously to stir emotion and to leave behind a deposit of opinion, there is much information about which judgment is not called upon to respond, and where even if it wanted to, it cannot act effectively so dispersive is the material about which it is called upon to exert itself. The average person is surrounded today by readymade intellectual goods as he is by readymade foods, articles, and all kinds of gadgets. He has not the personal share in making either intellectual or material goods that his pioneer ancestors had. Consequently they knew better what they themselves were about, though they knew infinitely less concerning what the world at large was doing.

Self-government of the town-meeting type is adequate for management of local affairs, such as school buildings, district revenues, local roads and local taxation. Participation in these forms of self-government was a good preparation for self-government on a larger scale. But such matters as roads and schools under existing conditions have more than local import even in country districts; and while participation in town meetings is good as far as it arouses public spirit, it cannot provide the information that enables a citizen to be an intelligent judge of national affairs—now also affected by world conditions. Schooling in literacy is no substitute for the dispositions which were formerly provided by direct experiences of an educative quality. The void created by lack of relevant personal experiences combines with the confusion produced by impact of multitudes of unrelated incidents to create attitudes which are responsive to organized propaganda, hammering in day after day the same few and relatively simple beliefs asseverated to be "truths" essential to national welfare. In short, we have to take into account the attitudes of human nature that have been created by the immense development in mechanical instrumentalities if we are to understand the present power of organized propaganda.

The effect of the increase in number and diversity of unrelated facts that now play pretty continuously upon the average person is more easily grasped than is the influence of popular generalities, not checked by observed facts, over the interpretation put upon practical events, one that provokes acquiescence rather than critical inquiry. One chief reason for underestimation of the influence of generalities or "principles" is that they are so embodied in habits that those actuated by them are hardly aware of their existence. Or, if they are aware of them, they take them to be self-evident truths of common sense. When habits are so ingrained as to be second nature, they seem to have all of the inevitability that belongs to the movement of the fixed stars. The "principles" and standards which are stated in words and which circulate widely at a given time are usually only formulations of things which men do not so much believe in the intellectual sense of belief as live by unconsciously. Then when men who have lived under different conditions and have formed different life habits put forth different "principles," the latter are rejected as sources of some contagion introduced by foreigners hostile to our institutions.

Opinions are at once the most superficial and the most steelplated of all human affairs. This difference between them is due to connection or lack of connection with habits that operate all but unconsciously. Verbal habits also exist and have power. Men continue to give assent to formulae after they have ceased to be more than linguistic rituals. Even lip-service has practical effect, that of creating intellectual and emotional divisions. The latter may not be deliberate hypocrisy. But they constitute that kind of insincerity, that incompatibility of actions with professions, which startles us in those cases in which it is clear that a person "believes" what he says in the sense that he is not even aware of its inconsistency with what he does. These gaps, these insincerities, become deeper and wider in times like the present when great change in events and practical affairs is attended with marked cultural lags in verbal formulations. And the persons who have first deceived themselves are most effective in misleading others. One of the most perplexing of human phenomena is the case of persons who do "in good faith" the sort of things which logical demonstration can easily prove to be incompatible with good faith.

Insincerities of this sort are much more frequent than deliberate hypocrisies and more injurious. They exist on a wide scale when there has been a period of rapid change in environment accompanied by change in what men do in response and by a change in overt habits, but without corresponding readjustment of the basic emotional and moral attitudes formed in the period prior to change of environment. This "cultural lag" is everywhere in evidence at the present time. The rate of change in conditions has been so much greater than anything the world has known before that it is estimated that the last century has seen more changes in the conditions under which people live and associate than occurred in thousands of previous years. The pace has been so swift that it was practically impossible for underlying traditions and beliefs to keep step. Not merely individuals here and there but large numbers of people habitually respond to conditions about them by means of actions having no connection with their familiar verbal responses. And yet the latter express dispositions saturated with emotions that find an outlet in words but not in acts.

No estimate of the effects of culture upon the elements that now make up freedom begins to be adequate that does not take into account the moral and religious splits that are found in our very make-up as persons. The problem of creation of genuine democracy cannot be successfully dealt with in theory or in practice save as we create intellectual and moral integration out of present disordered conditions. Splits, divisions, between attitudes emotionally and congenially attuned to the past and habits that are forced into existence because of the necessity of dealing with present conditions are a chief cause of continued profession of devotion to democracy by those who do not think nor act day by day in accord with the moral demands of the profession. The consequence is a further weakening of the environing conditions upon which genuine democracy occurs, whether the division is found in business men, in clergymen, in educators or in politicians. The serious threat to our democracy is not the existence of foreign totalitarian states. It is the existence within our own personal attitudes and within our own institutions of conditions similar to those which have given a victory to external authority, discipline, uniformity and dependence upon The Leader in foreign countries. The battlefield is also accordingly here—within ourselves and our institutions.

3. The American Background

While the sudden appearance of dictatorships and totalitarian states in Europe has raised such questions as have been asked, events in our country have put similar questions directly to ourselves. There is now raised the question of what was actually back of the formulation of the democratic faith a century and a half ago. Historians of the events that led up to the Declaration of Independence, the creation of the Confederation, and the adoption of the Federal Constitution tell us that what actually moved the leaders of the Rebellion against Great Britain were specific restrictions placed on industry and trade, together with levying of obnoxious taxes; and that what figured in doctrinal formulation as limitations upon inherent rights to freedom were in fact burdens imposed upon industrial pursuits from which persons of prestige and influence suffered economic losses.

Historians do not draw from their report of the concrete conditions, which, according to them, brought about the Revolution, the cynical conclusion that the ideas put forth about freedom, self-government and republican institutions were deliberate insincerities, intended to gull those who might otherwise have been indifferent in the struggle. It was rather that leaders generalized the particular restrictions from which they suffered into the general idea of oppression; and in similar fashion extended their efforts to get liberation from specific troubles into a struggle for liberty as a single all-embracing political ideal.

The distance, the physical distance, between American settlers and British officials was so generalized that it became a symbol of the idea that all government not self-imposed is foreign to human nature and to human rights. In the language of modern psychology, a local struggle of a group to obtain release from certain specific abuses was "rationalized" into a universal struggle of humanity to obtain freedom in the abstract; a rationalization which, like other idealizations springing up in times of crisis, enabled men better to endure hardship and summon up energy for a struggle continued long enough to get rid of immediate abuses. They do not, as historians, draw the inference that anything that goes by the name of an active love for liberty is in fact but an effort to get liberation from some specific evil; and that when that evil is got rid of, men turn from love of liberty to enjoyment of the specific goods they happen to possess. But their account of facts suggests a conclusion of this sort.

Nor have these historians drawn the conclusion that economic forces are the only forces that move men to collective action, and that the state of forces of production is the ultimate factor in determining social relations. Historians have not ventured so far afield into broad generalizations. But in their capacity as historians they have pointed out the effect of specific economic factors in producing the Revolution; and of changed economic conditions, after the confusion of the period of the Confederation, in producing special provisions of the Constitution. They have called attention to the enduring influence upon political events of conflict of interests between farmers and traders. They show, for example, that the difference in the policies advocated by the Republican and Federal parties respectively during the first thirty or forty years of the Republic represent a difference in the interests of agricultural and commercial sections and groups: conflicts reflected in the party attitudes toward centralized and decentralized government, the power of the judiciary, especially of the supreme court, free trade and protective tariff, foreign policies with regard to France and Great Britain, etc.

The striking differences in temper between the Declaration of Independence and the Constitution are cited. That the first should be much the more radical in tone is easily explicable by the fact that it was written by the man who was the firmest and most explicit of all the leaders of the movement in faith in democracy. Conditions conspired to make him the spokesman at this juncture as changed conditions brought others to the front in the Constitutional Convention while he was absent in France. In one case, it was necessary to rally all the forces in the country in the name of freedom against a foreign foe. In the other case, the most urgent need of men of established position seemed to be protection of established economic interests against on-slaughts of a populace using liberty as a cloak for an attack upon order and stability. There was also need of compromise to unite various sections in a single federal government. Even during his own lifetime the author of the Declaration of Independence feared lest monarchical and oligarchical tendencies should undermine republic institutions.

Marxist social philosophy has made a sweeping generalization where historians have been content to point out specific economic conditions operating in specific emergencies. The Marxist has laid down a generalization that is supposed to state the law governing the movement and final outcome of all the social changes with which historians are occupied in detail. The generalization to which historians have pointed is rather a practical maxim: If you wish to secure a certain political result, you must see to it that economic conditions are such as to tend to produce that result. If you wish to establish and maintain political self-government, you must see to it that conditions in industry and finance are not such as to militate automatically against your political aim.

This position leaves room for a great variety of shades of political opinion and practical policies, all the way from political action to curb tendencies toward monopolies when the latter gain undue strength to attempts to "socialize" industry and finance. The Marxist position, on the other hand, lays down a universal law claimed to be scientific. It derives its practical policies from adherence, actual or alleged, to the "law" which is formulated.

Whether the effect of the economic factor upon political conditions is taken in its moderate or its extreme form, the facts involved tremendously complicate the problem of democratic freedom as it existed when the Union was formed. The original democratic theory was simple in its formulation because the conditions under which it took effect were simple. As theory, it postulated a widespread desire in human nature for personal freedom, for release from dominion over personal beliefs and conduct that is exercised from sources external to the individual. Combined with belief in this desire was the belief, generated by the conditions that had provoked the struggle for independence, that the chief enemy to realization of the desire was the tendency of government officials to extend their power without limit. Guarantees against this abuse were then supposed to be enough to establish republican government.

The latter belief was a manifestation of the existing struggle to obtain independence from British rule. It was strengthened by memories of conditions which had induced many persons to emigrate from the old country. In the case of Jefferson, the most intellectual and the most definitely explicit of all the American leaders, it was strengthened by what he personally observed during his residence in France. What he experienced there led him to give unqualified support to the saying that in a country with an oppressive government everyone is either hammer or anvil. The doctrine received negative support, if I may put the matter in that way, from the fact that there was in the late eighteenth century no other organized foe to freedom visible above the horizon—although Jefferson anticipated with dread the rise of such an enemy in the growth of manufacturing and commerce and the growth of cities of large populations.

In any event, the heart of the doctrine as a theory was a virtual identification of freedom with the very state of being an individual; and the extent of freedom that existed was taken to be the measure of the degree in which individuality was realized. It is possible to interpret this attitude and faith in two different ways. According to one view, it was an expression of pioneer conditions; it was appropriate to those conditions but was thoroughly naïve as a universal truth about the individual and about government. According to the other view, while the idea had some of the qualities of a dream, yet it expresses a principle to be maintained by deliberative effort if mankind is to have a truly human career. Call it dream or call it vision, it has been interwoven in a tradition that has had an immense effect upon American life.

However, the influence of tradition is two-fold. On the one hand, it leads to effort to perpetuate and strengthen the conditions which brought it into existence. But, on the other hand, a tradition may result in habits that obstruct observation of what is actually going on; a mirage may be created in which republican institutions are seen as if they were in full vigor after they have gone into a decline. There are now persons who think that the anti-democratic effect of economic development has so far destroyed essential democracy that only by the democratization or "socialization" of industry and finance can political democracy be restored. Whatever be thought of this view, its existence marks an immense change in conditions. To the Founding Fathers control of production and distribution of commodities and services by means of any political agency whatsoever would have seemed the complete nullification of all they were fighting for. A similar belief is still put forward with especial strength when a movement, even a moderate one, is made toward social control of business by political action—which is then denounced as the destruction of "Americanism." No matter which side (if either) is right, the division is not helpful to the democratic cause.

We are not concerned to decide which one of the different schools of social theory is correct. We are not even concerned at this point to judge whether governmental action is necessarily hostile to the maintenance of personal freedom or whether the latter becomes an empty shell if it is without organized political backing. The point is the complication of the earlier situation regarding freedom which is made evident when it is possible for men to urge that preservation of democratic institutions requires just that extension of governmental functions which to the authors of our tradition was the enemy to be fought. Whatever school of social philosophy be right, the situation has been transformed since the day when the problem of freedom and democracy presented itself as essentially a *personal* problem capable of being decided by strictly personal choice and action. For, according to the earlier idea, about all that was needed was to keep alive a desire for freedom, which is inherent in the very constitution of individuals, and jealously to watch the actions of governmental officials. Given these basic conditions, the means required for perpetuation of self-government were simple. They were exhausted in personal responsibility of officials to the citizens for whom they are but delegates; general suffrage; frequent elections so that officials would have to give frequent accounts of the way they had used their powers; majority rule; and keeping the units of government as small as possible so that people would know what their representatives were up to. These measures, combined with complete abolition of whatever traces of the feudal system had been brought over from England, were sufficient, provided only a Bill of Rights was adopted and kept in force. For the Bill of Rights gave guarantees against certain specific encroachments of governmental officials upon personal freedom—such as arbitrary arrest. It instituted the moral and psychological conditions of self-government by securing the rights of free speech, free press, free assembly, free choice of creed. Given the maintenance of these rights, the few and simple governmental mechanisms mentioned would make secure the cause of free institutions.

That the conditions which influence the working of governmental mechanisms and the maintenance of the liberties constituting the Bill of Rights are infinitely more complex than they were a century and a half ago is evident beyond need for argument. Whether one is a believer in the necessity for increased social control of economic activities or in allowing the maximum possible of private initiative in industry and exchange, both sides must admit that impersonal forces have been set in motion on a scale undreamed of in the early days of the Republic.

Whatever else is reasonably settled or is unsettled, it is certain that the ratio of impersonal to personal activities in determining the course of events has enormously increased. The machine as compared with the hand tool is an impersonal agency. Free land and an abundance of unappropriated and unused natural resources—things which brought men in face-to-face personal connection with Nature and which also kept individual persons in pretty close contact with one another—have been replaced by impersonal forces working on a vast scale, with causes and effects so remote as not to be perceptible. A symbolic example is the change in production between the day when a comparatively small number of "hired hands" worked side by side with their employer in a shop, and modern factories with hundreds or thousands of laborers who never see the owners (who moreover, as scattered shareholders, do not even know one another); and who come in contact with those immediately responsible for the conduct of the work only through delegates. Need for large capital to carry on mass production has also separated even personal financial liability from ownership. The whole significance of property has changed. "Private" property, in its old sense, has disappeared. Or, if another illustration is needed, there is the replacement of village life where everyone knew everybody else's character by congested cities in which persons do not know the persons who live on the same floor with them; and where, on the political side, they are called upon to vote for a large number of persons many of whom they cannot identify even by name.

The point is the intervention of an indefinite number of indefinitely ramifying conditions between what a person does and the consequences of his actions, including even the consequences which return upon him. The intervals in time and space are so extensive that the larger number of factors that decide the final outcome cannot be foreseen. Even when they can be anticipated, the results are produced by factors over which the average person has hardly any more control than he has over those which produce earthquakes. The recurrence of large-scale unemployment with sharp curtailment of production and the consequent instability of the conditions of both employer and employed is a convincing example. When all allowance is made for shiftlessness and incompetency of employees and for recklessness on the part of the employer, the recurrence of these crises cannot be understood save as evidence of the working of forces operating beyond the possibility of personal control. The current proposal to take away the vote from persons on relief, if it were supplemented by a proposal to deprive of suffrage all employers who are not paying their debts, would carry out the Biblical remark about taking away from those who have not even that which they seem to have.

When conditions that make for unemployment are as extensively ramified as they are at present, political action assumes an importance for workers, employed and unemployed, that it does not have when conditions are settled and opportunity for employment is fairly general and secure. There are movements in all industrialized countries to provide work by governmental projects; there are schemes for offsetting, by doles and official relief, evils that have resulted from the failure of industrialists and financial captains to provide the means of livelihood. The chiefly palliative nature of these measures is an evidence that symptoms rather than causes are dealt with; and this fact is in turn further proof that fundamental economic conditions are so far out of control that emergency measures are resorted to. The fact that evils are not remedied and in some respects are aggravated calls out a reaction in favor of return to individual initiative—that is, leaving the course of events to determination by those who have a store of resources in reserve.

There is little to prevent this reaction from making temporary headway. For the chief phenomenon in American politics at the present time is that voters are moved primarily by the ills which are easily seen to be those from which they and the country at large are suffering. Since the evils are attributed more or less to the action of the party in power, there is a succession of swings back and forward as the relative impotency of this and that party and of this and that line of policy to regulate economic conditions, sufficiently to prevent widespread disaster, becomes clear. This impotency of existing political forms to direct the working and the social effects of modern industry has operated to generate distrust of the working of parliamentary institutions and all forms of popular government. It explains why democracy is now under attack from both the right and the left. There is no reason to suppose that a country as highly industrialized as the United States is immune.

While the possessing class is relatively more secure, yet its members are also profoundly unsettled by recurring cyclic depression. Emergence in political life of populist movements, square deals, new deals, accompanies depressions on the part of those most directly affected—farmers, factory laborers, etc., who are kept from uniting politically by divergence of immediate interests. But it would be foolish to suppose that the well-to-do class, the class of employers and investors, is not unsettled in a way that stirs it to political action to strengthen its hold on the agencies of political action. As the activities increase of the groups which are radical from the standpoint of the possessing class, and especially as they fail to effect a fundamental remedy of the situation, the activities of the favored economic class increase. When disorders appear on any considerable scale, the adherence of the middle class to the side of "law and order" is won. Ironically enough, the desire for security which proceeds from the two groups of very different economic status combines to increase readiness to surrender democratic forms of action. The coalescence of desire for security from two opposite sources has been a factor in the substitution of dictators for parliaments in European countries. The danger of the rise of an American Fascist movement in this country comes from a similar source. It is absurd to suppose that the class having relatively the superior economic status can promote a dictatorship unless it has strong popular support—which means the support of those relatively at a disadvantage. "Security" is a word covering a great diversity of interests, and all of them have a bearing upon the conditions required for maintenance of democracy.

In brief, economic developments which could not possibly have been anticipated when our political forms took shape have created confusion and uncertainty in the working of the agencies of popular government, and thereby have subjected the idea of democracy to basic strain. The change in conditions goes far beyond the particular consequences which Jefferson feared as a result of growth of manufacturing and trade at the expense of agriculture. The strengthening of the political power of laborers that occurred in Great Britain as the consequence of industrialization, and the part played by this factor in the liberalization of government, were not anticipated by him. In so far, there is no special cause for surprise in the fact that the interests originally represented by Jefferson and Hamilton have now changed places with respect to exercise of federal political power. For Jeffersonian principles of self-government, of the prime authority of the people, of general happiness or welfare as the end of government, can be appealed to in support of policies that are opposite to those urged by Jefferson in his day.

The real problem is deeper. There is no well-defined continuity of political movement because of the confusion that exists in general social movements. That the general trend is toward increase of public control of private industry and finance in the United States as in other countries is undeniable. But the movement is not clear-cut in theory nor are its consequences consistent in practice. In fact, there is one thesis of Herbert Spencer that could now be revived with a good deal of evidence in its support: namely, the economic situation is so complex, so intricate in the interdependence of delicately balanced factors, that planned policies initiated by public authority are sure to have consequences totally unforeseeable,—often the contrary of what was intended—as has happened in this country rather notably in connection with some of the measures undertaken for control of agricultural production.

So far I have been speaking of the fairly direct impact of economic conditions upon democratic political habits and beliefs. The mining and sapping have not begun to go so far in this country as in European countries which have adopted some form of National Socialism. But uncertainty and confusion and increasing scepticism about the relevancy of political democracy to present conditions, have been created. In this connection another effect of change from conditions which relatively were capable of being seen and regulated by personal skill and personal insight must be noted. The comparative helplessness of persons in their strictly singular capacities to influence the course of events expresses itself in formation of combinations in order to secure protection from too destructive impact of impersonal forces. That groups now occupy much the same place that was occupied earlier by individuals is almost a commonplace of writers on sociology. For example, trades unions for collective bargaining in regulation of wages, hours and physical conditions of work are produced on one side; pools, mergers, syndicates, trusts and employers' associations, often with command of armed strikebreakers, are generated on the other side. The theory of the self-actuated and self-governing individual receives a rude shock when massed activity has a potency which individual effort can no longer claim.

The growth of organized combinations has had an effect on that part of democratic doctrine which held that all men should be free as well as equal. The doctrine of equality never meant what some of its critics supposed it to mean. It never asserted equality of natural gifts. It was a moral, a political and legal principle, not a psychological one. Thomas Jefferson believed as truly in a "natural aristocracy" as did John Adams. The existence of marked psychological inequalities was indeed one of the reasons why it was considered so important to establish political and legal equality. For otherwise those of superior endowment might, whether intentionally or without deliberation, reduce those of inferior capacity to a condition of virtual servitude. The words "nature" and "natural" are among the most ambiguous of all the words used to justify courses of action. Their very ambiguity is one source of their use in defense of any measure and end regarded as desirable. The words mean what is native, what is original or innate, what exists at birth in distinction from what is acquired by cultivation and as a consequence of experience. But it also means that which men have got used to, inured to by custom, that imagination can hardly conceive of anything different. Habit is second nature and second nature under ordinary circumstances as potent and urgent as first nature. Again, nature has a definitely moral import; that which is *normal* and hence is right; that which should be.

The assertion that men are free and equal by nature unconsciously, possibly deliberately, took advantage of the prestige possessed by what is "natural" in the first two senses to reinforce the moral force of the word. That "naturalness" in the moral sense provided the imperative ethical foundation of politics and law was, however, the axiomatic premise of democratic theory. Exercise of a liberty which was taken to be a moral right has in the course of events, especially economic events, seriously threatened the moral right to legal and political equality. While we may not believe that the revolutionary effect of steam, electricity, etc., has nullified moral faith in equality, their operation has produced a new difficult problem. The effect of statutes, of administrative measures, of judicial decisions, upon the maintenance of equality and freedom cannot be estimated in terms of fairly direct personal consequences. We have first to estimate their effects upon complicated social conditions (largely a matter of guesswork), and then speculate what will be the effect of the new social conditions upon individual persons.

Even if everybody, no matter how unequal in other endowments, possessed in like measure the faculty of reason or of common sense with which the optimistic rationalism of the eighteenth century supposed men to be equipped, the faculty would not go far in judging causes and effects of political and legal action at the present time. What purports to be experiment in the social field is very different from experiment in natural science; it is rather a process of trial and error accompanied with some degree of hope and a great deal of talk. Legislation is a matter of more or less intelligent improvisation aiming at palliating conditions by means of patchwork policies. The apparent alternative seems to be a concentration of power that points toward ultimate dictatorship. Since at best legislation can only pass measures in general terms, which are not self-interpreting much less self-applying, and since it is a costly and uncertain process to wait upon decisions of the courts to ascertain what laws mean in the concrete, administrative bodies possessed of large powers are multiplied—in spite of their inconsistency with the doctrine of the three-fold division of powers that is still the nominal constitutional theory. Persons of a liberal outlook, captured by fear of dictatorship, join with persons whose special and anti-social interests are unfavorably affected by the action of these commissions and indulge in wholesale attack—failing to see that new administrative bodies are so imperatively needed that the real problem is that of building up an intelligent and capable civil-service under conditions that will operate against formation of rigid bureaucracies.

The point which is here pertinent is that early theory and practice assumed an inherent, and so to say pre-established, harmony between liberty and equality. As liberty has been practiced in industry and trade, the economic inequalities produced have reacted against the existence of equality of opportunity. Only those who have a special cause to plead will hold that even in the most democratic countries, under the most favorable conditions, have children of the poor the same chances as those of the well-to-do, even in a thing like schooling which is supported at public expense. And it is no consoling offset that the children of the rich often suffer because of the one-sided conditions under which they grow up.

The way in which the problem of the relation of liberty and equality was earlier conceived is perhaps most clearly exhibited in the pains taken in the French Revolution to prevent combinations and associations from growing up, even those of a voluntary sort; so convinced were the leaders of the revolutionary doctrine of Liberty, Equality and Fraternity that combinations are hostile to liberty. The laws against trade unions as conspiracies, which existed in England, had a very different source. But fear of combination and organization from whatever source it has emanated, liberal or reactionary, gives evidence of the existence of a problem. Even the late President Eliot voiced a not uncommon belief of a certain type of liberal in his jealous fear lest the growth of labor unions put restrictions upon the liberty of wage-earners to work when and where and how they individually liked, an attitude that still appears on a large scale when it is a question of the closed shop. Persons who are favorable "in principle" to collective bargaining shrink when the principle is systematically applied. Once more the point here pertinent is not who is right and who is wrong, but the fact that the conditions of industry and commerce produced by existing technologies have created in a wholly unanticipated way the problem of the relation of organization and freedom—with what philosophers call an antinomy as a result.

For there are convincing arguments both that individuals can be free only in connection with large-scale organizations and that such organizations are limitations of freedom. In any case, the organized associations of wage-workers in labor unions and of capitalistic employers in pools, combines, mergers, trusts, syndicates, gentlemen's agreements, are two aspects of the same process; while that indefinite amorphous thing called the consuming public tends by turns to be about equally suspicious of both, according to which one seems most active at a given time in producing a visible inconvenience. Just how mass-production and mass-distribution together with elimination of spatial barriers by speedy transportation and communication could have come into existence without consolidation and concentration on a large scale it is impossible to explain. And yet many who adhere to the letter rather than to the spirit of the early formulation of democratic faith will be found deploring or denouncing one or the other of the two forms of organizations that had come into existence as destructive of the ideals of liberty and equality—a fact which proves that a new type of problem has come into existence, whatever be its solution.

Growing distrust of the efficacy of parliamentary bodies is, as has been intimated, a result of the increased complexity of events. How can a collection of men, selected chiefly upon grounds of party availability, have either the knowledge or the skill required to cope with such extensive interlocking conditions as now exist? Some measure of conflict between the legislative body and the executive is an old story in American life whenever the President has happened to have strong convictions of his own; and it is a fact of a wider history than the American that in the case of such a conflict the executive tends to set himself up as an agent of the masses and the legislative body to be so selected as to be close to special interests. Difficulties in the way of effective action by law-making bodies in meeting actual conditions are increased by the general belief that they, with the courts and with administrative bodies, are favorable to special interests, by association and by education and at times by corruption. Distrust gives both the rabble-rouser and the would-be dictator their opportunities. The former speaks in words for the oppressed mass against oppression; in historic fact he has usually been an agent, willing or unknowing, of a new form of oppression. As Huey Long is reported to have said, Fascism would come in this country under the name of protecting democracy from its enemies.

Any adequate discussion of the present relations of politics and economics would have to extend to conditions in village, city, county, state and nation, and its conclusions would fill volumes. Its conclusions would enforce in detail the thesis that the interconnections and interdependence of industry and government puts a radically new face upon the problem of democratic policies. I shall mention but one more fact of those that could be cited. Modern industry could not have reached its present development without legalization of the corporation. The corporation is a creature of the state: that is, of political action. It has no existence save by the action of legislatures and courts. Many of the earlier arguments for limitation and extreme decentralization of political power were virtually outlawed when the first statute authorizing the formation of business corporations was passed. The bitter struggle in this country between business interests and governmental actions has been in large degree a struggle to see whether the child begot by the state or the progenitor should control the subsequent activities of the parent. Operation of the state-created corporation under the decisions of the courts is proof positive that the careers of politics and business cross and mix in intimate and manifold ways, all of them unforeseeable when our governmental arrangements took shape. Epigrams about the difference between the day of the stagecoach and of the railway and airplane are at best only suggestions of the enormous change in human relationships that has been produced by change in the means by which industry is carried on. The new relations require a new determination of rights and duties. The determination of them made during the time when the chief problem was that of maintaining peaceful relations between persons as persons is not adequate to determine rights and obligations when large combinations have largely replaced individual persons as the units of effective action. The very necessity for change only makes urgent the question of whether the existing agencies of democracy are competent to effect the change.

This is the basic question pointed to by the considerations which have been barely sketched. It is the problem which has precedence over the various plans and policies that are urged from one quarter or another. Consider, as an example, the argument that since the *processes* of industry, on the side of both labor and capital, have become collective, ownership and control must also be collective, resulting in elimination of private income from rent, interest and dividends. From the standpoint of democracy, this end, which is put forward in the interest of maintenance of democracy, raises the problem of the possibility of its execution by democratic methods. Can the change be effected by democratic means? After it is effected, supposing that it is, can production and distribution of goods and services be effected except by a centralized power that is destructive of democracy? The first of these two questions finds a profound split existing among professed socialists. Some of them hold the transition can be effected by recognized democratic means. But a larger and at present more vigorous section holds that democratic states are inherently bound up with just the things to be eliminated. Hence it is absurd—or, worse, deliberate deception—to believe the change can be effected by any means save violent overthrow of existing political governments and transfer of power to representatives of workers, urban factory workers at that. According to this view, the political state always has been and by its very nature is an arm of the dominant political class, and as long as that class is bourgeois capitalism, it is axiomatic with them that change must proceed from its complete overthrow.

Suppose the great change has come about, whether by one procedure or the other, what then? Asking the question is almost equivalent to calling attention to the relatively slight attention the underlying issue has received. For the most part the answer is to the effect that sufficient to the day is the evil or the good thereof. Since it would be utopian to try to imagine the details of a social state such as has never existed, energies should be taken up either with bringing about the violent revolution or with the educative process required for a peaceful transition to a socialist society. Many socialists of the latter type remain within our democratic tradition in believing that the continued use of democratic methods will mature those methods so that they will be effective in dealing with special problems as the latter arise. Nevertheless, the fact that popular ideas about socialism identify it with state or government socialism, while democratic socialists are strongly opposed to the latter—unless perhaps as a transitional stage—shows that the problem has not had a great deal of attention, syndicalist socialists being the faction that has considered it most explicitly.

So far social control of industry has mostly taken the form of regulation or ownership exercised under governmental auspices by governmental officials. This is so in National Socialist, in Bolshevist Socialist countries, and in democratic countries. Neither theory nor practical experience has as yet shown that state socialism will be essentially different from state capitalism. Even if we are obliged to abandon permanently the earlier belief that governmental action is by its own momentum hostile to free self-government, we are far from having refuted the evidence of history that officials who have political power will use it arbitrarily. Belief in what is sometimes called taking industry out of private hands is naïve until it is shown that the new private—or personal—hands to which it is confided are so controlled that they are reasonably sure to work in behalf of public ends. I am not saying the problem cannot be solved democratically nor that "socialization" of industry is bound to be followed by the regimentation so freely predicted by adherents of *laissez-faire* individualism. What I am saying is that the issue of democracy has taken a new form, where not much experience is available about the relation of economic factors, as they now operate, to democratic ends and methods.

In the absence of adequate experience, the tendency is to set up wholesale theories in opposition to one another; the current statement of the human problem as individualism versus socialism being both a reflex expression of the divisions in the economic factors of present society, and an example of wholesale opposition. In such an opposition of ideas, each theory thrives on the weaknesses of the other one; confusion is thereby increased. If it is utopian to expect a new social order will be ushered in as soon as industry is "socialized"—with little idea of what that means save negatively, or abolition of private profit, interest, rent and returns from fixed investment—it is highly unrealistic to go on repeating phrases about the connection of industry with personal independence, initiative and other desirable qualities that had a meaning in agrarian pioneer conditions. The idea of a pre-established harmony between the existing so-called capitalistic regime and democracy is as absurd a piece of metaphysical speculation as human history has ever evolved.

The strife of interests, parties and factions is especially harmful since the problem is a common human one, the ways in which it is dealt with and their results affecting all alike. The first necessity is study of the scientifically cooperative type. It is theoretically conceivable that strife of interests might bring to clearer recognition the different interests that are involved and that have to be harmonized in any enduring solution. As long, however, as conflict is conducted on the assumption, upon each side, that there is already possession of the truth, a position that amounts to denial for the need of any scientific examination of conditions in order to determine the policies that should be undertaken, the rivalry of parties will be a source of division and confusion.

The discussion of this chapter has been one-sided in its emphasis upon the economic phase of our culture. But industrialization and commercialization play such a part in determining the qualities of present culture that the primary need for analysis of its conditions is made especially clear. The facts that justify economic emphasis do not prove, however, that the issue of cooperative democratic freedom can be settled by dealing directly and exclusively with the economic aspect, if only because command of the means which would be needed to effect desirable changes in industry and in the distribution of income can be achieved only by the aid of correlative changes in science, morals and other phases of our common experience. The facts bring out in sharp outline that as yet the full conditions, economic and legal, for a completely democratic experience have not existed. Upon both the negative and the positive side, the facts suggest the importance of critical examination of the theory that attaches supremacy to economic factors in isolation. The significance of interaction will appear more clearly in the contrast.

4. Totalitarian Economics and Democracy

Social movements that have a new direction are accompanied by simplifications. Imagination ignores things that might obscure singleness of vision; plans ignore whatever gets in the way of concentrated energy. Later on, the things that were left out of the reckoning are noted. They are then seen to be involved in the failure to realize the original program. Disappointment and frustration succeed a period of enthusiasms; hope is followed by sober and critical second thought. There is often discouragement as to the practical value of any large social outlook. What is thought to be hard realism and is certainly an emotional disillusionment comes after a period of romantic idealism. We were in that state to a considerable degree until the rise of totalitarian states issued a challenge that compels us to reconsider fundamental principles.

It is easy to overlook later advantages that were obtained by an earlier simplification. Benefits wrought and harm done are wrongly located both at the time of origin and of later criticism. Simplification is beneficial as far as it brings about clear recognition of some new operative tendency in human affairs, a fuller and freer operation of which would occasion enrichment of human life. The exaggeration tends to make the new factor stand out in relief; acknowledgment of it then becomes a positive influence in furthering it, so that it works deliberately instead of more or less unconsciously. Harm comes from the fact that the theory framed is stated in absolute terms, as one which applies at all places and times, instead of under the contemporary conditions and having definite limits. Later, when conditions have undergone such a change that the idea does not work, a reaction sets in which is equally wholesale. The original idea is dismissed as pure illusion; some newer movement, going contrary to the conditions which evoked the earlier idea, is then often given similar absoluteness.

Since the rise of natural science and its attendant technologies, simplifications on the side of theory have been of two general classes. Theories have simplified in exaggeration of either the human factor, the constituents derived from human nature, or the "external" environing factor. Popular ideas are usually a more or less confused and inconsistent compromise, drawing some elements from each point of view and combining them in a haphazard way. Clarification may, then, be had if in this chapter and the next, we consider two types of theory that carry one-sided simplifications to extremes, extremes which are logical, given the premises, but which mislead action because of the absolute quality of the premises. The kind of theory thus formed contrasts radically with the procedure in which social events are seen to be *interactions* of components of human nature on one side with cultural conditions on the other. Events are explained as if one factor or other in the interaction were the whole thing. In this chapter, I shall criticize the type of social theory which reduces the human factor as nearly as possible to zero; since it explains events and frames policies exclusively in terms of conditions provided by the environment. Marxism is taken as the typical illustration of the absolutism which results when this factor in the interaction is isolated and made supreme. It provides a typical illustration both because of its present vogue, and because it claims to represent the only strictly scientific theory of social change and thereby the method by which to effect change in the future.

Since the theory is involved in practical and party controversies in which feelings are excited, it is almost useless to say that the theory is here discussed as an illustration of what may be called "objective" or "realistic" absolutism, and for the sake of the light which thereby is thrown upon the actual problems of the present. For its adherents, by reason of the very nature of the theory, readily become so absolutistic in their attitude that they can see only a display of class-bias, unconscious or deliberate, in any criticism of their theory—an attitude now summed up in calling any opposition pro-Fascist. With those not committed it may promote understanding if I say that the criticism is not aimed at denying the role of economic factors in society nor at denying the tendency of the present economic regime to produce consequences adverse to democratic freedom. These things are rather taken for granted. Criticism aims to show what happens when this undeniable factor is isolated and treated as *the* cause of *all* social change. One may hold that if there is to be genuine and adequate democracy there must be a radical transformation of the present controls of production and distribution of goods and services, and may nevertheless accept the criticisms to be made—indeed may make or accept the criticisms *because* one believes the transformation is required.

The Marxist isolation of one factor (one which actually operates only in interaction with another one) takes the form of holding that the state of the forces of economic productivity at a given time ultimately determines all forms of social activities and relations, political, legal, scientific, artistic, religious, moral. In its original formulation, there was an important qualification which later statements have tended to ignore. For it was admitted that when political relations, science, etc., are once produced, they operate as causes of subsequent events, and in this capacity are capable of modifying in some degree the operation of the forces which originally produced them.

The subsequent ignoring of this qualification, the relegation of it to a footnote, was not wholly accidental. For there were practical reasons for paying little attention to it. If the qualification be admitted, observation of existing conditions (not the theory in the abstract) can alone tell just what consequences at a given time are produced by secondary effects which have now themselves acquired the standing of causes. The only way to decide would be to investigate, and by investigation in the concrete decide just what effects are due, say, to science, and just what to the naked, so to say, forces of economic production. To adopt and pursue this method would be in effect to abandon the all-comprehensive character of economic determination. It would put us in the relativistic and pluralistic position of considering a number of interacting factors—of which a very important one is undoubtedly the economic.

Marx would have a distinguished historic position if the qualification were admitted in even fuller extent than he allowed for. He would not have been the first by any means to recognize the importance of economic conditions in determination of political and legal forms. Their close connection was almost a commonplace of the political philosophy of Aristotle. It was restated in a different form by English writers who influenced the ideas of the founders of the American republic. The latter uniformly emphasized connection between a certain state of the distribution of property and secure maintenance of popular government. But Marx did go back of property relations to the working of the forces of production as no one before him had done. He also discriminated between the state of the forces of product*ivity* and the actual state of production existing at a given time, pointing out the lag often found in the latter. He showed in considerable detail that the cause of the lag is subordination of productive forces to legal and political conditions holding over from a previous regime of production. Marx's criticism of the present state of affairs from this last point of view was penetrating and possessed of enduring value.

The great merit, however, of the Marxist simplification, for those who accept it in its extreme form, is the fact that it combines the romantic idealism of earlier social revolutionaries with what purports to be a thoroughly "objective" scientific analysis, expressed in formulation of a single all-embracing "law," a law which moreover sets forth the proper method to be followed by the oppressed economic class in achieving its final liberation. For the theory went far beyond presenting a point of view to be employed in historical and sociological investigations. It claimed to state the one and only law in accordance with which economic relations determine the course of social change. This law is that of the existence of classes which are economically determined, which are engaged in constant warfare with one another, the outcome of which is direction of social change toward the liberation of producers from the bonds which have kept them subjugated in the past. Final creation of a classless society is to be the outcome.

It is quite possible to accept the idea of some sort of economic determinism. But that acceptance does not constitute one a Marxian, since the essence of the latter is the view that class warfare is the channel through which economic forces operate to effect social change and progress. This "law" was not derived nor supposed to be derived from study of historical events. It was derived from Hegelian dialectical metaphysics. The method of its derivation is indicated by the saying of Marx that he stood Hegel on his head. Hegel's system is one of dialectic idealism, in which logical categories, through the movement inherent in any partial and incomplete formulation of the rational structure of the universe, generate their own opposites, while the union of these opposites constitutes a higher and more adequate grasp of the nature of things, until finally all possible points of view with all their seeming conflicts are "organic" constituents of one all-comprehensive system.

Marx converted dialectic idealism into dialectic material-ism—where the dialectic of conflict as the means of ultimate union and harmony is preserved, while the moving forces are economic classes, not ideas. Its "materialism" is therefore as dif-ferent from "vulgar" materialism, based solely on conclusions of physical science, as the ultimate socialism, or the final synthesis of classless society is different from the "utopian" socialism of earlier communists:—utopian because they gave power and im-petus to human preferences of values, thereby assigning causal power to moral factors. To Marx the economic movement is nec-essarily as self-determined toward its ultimate goal as the move-ment of logical categories had been in the Hegelian system. Marxism thus not only dropped the idealistic rationalism of the Hegelian system and violently condemned it, but he also, in the name of science, denied moving power to human valuations.

In lieu of one type of romantic absolutism, it developed another type more in harmony with the prestige which science and scien-tific law were gaining. It was a wonderful intellectual achievement to formulate laws for all social phenomena; it was still more wonderful to set forth one law working with absolute necessity, grasp of which enabled men to observe the "contradictions" in existing bourgeois capitalism, while it indicated with certainty the goal to which the contradictions by their own dialectic were carrying society. The law of history became the law for revolu-tionary action:—and all was accomplished that can possibly be accomplished in behalf of a clear vision of a goal and the con-centration of emotion and energy in its behalf.

The idea of causal necessity in social phenomena and of devel-opment or "evolution" were in the intellectual atmosphere a century ago, the latter anteceding the Darwinian notion of bio-logical development. Kant had taught that the idea of causal ne-cessity is a prerequisite for natural science; German scientists at least accepted the idea without question, especially as Kant also made a sharp division between the fields of science and that of morals where freedom reigned. Hume's criticism of the idea of necessity was unwelcome even when it was known, because of its association with scepticism. In any case Kant seemed to have made an adequate reply to Hume.

In almost every quarter attempts were made to create a science of social phenomena, for which undertaking the idea of necessary law was deemed indispensable. Auguste Comte introduced the word *Sociology* as a name for a comprehensive synthesis, while he found its basis in the "law" of three necessary stages of development. At a later period, Herbert Spencer had no difficulty in finding a single formula to cover all phenomena, cosmic, biological, psychological, social. The earlier attempts at introducing scientific arrangement into human events made use of the principle of stages of necessary "evolution" in some form or other.

The forties of the last century were also the time of promising radical political movements, all of which had a marked economic slant, while some were avowedly socialistic and communistic, especially at that time in France. There was a period in Germany when Hegel's philosophy was so dominant that all important differences were those between wings of the Hegelian school. All of these circumstances put together, it is not surprising that Marx saw in the Hegelian dialectic a principle which, when it was given economic interpretation, provided a sure basis for a science of social changes, while at the same time, it furnished the revolutionary movement a supreme directive for its practical activities.

As has been said, important social movements develop some sort of philosophy by which to guide, nominally, at least, their practical efforts and also to justify them *ex post facto*. German culture has been especially ardent and prolific in this direction, all attempts to deal with actual conditions on any other basis being regarded as proof that those engaged in them are mere "empiricists," a term of condemnation about equivalent to calling them quacks. In Marxism those who accepted any law except one having exclusively material support were utopian dreamers. The fact then that the dialectical formula was borrowed from the most metaphysical, in a non-scientific sense, of all modern philosophers was no deterrent to the vogue of the Marxist synthesis, since its practical character seemed to be vouched for not only by actual economic conditions and by Marx's predictions, but in particular by the increase in class conflict that was taking place.

The idea of class war took on a peculiarly timely quality because of its teaching that the then existing class struggle was that of bourgeoisie capitalists with the proletariat, the class of factory wage-workers having neither land nor any form of reserve capital. Moreover, Marx's study of the concrete facts of the factory system in Great Britain backed up his general theory with a considerable number of economic generalizations which proved sound on any theory:—such as the existence of economic cycles with crises of increasing severity, a tendency toward combination and concentration, etc. The simplified Romanticism of the principle of a negation of negations taught that class war would, through the mediation of a temporary dictatorship of the proletariat, finally usher in a classless society. In the latter the state as a political coercive power would wither away, all political agencies becoming organs of democratic administration of affairs of common interest. Even the anarchist with his opposition to all coercive power could find satisfaction in contemplation of this ultimate outcome.

Marxists object vigorously and naturally to any suggestion of an identification of their creed with theological systems of the past. But all absolutisms tend to assume a theological form and to arouse the kind of emotional ardor that has accompanied crusading religions in the past. The theological concerns and conflicts of the earlier centuries of our era involved, moreover, contemporary interests not now recoverable in imagination. That is, they were more "practical" in fact than they now appear in retrospect. Similarly the monolithic and in itself speculative Marxist doctrine took on immediate practical coloring in connection with existing economic conditions and new forms of oppressions they had produced. There is nothing novel or peculiar in a combination of theory and practice in which practical events give definite color to an abstract theory, while the theory serves as a fountainhead of inspiration to action, providing also rallying cries and slogans. Exegesis can always serve to bridge gaps and inconsistencies; and every absolutistic creed demonstrates that no limits can be put to exegetical ingenuity. What actually happens can, accordingly, be brought into harmony with dogma while the latter is covertly accommodated to events.

There is no need to go into the full scope of Marxist philosophy upon its theoretical side. What is of concern here is the support alleged to be given by it to a strictly *scientific* form of social development, one which is inevitable *because* scientific. As is said of literary products, Marxism is "dated" in the matter of its claims to be peculiarly scientific. For just as *necessity* and search for a *single* all-comprehensive law was typical of the intellectual atmosphere of the forties of the last century, so *probability* and *pluralism* are the characteristics of the present state of science. That the older interpretation of the idea of causal necessity has undergone a shock does not need to be told to those acquainted with recent developments. It is not necessary, however, to go to the point of throwing the idea entirely overboard to make the point which is significant for the present topic.

There is a worldwide difference between the idea that causal sequences will be found in any given set of events taken for investigation, and the idea that *all* sets of events are linked together into a *single* whole by *one* causal law. Even if it be admitted that the former principle is a necessary postulate of scientific inquiry, the latter notion is metaphysical and *extra*-scientific. When natural science was first struggling to achieve its independence, and later when an attempt was made to take social phenomena out of the domain of arbitrary free-will, those who wanted to promote the new struggles borrowed from dominant theology the idea which the latter had made familiar, that of a single all-embracing causal force. The nature of the force and the way it worked were radically altered in the new apologetics for science. But the requirements of habit were satisfied in maintaining the old forms of thought—just as the first "horseless carriages" kept the shape of the carriages they displaced. The void left by surrender first of a supernatural force, and then of Nature (which had replaced Deity during the periods of deistic rationalism) are thus made good. Only gradually did the work of science and the specific conclusions it reached make it clear that science was not a competitor with theology for a single ultimate explanation, so that the justification was no longer resorted to.

The surrender does not mean that search for broad generalizations has been given up. It means that the nature and function of these generalizations have changed. They are now, in effect and function, formulae for effecting transformations from one field to another, the qualitative difference of the fields being maintained. The doctrine of the conservation of energy represents, for example, an exceedingly comprehensive generalization. In terms of the now discarded philosophy of science, it would be said to set up a force which is at once electrical, mechanical, thermal, etc., and yet none of them, but a kind of nondescript Thing-in-itself back of all of them. In actual scientific procedure, it is a formula for converting any one of these forms of energy into any other, provided certain conditions are satisfied.

The same principle holds good of the recently discovered transmutation of chemical elements. It does not wipe out the differences of quality that mark off phenomena from one another but sets forth the conditions under which one kind is changed into another kind. Differences in the practical operations that are based upon science correspond with the change that has come about in theory—as the techniques of modern chemical industry are different from the dreams of the alchemists. No one today would think of undertaking a definite invention, the heavier-than-air flying boat, the internal combustion engine, and so on, by setting out from an alleged universal law of the working of some single ultimate force. The inventor who translates an idea into a working technological device starts from examination of special materials and tries special methods for combining them.

The practical techniques derived from the Marxist single all-embracing law of a single causative force follow the pattern discarded in scientific inquiry and in scientific engineering. What is necessary according to it is to promote class war in as great a variety of ways and on as many occasions as possible. For the essence of the theory, according to the dialectical method, is not recognition of class conflicts as *facts*—in which respect it provided a needed correction of the early nineteenth century notion of universal harmony and universal interdependence. Its distinguishing trait is that social progress is made by intensifying the conflict between the capitalistic employing classes and the proletarian employed class, so that the supreme principle of morals is to strengthen the power of the latter class.

The physical analogy is about like this: suppose that there had once been a theory that "nature abhors friction." It is then discovered that no mechanical work is done without resistance, and that there is no resistance without friction. It is then concluded that by abolishing lubrication and magnifying friction, a state of universal friction will by its own inner dialectic result in an adjustment of energies to one another which will provide the best possible conditions for doing useful work. Society *is* marked by conflict and friction of interests; interests may by some stretching and more consolidation be used to define classes. It may also be admitted that the conflict between them has under certain conditions served as a stimulus to social progress; it might even be admitted that a society in which there was no opposition of interests would be sunk in a condition of hopeless lethargy. But the idea of obtaining universal harmony by the greatest possible intensification of conflicts would remain analogous to the physical illustration given. Persons who are not Marxists often identify the proposition that serious strife of economic interests exists with the genuine Marxist thesis that it is the sole agency by which social change is effected in the desirable direction of a classless society.

The criticism made is not directed then to any generalization made by Marx on the basis of observation of actual conditions. On the contrary, the implication of the criticism is the necessity for *continued* observation of actual conditions, with testing and revision of all earlier generalization on the basis of what is now observed. The inherent theoretical weakness of Marxism is that it supposed a generalization that was made at a particular date and place (and made even then only by bringing observed facts under a premise drawn from a metaphysical source) can obviate the need for continued resort to observation, and to continual revision of generalizations in their office of working hypotheses. In the name of science, a thoroughly anti-scientific procedure was formulated, in accord with which a generalization is made having the nature of ultimate "truth," and hence holding good at all times and places.

Laissez-faire individualism indulged in the same kind of sweeping generalization but in the opposite direction. Doubtless, in accordance with the law of the union of opposites, this background played its part in creating a cultural atmosphere favorable to Marxism. But two opposite errors do not constitute one truth, especially when both errors have the same root. With some disregard for historic facts, the Marxist doctrine might even be regarded as a generalized version of that aspect of classic economic theory which held that completely free competition in the open market would automatically produce universal harmony of persons and nations, Marx converting competition of individuals into war of classes.

Marxism has, then, been selected as an illustration of the monistic block-universe theory of social causation. A few years ago the laissez-faire view, developed out of ideas of Adam Smith when they were wedded to ideas of utilitarian morals and psychology, would have been appropriately taken. The Russian Revolution is chiefly accountable for having brought Marxism to the foreground. Being conducted in the name of Marx, it claimed to be a large scale demonstration of the validity of the Marxist theory. The Union of Soviet Socialist Republics has fastened attention upon the theory as no idea ever succeeds on its own account in obtaining notice. It caused Marxism to be a terrifying menace in some quarters while giving it enormous prestige in other quarters. It led to a disruption of old socialist parties, as the Russian Revolution was held up in other countries as proof of the Marxist theory of class war and the dictatorship of the proletariat. The issue raised by events in Russia gave actuality to Marxist doctrine in every country of the globe.

An event of this sort cannot occur without arousing intense feeling, and corresponding conflicts of interpretation. In the present case, the division extends not only to the theory but to the facts of the situation. One can find data, real or alleged, to support almost any view as to the actual situation in the U.S.S.R., according to the source one takes to be authoritative. Facts, including statistics, are cited to show that extraordinary progress has been made in industrialization of the country and mechanization of agricultural pursuits, with an immense gain in productivity, and, what is more important, in creation of a genuine workers' republic, attended with striking rise in the material and cultural standards of living of the great mass of the population. But one may also find evidence to support the view that the dictatorship of the proletariat became first that of a party over the proletariat and then the dictatorship of a small band of bureaucrats over the party, until the latter, to maintain power, has adopted, with greatly improved technical skill in execution, all the repressive measures of the overthrown Czarist despotism. One can find evidence that, under a regime of governmental, instead of social, control, economic classes marked by great inequality of income are growing up. Such questions of fact are not settled by argument. Hence though there is no doubt in my own mind as to the conclusion available evidence points to, I shall not here attempt to take a stand on the particular issues of fact which are involved.

Certain facts that are not denied suffice as far as the present topic and problem are concerned. A monistic theory is accompanied in its practical execution by one-party control of press, schools, radio, the theater and every means of communication, even to effective restrictions imposed on private gatherings and private conversations. One of the reasons for the great difference in opinion about the state of facts—the point just mentioned—is the fact that effective dictatorship (and an ineffective dictatorship is not a dictatorship at all) exercises complete command over the press, over travel, over letters and personal communications. In consequence, only a few have access to the sources of information about political methods, and that few is just the group with the greatest interest in preventing free inquiry and report.

This suppression of freedom of belief and of speech, press and assembly is not among the facts in dispute for it is of the essence of the dictatorship, which in turn is of the essence of the doctrine the Revolution claims to have put in force. Nor is ruthless persecution and punishment of all dissenters one of the disputed facts. A succession of trials has eliminated from life (as well as from political action) every one of the men and women who brought on the Revolution, save a few relatively minor characters. The *justification* of the action is one of the things in controversy, but not the fact of the exile, imprisonment or execution of every important earlier leader. As a criterion for judging the theory back of revolutionary method of class war, it would not seem to make a great deal of difference whether we decide these men were traitors to their own cause of the liberation of humanity, or are victims of the desire of a clique to keep in their hands a monopoly of all power—great as will be the difference in our judgment about the character of the persons involved.

Events not in dispute confirm the conclusion drawn from other historical instances that absolute principles are intolerant of dissent, for dissent from "The Truth" is more than an intellectual error. It is proof of an evil and dangerous will. When the dominant dogma is definitely theological, the evil will is described in one set of terms; when it is political, the phraseology is different, "counter-revolution" taking the place of "heresy."

The psychological and moral dispositions stimulated and the

kind of activities in which they are expressed are extraordinarily similar. No general theory, moreover, is self-translating in application to particular events. Some body of persons must exist to state just what its significance is in its bearing upon this and that situation, and a body that merely interprets is impotent unless it has power to enforce decisions. The extreme danger of giving any body of persons power for whose exercise they are not accountable is a commonplace in a democracy. Arbitrary irresponsibility varies in direct ratio to the claim for absoluteness on the part of the principle in behalf of which power is exercised. To sustain the principle against heresy, or counter-revolutionary action, it finally becomes necessary to clothe the human officials that are supposed to represent the principle with the finality of the professed end. Divinity once hedged about kings. An earlier repudiation in Russia of glorification of individual persons, because of the immensely superior importance of collective action, gives way to Byzantine adulation of the Leader.

That the state, as governmental coercive power, is not withering away is another indisputable fact. Instead there has been an increase of the intensity and range of state action; the independent activity of factions within the party, of trade unions and of the original soviets is now judged to be, if not counter-revolutionary, at least hostile to the maintenance of the dictatorship of the proletariat. It is a part of original Marxist doctrine that no class having power surrenders it without being compelled to do so by superior force. The application of this particular phase of the doctrine to those who now wield power is one of the "contradictions" attending the dialectical theory. It might be worth while to ask whether the constant splintering of professed Marxists into factions that fight one another as bitterly as they fight their professed foe does not bear a similar relation to the doctrine of class war.

For while it was part of the original doctrine that personal hatred is outside the scope of the impersonal sweep of economic forces, it is doubtful if there is any case in history of *odium theologicum* that surpasses in intensity the venom displayed by convinced disciples of the orthodox Marxist creed toward dissenters, the venom being even greater against those who agree in some respects than towards professed representatives of capitalism. For the former are heretics, while the latter are simply believers in a faith that is natural to them. Like pagans, as distinct from heretics, they do not know any better. Verbal abuse in countries like the United States is the substitute for the physical power exerted where dictatorship exists, the mildest epithet being that of Fascist or friend of Fascism.

The large measure of sympathy shown by liberals in our own country toward Russian totalitarianism—to the extent of asserting the country is essentially a democracy with which common cause should be made against Fascist states—is not surprising. There are undoubted advances made in many directions in the U.S.S.R., since the overthrow of Czardom. They are visible and well-publicized, while the conduct of political affairs is a sealed book. More influential still is the fact that those persons who see the obstructive power of the existing economic system in our country are moved by the fact that one country has done something about overthrowing that system. Also we are not in the habit of taking social and political philosophies very seriously. We take them empirically and "pragmatically," as useful rallying-cries. We do not realize that continental Europeans, especially those educated under the influence of German ideas, have a still greater contempt for action which is "empirically" directed than we have for abstract theory. Again, when events occur that are obviously unfortunate, it is easy to explain them as a result of survival of tendencies bred in the earlier despotism or as expressions of a mentality which is still quasi-Asiatic—although in fact these are the attitudes which have made it possible for a monolithic theory of the Marxist type to flourish.

While nothing said discounts the effect of economic factors upon other components of culture (and certainly not upon political ones at the present time), nevertheless democratic methods are proved, even if they lack adequate substance, to be indispensable to effecting economic change in the interest of freedom. In common with many others, I have from time to time pointed out the harmful consequences the present regime of industry and finance has upon the reality of democratic ends and methods. I have nothing to retract. But conditions in totalitarian countries have brought home the fact, not sufficiently realized by critics, myself included, that the forms which still exist encourage freedom of discussion, criticism and voluntary associations, and thereby set a gulf between a country having suffrage and popular representation and a country having dictatorships, whether of the right or left—the differences between the two latter growing continually less as they borrow each other's techniques.

The Marxist theory holds that government in so-called democratic states is only the organ of a capitalist class, using legislatures, courts, army and police to do its will and maintain its class supremacy. But the effect of constant criticism of governmental action; of more than one political party in formulating rival policies; of frequent elections; of the discussion and public education that attend majority rule, and above all the fact that political action is but one factor in the interplay of a number of cultural factors, have a value that critics of partial democracy have not realized. And this point is strengthened when we accept the criticism that much of our political democracy is more formal than substantial, provided it is placed in contrast with totalitarian political control. Subordination of the political to the economic has a meaning for those trained to take for granted the operation of an indefinite plurality of social tendencies, many of which are neither political nor economic, that it cannot possibly have in countries that are without the democratic tradition. It is difficult for even English people to understand why and how it is that politics are not the absorbing interest in this country they are in England. If the result with us is often looseness of cohesion and indefiniteness in direction of action, there is generated a certain balance of judgment and some sort of equilibrium in social affairs. We take for granted the action of a number of diverse factors in producing any social result. There are temporary waves of insistence upon this and that particular measure and aim. But there is at least enough democracy so that in time any one tendency gets averaged up in interplay with other tendencies. An average presents qualities that are open to easy criticism. But as compared with the fanaticism generated by monistic ideas when they are put into operation, the averaging of tendencies, a movement toward a mean, is an achievement of splendor. However, the habit of imagination that is bred makes it easier than it otherwise would be to idealize conditions in a country which, like Russia, aims at a monolithic structure. The "common man" may be common but for that reason he strikes a certain balance, and the balance struck is a greater safeguard of democracy than any particular law can be, even if written into the Constitution.

The moral is not unintelligent glorification of empirical, pluralistic, and pragmatic method. On the contrary, the lesson to be learned is the importance of ideas and of a plurality of ideas employed in experimental activity as working hypotheses. Thoughtless empiricism provides opportunity for secret manipulation behind the visible scene. When we assume that we are following common sense policies, in the most honorable sense of common sense, we may in fact, unless we direct observation of conditions by means of general ideas, be in process of being led around by the nose by agencies purporting to be democratic, but whose activities are subversive of freedom: a generalized warning which, when translated into concrete words, should make us wary toward those who talk glibly about the "American way of life," after they have identified Americanism with a partisan policy in behalf of concealed economic aims.

The experimental method of science is the exemplification of empirical method when experience has reached maturity. It is opposed equally to "vulgar" empiricism which recognizes only rule-of-thumb action, depending upon a succession of trial-and-error acts that are unregulated by connection with an idea which is both expressed and tested, and to that absolutism which insists there is but one Truth and that truth one already revealed and possessed by some group or party. Mr. John Strachey, an Englishman, not a Russian, may be quoted upon the extent to which present "Communist" thought is authoritarian and monistic—that is, ruled by an ideal of uniformity. For he says that communistic parties even outside of Russia, e.g., in this country, in "refusal to tolerate the co-existence of incompatible opinions . . . are simply asserting the claim that socialism is scientific." It would be difficult, probably impossible, to find a more direct and elegantly finished denial of all the qualities that make ideas and theories either scientific or democratic than is contained in this statement. It helps explain why literary persons have been chiefly the ones in this country who have fallen for Marxist theory, since they are the ones who, having the least amount of scientific attitude, swallow most readily the notion that "science" is a new kind of infallibility.

To repeat a statement already made in another connection, no generalization which, like Marxism, claims to state the final truth about changes (whether physical or social), can set forth the significance of the general idea that is accepted in connection with actual events as they happen. For the purpose of day by day *action*, the sole value of a theory is the significance given to concrete events, when they are viewed in the light of the theory, in the concrete relations they sustain to one another. It is no accident that the final effect of uniformity of ideas is to set up some selected body of persons above the theoretical generalization. Those who determine what the theory signifies in terms of the one important thing—namely, *what should be done*—are supreme over the theory even when they claim to act in subjection to it. The demand for uniformity of opinion, "the refusal to tolerate the existence of incompatible opinions," demands first that there be a party and then a select council of persons within the party, to decide just what after all is The Truth with respect to events as they arise—together with a truly theological technique of exegesis to explain the perfect consistency existing among a succession of inconsistent policies. Thus there has been the change from the earlier denunciation of democracy as identical with middle class capitalism and the labeling of all other socialists as Social-Fascists, to the present policy of a Popular Front, and to the presentation of Bolshevism as twentieth century democracy. And, again, change from denunciation of Nazi Germany to the beginnings of a virtual alliance with it, but now in the wholly praiseworthy interest of world peace, following upon the former orthodox doctrine that only communism can institute peace after a succession of wars international and civil. Scientific method in operating with working hypotheses instead of with fixed and final Truth is not forced to have an Inner Council to declare just what is the Truth nor to develop a system of exegesis which rivals the ancient theological way of explaining away apparent inconsistencies. It welcomes a clash of "incompatible opinions" as long as they can produce observed facts in their support.

Since Marxism has been taken as the example of a uniformitarian theory, basing itself upon "objective" factors of the environment in separation from their interaction with the factors of human nature, something will be said in closing about the ignoring of human qualities. For it contradicts the statement sometimes made that the essence of Marxism, at least as a practical doctrine, is appeal to the motive of self-interest. This statement is made as an accusation by non-Marxists, while it sometimes appears in what profess to be Marxist documents. But actually it comes close to reversing actual Marxist doctrine—the doctrine that the state of the forces of production is the sole causal force. For according to this view, all the factors of human nature are shaped from without by "materialistic," that is economic, forces. To give independent validity to any component of human nature would be, from the Marxist standpoint, a relapse into the "idealistic" type of theory that Marxism came to destroy.

A much juster criticism would be that Marxism systematically neglects everything on the side of human nature with respect to its being a factor having efficacy, save as it is previously determined by the state of the forces of production. In claiming to replace "Utopian" socialisms, Marxism throws out psychological as well as moral considerations. Whether the theory is in fact able to live up to this claim—without which its "materialism" is meaningless—is another matter. For it would seem as if certain organic needs and appetites at least were required to set the "forces of production" moving. But if this bio-psychological factor is admitted, then it must *interact* with "external" factors, and there is no particular point at which its operation can be said to cease.

The point involved has a practical as well as theoretical force. Take for example the matter of classes and of class-*consciousness*, the latter being an imperatively required condition in the Marxist theory. According to orthodox Marxism, the class consciousness of the proletariat is generated by the fact that the state of economic forces represented by large-scale factory production throws wage-workers closely together with little or no direct intercourse with employers—such as existed, for example, in shops where hand tools were used. Physical conditions thus demarcate economic classes, and throw into relief the conflict of interests between employers and employees, together with the community of interests, if only in misery, that bind together the latter. Now as an observation there is an undeniable element of truth in this position—especially in contrast with the favorite editorial exhortation that there can be no conflict between "Capital" and "Labor" since each depends on the other. But the facts involved in the observation are not compatible with the ultimate theory. The formation of a class, especially of class consciousness, depends upon the operation of psychological factors which are not mentioned—and which the theory rules out.

The fact is that Marx and every Marxist after him unconsciously assumes the existence and operation of factors in the constitution of human nature which must cooperate with "external" economic or "material" conditions in producing what actually happens. Explicit recognition of these factors would give the theory a different practical slant. It would have put the things emphasized by Marx in a different perspective. The fact seems to be that Marx himself unconsciously took over the current psychology of his time, standing also on *its* head the optimistic psychology of laissez-faire liberalism. Overt recognition of the psychological factors entails introduction of values and judgments of valuation into a theory of social movement—as is shown later.

Any monolithic theory of social action and social causation tends to have a ready-made answer for problems that present themselves. The wholesale character of this answer prevents critical examination and discrimination of the particular facts involved in the actual problem. In consequence, it dictates a kind of all-or-none practical activity, which in the end introduces new difficulties. I suggest as illustrations two sets of events that have played a great part in the history of the U.S.S.R. According to the theory, the members of the agricultural class, as far as they own land, belong to the bourgeoisie, although of the "petty" subdivision. Only factory workers, congregated in cities, belong to the proletariat. By theory then class war exists between city workers and most of the rural population. There is a genuine psychological and political problem involved in getting these two groups of human beings together for common social action. But the wholesale or monistic character of the theoretical premise prevents exploration of the problem *as* a problem. It is settled in advance that the class conflict is of such a nature that success of the revolutionary movement is bound up with domination of the urban wage worker over the rural population. Anybody who has followed Russian history knows that an already difficult problem has been tremendously exacerbated by acceptance of this absolute principle—in spite of considerable flexibility on Lenin's part in applying it.

The other example is the question of the possibility of building socialism in one country at a time when the state of forces of production is international. Here again there is a difficult problem with respect to the policies to be adopted in adjusting domestic and foreign relations. The all-or-none theory led in Russia to a complete political break-up in the formation of two completely hostile factions within the original Communist Party. Negotiations, compromise, working out of a policy on the basis of study of actual conditions was ruled out in advance. Even when the original orthodox Marxism was abandoned in favor of an effort to build socialism in one country—a policy for which on practical grounds a great deal could be said—it had to be proved that this policy was the one and the only one authorized by the all-or-none theory which cannot "tolerate incompatible opinions" because of the "scientific" character of the doctrine. The most effective way of proving the point was to behead all those who took a contrary view as traitors and counter-revolutionaries.

It is ironical that the theory which has made the most display and the greatest pretense of having a scientific foundation should be the one which has violated most systematically every principle of scientific method. What we may learn from the contradiction is the potential alliance between scientific and democratic method and the need of consummating this potentiality in the techniques of legislation and administration. It is of the nature of science not so much to tolerate as to welcome diversity of opinion, while it insists that inquiry brings the evidence of observed facts to bear to effect a consensus of conclusions—and even then to hold the conclusion subject to what is ascertained and made public in further new inquiries. I would not claim that any existing democracy has ever made complete or adequate use of scientific method in deciding upon its policies. But freedom of inquiry, toleration of diverse views, freedom of communication, the distribution of what is found out to every individual as the ultimate intellectual consumer, are involved in the democratic as in the scientific method. When democracy openly recognizes the existence of *problems* and the need for probing them *as* problems as its glory, it will relegate political groups that pride themselves upon refusing to admit incompatible opinions to the obscurity which already is the fate of similar groups in science.

5.   Democracy and Human Nature

It is not accidental that the rise of interest in human nature coincided in time with the assertion in political matters of the rights of the people as a whole, over against the rights of a class supposedly ordained by God or Nature to exercise rule. The full scope and depth of the connection between assertion of democracy in government and new consciousness of human nature cannot be presented without going into an opposite historic background, in which social arrangements and political forms were taken to be an expression of Nature—but most decidedly not of *human* nature. There would be involved an account, upon the side of theory, of the long history of the idea of *Laws of Nature* from the time of Aristotle and the Stoics to the formulators of modern jurisprudence in the sixteenth and seventeenth centuries.

The story of this development and of the shift, in the eighteenth century, from Natural Law to Natural Rights is one of the most important chapters in the intellectual and moral history of mankind. But to delve into it would here take us too far away from the immediate theme. I must content myself then with emphatic reassertion of the statement that regard for *human* nature as the source of legitimate political arrangements is comparatively late in European history; that when it arose it marked an almost revolutionary departure from previous theories about the basis of political rule and citizenship and subjection—so much so that the fundamental difference between even ancient republican and modern democratic governments has its source in the substitution of human nature for cosmic nature as the foundation of politics. Finally changes and the need for further change in democratic theory are connected with an inadequate theory of the constitution of human nature and its component elements in their relation to social phenomena.

The subject matter which follows is that of a drama in three acts, of which the last is the unfinished one now being enacted in which we, now living, are the participants. The first act, as far as it is possible to tell its condensed story, is that of a one-sided simplification of human nature which was used to promote and justify the new political movement. The second act is that of the reaction against the theory and the practices connected with it, on the ground that it was the forerunner of moral and social anarchy, the cause of dissolution of the ties of cohesion that bind human beings together in organic union. The third act, now playing, is that of recovery of the moral significance of the connection of human nature and democracy, now stated in concrete terms of existing conditions and freed from the one-sided exaggerations of the earlier statement. I give this summary first because in what follows I have been compelled to go in some detail into matters that if pursued further are technically theoretical.

I begin by saying that the type of theory which isolated the "external" factor of interactions that produce social phenomena is paralleled by one which isolated the "internal" or human factor. Indeed, if I had followed the historic order the latter type of theory would have been discussed first. And this type of theory is still more widely and influentially held than we might suppose. For its vogue is not now adequately represented by those professional psychologists and sociologists who claim that all social phenomena are to be understood in terms of the mental operations of individuals, since society consists in the last analysis only of individual persons. The practically effective statement of the point of view is found in economic theory, where it furnished the backbone of laissez-faire economics; and in the British political liberalism which developed in combination with this economic doctrine. A particular view of human motives in relation to social events, as explanations of them and as the basis of all sound social policy, has not come to us labeled psychology. But as a theory about human nature it is essentially psychological. We still find a view put forth as to an intrinsic and necessary connection between democracy and capitalism which has a psychological foundation and temper. For it is only because of belief in a certain theory of human nature that the two are said to be Siamese twins, so that attack upon one is a threat directed at the life of the other.

The classic expression of the point of view which would explain social phenomena by means of psychological phenomena is that of John Stuart Mill in his *Logic*—a statement that probably appeared almost axiomatic when it was put forth. "All phenomena of society are phenomena of human nature . . . and if therefore the phenomena of human thought, feeling and action are subject to fixed laws, the phenomena of society cannot but conform to law." And again, "The laws of the phenomena of society are and can be nothing but the laws of the actions and passions of human beings united in the social state." And then, as if to state conclusively that being "united in the social state" makes no difference as to the laws of individuals and hence none in those of society, he adds, "Human beings in society have no properties but those which are derived from and may be resolved into the laws of the nature of individual man."

This reference to "individual man" discloses the nature of the particular simplification which controlled the views and the policies of this particular school. The men who expressed and entertained the type of philosophy whose method was summed up by Mill were in their time revolutionaries. They wished to liberate a certain group of individuals, those concerned in new forms of industry, commerce and finance, from shackles inherited from feudalism which were endeared by custom and interest to a powerful landed aristocracy. If they do not appear now to be revolutionary (operating to bring about social change by change in men's opinions not by force), it is because their views are now the philosophy of conservatives in every highly industrialized country.

They essayed an intellectual formulation of principles which would justify the success of the tendencies which present day revolutionaries call the bourgeois capitalism they are trying to overthrow. The psychology in question is not that of present textbooks. But it expressed the individualistic ideas that animated the economic and political theories of the radicals of the time. Its "individualism" supplied the background of a great deal of even the technical psychology of the present day—pretty much all of it, save that which has started on a new tack because of biological and anthropological considerations. At the time of its origin, it was not a bookish doctrine even when written down in books. The books were elaborations of ideas that were propounded in electoral campaigns and offered as laws to be adopted by parliament.

· Before engaging in any detailed statements, I want to recall a statement made earlier; namely, that the popular view of the constitution of human nature at any given time is a reflex of social movements which have either become institutionalized or else are showing themselves against opposing social odds and hence need intellectual and moral formulation to increase their power. I may seem to be going far afield if I refer to Plato's statement of the way by which to determine the constituents of human nature. The proper method, he said, was to look at the version of human nature written in large and legible letters in the organization of classes in society, before trying to make it out in the dim petty edition found in individuals. And so on the basis of the social organization with which he was acquainted he found that since in society there was a laboring class toiling to find the means of satisfying the appetites, a citizen soldiery class loyal even to death to the laws of the state, and a legislative class, so the human soul must be composed of appetite at the base—in both significations of "base"—of generous spirited impulses which looked beyond personal enjoyment, while appetite was engaged only in taking in and absorbing for its own satisfaction, and finally reason, the legislative power.

Having found these three things in the composition of human nature, he had no difficulty in going back to social organization and proving that there was one class which had to be kept in order by rules and laws imposed from above, since otherwise its action was without limits, and would in the name of liberty destroy harmony and order; another class, whose inclinations were all towards obedience and loyalty to law, towards right beliefs, although itself incapable of discovering the ends from which laws are derived; and at the apex, in any well-ordered organization, the rule of those whose predominant natural qualities were reason, after that faculty had been suitably formed by education.

It would be hard to find a better illustration of the fact that any movement purporting to discover the psychological causes and sources of social phenomena is in fact a reverse movement, in which current social tendencies are read back into the structure of human nature; and are then used to explain the very things from which they are deduced. It was then "natural" for the men who reflected the new movement of industry and commerce to erect the appetites, treated by Plato as a kind of necessary evil, into the cornerstone of social well-being and progress. Something of the same kind exists at present when love of power is put forward to play the role taken a century ago by self-interest as the dominant "motive"—and if I put the word motive in quotation marks, it is for the reason just given. What are called motives turn out upon critical examination to be complex attitudes patterned under cultural conditions, rather than simple elements in human nature.

Even when we refer to tendencies and impulses that actually are genuine elements in human nature we find, unless we swallow whole some current opinion, that of themselves they explain nothing about social phenomena. For they produce consequences only as they are shaped into acquired dispositions by interaction with environing cultural conditions. Hobbes, who was the first of the moderns to identify the "state of nature" and its laws— the classic background of all political theories—with the raw uneducated state of human nature, may be called as witness. According to Hobbes, "In the nature of man we find three principal causes of quarrel. First competition, secondly diffidence, thirdly glory. The first maketh men invade for gain; the second for safety; and the third for reputation. The first use violence to make themselves the masters of other persons; the second to defend them; the third for trifles as a word, a smile, a different opinion or any other sign of undervalue, either direct in their persons or by reflection in their kindred, their friends, their nation."

That the qualities mentioned by Hobbes actually exist in human nature and that they may generate "quarrel," that is, conflict and war between states and civil war within a nation—the chronic state of affairs when Hobbes lived—is not denied. Insofar, Hobbes' account of the natural psychology which prevents the state of security which is a pre-requisite for civilized communities shows more insight than many attempts made today to list the traits of raw human nature that are supposed to cause social phenomena. Hobbes thought that the entire natural state of men in their relations to one another was a war of all against all, man being naturally to man "as a wolf." The intent of Hobbes was thus a glorification of deliberately instituted relations, authoritative laws and regulations which should rule not just overt actions, but the impulses and ideas which cause men to hold up certain things as ends or goods. Hobbes himself thought of this authority as a political sovereign. But it would be in the spirit of his treatment to regard it as glorification of culture over against raw human nature, and more than one writer has pointed out the likeness between his Leviathan and the Nazi totalitarian state.

There are more than one instructive parallelisms that may be drawn between the period in which Hobbes lived and the present time, especially as to insecurity and conflict between nations and classes. The point here pertinent, however, is that the qualities Hobbes selected as the causes of disorders making the life of mankind "brutish and nasty," are the very "motives" that have been selected by others as the cause of *beneficent* social effects; namely, harmony, prosperity, and indefinite progress. The position taken by Hobbes about competition as love of gain was completely reversed in the British social philosophy of the nineteenth century. Instead of being a source of war, it was taken to be the means by which individuals found the occupation for which they were best fitted; by which needed goods reached the consumer at least cost, and by which a state of ultimate harmonious interdependence would be produced—provided only competition were allowed to operate without "artificial" restriction. Even today one reads articles and hears speeches in which the cause of our present economic troubles is laid to political interference with the beneficent workings of private competitive effort for gain.

The object of alluding to these two very different conceptions of this component in human nature is not to decide or discuss which is right. The point is that both are guilty of the same fallacy. In itself, the impulse (or whatever name be given it) is neither socially maleficent nor beneficent. Its significance depends upon consequences actually produced; and these depend upon the conditions under which it operates and with which it interacts. The conditions are set by tradition, by custom, by law, by the kind of public approvals and disapprovals; by all conditions constituting the environment. These conditions are so pluralized even in one and the same country at the same period that love of gain (regarded as a trait of human nature) may be both socially useful and socially harmful. And, in spite of the tendency to set up cooperative impulses as thoroughly beneficial, the same thing is true of them—regarded simply as components of human nature. Neither competition nor cooperation can be judged as traits of human nature. They are names for certain relations among the actions of individuals as the relations actually obtain in a community.

This would be true even if there were tendencies in human nature so definitely marked off from one another as to merit the names given them and even if human nature were as fixed as it is sometimes said to be. For even in that case, human nature operates in a multitude of different environing conditions, and it is interaction with the latter that determines the consequences and the social significance and value, positive or negative, of the tendencies. The alleged fixity of the structure of human nature does not explain in the least the differences that mark off one tribe, family, people, from another—which is to say that in and of itself it explains no state of society whatever. It issues no advice as to what policies it is advantageous to follow. It does not even justify conservatism as against radicalism.

But the alleged unchangeableness of human nature cannot be admitted. For while certain needs in human nature are constant, the consequences they produce (because of the existing state of culture—of science, morals, religion, art, industry, legal rules) react back into the original components of human nature to shape them into new forms. The total pattern is thereby modified. The futility of exclusive appeal to psychological factors both to explain what takes place and to form policies as to what *should* take place, would be evident to everybody—had it not proved to be a convenient device for "rationalizing" policies that are urged on other grounds by some group or faction. While the case of "competition" urging men both to war and to beneficent social progress is most obviously instructive in this respect, examination of the other elements of Hobbes supports the same conclusion.

There have been communities, for example, in which regard for the honor of one's self, one's family, one's class, has been the chief conservator of all worth while social values. It has always been the chief virtue of an aristocratic class, civil or military. While its value has often been exaggerated, it is folly to deny that in interaction with certain cultural conditions, it has had valuable consequences. "Diffidence" or fear as a motive is an even more ambiguous and meaningless term as far as its consequences are concerned. It takes any form, from craven cowardice to prudence, caution, and the circumspection without which no intelligent foresight is possible. It may become reverence—which has been exaggerated in the abstract at times but which may be attached to the kind of objects which render it supremely desirable. "Love of power," to which it is now fashionable to appeal, has a meaning only when it applies to everything in general and hence explains nothing in particular.

Discussion up to this point has been intended to elicit two principles. One of them is that the views about human nature that are popular at a given time are usually derived from contemporary social currents; currents so conspicuous as to stand out or else less marked and less effective social movements which a special group believes *should* become dominant:—as for example, in the case of the legislative reason with Plato, and of competitive love of gain with classical economists. The other principle is that reference to components of original human nature, even if they actually exist, explains no social occurrence whatever and gives no advice or direction as to what policies it is better to adopt. This does not mean that reference to them must necessarily be of a "rationalizing" concealed apologetic type. It means that whenever it occurs with practical significance it has *moral* not psychological import. For, whether brought forward from the side of conserving what already exists or from that of producing change, it is an expression of valuation, and of purpose determined by estimate of values. When a trait of human nature is put forward on this basis, it is in its proper context and is subject to intelligent examination.

The prevailing habit, however, is to assume that a social issue does not concern values to be preferred and striven for, but rather something predetermined by the constitution of human nature. This assumption is the source of serious social ills. Intellectually it is a reversion to the type of explanation that governed physical science until say, the seventeenth century: a method now seen to have been the chief source of the long-continued retardation of natural science. For this type of theory consists of appeal to general forces to "explain" what happens.

Natural science began to progress steadily only when general forces were banished and inquiry was directed instead to ascertaining correlations that exist between observed changes. Popular appeal to, say, electricity, light or heat, etc., as a force to account for some particular event still exists, as to electricity to explain storms attended by thunder and lightning. Scientific men themselves often talk in similar words. But such general terms are in their case shorthand expressions. They stand for uniform relations between events that are observed to occur; they do not mark appeal to something behind what happens and which is supposed to produce it. If we take the case of the lightning flash and electricity, Franklin's identification of the former as of the electrical kind brought it into connection with things from which it had been formerly isolated, and knowledge about them was available in dealing with it. But instead of electricity being an explanatory force, knowledge that lightning is an electrical phenomenon opened a number of special problems, some of which are still unsolved.

If the analogy between the relatively sterile condition of natural science when this method prevailed and the present state of the social "sciences" is not convincing, the misdirection of inquiry that results may be cited in evidence. There is an illusion of understanding, when in reality there is only a general word that conceals lack of understanding. Social ideas are kept in the domain of glittering generalities. Opinion as distinct from knowledge breeds controversy. Since what is regarded as a cause is that which is used as an agency or instrumentality of production, there is no controlled method of bringing anything into existence and of preventing the occurrence of that not wanted, save as there is knowledge of the conditions of its occurrence. When men knew that a certain kind of friction produced fire, they had at command at least one means, rubbing of sticks together, for producing fire when they wanted it. And it goes without saying that greater acquaintance with causal conditions has multiplied men's practical ability to have fire when needed, and to use it for an increased number of ends. The principle applies to the relation of social theory and social action.

Finally theories supposed to explain the course of events are used to urge and justify certain practical policies. Marxism is, of course, a striking instance. But it is so far from being the only instance that non-Marxian and anti-Marxian social theories often exemplify the principle. Utilitarianism used the idea that pleasure and pain are the sole determinants of human action to advance a sweeping theory of legislation, judicial and penal procedure; namely, that they be directed to secure the greatest happiness of the greatest number. Explanation of events on the basis of free, unimpeded manifestation of wants was used on the practical side as active propaganda for an open-market economic regime with all political and legal measures adapted to it. Belief in the general character of the alleged "force" rendered it unnecessary to keep track of actual events so as to check the theory. If things happened that obviously went contrary to the creed, the inconsistency was not taken as a reason for examining it, but as the cue for alleging special reasons for the failure, so that the truth of the principle could be kept intact.

Mere general ideas can be argued for and against without the necessity of recourse to observation. The arguments are saved from being a mere matter of words only because there are certain emotional attitudes involved. When general ideas are not capable of being continuously checked and revised by observation of what actually takes place, they are, as a mere truism, in the field of opinion. Clash of opinions is in that case the occasion for controversy, not, as is now the case in natural science, a location of a problem and an occasion for making further observations. If any generalization can be safely laid down about intellectual matters and their consequences, it is that the reign of opinion, and of controversial conflicts, is a function of absence of methods of inquiry which bring new facts to light and by so doing establish the basis for consensus of beliefs.

Social events are sufficiently complex in any case so that the development of effective methods of observation, yielding generalization about correlation of events, is difficult. The prevailing type of theory adds the further handicap of making such observation unnecessary—save as this and that arbitrarily selected event is used in argumentative controversy. The prime necessity is to frame general ideas, first, to promote search for problems— as against the assumption of a ready-made solution in view of which there are no problems; and, secondly, to solve these problems by generalizations that state interactions between analytically observed events.

I return to the particular social philosophy which associates the economic regime actuated by effort to make private profit with the essential conditions of free and democratic institutions. It is not necessary to go back to the theory in its early English formulation at the hands of laissez-faire liberals. For in spite of the discrediting of the philosophy by events, efforts put forth in this country to establish so-called social control of business has led at present to its revival in an extremely naked form. One does not need to endorse the measures for control that are used to be aware of the fallacy of the theory upon which current objections to them are based. The theory is that capitalism, interpreted as the maximum range of free personal opportunity for production and exchange of goods and services is the Siamese twin of democracy. For the former is identical, so it is claimed, with the personal qualities of initiative, independence, vigor, that are the basic conditions of free political institutions. Hence, so it is argued, the check given to the operation of these personal qualities by governmental regulation of business activities is at the same time an attack upon the practical and moral conditions for the existence of political democracy.

I am not concerned here with the merits of the special arguments put forth in behalf of and against the measures employed. The point is that appeal to certain alleged human motivations in a wholesale way, such as "initiative, independence, enterprise" at large, obscures the need for observation of events in the concrete. If and when special events are observed, interpretation of them is predestined instead of growing out of what is observed. By keeping the issues in the realm of opinion, appeal to equally general wholesale views on the other side is promoted. Then we get a kind of head-on conflict between something called "individualism" on one side and "socialism" on the other. Examination of concrete conditions might disclose certain specifiable conditions under which both of the methods vaguely pointed at by these words would operate to advantage.

The current use of the word *enterprise* as an honorific term is especially instructive with regard to the attempt to draw support for policies from a reference to general inherent traits of human nature. For the only legitimate signification of "enterprise" is a neutral one, an *undertaking* the desirability of which is a matter of actual results produced, which accordingly need to be studied in the concrete. But *enterprise* is given the significance of a certain desirable trait of human nature, so that the issue is taken out of the field of observation into that of opinion plus a eulogistic emotion. "Enterprise" like "initiative" and like "industry" can be exerted in behalf of an indefinite number of objects; the words may designate the activities of an Al Capone or a racketeering labor union as well as a socially useful industrial undertaking.

The case is cited in some detail because it provides a striking example, first, of the conversion of an existing mode of social behavior into a psychological property of human nature; and, secondly, conversion of an alleged matter of psychological fact into a principle of value—a moral matter. Social problems that are set by conditions having definite spatial and temporal boundaries— which have to be determined by observation—are made into matters capable of absolute determination without reference to conditions of place and date. Hence they become matters of opinion and controversial argument—and as the latter decides nothing, the final tendency is to appeal to force as the ultimate arbiter.

The theory of the components of human nature used by the intellectual radicals of Great Britain to justify popular government and freedom included more than the self-interest motivation. It was officially held that sympathy with the gains and losses, the pleasures and pains of others, is a native part of the human endowment. The two components, self-interest and sympathy, opposite in quality, were ingeniously linked together in the complete doctrine—occasionally with explicit reference to the supposedly analogous centripetal and centrifugal components of Newtonian celestial mechanics. The self-interest phase supplied the foundation of the theory of public and governmental action; the sympathetic phase took care of the relations of individuals to one another in their private capacities. The doctrine taught that if political institutions were reformed to do away with special privileges and unfair favoritisms, the sympathetic motive would have a vastly enlarged field of effective and successful operation, since bad institutions were the chief cause that led men to find their personal advantage in acts injurious to others.

The theory was even more important in the reaction it called out than in itself. For "organic idealistic" philosophies developed in Germany during the nineteenth century, and now form the theoretical background and justification of totalitarianism. They took their clew and point of departure from the weaknesses of the theories that based politics and morals, in theory and in practice, upon alleged components of human nature. An adequate account of the form and substance of the reaction would take us into matters which cannot be set forth without going into technicalities. But its basis is simple.

The attempt to locate the source of authority of politics and morals in human nature was regarded as the source of anarchy, disorder, and conflict;—an attempt to build social institutions and personal relationships upon the most unstable of shifting quicksands. At the same time, the philosophers who formulated the new view were Protestants and Northerners. Hence their reaction did not move them to urge acceptance of the doctrines of the Roman Church as the bulwark against the dissolving tendencies of ultra-individualistic ideas and policies.

The French Revolution, with its excesses, was uniformly regarded in German thought as the logical outcome of the attempt to locate authority where nothing binding could be found. It was thus taken to be a practical large scale demonstration of the weakness inherent in the position. The most that could be said for the doctrine was what could be said in defense of the French Revolution—it helped to get rid of abuses that had grown up. As a positive and constructive principle, it was a tragic delusion. The statement of the Rights of Man setting forth the official creed of the Revolution was said to be a summary of the false doctrines that had produced all the characteristic evils of the age. The protest, as just said, refused to accept the doctrines of the Church as the basis for its criticisms and for the constructive measures it proposed. It was itself too deeply influenced by the conditions which had produced the individualism against which it revolted. The extent of this influence is why the movement is criticized by representatives of the Hellenic-medieval ideas as itself intensely "subjectivistic." It found the way to "reconcile" freedom and authority, individuality and law, by setting up an Absolute Self, Mind, Spirit, of which human beings are individually partial manifestations, a "truer" and fuller manifestation being found in social institutions, the state and the course of history. Since history is the final court of judgment and since it represents the movement of absolute Spirit, appeal to force to settle issues between nations is not "really" an appeal to force, but rather to the ultimate logic of absolute reason. The individualistic movement was a necessary transitional movement to bring men to recognition of the primacy and ultimacy of Spirit and Personality in the constitution of nature, man, and society. German organic idealism was to save all that is true in the movement, while eliminating its errors and dangers by lifting it up to the plane of absolute Self and Spirit. There is much that is technical in the movement; much of its detail can be explained only on the ground of special intellectual events. But its heart and core is found in its attempt to find a "higher" justification for individuality and freedom where the latter are merged with law and authority, which *must* be rational since they are manifestations of Absolute Reason. Contemporary totalitarianism has no difficulty in discovering that the Germanic racial spirit embodied in the German state is an adequate substitute, for all practical purposes, for the Hegelian Absolute Spirit.

Rousseau is usually, and in many respects properly, regarded as the prophet and intellectual progenitor of the French Revolution. But by one of those ironies with which history abounds he was also a step-father of the theory that came to full expression in Germany. He served in this capacity partly indirectly by his attack on culture which, as previously said, was the challenge that resulted in glorification of culture over against human nature. But he also acted positively and directly. For in his political writings he advanced the idea that a Common Will is the source of legitimate political institutions; that freedom and law are one and the same thing in the operations of the Common Will, for it must act for the Common Good and hence for the "real" or true Good of every individual.

If the latter set up their purely personal desires against the General Will, it was accordingly legitimate (indeed necessary) to "*force* them to be free." Rousseau intended his theory to state the foundation of self-governing institutions and majority rule. But his premise was employed to prove that the Common—or Universal—Will and Reason was embodied in the national state. Its most adequate incarnation was in those states in which the authority of law, order, and discipline had not been weakened by democratic heresies:—a view which was used in Germany after the Napoleonic conquest to create an aggressive national spirit in that country, one which provided the basis for systematic depreciation of French "materialistic" civilization as over against

German *Kultur*—a depreciation later extended to condemnation of democratic institutions in any country.

While this brief exposition of the reaction against the individualistic theory of human nature suggests the ground pattern of National Socialism, it also throws some light upon the predicament in which democratic countries find themselves. The fact that the individualistic theory was used a century and more ago to justify political self-government and then aided promotion of its cause does not constitute the theory a present trustworthy guide of democratic action. It is profitable to read today the bitterly vivid denunciations of Carlyle on the theory as it was originally put forth. He denounced with equal fierceness the attempt to erect political authority upon the basis of self-interest and private morals upon the exercise of sympathy. The latter was sentimentalism run riot and the former was "Anarchy plus the Constable"—the latter being needed to preserve even a semblance of outward order. His plea for discipline and order included even a plea for leadership by select persons.

The present predicament may be stated as follows: Democracy does involve a belief that political institutions and law be such as to take fundamental account of human nature. They must give it freer play than any non-democratic institutions. At the same time, the theory, legalistic and moralistic, about human nature that has been used to expound and justify this reliance upon human nature has proved inadequate. Upon the legal and political side, during the nineteenth century it was progressively overloaded with ideas and practices which have more to do with business carried on for profit than with democracy. On the moralistic side, it has tended to substitute emotional exhortation to act in accord with the Golden Rule for the discipline and the control afforded by incorporation of democratic ideals into *all* the relations of life. Because of lack of an adequate theory of human nature in its relations to democracy, attachment to democratic ends and methods has tended to become a matter of tradition and habit—an excellent thing as far as it goes, but when it becomes routine is easily undermined when change of conditions changes other habits.

Were I to say that democracy needs a new psychology of human nature, one adequate to the heavy demands put upon it by foreign and domestic conditions, I might be taken to utter an academic irrelevancy. But if the remark is understood to mean that democracy has always been allied with humanism, with faith in the potentialities of human nature, and that the present need is vigorous reassertion of this faith, developed in relevant ideas and manifested in practical attitudes, it but continues the American tradition. For belief in the "common man" has no significance save as an expression of belief in the intimate and vital connection of democracy and human nature.

We cannot continue the idea that human nature when left to itself, when freed from external arbitrary restrictions, will tend to the production of democratic institutions that work successfully. We have now to state the issue from the other side. We have to see that democracy means the belief that humanistic culture *should* prevail; we should be frank and open in our recognition that the proposition is a moral one—like any idea that concerns what *should* be.

Strange as it seems to us, democracy is challenged by totalitarian states of the Fascist variety on moral grounds just as it is challenged by totalitarianisms of the left on economic grounds. We may be able to defend democracy on the latter score, as far as comparative conditions are involved, since up to the present at least the Union of Soviet Socialist Republics has not "caught up" with us, much less "surpassed" us, in material affairs. But defense against the other type of totalitarianism (and perhaps in the end against also the Marxist type) requires a positive and courageous constructive awakening to the significance of faith in human nature for development of every phase of our culture:— science, art, education, morals and religion, as well as politics and economics. No matter how uniform and constant human nature is in the abstract, the conditions within which and upon which it operates have changed so greatly since political democracy was established among us, that democracy cannot now depend upon or be expressed in political institutions alone. We cannot even be certain that they and their legal accompaniments are actually democratic at the present time—for democracy is expressed in the attitudes of human beings and is measured by consequences produced in their lives.

The impact of the humanist view of democracy upon all forms of culture, upon education, science and art, morals and religion, as well as upon industry and politics, saves it from the criticism passed upon moralistic exhortation. For it tells us that we need to examine every one of the phases of human activity to ascertain what effects it has in release, maturing and fruition of the potentialities of human nature. It does not tell us to "re-arm morally" and all social problems will be solved. It says, Find out how all the constituents of our existing culture are operating and then see to it that whenever and wherever needed they be modified in order that their workings may release and fulfill the possibilities of human nature.

It used to be said (and the statement has not gone completely out of fashion) that democracy is a by-product of Christianity, since the latter teaches the infinite worth of the individual human soul. We are now told by some persons that since belief in the soul has been discredited by science, the moral basis for democracy supposed to exist must go into the discard. We are told that if there are reasons for preferring it to other arrangements of the relations of human beings to one another, they must be found in specialized external advantages which outweigh the advantages of other social forms. From a very different quarter, we are told that weakening of the older theological doctrine of the soul is one of the reasons for the eclipse of faith in democracy. These two views at opposite poles give depth and urgency to the question whether there are adequate grounds for faith in the potentialities of human nature and whether they can be accompanied by the intensity and ardor once awakened by religious ideas upon a theological basis. Is human nature intrinsically such a poor thing that the idea is *absurd*? I do not attempt to give any answer, but the word *faith* is intentionally used. For in the long run democracy will stand or fall with the possibility of maintaining the faith and justifying it by works.

Take, for example, the question of intolerance. Systematic hatred and suspicion of any human group, "racial," sectarian, political, denotes deep-seated scepticism about the qualities of human nature. From the standpoint of a faith in the possibilities of human nature possessing religious quality it is blasphemous. It may start by being directed at a particular group, and be supported in name by assigning special reasons why that group is not worthy of confidence, respect, and decent human treatment. But the underlying attitude is one of fundamental distrust of human nature. Hence it spreads from distrust and hatred of a particular group until it may undermine the conviction that any group of persons has any intrinsic right for esteem or recognition—which, then, if it be given, is for some special and external grounds, such as usefulness to our particular interests and ambitions. There is no physical acid which has the corrosive power possessed by intolerance directed against persons because they belong to a group that bears a certain name. Its corrosive potency gains with what it feeds on. An anti-humanist attitude is the essence of every form of intolerance. Movements that begin by stirring up hostility against a group of people end by denying to them all human qualities.

The case of intolerance is used as an illustration of the intrinsic connection between the prospects of democracy and belief in the potentialities of human nature—not for its own sake, important as it is on its own account. How much of our past tolerance was positive and how much of it a toleration equivalent to "standing" something we do not like, "putting up" with something because it involves too much trouble to try to change it? For a good deal of the present reaction against democracy is probably simply the disclosure of a weakness that was there before; one that was covered up or did not appear in its true light. Certainly racial prejudice against Negroes, Catholics, and Jews is no new thing in our life. Its presence among us is an intrinsic weakness and a handle for the accusation that we do not act differently from Nazi Germany.

The greatest practical inconsistency that would be revealed by searching our own habitual attitudes is probably one between the democratic method of forming opinions in political matters and the methods in common use in forming beliefs in other subjects. In theory, the democratic method is persuasion through public discussion carried on not only in legislative halls but in the press, private conversations and public assemblies. The substitution of ballots for bullets, of the right to vote for the lash, is an expression of the will to substitute the method of discussion for the method of coercion. With all its defects and partialities in determination of political decisions, it has worked to keep factional disputes within bounds, to an extent that was incredible a century or more ago. While Carlyle could bring his gift of satire into play in ridiculing the notion that men by talking to and at each other in an assembly hall can settle what is true in social affairs any more than they can settle what is true in the multiplication table, he failed to see that if men had been using clubs to maim and kill one another to decide the product of 7 times 7, there would have been sound reasons for appealing to discussion and persuasion even in the latter case. The fundamental reply is that social "truths" are so unlike mathematical truths that unanimity of uniform belief is possible in respect to the former only when a dictator has the power to tell others what they must believe—or profess they believe. The adjustment of interests demands that diverse interests have a chance to articulate themselves.

The real trouble is that there is an intrinsic split in our habitual attitudes when we profess to depend upon discussion and persuasion in politics and then systematically depend upon other methods in reaching conclusions in matters of morals and religion, or in anything where we depend upon a person or group possessed of "authority." We do not have to go to theological matters to find examples. In homes and in schools, the places where the essentials of character are supposed to be formed, the usual procedure is settlement of issues, intellectual and moral, by appeal to the "authority" of parent, teacher, or textbook. Dispositions formed under such conditions are so inconsistent with the democratic method that in a crisis they may be aroused to act in positively anti-democratic ways for anti-democratic ends; just as resort to coercive force and suppression of civil liberties are readily palliated in nominally democratic communities when the cry is raised that "law and order" are threatened.

It is no easy matter to find adequate authority for action in the demand, characteristic of democracy, that conditions be such as will enable the potentialities of human nature to reach fruition. Because it is not easy the democratic road is the hard one to take. It is the road which places the greatest burden of responsibility upon the greatest number of human beings. Backsets and deviations occur and will continue to occur. But that which is its weakness at particular times is its strength in the long course of human history. Just because the cause of democratic freedom is the cause of the fullest possible realization of human potentialities, the latter when they are suppressed and oppressed will in time rebel and demand an opportunity for manifestation. With the founders of American democracy, the claims of democracy were inherently one with the demands of a just and equal morality. We cannot now well use their vocabulary. Changes in knowledge have outlawed the significations of the words they commonly used. But in spite of the unsuitability of much of their language for present use, what they asserted was that self-governing institutions are the means by which human nature can secure its fullest realization in the greatest number of persons. The question of what is involved in self-governing methods is now much more complex. But for this very reason, the task of those who retain belief in democracy is to revive and maintain in full vigor the original conviction of the intrinsic moral nature of democracy, now stated in ways congruous with present conditions of culture. We have advanced far enough to say that democracy is a way of life. We have yet to realize that it is a way of personal life and one which provides a moral standard for personal conduct.

6.   Science and Free Culture

It is no longer possible to hold the simple faith of the Enlightenment that assured advance of science will produce free institutions by dispelling ignorance and superstition:—the sources of human servitude and the pillars of oppressive government. The progress of natural science has been even more rapid and extensive than could have been anticipated. But its technological application in mass production and distribution of goods has required concentration of capital; it has resulted in business corporations possessed of extensive legal rights and immunities; and, as is a commonplace, has created a vast and intricate set of new problems. It has put at the disposal of dictators means of controlling opinion and sentiment of a potency which reduces to a mere shadow all previous agencies at the command of despotic rulers. For negative censorship it has substituted means of propaganda of ideas and alleged information on a scale that reaches every individual, reiterated day after day by every organ of publicity and communication, old and new. In consequence, for practically the first time in human history, totalitarian states exist claiming to rest upon the active consent of the governed. While despotic governments are as old as political history, this particular phenomenon is as startlingly unexpected as it is powerful.

One of the earlier arguments for democracy is countered in the most disturbing way. Before the industrial revolution had made much headway it was a commonplace that oppressive governments had the support of only a relatively small class. Republican government, it was assumed, would have the broad support of the masses, so that the "people" who, as Rousseau expressed it, had been nothing would become everything. We are now told the contrary. Democracy is said to be but a numerical contrivance, resting upon shifting combinations of individuals who happen at a given time to make up a majority of voters. We are told that the moral consensus which exists only when there is unity of beliefs and aims, is conspicuously lacking in democracies, and is of the very essence of totalitarian states. The claim stands side by side with that of Marxist communists who say that since their views are inherently scientific, false opinions have no legitimate standing as against the authority of The Truth. But in a way the Fascist claim goes deeper since it pretends to extend below merely intellectual loyalties, to which science appeals, and lay hold of fundamental emotions and impulses.

There is an argument about science which so far has found comparatively little response in democratic countries, but which nevertheless puts a problem so basic that it will receive more and more attention as time goes by. It is said that the principles of laissez-faire individualism have governed the conduct of scientific inquiry; that the tastes and preferences of individual investigators have been allowed to regulate its course to such an extent that present intellectual confusion and moral chaos of the world exists because of tacit connivance of science with uncontrolled individualistic activity in industry.

The position is so extreme and goes so contrary to all we had come to believe that it is easily passed over as an aberration. But the view, because of its extreme character, may be taken to point to a genuine issue: just what are the social consequences of science? Are they not so important, because of technological applications, that the social interest is paramount over intellectual interest? Can the type of social control of industry urged by socialists be carried through without some kind of public regulation of the scientific investigations that are the source of the inventions determining the course of industry? And might not such regulation throttle the freedom of science? Those who say that the social effect of inventions (which exist only because of the findings of scientific inquiry) is so unsettling that the least which can be done is to declare a moratorium on science express the same problem with more moderation.

The claim is made in Russia that the direction taken by science has in the last hundred and fifty years been so determined by the interest of the dominant economic class, that science has been upon the whole an organ of bourgeois democracy:—not so consciously perhaps as in the case of government, the police and the army, but yet in substantial effect. Since it is impossible to draw any fixed line between the physical and the social sciences, and since the latter—both with respect to investigation and teaching—must be regulated in the interest of the politics of the new social order, it is impossible to allow the physical sciences to go their way apart without political regulation. Nazi Germany decrees what is scientific truth in anthropology regarding race, and Moscow determines that Mendelism is scientifically false, and dictates the course to be pursued by Genetics. Both countries look askance at the theory of Relativity, although on different grounds. Quite aside, however, from special cases, a general atmosphere of control of opinion cannot exist without reacting in pretty fundamental ways upon every form of intellectual activity—art too as well as science.

Even if we hold that extreme views are so extreme as to be distorted caricatures, there remains an actual problem. Can society, especially a democratic society, exist without a basic consensus and community of beliefs? If it cannot, can the required community be achieved without regulation of scientific pursuits exercised by a public authority in behalf of social unity?

In this connection the accusation of irresponsibility as to social consequences is brought against scientific men, and it is in this context that the underlying issue takes shape. It is argued (and some who take the position are themselves scientists) that the main directions of physical science during the past hundred years, increasingly so in the last half century, have been set, indirectly and directly, by the requirements of industry carried on for private profit. Consideration of the *problems* which have not received attention in comparison with those which have absorbed expenditure of intellectual energies will, it is said, prove the proposition.

Direct control has been exercised for the most part by governments. They have subsidized the kind of investigations that promise increased national power, either by promoting manufacturing and commerce as against other national states, or by fostering researches that strengthen military prowess. Indirect control has been exercised in subtler ways. The place of industry is so central in modern life that quite apart from questions handed directly over to scientific laboratories by industrial enterprises, it is psychologically impossible for men engaged in scientific research not to be most sensitive and most responsive to the *type* of

problems presented in practical effort to control natural energies;—which in the concrete means manufacturing and distributing goods. Moreover, a kind of positive halo surrounds scientific endeavors. For it has been held, not without grounds, that
general social—or at least national—welfare is thereby promoted. Germany led other countries in physical research; and it
was in Germany that scientific advances could be shown to have
contributed most directly to national strength and prestige. It
was thus possible for some intellectual observers, not particularly naïve, to hold up German universities as models to follow in
our own country.

It is not implied that personal economic interest has played
any important part in directing the researches of individual scientists. The contrary is notoriously the rule. But attention and
interest are not freely ranging searchlights that can be directed at
all parts of the natural universe with equal ease. They operate
within certain channels, and the general state of culture determines what and where the channels are. The "climate of opinion"
decides the direction taken by scientific activity as truly as physical climate decides what agricultural pursuits can be carried on.
Social imagination comes to have a certain tone and color; intellectual immunity in one direction and intellectual sensitivity in
other directions are the result. It has even been said, and with a
good deal of evidence in its support, that the prevailing mechanistic creed of science during the nineteenth century was an indirect product of the importance assumed by the machine in industrial production, so that now, when machine-production is
giving way to power-production, basic scientific "concepts" are
also changing.

I referred above to the role of nationalism in deciding the direction taken by science. The striking instance is of course the
organization of scientific men for aid to a nation in time of war.
The instance brings to a head tendencies that are going on in less
overt and more unconscious ways pretty much all the time, even
in times of nominal peace. Increase of the scope of governmental
activities in all industrialized countries, going on for some years
at an accelerated pace, has reinforced the alliance between national interest and scientific inquiry. It is certainly arguable that
when the choice at hand is between regulation of science by private economic interests and by nationalist interest, the latter

should have preference. It may be inferred that the open control of science exercised in totalitarian states is but a culmination of tendencies that have been going on in more or less covert ways for some time—from which it follows that the problem presented extends beyond the borders of those particular states.

Strangely enough, at first sight, the demand for direct social control of scientific inquiries and conclusion is unwittingly reinforced by an attitude quite commonly taken by scientific men themselves. For it is commonly said and commonly believed that science is completely neutral and indifferent as to the ends and values which move men to act: that at most it only provides more efficient means for realization of ends that are and must be due to wants and desires completely independent of science. It is at this point that the present climate of opinion differs so widely from that which marked the optimistic faith of the Enlightenment; the faith that human science and freedom would advance hand in hand to usher in an era of indefinite human perfectibility.

That the popular esteem of science is largely due to the aid it has given to men for attainment of things they wanted independently of what they had learned from science is doubtless true. Russell has stated in a vivid way the sort of thing that has enabled science to displace beliefs that had previously been held: "The world ceased to believe that Joshua caused the sun to stand still, because Copernican astronomy was useful in navigation; it abandoned Aristotle's physics, because Galileo's theory of falling bodies made it possible to calculate the trajectory of a cannonball. It rejected the theory of the flood because geology is useful in mining and so on." [1] That the quotation expresses the sort of thing that gave the conclusions of the new science prestige and following at a time when it badly needed some outside aid in getting a hearing can hardly be doubted. As illustrative material it is especially impressive because of the enormous authority enjoyed by the doctrines of Aristotle and of the Church. If even in the case where all the advantage was on the side of old doctrines, the demonstrated serviceability of science gave it the victory, we can easily judge the enhancement of the esteem in which science was held in matters where it had no such powerful foe to contend with.

Quite apart from the antagonism to science displayed by en-

1. Bertrand Russell, *Power*, p. 138.

trenched institutional interests that had previously obtained a monopoly over beliefs in, say, astronomy, geology and some fields of history, history proves the existence of so much indifference on the part of mankind to the quality of its beliefs and such lethargy towards methods that disturb old beliefs, that we should be glad that the new science has had such powerful adventitious aid. But it leaves untouched the question as to whether scientific knowledge has power to modify the ends which men prize and strive to attain. Is it proved that the findings of science—the best authenticated knowledge we have—add only to our power to realize desires already in existence? Or is this view derived from some previous theory about the constitution of human nature? Can it be true that desires and knowledge exist in separate non-communicating compartments? Do the facts which can undoubtedly be cited as evidence, such as the use of scientific knowledge indifferently to heal disease and prolong human life and to provide the instruments for wholesale destruction of life, really prove the case? Or are they specially selected cases that support a doctrine that originated on other grounds than the evidence of facts? Is there such a complete separation of human ends from human beliefs as the theory assumes?

The shock given old ideas by the idea that knowledge is incapable of modifying the quality of desires (and hence cannot affect the formation of ends and purposes) is not of course in itself a ground for denying it is sound. It may be that the old view is totally false. Nevertheless, the point is worth discussion. We do not have to refer to the theory of Plato that knowledge, or what passes as knowledge, is the sole final determinant of men's ideas of the Good and hence of their actions. Nor is it needful to refer to Bacon's vision of the organization of scientific knowledge as the prospective foundation of future social policies directed exclusively to the advance of human well-being. The simple fact is that all the deliberately liberal and progressive movements of modern times have based themselves on the idea that action is determined by ideas, up to the time when Hume said that reason was and should be the "slave of the passions"; or, in contemporary language, of the emotions and desires. Hume's voice was a lonely one when he uttered the remark. The idea is now echoed and re-echoed from almost every quarter. The classic economic school made wants the prime motors of human action, reducing reason to a power of calculating the means best fitted to satisfy the wants. The first effect of biology upon psychology was to emphasize the primacy of appetites and instincts. Psychiatrists have enforced the same conclusion by showing that intellectual disturbances originate in emotional maladjustments, and by exhibiting the extent of dictation of belief by desire.

It is one thing, however, to recognize that earlier theories neglected the importance of emotions and habits as determinants of conduct and exaggerated that of ideas and reason. It is quite another thing to hold that ideas (especially those warranted by competent inquiry) and emotions (with needs and desires) exist in separate compartments so that no interaction between them exists. When the view is as baldly stated it strikes one as highly improbable that there can be any such complete separation in the constitution of human nature. And while the idea must be accepted if the evidence points that way, no matter into what plight human affairs are forever plunged, the implications of the doctrine of complete separation of desire and knowledge must be noted. The assumption that desires are rigidly fixed is not one on its face consistent with the history of man's progress from savagery through barbarism to even the present defective state of civilization. If knowledge, even of the most authenticated kind, cannot influence desires and aims, if it cannot determine what is of value and what is not, the future outlook as to formation of desires is depressing. Denial that they can be influenced by knowledge points emphatically to the non-rational and anti-rational forces that will form them. One alternative to the power of ideas is habit or custom, and then when the rule of sheer habit breaks down—as it has done at the present time—all that is left is competition on the part of various bodies and interests to decide which shall come out ahead in a struggle, carried on by intimidation, coercion, bribery, and all sorts of propaganda, to shape the desires which shall predominantly control the ends of human action. The prospect is a black one. It leads one to consider the possibility that Bacon, Locke, and the leaders of the Enlightenment—typified by the act of Condorcet, writing, while imprisoned and waiting for death, about the role of science in the future liberation of mankind—were after all quite aware of the actual influence of appetite, habit, and blind desire upon action, but were engaged in holding up another and better way as the alternative to follow in the future.

That the course they anticipated has not come to fruition is obvious without argument. Bacon's action in using his own knowledge as a servant of the Crown in strengthening Great Britain in a military way against other nations now seems more prophetic of what has happened than what he put down in words. The power over Nature which he expected to follow the advance of science has come to pass. But in contradiction to his expectations, it has been largely used to increase, instead of reduce, the power of Man over Man. Shall we conclude that the early prophets were totally and intrinsically wrong? Or shall we conclude that they immensely underestimated the obduracy of institutions and customs antedating the appearance of science on the scene in shaping desires in their image? Have events after all but accentuated the problem of discovering the means by which authenticated beliefs shall influence desires, the formation of ends, and thereby the course of events? Is it possible to admit the power of propaganda to shape ends and deny that of science?

Looked at from one angle, the question brings us back to our fundamental issue: the relation of culture and human nature. For the fact which is decisive in answering the question whether verified knowledge is or is not capable of shaping desires and ends (as well as means) is whether the desires that are effective in settling the course of action are innate and fixed, or are themselves the product of a certain culture. If the latter is the case, the practical issue reduces itself to this: Is it possible for the scientific attitude to become such a weighty and widespread constituent of culture that, through the medium of culture, it may shape human desires and purposes?

To state the question is a long way from ability to answer it. But it is something to have the issue before us in its actual instead of in its factitious form. The issue ceases to be the indeterminate one of the relation of knowledge and desires in the native psychological constitution of man—indeterminate, among other reasons, because it is disputable whether there is any such thing as the latter apart from native biological constitution. It becomes the determinate one of the institution of the kind of culture in which scientific method and scientific conclusions are integrally incorporated.

The problem stated in this way puts in a different light the esteem gained by science because of its serviceability. That there are individuals here and there who have been influenced to esteem science because of some obvious contribution to satisfaction of their merely personal desires may well be a fact. That there are groups similarly influenced must be admitted. But the reasons why men have been willing to accept conclusions derived from science in lieu of older ideas are not exclusively or even mainly those of direct personal and class benefit. Improvements in navigation and mining have become part of the state of culture. It is in this capacity they have tended to displace beliefs that were congenial to an earlier state of culture. By and large the same thing is true of the application of physics and chemistry in more effective satisfaction of wants and in creation of new wants. While their application to produce increased efficiency in carrying on war has doubtlessly recommended those sciences to persons like rulers and generals, who otherwise would have been indifferent, the mass of persons have been moved to an attitude of favorable esteem by what has happened in the arts of peace. The decisive factor would seem to be whether the arts of war or of peace are to be in the future the ones that will control culture, a question that involves the need of discovering why war is such an important constituent of present culture.

I should be on controversial ground if I held up as evidence the belief that the technologies, which are the practical correlates of scientific theories, have now reached a point in which they can be used to create an era of abundance instead of the deficit-economies that existed before natural science developed, and that with an era of abundance and security the causes of conflict would be reduced. It may be mentioned as a hypothetical illustration. The kind of serviceability which is capable of generating high esteem for science *may* possibly be serviceability for general and shared, or "social," welfare. If the economic regime were so changed that the resources of science were employed to maintain security for all, the present view about the limitation of science might fade away. I imagine there are not many who will deny that esteem for science, even when placed upon the ground of serviceability alone, is produced at least in part by an admixture of general with private serviceability. If there is a skeptic let him consider the contribution made by science both actually and still more potentially to agriculture, and the social consequences of the change in production of foods and raw materials, thereby effected.

The other side of the ledger is marked by such a debit entry as the following from the English chemist Soddy: "So far the pearls of science have been cast before swine, who have given us in return millionaires and slums, armaments and the desolation of war." The contrast is real. If its existence seems to support the doctrine that science only supplies means for more efficient execution of already existing desires and purposes, it is because it points to the division which exists in our culture. The war that mobilizes science for wholesale destruction mobilizes it, also, for support of life and for healing the wounded. The desires and ends involved proceed not from native and naked human nature but from modifications it has undergone in interaction with a complex of cultural factors of which science is indeed one, but one which produces social consequences only as it is affected by economic and political traditions and customs formed before its rise.

For in any case, the influence of science on both means and ends is not exercised directly upon individuals but indirectly through incorporation within culture. In this function and capacity it is that scientific beliefs have replaced earlier unscientific beliefs. The position stated at its worst is that science operates as a part of folklore, not just as science. Even when put in this way, attention is invited to differences in folklore and to differences of the consequences that are produced by different folklores. And when it is admitted that the folklore may be one of aggressive nationalism, where the consequences of science as part of the prevailing folklore is war of the present destructive scope, we at least have the advantage of clear knowledge as to the location of the problem.

We have been considering science as a body of conclusions. We have ignored science in its quality of an attitude embodied in habitual will to employ certain methods of observation, reflection, and test rather than others. When we look at science from this point of view, the significance of science as a constituent of culture takes on a new color. The great body of scientific inquirers would deny with indignation that they are actuated in *their* esteem for science by its material serviceability. If they use words sanctioned by long tradition, they say they are moved by love of the truth. If they use contemporary phraseology, less grandiloquent in sound but of equivalent meaning, they say they are moved by a controlling interest in inquiry, in discovery, in following where the evidence of discovered facts points. Above all they say that this kind of interest excludes interest in reaching any conclusion not warranted by evidence, no matter how personally congenial it may be.

In short, it is a fact that a certain group of men, perhaps relatively not very numerous, have a "disinterested" interest in scientific inquiry. This interest has developed a morale having its own distinctive features. Some of its obvious elements are willingness to hold belief in suspense, ability to doubt until evidence is obtained; willingness to go where evidence points instead of putting first a personally preferred conclusion; ability to hold ideas in solution and use them as hypotheses to be tested instead of as dogmas to be asserted; and (possibly the most distinctive of all) enjoyment of new fields for inquiry and of new problems.

Every one of these traits goes contrary to some human impulse that is naturally strong. Uncertainty is disagreeable to most persons; suspense is so hard to endure that assured expectation of an unfortunate outcome is usually preferred to a long-continued state of doubt. "Wishful thinking" is a comparatively modern phrase; but men upon the whole have usually believed what they wanted to believe, except as very convincing evidence made it impossible. Apart from a scientific attitude, guesses, with persons left to themselves, tend to become opinions and opinions dogmas. To hold theories and principles in solution, awaiting confirmation, goes contrary to the grain. Even today questioning a statement made by a person is often taken by him as a reflection upon his integrity, and is resented. For many millennia opposition to views widely held in a community was intolerable. It called down the wrath of the deities who are in charge of the group. Fear of the unknown, fear of change and novelty, tended, at all times before the rise of scientific attitude, to drive men into rigidity of beliefs and habits; they entered upon unaccustomed lines of behavior—even in matters of minor moment—with qualms which exacted rites of expiation. Exceptions to accepted rules have either been ignored or systematically explained away when they were too conspicuous to ignore. Baconian idols of the tribe, the cave, the theater, and den have caused men to rush to conclusions, and then to use all their powers to defend from criticism and change the conclusions arrived at. The connection of common law with custom and its resistance to change are familiar facts. Even religious beliefs and rites which were at first more or less heretical deviations harden into modes of action it is impious to question, after once they have become part of the habits of a group.

If I mention such familiar considerations it is in part to suggest that we may well be grateful that science has had undeniable social serviceability, and that to some extent and in some places strong obstructions to adoption of changed beliefs have been overcome. But the chief reason for calling attention to them is the proof they furnish that in some persons and to some degree science has already created a new morale—which is equivalent to the creation of new desires and new ends. The existence of the scientific attitude and spirit, even upon a limited scale, is proof that science is capable of developing a distinctive type of disposition and purpose: a type that goes far beyond provision of more effective means for realizing desires which exist independently of any effect of science.

It is not becoming, to put it moderately, for those who are themselves animated by the scientific morale to assert that other persons are incapable of coming into possession of it and being moved by it.

Such an attitude is saved from being professional snobbery only when it is the result of sheer thoughtlessness. When one and the same representative of the intellectual class denounces any view that attaches inherent importance to the consequences of science, claiming the view is false to the spirit of science—and also holds that it is impossible for science to do anything to affect desires and ends, the inconsistency demands explanation.

A situation in which the fundamental dispositions and ends of a few are influenced by science while that of most persons and most groups is not so influenced proves that the issue is cultural. The difference sets a social problem: what are the causes for the existence of this great gap, especially since it has such serious consequences? If it is possible for persons to have their beliefs formed on the ground of evidence, procured by systematic and competent inquiry, nothing can be more disastrous socially than that the great majority of persons should have them formed by habit, accidents of circumstance, propaganda, personal and class bias. The existence, even on a relatively narrow scale, of a morale of fairmindedness, intellectual integrity, of will to subordinate personal preference to ascertained facts and to share with others what is found out, instead of using it for personal gain, is a challenge of the most searching kind. Why don't a great many more persons have this attitude?

The answer given to this challenge is bound up with the fate of democracy. The spread of literacy, the immense extension of the influence of the press in books, newspapers, periodicals, make the issue peculiarly urgent for a democracy. The very agencies that a century and a half ago were looked upon as those that were sure to advance the cause of democratic freedom, are those which now make it possible to create pseudo-public opinion and to undermine democracy from within. Callousness due to continuous reiteration may produce a certain immunity to the grosser kinds of propaganda. But in the long run negative measures afford no assurance. While it would be absurd to believe it desirable or possible for every one to become a scientist when science is defined from the side of subject matter, the future of democracy is allied with spread of the scientific attitude. It is the sole guarantee against wholesale misleading by propaganda. More important still, it is the only assurance of the possibility of a public opinion intelligent enough to meet present social problems.

To become aware of the problem is a condition of taking steps toward its solution. The problem is in part economic. The nature of control of the means of publicity enters directly; sheer financial control is not a favorable sign. The democratic belief in free speech, free press and free assembly is one of the things that exposes democratic institutions to attack. For representatives of totalitarian states, who are the first to deny such freedom when they are in power, shrewdly employ it in a democratic country to destroy the foundations of democracy. Backed with the necessary financial means, they are capable of carrying on a work of continuous sapping and mining. More dangerous, perhaps, in the end is the fact that all economic conditions tending toward centralization and concentration of the means of production and distribution affect the public press, whether individuals so desire or not. The causes which require large corporate capital to carry on modern business, naturally influence the publishing business.

The problem is also an educative one. A book instead of a paragraph could be given to this aspect of the topic. That the schools have mostly been given to imparting information ready-made, along with teaching the tools of literacy, cannot be denied. The methods used in acquiring such information are not those which develop skill in inquiry and in test of opinions. On the contrary, they are positively hostile to it. They tend to dull native curiosity, and to load powers of observation and experimentation with such a mass of unrelated material that they do not operate as effectively as they do in many an illiterate person. The problem of the common schools in a democracy has reached only its first stage when they are provided for everybody. Until what shall be taught and how it is taught is settled upon the basis of formation of the scientific attitude, the so-called educational work of schools is a dangerously hit-or-miss affair as far as democracy is concerned.

The problem—as was suggested earlier—is also one of art. It is difficult to write briefly on this aspect of the question without giving rise to false impressions. For of late there has been an active campaign, carried on in the name of the social function of art, for using the arts, the plastic arts as well as literature, in propaganda for special views which are dogmatically asserted to be socially necessary. In consequence, any reference to the topic may seem to have a flavor of commendation of something of the same kind, only exercised by way of a counter-campaign in behalf of democratic ideas. The point is different. It is a reminder that ideas are effective not as bare ideas but as they have imaginative content and emotional appeal. I have alluded to the extensive reaction that has set in against the earlier over-simplified rationalism. The reaction tended to go to an opposite extreme. In emphasizing the role of wants, impulse, habit, and emotion, it often denied any efficacy whatever to ideas, to intelligence. The problem is that of effecting the union of ideas and knowledge with the non-rational factors in the human make-up. Art is the name given to all the agencies by which this union is effected.

The problem is also a moral and religious one. That religions have operated most effectively in alliance with the fine arts was indicated earlier. Yet the historic influence of religions has often been to magnify doctrines that are not subject to critical inquiry and test. Their cumulative effect in producing habits of mind at odds with the attitudes required for maintenance of democracy is probably much greater than is usually recognized. Shrewd observers have said that one factor in the relatively easy victory of totalitarianism in Germany was the void left by decay of former theological beliefs. Those who had lost one external authority upon which they had depended were ready to turn to another one which was closer and more tangible.

To say that the issue is a moral one is to say that in the end it comes back to personal choice and action. From one point of view everything which has been said is a laboring of the commonplace that democratic government is a function of public opinion and public sentiment. But identification of its formation in the democratic direction with democratic extension of the scientific morale till it is part of the ordinary equipment of the ordinary individual indicates the issue is a moral one. It is individual persons who need to have this attitude substituted for pride and prejudice, for class and personal interest, for beliefs made dear by custom and early emotional associations. It is only by the choice and the active endeavor of many individuals that this result can be effected.

A former president of the United States once made a political stir by saying that "Public office is a public trust." The saying was a truism although one that needed emphasis. That possession of knowledge and special skill in intellectual methods is a public trust has not become a truism even in words. Scientific morale has developed in some persons to a point where it is a matter of course that what is found out is communicated to other persons who are also engaged in specialized research. But it has not developed to the point where wider responsibility for communication is acknowledged. Circumstances which have attended the historic growth of modern science explain why this is so, although they do not justify its continuance. Internal and external circumstances have brought about a social seclusion of science which from a certain standpoint is analogous to an earlier monastic seclusion.

The external circumstance was the opposition scientific men had to overcome before it was possible for them to carry on their work free from dictation or persecution. The internal circumstance was in part the need for extreme specialization of inquiries which necessarily accompanied the novelty of the new method; in part, it was a self-protective policy for maintaining the purity of a new, still immature and struggling attitude from contamination that proceeded from taking sides in practical affairs. This attitude had the blessing of the old and ingrained tradition of the "purity" of science as an exclusively theoretical subject; a subject aloof from practice, since reason and theory were so high above practice, which was, according to tradition, only material and utilitarian. The danger of loss of the impartiality of the scientific spirit through affiliation with some partisan and partial interest seemed to give significance to the established tradition about "purity," which, like traditional feminine chastity, needed all kinds of external safeguards to hedge it about. The need is not that scientific men become crusaders in special practical causes. Just as the problem with art is to unite the inherent integrity of the artist with imaginative and emotional appeal of ideas, so the present need is recognition by scientific men of social responsibility for contagious diffusion of the scientific attitude: a task not to be accomplished without abandoning once for all the belief that science is set apart from all other social interests as if possessed of a peculiar holiness.

Extension of the qualities that make up the scientific attitude is quite a different matter than dissemination of the results of physics, chemistry, biology and astronomy, valuable as the latter may be. The difference is the reason why the issue is a moral one. The question of whether science is capable of influencing the formation of ends for which men strive or is limited to increasing power of realizing those which are formed independently of it is the question whether science has intrinsic moral potentiality. Historically, the position that science is devoid of moral quality has been held by theologians and their metaphysical allies. For the position points unmistakably to the necessity for recourse to some other source of moral guidance. That a similar position is now taken in the name of science is either a sign of a confusion that permeates all aspects of culture, or is an omen of ill for democracy. If control of conduct amounts to conflict of desires with no possibility of determination of desire and purpose by scientifically warranted beliefs, then the practical alternative is competition and conflict between unintelligent forces for control of desire. The conclusion is so extreme as to suggest that denial in the name of science of the existence of any such things as moral facts may mark a transitional stage thoughtlessly taken to be final. It is quite true that science cannot affect moral values, ends, rules, principles as these were once thought of and believed in, namely, prior to the rise of science. But to say that there are no such things as moral facts because desires control formation and valuation of ends is in truth but to point to desires and interests as themselves moral facts requiring control by intelligence equipped with knowledge. Science through its physical technological consequences is now determining the relations which human beings, severally and in groups, sustain to one another. If it is incapable of developing moral techniques which will also determine these relations, the split in modern culture goes so deep that not only democracy but all civilized values are doomed. Such at least is the problem. A culture which permits science to destroy traditional values but which distrusts its power to create new ones is a culture which is destroying itself. War is a symptom as well as a cause of the inner division.

7.   Democracy and America

I make no apology for linking what is said in this chapter with the name of Thomas Jefferson. For he was the first modern to state in human terms the principles of democracy. Were I to make an apology, it would be that in the past I have concerned myself unduly, if a comparison has to be made, with the English writers who have attempted to state the ideals of self-governing communities and the methods appropriate to their realization. If I now prefer to refer to Jefferson it is not, I hope, because of American provincialism, even though I believe that only one who was attached to American soil and who took a consciously alert part in the struggles of the country to attain its independence, could possibly have stated as thoroughly and intimately as did Jefferson the aims embodied in the American tradition: "the definitions and axioms of a free government," as Lincoln called them. Nor is the chief reason for going to him, rather than to Locke or Bentham or Mill, his greater sobriety of judgment due to that constant tempering of theory with practical experience which also kept his democratic doctrine within human bounds.

The chief reason is that Jefferson's formulation is moral through and through: in its foundations, its methods, its ends. The heart of his faith is expressed in his words "Nothing is unchangeable but inherent and inalienable rights of man." The words in which he stated the moral basis of free institutions have gone out of vogue. We repeat the opening words of the Declaration of Independence, but unless we translate them they are couched in a language that, even when it comes readily to our tongue, does not penetrate today to the brain. He wrote: "These truths are self-evident: that all men are created equal; that they are endowed by their Creator with inherent and unalienable rights; that among these are life, liberty and the pursuit of happiness." Today we are wary of anything purporting to be self-evident truths; we are not given to associating politics with the plans of the Creator; the doctrine of natural rights which governed his style of expression has been weakened by historic and by philosophic criticism. To put ourselves in touch with Jefferson's position we have therefore to translate the word "natural" into *moral*. Jefferson was under the influence of the Deism of his time. Nature and the plans of a benevolent and wise Creator were never far apart in his reflections. But his fundamental beliefs remain unchanged in substance if we forget all special associations with the word *Nature* and speak instead of ideal aims and values to be realized— aims which, although ideal, are not located in the clouds but are backed by something deep and indestructible in the needs and demands of humankind.

Were I to try to connect in any detail what I have to say with the details of Jefferson's speeches and letters—he wrote no theoretical treatises—I should probably seem to be engaged in a partisan undertaking; I should at times be compelled to indulge in verbal exegesis so as to attribute to him ideas not present in his mind. Nevertheless, there are three points contained in what has to be said about American democracy that I shall here explicitly connect with his name. In the first place, in the quotation made, it was the *ends* of democracy, the rights of *man*—not of men in the plural—which are unchangeable. It was not the forms and mechanisms through which inherent moral claims are realized that are to persist without change. Professed Jeffersonians have often not even followed the words of the one whose disciples they say they are, much less his spirit. For he said: "I know that laws and institutions must go hand in hand with the progress of the human mind. . . . As new discoveries are made, new truths disclosed, and manners and opinions change with the change of circumstances, institutions must change also and keep pace with the times. We might as well require a man to wear the coat which fitted him when a boy, as civilized society to remain ever under the regime of their barbarous ancestors."

Because of the last sentence his idea might be interpreted to be a justification of the particular change in government he was championing against earlier institutions. But he goes on to say: "Each generation has a right to choose for itself the form of government it believes the most promotive of its own happiness." Hence he also said: "The idea that institutions established for the use of a nation cannot be touched or modified, even to make them answer their end . . . may perhaps be a salutary provision against the abuses of a monarch, but is most absurd against the nation itself." "A generation holds all the rights and powers their predecessors once held and may change their laws and institutions to suit themselves." He engaged in certain calculations based on Buffon, more ingenious than convincing, to settle upon a period of eighteen years and eight months that fixed the natural span of the life of a generation; thereby indicating the frequency with which it is desirable to overhaul "laws and institutions" to bring them into accord with "new discoveries, new truths, change of manners and opinions." The word *culture* is not used; Jefferson's statement would have been weakened by its use. But it is not only professed followers of Jefferson who have failed to act upon his teaching. It is true of all of us so far as we have set undue store by established mechanisms. The most flagrantly obvious violation of Jefferson's democratic point of view is found in the idolatry of the Constitution as it stands that has been sedulously cultivated. But it goes beyond this instance. As believers in democracy we have not only the right but the duty to question existing mechanisms of, say, suffrage and to inquire whether some functional organization would not serve to formulate and manifest public opinion better than the existing methods. It is not irrelevant to the point that a score of passages could be cited in which Jefferson refers to the American Government as an *experiment*.

The second point of which I would speak is closely bound up with an issue which has become controversial and partisan, namely, states rights versus federal power. There is no question of where Jefferson stood on that issue, nor as to his fear in general of governmental encroachment on liberty—inevitable in his case, since it was the cause of the Rebellion against British domination and was also the ground of his struggle against Hamiltonianism. But any one who stops with this particular aspect of Jefferson's doctrine misses an underlying principle of utmost importance. For while he stood for state action as a barrier against excessive power at Washington, and while on the *practical side* his concern with it was most direct, in his theoretical writings chief importance is attached to local self-governing units on something like the New England town-meeting plan. His project for general political organization on the basis of small units, small enough so that all its members could have direct communication with one another and take care of all community affairs was never acted upon. It never received much attention in the press of immediate practical problems.

But without forcing the significance of this plan, we may find in it an indication of one of the most serious of present problems regarding democracy. I spoke earlier of the way in which individuals at present find themselves in the grip of immense forces whose workings and consequences they have no power of affecting. The situation calls emphatic attention to the need for face-to-face associations, whose interactions with one another may offset if not control the dread impersonality of the sweep of present forces. There is a difference between a society, in the sense of an association, and a community. Electrons, atoms and molecules are in association with one another. Nothing exists in isolation anywhere throughout nature. Natural associations are conditions for the existence of a community, but a community adds the function of communication in which emotions and ideas are shared as well as joint undertakings engaged in. Economic forces have immensely widened the scope of associational activities. But it has done so largely at the expense of the intimacy and directness of communal group interests and activities. The American habit of "joining" is a tribute to the reality of the problem but has not gone far in solving it. The power of the rabblerouser, especially in the totalitarian direction, is mainly due to his power to create a factitious sense of direct union and communal solidarity—if only by arousing the emotion of common intolerance and hate.

I venture to quote words written some years ago: "Evils which are uncritically and indiscriminately laid at the door of industrialism and democracy might, with greater intelligence, be referred to the dislocation and unsettlement of local communities. Vital and thorough attachments are bred only in the intimacy of an intercourse which is of necessity restricted in range. . . . Is it possible to restore the reality of the less communal organizations and to penetrate and saturate their members with a sense of local community life? . . . Democracy must begin at home, and its home is the neighborly community." [1] On account of the vast ex-

1. *The Public and Its Problems*, pp. 212–13 [*Later Works* 2:367–68].

tension of the field of association, produced by elimination of distance and lengthening of temporal spans, it is obvious that social agencies, political and non-political, cannot be confined to localities. But the problem of harmonious adjustment between extensive activities, precluding direct contacts, and the intensive activities of community intercourse is a pressing one for democracy. It involves even more than apprenticeship in the practical processes of self-government, important as that is, which Jefferson had in mind. It involves development of local agencies of communication and cooperation, creating stable loyal attachments, to militate against the centrifugal forces of present culture, while at the same time they are of a kind to respond flexibly to the demands of the larger unseen and indefinite public. To a very considerable extent, groups having a functional basis will probably have to replace those based on physical contiguity. In the family both factors combine.

The third point of which I would make express mention as to Jefferson and democracy has to do with his ideas about property. It would be absurd to hold that his personal views were "radical" beyond fear of concentrated wealth and a positive desire for general distribution of wealth without great extremes in either direction. However, it is sometimes suggested that his phrase "pursuit of happiness" stood for economic activity, so that life, liberty, and property were the rights he thought organized society should maintain. But just here is where he broke most completely with Locke. In connection with property, especially property in land, he makes his most positive statements about the inability of any generation to bind its successors. Jefferson held that property rights are created by the "social pact" instead of representing inherent individual moral claims which government is morally bound to maintain.

The right to pursue happiness stood with Jefferson for nothing less than the claim of every human being to choose his own career and to act upon his own choice and judgment free from restraints and constraints imposed by the arbitrary will of other human beings—whether these others are officials of government, of whom Jefferson was especially afraid, or are persons whose command of capital and control of the opportunities for engaging in useful work limits the ability of others to "pursue happiness." The Jeffersonian principle of equality of rights without special favor to any one justifies giving supremacy to personal rights when they come into conflict with property rights. While his views are properly enough cited against ill-considered attacks upon the economic relations that exist at a given time, it is sheer perversion to hold that there is anything in Jeffersonian democracy that forbids political action to bring about equalization of economic conditions in order that the equal right of all to free choice and free action be maintained.

I have referred with some particularity to Jefferson's ideas upon special points because of the proof they afford that the source of the American democratic tradition is moral—not technical, abstract, narrowly political nor materially utilitarian. It is moral because based on faith in the ability of human nature to achieve freedom for individuals accompanied with respect and regard for other persons and with social stability built on cohesion instead of coercion. Since the tradition is a moral one, attacks upon it, however they are made, wherever they come from, from within or from without, involve moral issues and can be settled only upon moral grounds. In as far as the democratic ideal has undergone eclipse among us, the obscuration is moral in source and effect. The dimming is both a product and a manifestation of the confusion that accompanies transition from an old order to a new one for the arrival of the latter was heralded only as conditions plunged it into an economic regime so novel that there was no adequate preparation for it and which dislocated the established relations of persons with one another.

Nothing is gained by attempts to minimize the novelty of the democratic order, nor the scope of the change it requires in old and long cherished traditions. We have not even as yet a common and accepted vocabulary in which to set forth the order of moral values involved in realization of democracy. The language of Natural Law was once all but universal in educated Christendom. The conditions which gave it force disappeared. Then there was an appeal to natural rights, supposed by some to centre in isolated individuals—although not in the original American formulation. At present, appeal to the individual is dulled by our inability to locate the individual with any assurance. While we are compelled to note that his freedom can be maintained only through the working together toward a single end of a large number of different and complex factors, we do not know how to coordinate them on the basis of voluntary purpose.

The intimate association that was held to exist between individualism and business activity for private profit gave, on one side, a distorted meaning to individualism. Then the weakening, even among persons who nominally retain older theological beliefs, of the imaginative ideas and emotions connected with the sanctity of the individual, disturbed democratic individualism on the positive moral side. The moving energy once associated with things called spiritual has lessened; we use the word *ideal* reluctantly, and have difficulty in giving the word *moral* much force beyond, say, a limited field of mutually kindly relations among individuals. That such a syllogism as the following once had a vital meaning to a man of affairs like Jefferson today seems almost incredible: "Man was created for social intercourse, but social intercourse cannot be maintained without a sense of justice; then man must have been created with a sense of justice."

Even if we have an abiding faith in democracy, we are not likely to express it as Jefferson expressed his faith: "I have no fear but that the result of our experiment will be that men may be trusted to govern themselves without a master. Could the contrary of this be proved, I should conclude either there is no God or that he is a malevolent being." The belief of Jefferson that the sole legitimate object of government among men "is to secure the greatest degree of happiness possible to the general mass of those associated under it" was connected with his belief that Nature—or God—benevolent in intent, had created men for happiness on condition they attained knowledge of natural order and observed the demands of that knowledge in their actions. The obsolescence of the language for many persons makes it the more imperative for all who would maintain and advance the ideals of democracy to face the issue of the moral ground of political institutions and the moral principles by which men acting together may attain freedom of individuals which will amount to fraternal associations with one another. The weaker our faith in Nature, in its laws and rights and its benevolent intentions for human welfare, the more urgent is the need for a faith based on ideas that are now intellectually credible and that are consonant with present economic conditions, which will inspire and direct action with something of the ardor once attached to things religious.

Human power over the physical energies of nature has immensely increased. In moral ideal, power of man over physical nature should be employed to reduce, to eliminate progressively, the power of man over man. By what means shall we prevent its use to effect new, more subtle, more powerful agencies of subjection of men to other men? Both the issue of war or peace between nations, and the future of economic relations for years and generations to come in contribution either to human freedom or human subjection are involved. An increase of power undreamed of a century ago, one to whose further increase no limits can be put as long as scientific inquiry goes on, is an established fact. The thing still uncertain is what we are going to do with it. That it is power signifies of itself it is electrical, thermic, chemical. What will be done with it is a moral issue.

Physical interdependence has increased beyond anything that could have been foreseen. Division of labor in industry was anticipated and was looked forward to with satisfaction. But it is relatively the least weighty phase of the present situation. The career of individuals, their lives and security as well as prosperity is now affected by events on the other side of the world. The forces back of these events he cannot touch or influence—save perhaps by joining in a war of nations against nations. For we seem to live in a world in which nations try to deal with the problems created by the new situation by drawing more and more into themselves, by more and more extreme assertions of independent nationalist sovereignty, while everything they do in the direction of autarchy leads to ever closer mixture with other nations—but in war.

War under existing conditions compels nations, even those professedly the most democratic, to turn authoritarian and totalitarian as the World War of 1914–18 resulted in Fascist totalitarianism in non-democratic Italy and Germany and in Bolshevist totalitarianism in non-democratic Russia, and promoted political, economic and intellectual reaction in this country. The necessity of transforming physical interdependence into moral—into human—interdependence is part of the democratic problem: and yet war is said even now to be the path of salvation for democratic countries!

Individuals can find the security and protection that are prerequisites for freedom only in association with others—and then the organization these associations take on, as a measure of securing their efficiency, limits the freedom of those who have entered into them. The importance of organization has increased so much in the last hundred years that the word is now quite commonly used as a synonym for association and society. Since at the very best organization is but the mechanism through which association operates, the identification is evidence of the extent in which a servant has become a master; in which means have usurped the place of the end for which they are called into existence. The predicament is that individuality demands association to develop and sustain it and association requires arrangement and coordination of its elements, or organization—since otherwise it is formless and void of power. But we have now a kind of molluscan organization, soft individuals within and a hard constrictive shell without. Individuals voluntarily enter associations which have become practically nothing but organizations; and then conditions under which they act take control of what they do whether they want it or not.

Persons acutely aware of the dangers of regimentation when it is imposed by government remain oblivious of the millions of persons whose behavior is regimented by an economic system through whose intervention alone they obtain a livelihood. The contradiction is the more striking because the new organizations were for the most part created in the name of freedom, and, at least at the outset, by exercise of voluntary choice. But the kind of working-together which has resulted is too much like that of the parts of a machine to represent a cooperation which expresses freedom and also contributes to it. No small part of the democratic problem is to achieve associations whose ordering of parts provides the strength that comes from stability, while they promote flexibility of response to change.

Lastly, in this brief survey, there is the problem of the relation of human nature and physical nature. The ancient world solved the problem, in abstract philosophical theory, by endowing all nature, in its cosmic scope, with the moral qualities of the highest and most ideal worth in humanity. The theology and rites of the Church gave this abstract theory direct significance in the lives of the peoples of the western world. For it provided practical agencies by means of which the operation of the power creating and maintaining the universe were supposed to come to the support of individuals in this world and the next. The rise of physical science rendered an ever increasing number of men skeptical of the intellectual foundation provided by the old theory. The unsettlement, going by the name of the conflict of science and religion, proves the existence of the division in the foundations upon which our culture rests, between ideas in the form of knowledge and ideas that are emotional and imaginative and that directly actuate conduct.

This disturbance on the moral side has been enormously aggravated by those who are remote from the unsettlement due to intellectual causes. It comes home to everyone by the effects of the practical application of the new physical science. For all the physical features of the present regime of production and distribution of goods and services are products of the new physical science, while the distinctively *human* consequences of science are still determined by habits and beliefs established before its origin. That democracy should not as yet have succeeded in healing the breach is no cause for discouragement: provided there is effected a union of human possibilities and ideals with the spirit and methods of science on one side and with the workings of the economic system on the other side. For a considerable period laissez-faire individualism prevented the problem from being even seen. It treated the new economic movement as if it were simply an expression of forces that were fundamental in the human constitution but were only recently released for free operation. It failed to see that the great expansion which was occurring was in fact due to release of *physical* energies; that as far as human action and human freedom is concerned, a problem, not a solution, was thereby instituted: the problem, namely, of management and direction of the new physical energies so they would contribute to realization of human possibilities.

The reaction that was created by the inevitable collapse of a movement that failed so disastrously in grasp of the problem has had diverse results, the diversity of which is part of the present confused state of our lives. Production of the material means of a secure and free life has been indefinitely increased and at an accelerated rate. It is not surprising that there is a large group which attributes the gains which have accrued, actually and potentially, to the economic regime under which they have occurred—instead of to the scientific knowledge which is the source of physical control of natural energies. The group is large. It is composed not only of the immediate beneficiaries of the system but also of the much larger number who hope that they, or at least their children, are to have full share in its benefits. Because of the opportunities furnished by free land, large unused natural resources and the absence of fixed class differences (which survive in European countries in spite of legal abolition of feudalism), this group is particularly large in this country. It is represented by those who point to the higher standard of living in this country and by those who have responded to the greater opportunities for advancement this country has afforded to them. In short, this group, in both categories of its constituents, is impressed by actual gains that have come about. They have a kind of blind and touching faith that improvement is going to continue in some more or less automatic way until it includes them and their offspring.

Then there is a much smaller group who are as sensitive, perhaps more so, to the immense possibilities represented by the physical means now potentially at our command, but who are acutely aware of our failure to realize them; who see instead the miseries, cruelties, oppressions and frustrations which exist. The weakness of this group has been that it has also failed to realize the involvement of the new scientific method in producing the existing state of affairs, and the need for its further extensive and unremitting application to determine analytically—in detail—the causes of present ills, and to project means for their elimination. In social affairs, the wholesale mental attitude that has been referred to persists with little change. It leads to formation of ambitious and sweeping beliefs and policies. The human *ideal* is indeed comprehensive. As a standpoint from which to view existing conditions and judge the direction change should take, it cannot be too inclusive. But the problem of production of change is one of infinite attention to means; and means can be determined only by definite analysis of the conditions of each problem as it presents itself. Health is a comprehensive, a "sweeping" ideal. But progress toward it has been made in the degree in which recourse to panaceas has been abandoned and inquiry has been directed to determinate disturbances and means for dealing with them. The group is represented at its extreme by those who believe there is a necessary historical law which governs the course of events so that all that is needed is deliberate acting in accord with it. The law by which class conflict produces by its own dialectic its complete opposite becomes then the supreme and sole regulator for determining policies and methods of action.

That more adequate knowledge of human nature is demanded if the release of physical powers is to serve human ends is undeniable. But it is a mistake to suppose that this knowledge of itself enables us to control human energies as physical science has enabled us to control physical energies. It suffers from the fallacy into which those have fallen who have supposed that physical energies put at our disposal by science are sure to produce human progress and prosperity. A more adequate science of human nature might conceivably only multiply the agencies by which some human beings manipulate other human beings for their own advantage. Failure to take account of the moral phase of the problem, the question of values and ends, marks, although from the opposite pole, a relapse into the fallacy of the theorists of a century ago who assumed that "free"— that is to say, politically unrestrained—manifestation of human wants and impulses would tend to bring about social prosperity, progress, and harmony. It is a counterpart fallacy to the Marxist notion that there is an economic or "materialistic," dialectic of history by which a certain desirable (and in that sense moral) end will be brought about with no intervention of choice of values and effort to realize them. As I wrote some years ago, "the assimilation of human science to physical science represents only another form of absolutistic logic, a kind of physical absolutism."

Social events will continue, in any case, to be products of interaction of human nature with cultural conditions. Hence the primary and fundamental question will always be what sort of social results we supremely want. Improved science of human nature would put at our disposal means, now lacking, for defining the problem and working effectively for its solution. But save as it should reinforce respect for the morale of science, and thereby extend and deepen the incorporation of the attitudes which form the method of science into the disposition of individuals, it might add a complication similar to that introduced by improved physical science. Anything that obscures the fundamentally moral nature of the social problem is harmful, no matter whether it proceeds from the side of physical or of psychological theory. Any doctrine that eliminates or even obscures the function of choice of values and enlistment of desires and emotions in behalf of those chosen weakens personal responsibility for judgment and for action. It thus helps create the attitudes that welcome and support the totalitarian state.

I have stated in bare outline some of the outstanding phases of the problem of culture in the service of democratic freedom. Difficulties and obstacles have been emphasized. This emphasis is a result of the fact that a *problem* is presented. Emphasis upon the problem is due to belief that many weaknesses which events have disclosed are connected with failure to see the immensity of the task involved in setting mankind upon the democratic road. That with a background of millennia of non-democratic societies behind them, the earlier advocates of democracy tremendously simplified the issue is natural. For a time the simplification was an undoubted asset. Too long continued it became a liability.

Recognition of the scope and depth of the problem is neither depressing nor discouraging when the democratic movement is placed in historic perspective. The ideas by which it formulated itself have a long history behind them. We can trace their source in Hellenic humanism and in Christian beliefs; and we can also find recurrent efforts to realize this or that special aspect of these ideas in some special struggle against a particular form of oppression. By proper selection and arrangement, we can even make out a case for the idea that all past history has been a movement, at first unconscious and then conscious, to attain freedom. A more sober view of history discloses that it took a very fortunate conjunction of events to bring about the rapid spread and seemingly complete victory of democracy during the nineteenth century. The conclusion to be drawn is not the depressing one that it is now in danger of destruction because of an unfavorable conjunction of events. The conclusion is that what was won in a more or less external and accidental manner must now be achieved and sustained by deliberate and intelligent endeavor.

The contrast thus suggested calls attention to the fact that underlying persistent attitudes of human beings were formed by traditions, customs, institutions, which existed when there was no democracy—when in fact democratic ideas and aspirations tended to be strangled at birth. Persistence of these basic dispositions accounts, on one side, for the sudden attack upon democracy; it is a reversion to old emotional and intellectual habits; or rather it is not so much a reversion as it is a manifestation of attitudes that have been there all the time but have been more or less covered up. Their persistence also explains the depth and range of the present problem. The struggle for democracy has to be maintained on as many fronts as culture has aspects: political, economic, international, educational, scientific and artistic, religious. The fact that we now have to accomplish of set purpose what in an earlier period was more or less a gift of grace renders the problem a moral one to be worked out on moral grounds.

Part of the fortunate conjunction of circumstances with respect to us who live here in the United States consists, as has been indicated, of the fact that our forefathers found themselves in a new land. The shock of physical dislocation effected a very considerable modification of old attitudes. Habits of thought and feeling which were the products of long centuries of acculturation were loosened. Less entrenched dispositions dropped off. The task of forming new institutions was thereby rendered immensely easier. The readjustment thus effected has been a chief factor in creating a general attitude of adaptability that has enabled us, save for the Civil War, to meet change with a minimum of external conflict and, in spite of an heritage of violence, with good nature. It is because of such consequences that the geographical New World may become a New World in a human sense. But, all the more on this account, the situation is such that most of the things about which we have been complacent and self-congratulatory now have to be won by thought and effort, instead of being results of evolution of a manifest destiny.

In the present state of affairs, a conflict of the moral Old and New Worlds is the essence of the struggle for democracy. It is not a question for us of isolationism, although the physical factors which make possible physical isolation from the warring ambitions of Europe are a factor to be cherished in an emergency. The conflict is not one waged with arms, although the question whether we again take up arms on European battlefields for ends that are foreign to the ends to which this country is dedicated will have weight in deciding whether we win or lose our own battle on our own ground. It is possible to stay out for reasons that have nothing to do with the maintenance of democracy, and a good deal to do with pecuniary profit, just as it is possible to be deluded into participation in the name of fighting for democracy. The conflict as it concerns the democracy to which our history commits us is *within* our own institutions and attitudes. It can be won only by extending the application of democratic methods, methods of consultation, persuasion, negotiation, communication, cooperative intelligence, in the task of making our own politics, industry, education, our culture generally, a servant and an evolving manifestation of democratic ideas. Resort to military force is a first sure sign that we are giving up the struggle for the democratic way of life, and that the Old World has conquered morally as well as geographically—succeeding in imposing upon us its ideals and methods.

If there is one conclusion to which human experience unmistakably points it is that democratic ends demand democratic methods for their realization. Authoritarian methods now offer themselves to us in new guises. They come to us claiming to serve the ultimate ends of freedom and equity in a classless society. Or they recommend adoption of a totalitarian regime in order to fight totalitarianism. In whatever form they offer themselves, they owe their seductive power to their claim to serve ideal ends. Our first defense is to realize that democracy can be served only by the slow day by day adoption and contagious diffusion in every phase of our common life of methods that are identical with the ends to be reached and that recourse to monistic, wholesale, absolutist procedures is a betrayal of human freedom no matter in what guise it presents itself. An American democracy can serve the world only as it demonstrates in the conduct of its own life the efficacy of plural, partial, and experimental methods in securing and maintaining an ever-increasing release of the powers of human nature, in service of a freedom which is cooperative and a cooperation which is voluntary.

We have no right to appeal to time to justify complacency about the ultimate result. We have every right to point to the long non-democratic and anti-democratic course of human history and to the recentness of democracy in order to enforce the immensity of the task confronting us. The very novelty of the experiment explains the impossibility of restricting the problem to any one element, aspect, or phase of our common everyday life. We have every right to appeal to the long and slow process of time to protect ourselves from the pessimism that comes from taking a short-span temporal view of events—under one condition. We must know that the dependence of ends upon means is such that the only *ultimate* result is the result that is attained today, tomorrow, the next day, and day after day, in the succession of years and generations. Only thus can we be sure that we face our problems in detail one by one as they arise, with all the resources provided by collective intelligence operating in cooperative action. At the end as at the beginning the democratic method is as fundamentally simple and as immensely difficult as is the energetic, unflagging, unceasing creation of an ever-present new road upon which we can walk together.

Theory of Valuation

Theory of Valuation

I. Its Problems

A skeptically inclined person viewing the present state of the discussion of valuing and values might find reason for concluding that a great ado is being made about very little, possibly about nothing at all. For the existing state of discussion shows not only that there is a great difference of opinion about the proper theoretical interpretation to be put upon facts, which might be a healthy sign of progress, but also that there is great disagreement as to what the facts are to which theory applies, and indeed whether there are any facts to which a theory of value can apply. For a survey of the current literature of the subject discloses that views on the subject range from the belief, at one extreme, that so-called "values" are but emotional epithets or mere ejaculations, to the belief, at the other extreme, that a priori necessary standardized, rational values are the principles upon which art, science, and morals depend for their validity. And between these two conceptions lies a number of intermediate views. The same survey will also disclose that discussion of the subject of "values" is profoundly affected by epistemological theories about idealism and realism and by metaphysical theories regarding the "subjective" and the "objective."

Given a situation of this sort, it is not easy to find a starting-point which is not compromised in advance. For what seems on the surface to be a proper starting-point may in fact be simply the conclusion of some prior epistemological or metaphysical theory. Perhaps it is safest to begin by asking how it is that the problem of valuation-theory has come to bulk so largely in recent

[First published as vol. 2, no. 4, *International Encyclopedia of Unified Science* (Chicago: University of Chicago Press, 1939), 67 pp.]

discussions. Have there been any factors in intellectual history which have produced such marked changes in scientific attitudes and conceptions as to throw the problem into relief?

When one looks at the problem of valuation in this context, one is at once struck by the fact that the sciences of astronomy, physics, chemistry, etc., do not contain expressions that by any stretch of the imagination can be regarded as standing for value-facts or conceptions. But, on the other hand, all deliberate, all planned human conduct, personal and collective, seems to be influenced, if not controlled, by estimates of value or worth of ends to be attained. Good sense in practical affairs is generally identified with a sense of relative values. This contrast between natural science and human affairs apparently results in a bifurcation, amounting to a radical split. There seems to be no ground common to the conceptions and methods that are taken for granted in all physical matters and those that appear to be most important in respect to human activities. Since the propositions of the natural sciences concern matters-of-fact and the relations between them, and since such propositions constitute the subject matter acknowledged to possess preeminent scientific standing, the question inevitably arises whether scientific propositions about the direction of human conduct, about any situation into which the idea of *should* enters, are possible; and, if so, of what sort they are and the grounds upon which they rest.

The elimination of value-conceptions from the science of non-human phenomena is, from a historical point of view, comparatively recent. For centuries, until, say, the sixteenth and seventeenth centuries, nature was supposed to be what it is because of the presence within it of *ends*. In their very capacity as ends they represented complete or *perfect* Being. All natural changes were believed to be striving to actualize these ends as the goals toward which they moved by their own nature. Classic philosophy identified *ens, verum,* and *bonum,* and the identification was taken to be an expression of the constitution of nature as the object of natural science. In such a context there was no call and no place for any *separate* problem of valuation and values, since what are now termed values were taken to be integrally incorporated in the very structure of the world. But when teleological considerations were eliminated from one natural science after another, and finally from the sciences of physiology and biology, the problem of value arose as a separate problem.

If it is asked why it happened that, with the exclusion from nature of conceptions of ends and of striving to attain them, the conception of values did not entirely drop out—as did, for example, that of phlogiston—the answer is suggested by what has been said about the place of conceptions and estimates of value in distinctively human affairs. Human behavior *seems* to be influenced, if not controlled, by considerations such as are expressed in the words 'good-bad,' 'right-wrong,' 'admirable-hideous,' etc. All conduct that is not simply either blindly impulsive or mechanically routine seems to involve valuations. The problem of valuation is thus closely associated with the problem of the structure of the sciences of *human* activities and *human* relations. When the problem of valuation is placed in this context, it begins to be clear that the problem is one of moment. The various and conflicting theories that are entertained about valuation also take on significance. For those who hold that the field of scientifically warranted propositions is exhausted in the field of propositions of physics and chemistry will be led to hold that there are no genuine value-propositions or judgments, no propositions that state (affirm or deny) anything about values capable of support and test by experimental evidence. Others, who accept the distinction between the nonpersonal field and the personal or human field as one of two separate fields of existence, the physical and the mental or psychical, will hold that the elimination of value-categories from the physical field makes it clear that they are located in the mental. A third school employs the fact that value-expressions are not found in the physical sciences as proof that the subject matter of the physical sciences is only partial (sometimes called merely "phenomenal") and hence needs to be supplemented by a "higher" type of subject matter and knowledge in which value-categories are supreme over those of factual existence.

The views just listed are typical but not exhaustive. They are listed not so much to indicate the theme of discussion as to help delimit the central problem about which discussions turn, often, apparently, without being aware of their source; namely, the problem of the possibility of genuine propositions about the direction of human affairs. Were it possible, it would probably be desirable to discuss this problem with a minimum of explicit reference to value-expressions. For much ambiguity has been imported into discussion of the latter from outside epistemological and psychological sources. Since this mode of approach is not possible under existing circumstances, this introductory section will conclude with some remarks about certain linguistic expressions purporting to designate distinctive value-facts.

1. The expression 'value' is used as a verb and a noun, and there is a basic dispute as to which sense is primary. If there are things that are values or that have the property of value apart from connection with any activity, then the verb 'to value' is derivative. For in this case an act of apprehension is called valuation simply because of the object it grasps. If, however, the active sense, designated by a verb, is primary, then the noun 'value' designates what common speech calls a *valuable*—something that is the object of a certain kind of activity. For example, things which exist independently of being valued, like diamonds or mines and forests, are valuable when they are the objects of certain human activities. There are many nouns designating things not in their primary existence but as the material or objectives (as when something is called a target) of activities. The question whether this holds in the case of a thing (or the property) called value is one of the matters involved in controversy. Take, for example, the following quotations. Value is said to be "best defined as the qualitative content of an apprehending process. . . . It is a given qualitative content present to attention or intuition." This statement would seem to take 'value' as primarily a noun, or at least an adjective, designating an object or its intrinsic quality. But when the same author goes on to speak of the process of intuiting and apprehending, he says: "What seems to distinguish the act of valuing from the bare act of intuiting is that the former is qualified, to a noticeable degree, by feeling. . . . It consciously discriminates some specific content. But the act of valuing is also emotional; it is the conscious expression of an interest, a motor-affective attitude." This passage gives the opposite impression of the one previously cited. Nor is the matter made clearer when it is further said that "the value-quality or content of the experience has been distinguished from the value-act or psychological attitude of which this content is the immediate object"—a position that seems like an attempt to solve a problem by riding two horses going in opposite directions.

Furthermore, when attention is confined to the usage of the verb 'to value,' we find that common speech exhibits a double usage. For a glance at the dictionary will show that in ordinary speech the words 'valuing' and 'valuation' are verbally employed to designate both *prizing*, in the sense of holding precious, dear (and various other nearly equivalent activities, like honoring, regarding highly), and *appraising* in the sense of *putting* a value upon, *assigning* value to. This is an activity of rating, an act that involves comparison, as is explicit, for example, in appraisals in money terms of goods and services. The double meaning is significant because there is implicit in it one of the basic issues regarding valuation. For in *prizing*, emphasis falls upon something having definite *personal* reference, which, like all activities of distinctively personal reference, has an aspectual quality called emotional. Valuation as *appraisal,* however, is primarily concerned with a relational property of objects so that an intellectual aspect is uppermost of the same general sort that is found in '*estimate*' as distinguished from the personal-emotional word '*esteem*.' That the same verb is employed in both senses suggests the problem upon which schools are divided at the present time. Which of the two references is basic in its implications? Are the two activities separate or are they complementary? In connection with etymological history, it is suggestive (though, of course, in no way conclusive) that 'praise,' 'prize,' and 'price' are all derived from the same Latin word; that 'appreciate' and 'appraise' were once used interchangeably; and that 'dear' is still used as equivalent both to 'precious' and to 'costly' in monetary price. While the dual significance of the word as used in ordinary speech raises a problem, the question of linguistic usage is further extended—not to say confused—by the fact that current theories often identify the verb 'to value' with 'to enjoy' in the sense of receiving pleasure or gratification from something, finding it agreeable; and also with 'to enjoy' in the active sense of *concurring* in an activity and its outcome.

2. If we take certain words commonly regarded as value-expressions, we find no agreement in theoretical discussions as to their proper status. There are, for example, those who hold that 'good' means *good for,* useful, serviceable, helpful; while 'bad' means harmful, detrimental—a conception which contains implicitly a complete theory of valuation. Others hold that a sharp difference exists between good in the sense of 'good for' and that which is 'good in itself.' Again, as just noted, there are those who

hold that 'pleasant' and 'gratifying' are value-expressions of the first rank, while others would not give them standing as primary value-expressions. There is also dispute as to the respective status of 'good' and 'right' as value-words.

The conclusion is that verbal usage gives us little help. Indeed, when it is used to give direction to the discussion, it proves confusing. The most that reference to linguistic expressions can do at the outset is to point out certain problems. These problems may be used to delimit the topic under discussion. As far, then, as the terminology of the present discussion is concerned, the word 'valuation' will be used, both verbally and as a noun, as the most neutral in its theoretical implications, leaving it to further discussion to determine its connection with *prizing, appraising, enjoying,* etc.

II. Value-Expression as Ejaculatory

Discussion will begin with consideration of the most extreme of the views which have been advanced. This view affirms that value-expressions cannot be constituents of propositions, that is, of sentences which affirm or deny, because they are purely ejaculatory. Such expressions as 'good,' 'bad,' 'right,' 'wrong,' 'lovely,' 'hideous,' etc., are regarded as of the same nature as interjections; or as phenomena like blushing, smiling, weeping; or/and as stimuli to move others to act in certain ways—much as one says "Gee" to oxen or "Whoa" to a horse. They do not say or state anything, not even about feelings; they merely evince or manifest the latter.

The following quotations represent this view: "If I say to someone, 'You acted wrongly in stealing that money,' I am not *stating* anything more than if I had simply said 'You stole that money.' . . . It is as if I had said 'You stole that money' in a peculiar tone of horror, or written it with the addition of some special exclamation marks. The tone . . . merely serves to show that the expression is attended by certain feelings in the speaker." And again: "Ethical terms do not serve only to express feelings. They are calculated also to arouse feeling and so to stimulate action. . . . Thus the sentence 'It is your duty to tell the truth' may be regarded both as the expression of a certain sort of ethical feeling about truthfulness and as the expression of the command 'Tell the truth.' . . . In the sentence 'It is good to tell the truth' the command has become little more than a suggestion." On what grounds the writer calls the terms and the "feelings" of which he speaks "ethical" does not appear. Nevertheless, applying this adjective to the feelings seems to involve some objective ground for discriminating and identifying them as of a certain kind, a conclusion inconsistent with the position taken. But, ignoring this fact, we pass on to a further illustration: "In saying 'tolerance is a virtue' I should not be making a statement about my own feelings or about anything else. I should simply be evincing my own feelings, which is not at all the same thing as saying that I have them." Hence "it is impossible to dispute about questions of value," for sentences that do not say or state anything whatever cannot, a fortiori, be incompatible with one another. Cases of apparent dispute or of opposed statements are, if they have any meaning at all, reducible to differences regarding the facts of the case—as there might be a dispute whether a man performed the particular action called stealing or lying. Our hope or expectation is that if "we can get an opponent to agree with us about the empirical facts of the case he will adopt the same moral attitude towards them as we do"—though once more it is not evident why the attitude is called "moral" rather than "magical," "belligerent," or any one of thousands of adjectives that might be selected at random.

Discussion will proceed, as has previously been intimated, by analyzing the facts that are appealed to and not by discussing the merits of the theory in the abstract. Let us begin with phenomena that admittedly say nothing, like the first cries of a baby, his first smiles, or his early cooings, gurglings, and squeals. When it is said that they "express feelings," there is a dangerous ambiguity in the words 'feelings' and 'express.' What is clear in the case of tears or smiles ought to be clear in the case of sounds involuntarily uttered. They are not in themselves expressive. They are constituents of a larger organic condition. They are facts of organic behavior and are *not* in any sense whatever value-expressions. They may, however, be taken by other persons as *signs* of an organic state, and, so taken, *qua* signs or treated as *symptoms,* they evoke certain responsive forms of behavior in these other persons. A baby cries. The mother takes the cry as a sign the baby is hungry or that a pin is pricking it, and so acts to change the organic condition inferred to exist by using the cry as an evidential sign.

Then, as the baby matures, it becomes aware of the connection that exists between a certain cry, the activity evoked, and the consequences produced in response to it. The cry (gesture, posture) is now made *in order* to evoke the activity and in order to experience the consequences of that activity. Just as with respect to the original response there is a difference between the activity that is merely *caused* by the cry as a stimulus (as the cry of a child may awaken a sleeping mother before she is even aware there is a cry) and an activity that is evoked by the cry interpreted as a *sign* or evidence of something, so there is a difference between the original cry—which may properly be called purely ejaculatory—and the cry made on purpose, that is, with the intent to evoke a response that will have certain consequences. The latter cry exists in the medium of language; it is a linguistic sign that not only says something but is intended to say, to convey, to tell.

What is it which is then told or stated? In connection with this question, a fatal ambiguity in the word 'feelings' requires notice. For perhaps the view will be propounded that at most all that is communicated is the existence of certain feelings along perhaps with a desire to obtain other feelings in consequence of the activity evoked in another person. But any such view (*a*) goes contrary to the obvious facts with which the account began and (*b*) introduces a totally superfluous not to say empirically unverifiable matter. (*a*) For what we started with was not a feeling but an organic condition of which a cry, or tears, or a smile, or a blush, is a constituent part. (*b*) The word 'feelings' is accordingly either a strictly behavioral term, a name for the total organic state of which the cry or gesture is a part, or it is a word which is introduced entirely gratuitously. The phenomena in question are events in the course of the life of an organic being, not differing from taking food or gaining weight. But just as a gain in weight may be taken as a sign or evidence of proper feeding, so the cry may be taken as a sign or evidence of some special occurrence in organic life.

The phrase 'evincing feeling,' whether or not 'evincing' is

taken as a synonym of 'expressing,' has, then, no business in the report of what takes place. The original activity—crying, smiling, weeping, squealing—is, as we have seen, a part of a larger organic state, so the phrase does not apply to it. When the cry or bodily attitude is purposely made, it is not a feeling that is evinced or expressed. Overt linguistic behavior is undertaken so as to obtain a change in organic conditions—a change to occur as the result of some behavior undertaken by some other person. Take another simple example: A smacking of the lips is or may be part of the original behavioral action called taking food. In one social group the noise made in smacking the lips is treated as a sign of boorishness or of "bad manners." Hence as the young grow in power of muscular control, they are taught to inhibit this activity. In another social group smacking the lips and the accompanying noise are taken as a sign that a guest is properly aware of what the host has provided. Both cases are completely describable in terms of observable modes of behavior and their respective observable consequences.

The serious problem in this connection is why the word 'feelings' is introduced in the theoretical account, since it is unnecessary in report of what actually happens. There is but one reasonable answer. The word is brought in from an alleged psychological theory which is couched in mentalistic terms, or in terms of alleged states of an inner consciousness or something of that sort. Now it is irrelevant and unnecessary to ask in connection with events before us whether there are in fact such inner states. For, even if there be such states, they are by description wholly private, accessible only to private inspection. Consequently, even if there were a legitimate introspectionist theory of states of consciousness or of feelings as purely mentalistic, there is no justification for borrowing from this theory in giving an account of the occurrences under examination. The reference to "feelings" is superfluous and gratuitous, moreover, because the important part of the account given is the use of "value-expressions" to influence the conduct of others by evoking certain responses from them. From the standpoint of an empirical report it is meaningless, since the interpretation is couched in terms of something not open to public inspection and verification. If there are "feelings" of the kind mentioned, there cannot be any assurance that any given word when used by two different persons even refers to the same thing, since the thing is not open to common observation and description.

Confining further consideration, then, to the part of the account that has an empirical meaning, namely, the existence of organic activities which evoke certain responses from others and which are capable of being employed with a view to evoking them, the following statements are warranted: (1) The phenomena in question are *social* phenomena where 'social' means simply that there is a form of behavior of the nature of an interaction or transaction between two or more persons. Such an interpersonal activity exists whenever one person—as a mother or nurse—treats a sound made by another person incidentally to a more extensive organic behavior *as a sign,* and responds to it in that capacity instead of reacting to it in its primary existence. The interpersonal activity is even more evident when the item of organic personal behavior in question takes place *for the sake of* evoking a certain kind of response from other persons. If, then, we follow the writer in locating value-expressions where he located them, we are led, after carrying out the required elimination of the ambiguity of 'expression' and the irrelevance of 'feeling,' to the conclusions that value-expressions have to do with or are involved in the behavioral relations of persons to one another. (2) Taken as signs (and, a fortiori, when used as signs) gestures, postures, and words are linguistic symbols. They say something and are of the nature of propositions. Take, for example, the case of a person who assumes the posture appropriate to an ailing person and who utters sounds such as the latter person would ordinarily make. It is then a legitimate subject of inquiry whether the person is genuinely ailing and incapacitated for work or is malingering. The conclusions obtained as a result of the inquiries undertaken will certainly "evoke" from other persons very different kinds of responsive behavior. The investigation is carried on to determine what is the actual case of things that are empirically observable; it is not about inner "feelings." Physicians have worked out experimental tests that have a high degree of reliability. Every parent and schoolteacher learns to be on guard against the assuming by a child of certain facial "expressions" and bodily attitudes for the purpose of causing inferences to be drawn which are the source of favor on the part of the adult. In such cases (they could easily be extended to include more complex matters) the propositions that embody the inference are likely to be in error when only a short segment of behavior is observed and are likely to be warranted when they rest upon a prolonged segment or upon a variety of carefully scrutinized data—traits that the propositions in question have in common with all genuine physical propositions. (3) So far the question has not been raised as to whether the propositions that occur in the course of interpersonal behavioral situations are or are not of the nature of valuation-propositions. The conclusions reached are hypothetical. *If* the expressions involved are valuation-expressions, as this particular school takes them to be, *then* it follows (i) that valuation-phenomena are social or interpersonal phenomena and (ii) that they are such as to provide material for propositions about observable events—propositions subject to empirical test and verification or refutation. But so far the hypothesis remains a hypothesis. It raises the question whether the statements which occur with a view to influencing the activity of others, so as to call out from them certain modes of activity having certain consequences, are phenomena falling under the head of valuation.

Take, for example, the case of a person calling "Fire!" or "Help!" There can be no doubt of the intent to influence the conduct of others in order to bring about certain consequences capable of observation and of statement in propositions. The expressions, taken in their observable context, say something of a complex character. When analyzed, what is said is (i) that there exists a situation that will have obnoxious consequences; (ii) that the person uttering the expressions is unable to cope with the situation; and (iii) that an improved situation is anticipated in case the assistance of others is obtained. All three of these matters are capable of being tested by empirical evidence, since they all refer to things that are observable. The proposition in which the content of the last point (the anticipation) is stated is capable, for example, of being tested by observation of what happens in a particular case. Previous observations may substantiate the conclusion that in any case objectionable consequences are much less likely to happen if the linguistic sign is employed in order to obtain the assistance it is designed to evoke.

Examination shows certain resemblances between these cases

and those previously examined which, according to the passage quoted, contain valuation-expressions. The propositions refer directly to an *existing* situation and indirectly to a *future* situation which it is intended and desired to produce. The expressions noted are employed as intermediaries to bring about the desired change from present to future conditions. In the set of illustrative cases that was first examined, certain valuation-words, like 'good' and 'right,' explicitly appear; in the second set there are no *explicit* value-expressions. The cry for aid, however, when taken in connection with its existential context, affirms in effect, although not in so many words, that the situation with reference to which the cry is made is "bad." It is "bad" in the sense that it is objected to, while a future situation which is *better* is anticipated, provided the cry evokes a certain response. The analysis may seem to be unnecessarily detailed. But, unless in each set of examples the existential context is made clear, the verbal expressions that are employed can be made to mean anything or nothing. When the contexts are taken into account, what emerges are propositions assigning a relatively negative value to existing conditions; a comparatively positive value to a prospective set of conditions; and intermediate propositions (which may or may not contain a valuation-expression) intended to evoke activities that will bring about a transformation from one state of affairs to another. There are thus involved (i) aversion to an existing situation and attraction toward a prospective possible situation and (ii) a *specifiable and testable relation between the latter as an end and certain activities as means for accomplishing it.* Two problems for further discussion are thus set. One of them is the relation of active or behavioral attitudes to what may be called (for the purpose of identification) *liking* and *disliking,* while the other is the relation of valuation to things as means-end.

III. Valuation as Liking and Disliking

That liking and disliking in their connection with valuation are to be considered in terms of observable and identifiable modes of behavior follows from what is stated in the previous section. As behavioral the adjective 'affective-motor' is applicable, although care must be taken not to permit the "affective" quality to be interpreted in terms of private "feelings"—an interpretation that nullifies the active and observable element expressed in 'motor.' For the "motor" takes place in the public and observable world, and, like anything else taking place there, has observable conditions and consequences. When, then, the word 'liking' is used as a name for a mode of behavior (not as a name for a private and inaccessible feeling), what sort of activities does it stand for? What is its designatum? This inquiry is forwarded by noting that the words 'caring' and 'caring for' are, as modes of behavior, closely connected with 'liking,' and that other substantially equivalent words are 'looking out for or after,' 'cherishing,' 'being devoted to,' 'attending to,' in the sense of 'tending,' 'ministering to,' 'fostering'—words that all seem to be variants of what is referred to by 'prizing,' which, as we saw earlier, is one of the two main significations recognized by the dictionary. When these words are taken in the behavioral sense, or as naming activities that take place so as to maintain or procure certain conditions, it is possible to demarcate what is designated by them from things designated by such an ambiguous word as 'enjoy.' For the latter word may point to a condition of *receiving* gratification *from* something already in existence, apart from any affective-motor action exerted as a condition of its production or continued existence. Or it may refer to precisely the latter activity, in which case 'to enjoy' is a synonym for the activity of taking delight in an effort, having a certain overtone of relishing, which "takes pains," as we say, to perpetuate *the existence of conditions* from which gratification is received. Enjoying in this active sense is marked by energy expended to secure the conditions that are the source of the gratification.

The foregoing remarks serve the purpose of getting theory away from a futile task of trying to assign signification to words in isolation from objects as designata. We are led instead to evocation of specifiable existential situations and to observation of what takes place in them. We are directed to observe whether energy is put forth to call into existence or to maintain in existence certain conditions; in ordinary language, to note whether effort is evoked, whether pains are taken to bring about the existence of certain conditions rather than others, the need for expenditure of energy showing that there exist conditions adverse to what is wanted. The mother who professes to prize her child and to enjoy (in the active sense of the word) the child's companionship but who systematically neglects the child and does not seek out occasions for being with the child is deceiving herself; if she makes, in addition, demonstrative signs of affection—like fondling—only when others are present, she is presumably trying to deceive them also. It is by observations of behavior—which observations (as the last illustration suggests) may need to be extended over a considerable space-time—that the existence and description of valuations have to be determined. Observation of the amount of energy expended and the length of time over which it persists enables qualifying adjectives like 'slight' and 'great' to be warrantably prefixed to a given valuation. The direction the energy is observed to take, as toward and away from, enables grounded discrimination to be made between "positive" and "negative" valuations. If there are "feelings" existing in addition, their existence has nothing to do with any verifiable proposition that can be made about a valuation.

Because valuations in the sense of prizing and caring for occur only when it is necessary to bring something into existence which is lacking, or to conserve in existence something which is menaced by outside conditions, valuation *involves* desiring. The latter is to be distinguished from mere wishing in the sense in which wishes occur in the absence of effort. "If wishes were horses, beggars would ride." There is something lacking, and it would be gratifying if it were present, but there is either no energy expended to bring what is absent into existence or else, under the given conditions, no expenditure of effort would bring it into existence—as when the baby is said to cry for the moon, and when infantile adults indulge in dreams about how nice everything would be if things were only different. The *designata* in the cases to which the names 'desiring' and 'wishing' are respectively applied are basically different. When, accordingly, 'valuation' is defined in terms of desiring, the prerequisite is a treatment of desire in terms of the existential context in which it arises and functions. If 'valuation' is defined in terms of desire as something initial and complete in itself, there is nothing by which to discriminate one desire from another and hence no way in which to measure the worth of different valuations in comparison with one another. Desires are desires, and that is all that can be said. Furthermore, desire is then conceived of as *merely* personal and hence as not capable of being stated in terms of other objects or events. If, for example, it should happen to be noted that effort ensues upon desire and that the effort put forth changes existing conditions, these considerations would then be looked upon as matters wholly external to desire—provided, that is, desire is taken to be original and complete in itself, independent of an observable contextual situation.

When, however, desires are seen to arise only within certain existential contexts (namely, those in which some lack prevents the immediate execution of an active tendency) and when they are seen to function in reference to these contexts in such a way as to make good the existing want, the relation between desire and *valuation* is found to be such as both to make possible, and to require, statement in verifiable propositions. (i) The content and object of desires are seen to depend upon the particular context in which they arise, a matter that in turn depends upon the antecedent state of both personal activity and of surrounding conditions. Desires for food, for example, will hardly be the same if one has eaten five hours or five days previously, nor will they be of the same content in a hovel and a palace or in a nomadic or agricultural group. (ii) Effort, instead of being something that comes after desire, is seen to be of the very essence of the tension involved in desire. For the latter, instead of being merely personal, is an active relation of the organism to the environment (as is obvious in the case of hunger), a factor that makes the difference between genuine desire and mere wish and fantasy. It follows that valuation in its connection with desire is linked to existential situations and that it differs with differences in its existential context. Since its existence depends upon the situation, its adequacy depends upon its adaptation to the needs and demands imposed by the situation. Since the situation is open to observation, and since the consequences of effort-behavior as observed determine the adaptation, the adequacy of a given desire can be stated in propositions. The propositions are capable of empirical test because the connection that exists between a given desire and the conditions with reference to which it functions are ascertained by means of these observations.

The word 'interest' suggests in a forcible way the active connection between personal activity and the conditions that must be taken into account in the theory of valuation. Even in ety-

mology it indicates something in which both a person and surrounding conditions participate in intimate connection with one
another. In naming this something that occurs between them it
names a transaction. It points to an activity which takes effect
through the mediation of external conditions. When we think,
for example, of the interest of any particular group, say the bank-
ers' interest, the trade-union interest, or the interest of a political
machine, we think not of mere states of mind but of the group as
a pressure group having organized channels in which it directs
action to obtain and make secure conditions that will produce
specified consequences. Similarly in the case of singular persons,
when a court recognizes an individual as having an interest in
some matter, it recognizes that he has certain claims whose enforcement will affect an existential issue or outcome. Whenever a
person has an interest in something, he has a stake in the course
of events and in their final issue—a stake which leads him to take
action to bring into existence a particular result rather than
some other one.

It follows from the facts here adduced that the view which
connects valuation (and "values") with desires and interest is but
a starting-point. It is indeterminate in its bearing upon the theory of valuation until the nature of interest and desire has been
analyzed, and until a method has been established for determining the constituents of desires and interests in their concrete particular occurrence. Practically all the fallacies in the theories that
connect valuation with desire result from taking "desire" at
large. For example, when it is said (quite correctly) that "values
spring from the immediate and inexplicable reaction of vital impulse and from the irrational part of our nature," what is actually
stated is that vital impulses are a *causal condition* of the existence of desires. When "vital impulse" is given the only interpretation which is empirically verifiable (that of an organic biological tendency), the fact that an "irrational" factor is the causal
condition of valuations proves that valuations have their roots
in an existence which, like any existence *taken in itself,* is *a*-
rational. Correctly interpreted, the statement is thus a reminder
that organic tendencies are existences which are connected with
other existences (the word 'irrational' adds nothing to "*existence*" as such) and hence are observable. But the sentence cited

is often interpreted to mean that vital impulses *are* valuations—an interpretation which is incompatible with the view which connects valuations with desires and interests, and which, by parity of logic, would justify the statement that trees are seeds since they "spring from" seeds. Vital impulses are doubtless conditions *sine qua non* for the existence of desires and interests. But the latter include foreseen consequences along with ideas in the form of signs of the measures (involving expenditure of energy) required to bring the ends into existence. When valuation is identified with the activity of desire or interest, its identification with vital impulse is denied. For its identification with the latter would lead to the absurdity of making every organic activity of every kind an act of valuation, since there is none that does not involve some "vital impulse."

The view that "a value is any object of any interest" must also be taken with great caution. On its face it places all interests on exactly the same level. But, when interests are examined in their concrete makeup in relation to their place in some situation, it is plain that everything depends upon the objects involved in them. This in turn depends upon the care with which the needs of existing situations have been looked into and upon the care with which the ability of a proposed act to satisfy or fulfil just those needs has been examined. That all interests stand on the same footing with respect to their function as valuators is contradicted by observation of even the most ordinary of everyday experiences. It may be said that an interest in burglary and its fruits confers value upon certain objects. But the valuations of the burglar and the policeman are not identical, any more than the interest in the fruits of productive work institutes the same values as does the interest of the burglar in the pursuit of his calling—as is evident in the action of a judge when stolen goods are brought before him for disposition. Since interests occur in definite existential contexts and not at large in a void, and since these contexts are situations within the life-activity of a person or group, interests are so linked with one another that the valuation-capacity of any one is a function of the set to which it belongs. The notion that a value is equally any object of any interest can be maintained only upon a view that completely isolates them from one another—a view that is so removed from readily observed facts that its existence can be explained only as a corollary of the introspectionist psychology which holds that desires and interests are but "feelings" instead of modes of behavior.

IV. Propositions of Appraisal

Since desires and interests are activities which take place in the world and which have effects in the world, they are observable in themselves and in connection with their observed effects. It might seem then as if, upon any theory that relates valuation with desire and interest, we had now come within sight of our goal—the discovery of valuation-propositions. Propositions *about* valuations have, indeed, been shown to be possible. But they are valuation-propositions only in the sense in which propositions about potatoes are potato-propositions. They are propositions about matters-of-fact. The fact that these occurrences happen to be valuations does not make the propositions valuation-propositions in any distinctive sense. Nevertheless, the fact that such matter-of-fact propositions can be made is of importance. For, unless they exist, it is doubly absurd to suppose that valuation-propositions in a *distinctive* sense can exist. It has also been shown that the subject matter of personal activities forms no theoretical barrier to institution of matter-of-fact propositions, for the behavior of human beings is open to observation. While there are practical obstacles to the establishment of valid general propositions about such behavior (i.e., about the relations of its constituent acts), its conditions and effects may be investigated. Propositions about valuations made in terms of their conditions and consequences delimit the problem as to existence of valuation-propositions in a *distinctive* sense. Are propositions about existent valuations themselves capable of being appraised, and can the appraisal when made enter into the constitution of further valuations? That a mother prizes or holds dear her child, we have seen, may be determined by observation; and the conditions and effects of different kinds of prizing or caring for may, in theory, be compared and contrasted with one another. In case the final outcome is to show that some kinds of acts of prizing are *better* than others, valuation-acts are themselves evaluated, and the evaluation may modify further direct acts of prizing. If this condition is satisfied, then propositions about valuations that actually take place become the subject matter of valuations in a distinctive sense, that is, a sense that marks them off both from propositions of physics and from historical propositions about what human beings have in fact done.

We are brought thus to the problem of the nature of appraisal or evaluation which, as we saw, is one of the two recognized significations of 'valuation.' Take such an elementary appraisal proposition as "This plot of ground is worth $200 a front foot." It is different in form from the proposition, "It has a frontage of 200 feet." The latter sentence states a matter of accomplished fact. The former sentence states a rule for determination of an act to be performed, its reference being to the future and not to something already accomplished or done. If stated in the context in which a tax-assessor operates, it states a regulative condition for levying a tax against the owner; if stated by the owner to a real estate dealer, it sets forth a regulative condition to be observed by the latter in offering the property for sale. The future act or state is not set forth as a prediction of what will happen but as something which *shall* or *should* happen. Thus the proposition may be said to lay down a norm, but "norm" must be understood simply in the sense of a condition *to be* conformed to in definite forms of future action. That rules are all but omnipresent in every mode of human relationship is too obvious to require argument. They are in no way confined to activities to which the name 'moral' is applied. Every recurrent form of activity, in the arts and professions, develops rules as to the best way in which to accomplish the ends in view. Such rules are used as criteria or "norms" for judging the value of proposed modes of behavior. The existence of rules for valuation of modes of behavior in different fields as wise or unwise, economical or extravagant, effective or futile, cannot be denied. The problem concerns not their existence as general propositions (since every rule of action is general) but whether they express only custom, convention, tradition, or are capable of stating relations between things as means and other things as consequences, which relations are themselves grounded in empirically ascertained and tested existential relations such as are usually termed those of cause and effect.

In the case of some crafts, arts, and technologies, there can be no doubt which of these alternatives is correct. The medical art, for example, is approaching a state in which many of the rules laid down for a patient by a physician as to what it is *better* for him to do, not merely in the way of medicaments but of diet and habits of life, are based upon experimentally ascertained principles of chemistry and physics. When engineers say that certain materials subjected to certain technical operations are *required* if a bridge capable of supporting certain loads is to be built over the Hudson River at a certain point, their advice does not represent their personal opinions or whims but is backed by acknowledged physical laws. It is commonly believed that such devices as radios and automobiles have been greatly improved (bettered) since they were first invented, and that the betterment in the relation of means to consequences is due to more adequate scientific knowledge of underlying physical principles. The argument does not demand the belief that the influence of custom and convention is entirely eliminated. It is enough that such cases show that it is possible for rules of appraisal or evaluation to rest upon scientifically warranted physical generalizations and that the ratio of rules of this type to those expressing mere customary habits is on the increase.

In medicine a quack may cite a number of alleged cures as evidential ground for taking the remedies he offers. Only a little examination is needed to show in what definite respects the procedures he recommends differ from those said to be "good" or to be "required" by competent physicians. There is, for example, no analysis of the cases presented as evidence to show that they are actually like the disease for the cure of which the remedy is urged; and there is no analysis to show that the recoveries which are said (rather than proved) to have taken place were in fact due to taking the medicine in question rather than to any one of an indefinite number of other causes. Everything is asserted wholesale with no analytic control of conditions. Furthermore, the first requirement of scientific procedure—namely, full publicity as to materials and processes—is lacking. The sole justification for citing these familiar facts is that their contrast with competent medical practice shows the extent to which the rules of procedure in the latter art have the warrant of tested empirical propositions. Appraisals of courses of action as better and worse, more and less serviceable, are as experimentally justified as are nonvaluative propositions about impersonal subject matter. In advanced engineering technologies propositions that state the *proper* courses of action to be adopted are evidently grounded in generalizations of physical and chemical science; they are often referred to as *applied* science. Nevertheless, propositions which lay down rules for procedures as being fit and good, as distinct from those that are inept and bad, are different in form from the scientific propositions upon which they rest. For they are rules for the use, in and by human activity, of scientific generalizations as means for accomplishing certain desired and intended ends.

Examination of these appraisals discloses that they have to do with things as they sustain to each other the relation of *means to ends or consequences*. Wherever there is an appraisal involving a rule as to better or as to needed action, there is an end to be reached: the appraisal is a valuation of things with respect to their serviceability or needfulness. If we take the examples given earlier, it is evident that real estate is appraised for the purpose of levying taxes or fixing a selling price; that medicinal treatments are appraised with reference to the end of effecting recovery of health; that materials and techniques are valued with respect to the building of bridges, radios, motorcars, etc. If a bird builds its nest by what is called pure "instinct," it does not have to appraise materials and processes with respect to their fitness for an end. But if the result—the nest—is contemplated as an object of desire, then either there is the most arbitrary kind of trial-and-error operations or there is consideration of the fitness and usefulness of materials and processes to bring the desired object into existence. And this process of weighing obviously involves comparison of different materials and operations as alternative possible means. In every case, except those of sheer "instinct" and complete trial and error, there are involved observation of actual materials and estimate of their potential force in production of a particular result. There is always some observation of the *outcome attained* in comparison and contrast with that intended, such that the comparison throws light upon the actual fitness of the things employed as means. It thus makes possible a better judgment in the future as to their fitness and usefulness. On the basis of such observations certain modes of conduct are adjudged silly, imprudent, or unwise, and other modes of conduct sensible, prudent, or wise, the discrimination being made upon the basis of the validity of the estimates reached about the relation of things as means to the end or consequence actually reached.

The standing objection raised against this view of valuation is that it applies only to things *as means*, while propositions that are genuine valuations apply to things as *ends*. This point will be shortly considered at length. But it may be noted here that ends are appraised in the same evaluations in which things as means are weighed. For example, an end suggests itself. But, when things are weighed as means toward that end, it is found that it will take too much time or too great an expenditure of energy to achieve it, or that, if it were attained, it would bring with it certain accompanying inconveniences and the promise of future troubles. It is then appraised and rejected as a "bad" end.

The conclusions reached may be summarized as follows: (1) There are propositions which are not merely about valuations that have actually occurred (about, i.e., prizings, desires, and interests that have taken place in the past) but which describe and define certain things as good, fit, or proper in a definite existential relation: these propositions, moreover, are *generalizations,* since they form rules for the proper use of materials. (2) The existential relation in question is that of means-ends or means-consequences. (3) These propositions in their generalized form may rest upon scientifically warranted empirical propositions and are themselves capable of being tested by observation of results actually attained as compared with those intended.

The objection brought against the view just set forth is that it fails to distinguish between things that are good and right in and of themselves, immediately, intrinsically, and things that are simply good *for* something else. In other words, the latter are useful for attaining the things which have, so it is said, value in and of themselves, since they are prized for their own sake and not as means to something else. This distinction between two different meanings of 'good' (and 'right') is, it is claimed, so crucial for the whole theory of valuation and values that failure to make the distinction destroys the validity of the conclusions that have been set forth. This objection definitely puts before us for consideration the question of the relations to each other of the categories of *means* and *end*. In terms of the dual meaning of 'valuation' already mentioned, the question of the relation of *prizing* and *appraising* to one another is explicitly raised. For, according to the objection, appraising applies only to *means,* while prizing applies to things that are *ends,* so that a difference must be recognized between valuation in its full pregnant sense and evaluation as a secondary and derived affair.

Let the connection between prizing and valuation be admitted and also the connection between desire (and interest) and prizing. The problem as to the relation between appraisal of things as means and prizing of things as ends then takes the following form: Are desires and interests ('likings,' if one prefers that word), which directly effect an institution of end-values, independent of the appraisal of things as means or are they intimately influenced by this appraisal? If a person, for example, finds after due investigation that an immense amount of effort is required to procure the conditions that are the means required for realization of a desire (including perhaps sacrifice of other end-values that might be obtained by the same expenditure of effort), does that fact react to modify his original desire and hence, by definition, his valuation? A survey of what takes place in any deliberate activity provides an affirmative answer to this question. For what is deliberation except weighing of various alternative desires (and hence end-values) in terms of the conditions that are the means of their execution, and which, as means, determine the consequences actually arrived at? There can be no control of the operation of foreseeing consequences (and hence of forming ends-in-view) save in terms of conditions that operate as the causal conditions of their attainment. The proposition in which any object adopted as an end-in-view is statable (or explicitly stated) is *warranted* in just the degree to which existing conditions have been surveyed and appraised in their capacity as means. The sole alternative to this statement is that no deliberation whatsoever occurs, no ends-in-view are formed, but a person acts directly upon whatever impulse happens to present itself.

Any survey of the experiences in which ends-in-view are formed, and in which earlier impulsive tendencies are shaped through deliberation into a *chosen* desire, reveals that the object finally valued as an end to be reached is determined in its concrete makeup by appraisal of existing conditions as means. However, the habit of completely separating the conceptions of ends from that of means is so ingrained because of a long philosophical tradition that further discussion is required.

1. The common assumption that there is a sharp separation between things, on the one hand, as useful or helpful, and, on the other hand, as *intrinsically* good, and hence that there exists a separation between propositions as to what is expedient, prudent, or advisable and what is inherently desirable, does not, in any case, state a *self-evident* truth. The fact that such words as 'prudent,' 'sensible,' and 'expedient,' in the long run, or after survey of all conditions, merge so readily into the word 'wise' suggests (though, of course, it does not prove) that ends framed in separation from consideration of things as means are foolish to the point of irrationality.

2. Common sense regards some desires and interests as shortsighted, "blind," and others, in contrast, as enlightened, farsighted. It does not for a moment lump all desires and interests together as having the same status with respect to end-values. Discrimination between their respective shortsightedness and farsightedness is made precisely on the ground of whether the object of a given desire is viewed as, in turn, itself a conditioning means of further consequences. Instead of taking a laudatory view of "immediate" desires and valuations, common sense treats refusal to mediate as the very essence of short-view judgment. For treating the end as *merely* immediate and exclusively final is equivalent to refusal to consider what will happen after and because a particular end is reached.

3. The words 'inherent,' 'intrinsic,' and 'immediate' are used ambiguously, so that a fallacious conclusion is reached. Any quality or property that actually belongs to any object or event is properly said to be immediate, inherent, or intrinsic. The fallacy consists in interpreting what is designated by these terms as out of relation to anything else and hence as absolute. For example, *means* are by definition relational, mediated, and mediating, since they are intermediate between an existing situation and a situation that is to be brought into existence by their use. But the relational character of the *things* that are employed as means does not prevent the things from having their own immediate qualities. In case the things in question are prized and cared for, then, according to the theory that connects the property of value

with prizing, they necessarily have an immediate quality of value. The notion that, when means and instruments are valued, the value-qualities which result are only instrumental is hardly more than a bad pun. There is nothing in the nature of prizing or desiring to prevent their being directed to things which are means, and there is nothing in the nature of means to militate against their being desired and prized. In empirical fact, the measure of the value a person attaches to a given end is not what he *says* about its preciousness but the care he devotes to obtaining and using the *means* without which it cannot be attained. No case of notable achievement can be cited in any field (save as a matter of sheer accident) in which the persons who brought about the end did not give loving care to the instruments and agencies of its production. The dependence of ends attained upon means employed is such that the statement just made reduces in fact to a tautology. Lack of desire and interest are proved by neglect of, and indifference to, required means. As soon as an attitude of desire and interest has been developed, then, because without full-hearted attention an end which is professedly prized will not be attained, the desire and interest in question automatically attach themselves to whatever other things are seen to be required means of attaining the end.

The considerations that apply to 'immediate' apply also to 'intrinsic' and 'inherent.' A quality, including that of value, is inherent if it actually belongs to something, and the question of whether or not it belongs is one of *fact* and not a question that can be decided by dialectical manipulation of the concept of inherency. If one has an ardent desire to obtain certain things as means, then the quality of value belongs to, or inheres in, those things. For the time being, producing or obtaining those means *is* the end-in-view. The notion that only that which is out of relation to everything else can justly be called *inherent* is not only itself absurd but is contradicted by the very theory that connects the value of objects as ends with desire and interest, for this view expressly makes the value of the end-object relational, so that, if the inherent is identified with the nonrelational, there are, according to this view, no inherent values at all. On the other hand, if it is the fact that the quality exists in this case, because that to which it belongs is conditioned by a relation, then the relational character of means cannot be brought forward as evidence that their value is not inherent. The same considerations apply to the terms 'intrinsic' and 'extrinsic' as applied to value-qualities. Strictly speaking, the phrase 'extrinsic value' involves a contradiction in terms. Relational properties do not lose their intrinsic quality of being just what they are because their coming into being is *caused* by something 'extrinsic.' The theory that such is the case would terminate logically in the view that there are no intrinsic qualities whatever, since it can be shown that such intrinsic qualities as *red, sweet, hard,* etc., are causally conditioned as to their occurrence. The trouble, once more, is that a dialectic of concepts has taken the place of examination of actual empirical facts. The extreme instance of the view that to be intrinsic is to be out of any relation is found in those writers who hold that, since values *are* intrinsic, they cannot depend upon *any* relation whatever, and certainly not upon a relation to human beings. Hence this school attacks those who connect value-properties with desire and interest on exactly the same ground that the latter equate the distinction between the values of means and ends with the distinction between instrumental and intrinsic values. The views of this extreme nonnaturalistic school may, accordingly, be regarded as a definite exposure of what happens when an analysis of the abstract concept of 'intrinsicalness' is substituted for analysis of empirical occurrences.

The more overtly and emphatically the valuation of objects as ends is connected with desire and interest, the more evident it should be that, since desire and interest are ineffectual save as they cooperatively interact with environing conditions, valuation of desire and interest, as means correlated with other means, is the sole condition for valid appraisal of objects as ends. If the lesson were learned that the object of scientific knowledge is *in any case* an ascertained correlation of changes, it would be seen, beyond the possibility of denial, that anything taken *as end* is in its own content or constituents a correlation of the energies, personal and extra-personal, which operate as means. An end as an *actual* consequence, as an existing outcome, is, like any other occurrence which is scientifically analyzed, nothing but the interaction of the conditions that bring it to pass. Hence it follows necessarily that the *idea* of the object of desire and interest, the *end-in-view* as distinct from the end or outcome actually effected, is warranted in the precise degree in which it is formed in terms of these operative conditions.

4. The chief weakness of current theories of valuation which relate the latter to desire and interest is due to failure to make an empirical analysis of concrete desires and interests as they actually exist. When such an analysis is made, certain relevant considerations at once present themselves.

(i) Desires are subject to frustration and interests are subject to defeat. The likelihood of the occurrence of failure in attaining desired ends is in direct ratio to failure to form desire and interest (and the objects they involve) on the basis of conditions that operate either as obstacles (negatively valued) or as positive resources. The difference between reasonable and unreasonable desires and interests is precisely the difference between those which arise casually and are not reconstituted through consideration of the conditions that will actually decide the outcome and those which are formed on the basis of existing liabilities and potential resources. That desires as they first present themselves are the product of a mechanism consisting of native organic tendencies and acquired habits is an undeniable fact. All growth in maturity consists in *not* immediately giving way to such tendencies but in remaking them in their first manifestation through consideration of the consequences they will occasion *if* they are acted upon— an operation which is equivalent to judging or evaluating them as means operating in connection with extra-personal conditions as also means. Theories of valuation which relate it to desire and interest cannot both eat their cake and have it. They cannot continually oscillate between a view of desire and interest that identifies the latter with impulses just as they happen to occur (as products of organic mechanisms) and a view of desire as a modification of a raw impulse through foresight of its outcome; the latter alone being desire, the whole difference between impulse and desire is made by the presence in desire of an end-in-view, of objects *as* foreseen consequences. The foresight will be dependable in the degree in which it is constituted by examination of the conditions that will in fact decide the outcome. If it seems that this point is being hammered in too insistently, it is because the issue at stake is nothing other and nothing less than the possibility of distinctive valuation-propositions. For it cannot be denied that propositions having evidential warrant and experimental test are possible in the case of evaluation of things as means. Hence it follows that, if these propositions enter into the formation of the interests and desires which are valuations of ends, the latter are thereby constituted the subject matter of authentic empirical affirmations and denials.

(ii) We commonly speak of "learning from experience" and the "maturity" of an individual or a group. What do we mean by such expressions? At the very least, we mean that in the history of individual persons and of the human race there takes place a change from original, comparatively unreflective, impulses and hard-and-fast habits to desires and interests that incorporate the results of critical inquiry. When this process is examined, it is seen to take place chiefly on the basis of careful observation of differences found between desired and proposed ends (ends-*in-view*) and attained ends or actual consequences. Agreement between what is wanted and anticipated and what is actually obtained confirms the selection of conditions which operate as means to the desired end; discrepancies, which are experienced as frustrations and defeats, lead to an inquiry to discover the causes of failure. This inquiry consists of more and more thorough examination of the conditions under which impulses and habits are formed and in which they operate. The result is formation of desires and interests which are what they are through the union of the affective-motor conditions of action with the intellectual or ideational. The latter is there in any case if there is an end-in-view of any sort, no matter how casually formed, while it is adequate in just the degree in which the end is constituted in terms of the conditions of its actualization. For, wherever there is an *end-in-view* of any sort whatever, there is affective-*ideational*-motor activity; or, in terms of the dual meaning of valuation, there is union of prizing and appraising. Observation of results obtained, of *actual* consequences in their agreement with and difference from ends anticipated or held in view, thus provides the conditions by which desires and interests (and hence valuations) are matured and tested. Nothing more contrary to common sense can be imagined than the notion that we are incapable of changing our desires and interests by means of learning what the consequences of acting upon them are, or, as it is sometimes put, of *indulging* them. It should not be necessary to point in evidence to the spoiled child and the adult who cannot "face reality." Yet, as far as valuation and the theory of values are concerned, any theory which isolates valuation of ends from appraisal of means equates the spoiled child and the irresponsible adult to the mature and sane person.

(iii) Every person in the degree in which he is capable of learning from experience draws a distinction between what is desired and what is desirable whenever he engages in formation and choice of competing desires and interests. There is nothing far-fetched or "moralistic" in this statement. The contrast referred to is simply that between the object of a desire as it first presents itself (because of the existing mechanism of impulses and habits) and the object of desire which emerges as a revision of the first-appearing impulse, after the latter is critically judged in reference to the conditions which will decide the actual result. The "desirable," or the object which *should* be desired (valued), does not descend out of the a priori blue nor descend as an imperative from a moral Mount Sinai. It presents itself because past experience has shown that hasty action upon uncriticized desire leads to defeat and possibly to catastrophe. The "desirable" as distinct from the "desired" does not then designate something at large or a priori. It points to the difference between the operation and consequences of unexamined impulses and those of desires and interests that are the product of investigation of conditions and consequences. Social conditions and pressures are part of the conditions that affect the execution of desires. Hence they have to be taken into account in framing ends in terms of available means. But the distinction between the "is" in the sense of the object of a casually emerging desire and the "should be" of a desire framed in relation to actual conditions is a distinction which in any case is bound to offer itself as human beings grow in maturity and part with the childish disposition to "indulge" every impulse as it arises.

Desires and interests are, as we have seen, themselves causal conditions of results. As such they are potential means and have to be appraised as such. This statement is but a restatement of points already made. But it is worth making because it forcibly indicates how far away some of the theoretical views of valuation are from practical common-sense attitudes and beliefs. There is an indefinite number of proverbial sayings which in effect set forth the necessity of not treating desires and interests as final in their first appearance but of treating them as means—that is, of appraising them and forming objects or ends-in-view on the ground of what consequences they will tend to produce in practice. "Look before you leap"; "Act in haste, repent at leisure"; "A stitch in time saves nine"; "When angry count ten"; "Do not put your hand to the plow until the cost has been counted"—are but a few of the many maxims. They are summed up in the old saying, "*Respice finem*"—a saying which marks the difference between simply *having* an end-in-view for which *any* desire suffices, and *looking,* examining, to make sure that the consequences that will actually result are such as will be actually prized and valued when they occur. Only the exigencies of a preconceived theory (in all probability one seriously infected by the conclusions of an uncritically accepted "subjectivistic" psychology) will ignore the concrete differences that are made in the content of "likings" and "prizings," and of desires and interests, by evaluating them in their respective causal capacities when they are taken as means.

V. Ends and Values

It has been remarked more than once that the source of the trouble with theories which relate value to desire and interest, and then proceed to make a sharp division between prizing and appraisal, between ends and means, is the failure to make an empirical investigation of the actual conditions under which desires and interests arise and function, and in which end-objects, ends-in-view, acquire their actual contents. Such an analysis will now be undertaken.

When we inquire into the actual emergence of desire and its object and the value-property ascribed to the latter (instead of merely manipulating dialectically the general concept of desire), it is as plain as anything can be that desires arise only when "there is something the matter," when there is some "trouble" in an existing situation. When analyzed, this "something the matter" is found to spring from the fact that there is something lacking, wanting, in the existing situation as it stands, an absence which produces conflict in the elements that do exist. When things are going completely smoothly, desires do not arise, and there is no occasion to project ends-in-view, for "going smoothly" signifies that there is no need for effort and struggle. It suffices to let things take their "natural" course. There is no occasion to investigate what it would be better to have happen in the future, and hence no projection of an end-object.

Now vital impulses and acquired habits often operate without the intervention of an end-in-view or a purpose. When someone finds that his foot has been stepped on, he is likely to react with a push to get rid of the offending element. He does not stop to form a definite desire and set up an end to be reached. A man who has started walking may continue walking from force of an acquired habit without continually interrupting his course of action to inquire what object is to be obtained at the next step. These rudimentary examples are typical of much of human activity. Behavior is often so direct that no desires and ends intervene and no valuations take place. Only the requirements of a preconceived theory will lead to the conclusion that a hungry animal seeks food because it has formed an idea of an end-object to be reached, or because it has evaluated that object in terms of a desire. Organic tensions suffice to keep the animal going until it has found the material that relieves the tension. But if and when *desire* and *an end-in-view* intervene between the occurrence of a vital impulse or a habitual tendency and the execution of an activity, then the impulse or tendency is to some degree modified and transformed: a statement which is purely tautological, since the occurrence of a desire related to an end-in-view *is* a transformation of a prior impulse or routine habit. It is only in such cases that valuation occurs. This fact, as we have seen, is of much greater importance than it might at first sight seem to be in connection with the theory which relates valuation to desire and interest,[1] for it proves that valuation takes place only when there is something the matter; when there is some trouble to be done away with, some need, lack, or privation to be made good, some conflict of tendencies to be resolved by means of changing existing conditions. This fact in turn proves that there is present an intellectual factor—a factor of inquiry—whenever there is valuation, for the end-in-view is formed and projected as that which, if acted upon, will supply the existing need or lack and resolve the existing conflict. It follows from this that the difference in different desires and their correlative ends-in-view depends upon two things. The first is the adequacy with which inquiry into the lacks and conflicts of the existing situation has been carried on. The second is the adequacy of the inquiry into

1. Cf. pp. 217 ff., above.

the likelihood that the particular end-in-view which is set up will, if acted upon, actually fill the existing need, satisfy the requirements constituted by what is needed, and do away with conflict by directing activity so as to institute a unified state of affairs.

The case is empirically and dialectically so simple that it would be extremely difficult to understand why it has become so confused in discussion were it not for the influence of irrelevant theoretical preconceptions drawn in part from introspectionist psychology and in part from metaphysics. Empirically, there are two alternatives. Action may take place with or without an end-in-view. In the latter case, there is overt action with no intermediate valuation; a vital impulse or settled habit reacts directly to some immediate sensory stimulation. In case an end-in-view exists and is valued, or exists in relation to a desire or an interest, the (motor) activity engaged in is, tautologically, mediated by the anticipation of the consequences which *as a foreseen end* enter into the makeup of the desire or interest. Now, as has been so often repeated, things can be anticipated or foreseen *as ends* or outcomes only in terms of the conditions by which they are brought into existence. It is simply impossible to have an end-in-view or to anticipate the consequences of any proposed line of action save upon the basis of some, however slight, consideration of the means by which it can be brought into existence. Otherwise, there is no genuine desire but an idle fantasy, a futile wish. That vital impulses and acquired habits are capable of expending themselves in the channels of daydreaming and building castles in the air is unfortunately true. But by description the contents of dreams and air castles are *not* ends-in-view, and what makes them fantasies is precisely the fact that they are *not* formed in terms of actual conditions serving as means of their actualization. *Propositions in which things (acts and materials) are appraised as means enter necessarily into desires and interests that determine end-values.* Hence the importance of the inquiries that result in the appraisal of things as means.

The case is so clear that, instead of arguing it directly, it will prove more profitable to consider how it is that there has grown up the belief that there are such things as ends having value apart from valuation of the means by which they are reached.

1. The mentalistic psychology which operates "to reduce"

affective-motor activities to mere *feelings* has also operated in the interpretations assigned to *ends-in-view, purposes,* and *aims.* Instead of being treated as anticipations of consequences of the same order as a prediction of future events and, in any case, as depending for their contents and validity upon such predictions, they have been treated as merely mental states; for, when they are so taken (and only then), ends, needs, and satisfactions are affected in a way that distorts the whole theory of valuation. An end, aim, or purpose as a *mental* state *is* independent of the biological and physical means by which it can be realized. The want, lack, or privation which exists wherever there is desire is then interpreted as a mere state of "mind" instead of as something lacking or absent *in the situation*—something that must be supplied if the empirical situation is to be complete. In its latter sense, the needful or required is that which is *existentially necessary* if an end-in-view is to be brought into actual existence. *What* is needed cannot in this case be told by examination of a state of mind but only by examination of actual conditions. With respect to interpretation of "satisfaction" there is an obvious difference between it as a state of mind and as fulfilment of conditions, i.e., as something that meets the conditions imposed by the conjoint potentialities and lacks of the situation in which desire arises and functions. Satisfaction of desire signifies that the lack, characteristic of the situation evoking desire, has been so met that the means used make sufficient, in the most literal sense, the conditions for accomplishing the end. Because of the subjectivistic interpretation of end, need, and satisfaction, the verbally correct statement that valuation is a *relation* between a personal attitude and extra-personal things—a relation which, moreover, includes a motor (and hence physical) element—is so construed as to involve separation of means and end, of appraisal and prizing. A "value" is then affirmed to be a "feeling"—a feeling which is not, apparently, the feeling of anything but itself. If it were said that a "value" is *felt,* the statement *might* be interpreted to signify that a certain existing relation between a personal motor attitude and extra-personal environing conditions is a matter of direct experience.

2. The shift of ground between valuation as *desire-interest* and as *enjoyment* introduces further confusion in theory. The shift is facilitated because in fact there exist both enjoyments of things

directly possessed *without* desire and effort and enjoyments of things that are possessed only *because* of activity put forth to obtain the conditions required to satisfy desire. In the latter case, the enjoyment is in functional relation to desire or interest, and there is no violation of the definition of valuation in terms of desire-interest. But since the same *word*, 'enjoyment,' is applied also to gratifications that arise quite independently of prior desire and attendant effort, the ground is shifted so that "valuing" is identified with any and every state of enjoyment no matter how it comes about—including gratifications obtained in the most casual and accidental manner, "accidental" in the sense of coming about apart from desire and intent. Take, for example, the gratification of learning that one has been left a fortune by an unknown relative. There is *enjoyment*. But if valuation is defined in terms of desire and interest, there is no valuation, and in so far no "value," the latter coming into being only when there arises some desire as to what shall be done with the money and some question as to formation of an end-in-view. The two kinds of enjoyment are thus not only different but their respective bearings upon the theory of valuation are incompatible with each other, since one is connected with direct possession and the other is conditioned upon prior lack of possession—the very case in which desire enters.

For sake of emphasis, let us repeat the point in a slightly varied illustration. Consider the case of a man gratified by the unexpected receipt of a sum of money, say money picked up while he is walking on the street, an act having nothing to do with his purpose and desire at the moment he is performing it. If values are connected with desire in such a way that the connection is involved in their definition, there is, so far, no valuation. The latter begins when the finder begins to consider *how* he shall prize and care for the money. Shall he prize it, for example, as a means of satisfying certain wants he has previously been unable to satisfy, or shall he prize it as something held in trust until the owner is found? In either case, there is, by definition, an act of valuation. But it is clear that the property of value is attached in the two cases to very different objects. Of course, the uses to which money is put, the ends-in-view which it will serve, are fairly standardized, and in so far the instance just cited is not especially well chosen. But take the case of a child who has found a bright smooth stone. His sense of touch and of sight is gratified. But there is no valuation because no desire and no end-in-view, until the question arises of what shall be done with it; until the child *treasures* what he has accidentally hit upon. The moment he begins to prize and care for it he puts it to some use and thereby employs it as a *means* to some end, and, depending upon his maturity, he estimates or values it *in that relation,* or as means to end.

The confusion that occurs in theory when shift is made from valuation related to desire and interest, to "enjoyment" independent of any relation to desire and interest is facilitated by the fact that attainment of the objectives of desire and interest (of valuation) is itself enjoyed. The nub of the confusion consists in isolating enjoyment from the conditions under which it occurs. Yet the enjoyment that is the consequence of fulfilment of a desire and realization of an interest is what it is because of satisfaction or making good of a need or lack—a satisfaction conditioned by effort directed by the idea of something as an end-in-view. In this sense "enjoyment" involves inherent connection with *lack* of possession; while, in the other sense, the "enjoyment" is that of sheer possession. Lack of possession and possession are tautologically incompatible. Moreover, it is a common experience that the object of desire when attained is *not* enjoyed, so common that there are proverbial sayings to the effect that enjoyment is in the seeking rather than in the obtaining. It is not necessary to take these sayings literally to be aware that the occurrences in question prove the existence of the difference between value as connected with desire and value as mere enjoyment. Finally, as matter of daily experience, enjoyments provide the primary material of *problems* of valuation. Quite independently of any "moral" issues, people continually ask themselves whether a given enjoyment is worth while or whether the conditions involved in its production are such as to make it a costly indulgence.

Reference was made earlier to the confusion in theory which results when "values" are *defined* in terms of vital impulses. (The ground offered is that the latter are conditions of the existence of values in the sense that they "spring from" vital impulse.) In the text from which the passage was quoted there occurs in close connection the following: "The ideal of rationality is itself as arbitrary, as much dependent upon the needs of a finite organization, as any other ideal." Implicit in this passage are two extraordinary conceptions. One of them is that an ideal is arbitrary if it is causally conditioned by actual existences and is relevant to actual needs of human beings. This conception is extraordinary because naturally it would be supposed that an ideal is arbitrary in the degree in which it is *not* connected with things which exist and is not related to concrete existential requirements. The other astounding conception is that the ideal of rationality is "arbitrary" because it is so conditioned. One would suppose it to be peculiarly true of the ideal of rationality that it is to be judged as to its reasonableness (versus its arbitrariness) on the ground of its function, of what it does, not on the ground of its origin. If rationality as an ideal or generalized end-in-view serves to direct conduct so that things experienced in consequence of conduct so directed are more reasonable in the concrete, nothing more can be asked of it. Both of the implied conceptions are so extraordinary that they can be understood only on the ground of some unexpressed preconceptions. As far as one can judge, these preconceptions are (i) that an ideal *ought* to be independent of existence, that is, a priori. The reference to the origin of ideals in vital impulses is in fact an effective criticism of this a priori view. But it provides a ground for calling ideas arbitrary only if the a priori view is accepted. (ii) The other preconception would seem to be an acceptance of the view that there are or ought to be "ends-in-themselves"; that is to say, ends or ideals that are not also means, which, as we have already seen, is precisely what an ideal is, if it is judged and valued in terms of its function. The sole way of arriving at the conclusion that a generalized end-in-view or ideal is arbitrary because of existential and empirical origin is by first laying down as an ultimate criterion that an end should also *not* be a means. The whole passage and the views of which it is a typical and influential manifestation is redolent of the survival of belief in "ends-in-themselves" as the solely and finally legitimate kind of ends.

VI. The Continuum of Ends-Means

Those who have read and enjoyed Charles Lamb's essay on the origin of roast pork have probably not been conscious that their enjoyment of its absurdity was due to perception of the absurdity of any "end" which is set up apart from the means by which it is to be attained and apart from its own further function as means. Nor is it probable that Lamb himself wrote the story as a deliberate travesty of the theories that make such a separation. Nonetheless, that is the whole point of the tale. The story, it will be remembered, is that roast pork was first enjoyed when a house in which pigs were confined was accidentally burned down. While searching in the ruins, the owners touched the pigs that had been roasted in the fire and scorched their fingers. Impulsively bringing their fingers to their mouths to cool them, they experienced a new taste. Enjoying the taste, they henceforth set themselves to building houses, inclosing pigs in them, and then burning the houses down. Now, if ends-in-view are what they are entirely apart from means, and have their value independently of valuation of means, there is nothing absurd, nothing ridiculous, in this procedure, for the end attained, the *de facto* termination, *was* eating and enjoying roast pork, and that was just the end desired. Only when the end attained is estimated in terms of the means employed—the building and burning-down of houses in comparison with other available means by which the desired result in view might be attained—is there anything absurd or unreasonable about the method employed.

The story has a direct bearing upon another point, the meaning of 'intrinsic.' *Enjoyment* of the taste of roast pork may be said to be immediate, although even so the enjoyment would be a somewhat troubled one, for those who have memory, by the thought of the needless cost at which it was obtained. But to pass from immediacy of enjoyment to something called "intrinsic value" is a leap for which there is no ground. The *value* of enjoyment of an object *as* an attained end is a value of something which in being an end, an outcome, stands in relation to the means of which it is the consequence. Hence if the object in question is prized *as* an end or "final" value, it is valued *in this relation* or as mediated. The first time roast pork was enjoyed, it was *not* an end-value, since by description it was not the result of desire, foresight, and intent. Upon subsequent occasions it was, by description, the outcome of prior foresight, desire, and effort, and hence occupied the position of an end-in-view. There are occasions in which previous effort enhances enjoyment of what is attained. But there are also many occasions in which persons find that, when they have attained something as an end, they have paid too high a price in effort and in sacrifice of other ends. In such situations *enjoyment* of the end attained is itself *valued*, for it is not taken in its immediacy but in terms of its cost—a fact fatal to its being regarded as "an end-in-itself," a self-contradictory term in any case.

The story throws a flood of light upon what is usually meant by the maxim "the end justifies the means" and also upon the popular objection to it. Applied in this case, it would mean that the value of the attained end, the eating of roast pork, was such as to warrant the price paid in the means by which it was attained—destruction of dwelling-houses and sacrifice of the values to which they contribute. The conception involved in the maxim that "the end justifies the means" is basically the same as that in the notion of ends-in-themselves; indeed, from a historical point of view, it is the fruit of the latter, for only the conception that certain things are ends-in-themselves can warrant the belief that the relation of ends-means is unilateral, proceeding exclusively from end to means. When the maxim is compared with empirically ascertained facts, it is equivalent to holding one of two views, both of which are incompatible with the facts. One of the views is that only the specially selected "end" held in view will actually be brought into existence by the means used, something miraculously intervening to prevent the means employed from having their other usual effects; the other (and more probable) view is that, as compared with the importance of the selected and uniquely prized end, other consequences may be completely ignored and brushed aside no matter how intrinsically obnoxious they are. This arbitrary selection of some one part of the attained consequences as *the* end and hence as the warrant of means used (no matter how objectionable are their *other* consequences) is the fruit of holding that *it*, as *the* end, is an end-in-itself, and hence possessed of "value" irrespective of all its existential relations. And this notion is inherent in *every* view that assumes that "ends" can be valued apart from appraisal of the things used as means in attaining them. The sole alternative to the view that *the* end is an arbitrarily selected part of actual consequences which *as* "the end" then justifies the use of means irrespective of the other consequences they produce, is that desires, ends-in-view, and consequences achieved be valued in turn as means of further consequences. The maxim referred to, under the guise of saying that ends, in the sense of actual consequences, provide the warrant for means employed—a correct position—actually says that some fragment of these actual consequences—a fragment arbitrarily selected because the heart has been set upon it—authorizes the use of means to obtain *it*, without the need of foreseeing and weighing other ends as consequences of the means used. It thus discloses in a striking manner the fallacy involved in the position that ends have value independent of appraisal of means involved and independent of their own further causal efficacy.

We are thus brought back to a point already set forth. In all the physical sciences (using 'physical' here as a synonym for *nonhuman*) it is now taken for granted that all "effects" are also "causes," or, stated more accurately, that nothing happens which is *final* in the sense that it is not part of an ongoing stream of events. If this principle, with the accompanying discrediting of belief in objects that are ends but not means, is employed in dealing with distinctive human phenomena, it necessarily follows that the distinction between ends and means is temporal and relational. Every condition that has to be brought into existence in order to serve as means is, *in that connection,* an object of desire and an end-in-view, while the end actually reached is a means to future ends as well as a test of valuations previously made. Since the end attained is a condition of further existential occurrences, it must be appraised as a potential obstacle and potential resource. If the notion of some objects as ends-in-themselves were abandoned, not merely in words but in all practical implications, human beings would for the first time in history be in a position to frame ends-in-view and form desires on the basis of empirically grounded propositions of the temporal relations of events to one another.

At any given time an adult person in a social group has certain ends which are so standardized by custom that they are taken for granted without examination, so that the only problems arising concern the best means for attaining them. In one group money-making would be such an end; in another group, possession of political power; in another group, advancement of scientific knowledge; in still another group, military prowess, etc. But such ends in any case are (i) more or less blank frameworks where the nominal "end" sets limits within which definite ends will fall, the latter being determined by appraisal of things as means; while (ii) as far as they simply express habits that have become established without critical examination of the relation of means and ends, they do not provide a model for a theory of valuation to follow. If a person moved by an experience of intense cold, which is highly objectionable, should momentarily judge it worth while to get warm by burning his house down, all that saves him from an act determined by a "compulsion neurosis" is the intellectual realization of what other consequences would ensue with the loss of his house. It is not necessarily a sign of insanity (as in the case cited) to isolate some event projected as an end out of the context of a world of moving changes in which it will in fact take place. But it is at least a sign of immaturity when an individual fails to view his end as also a moving condition of further consequences, thereby treating it as *final* in the sense in which 'final' signifies that the course of events has come to a complete stop. Human beings do indulge in such arrests. But to treat them as models for forming a theory of ends is to substitute a manipulation of ideas, abstracted from the contexts in which they arise and function, for the conclusions of observation of concrete facts. It is a sign either of insanity, immaturity, indurated routine, or of a fanaticism that is a mixture of all three.

Generalized ideas of ends and values undoubtedly exist. They exist not only as expressions of habit and as uncritical and probably invalid ideas but also in the same way as valid general ideas arise in any subject. Similar situations recur; desires and interests are carried over from one situation to another and progressively consolidated. A schedule of general ends results, the involved values being "abstract" in the sense of not being directly connected with any particular existing case but not in the sense of independence of all empirically existent cases. As with general ideas in the conduct of any natural science, these general ideas are used as intellectual instrumentalities in judgment of particular cases as the latter arise; they are, in effect, tools that direct and facilitate examination of things in the concrete while they are also developed and tested by the results of their application in these cases. Just as the natural sciences began a course of sure development when the dialectic of concepts ceased to be employed to arrive at conclusions about existential affairs and was employed instead as a means of arriving at a hypothesis fruitfully applicable to particulars, so it will be with the theory of human activities and relations. There is irony in the fact that the very continuity of experienced activities which enables general ideas of value to function as rules for evaluation of particular desires and ends should have become the source of a belief that desires, by the bare fact of their occurrence, confer value upon objects as ends, entirely independent of their contexts in the continuum of activities.

In this connection there is danger that the idea of "finality" be manipulated in a way analogous to the manipulation of the concepts of "immediacy" and "intrinsic" previously remarked upon. A value is *final* in the sense that it represents the conclusion of a process of analytic appraisals of conditions operating in a concrete case, the conditions including impulses and desires on one side and external conditions on the other. Any conclusion reached by an inquiry that is taken to warrant the conclusion is "final" for that case. "Final" here has logical force. The quality or property of value that is correlated with the *last* desire formed in the process of valuation is, tautologically, ultimate for that particular situation. It applies, however, to a specifiable temporal *means-end relation* and not to something which is an end per se. There is a fundamental difference between a final property or quality and the property or quality of finality.

The objection always brought against the view set forth is that, according to it, valuation activities and judgments are involved in a hopeless *regressus ad infinitum*. If, so it is said, there is no end which is not in turn a means, foresight has no place at which it can stop, and no end-in-view can be formed except by the most arbitrary of acts—an act so arbitrary that it mocks the claim of being a genuine valuation-proposition.

This objection brings us back to the conditions under which desires take shape and foreseen consequences are projected as ends to be reached. These conditions are those of need, deficit, and conflict. Apart from a condition of tension between a person and environing conditions there is, as we have seen, no occasion for evocation of desire for something else; there is nothing to induce the formation of an end, much less the formation of one end rather than any other out of the indefinite number of ends theoretically possible. Control of transformation of active tendencies into a desire in which a particular end-in-view is incorporated, is exercised by the needs or privations of an actual situation as its requirements are disclosed to observation. The "value" of different ends that suggest themselves is estimated or measured by the capacity they exhibit to guide action in making good, *satisfying*, in its literal sense, existing lacks. Here is the factor which cuts short the process of foreseeing and weighing ends-in-view in their function as means. Sufficient unto the day is the evil thereof and sufficient also is the *good* of that which does away with the existing evil. Sufficient because it is the means of instituting a complete situation or an integrated set of conditions.

Two illustrations will be given. A physician has to determine the value of various courses of action and their results in the case of a particular patient. He forms ends-in-view having the value that justifies their adoption, on the ground of what his examination discloses is the "matter" or "trouble" with the patient. He estimates the worth of what he undertakes on the ground of its capacity to produce a condition in which these troubles will not exist, in which, as it is ordinarily put, the patient will be "restored to health." He does not have an idea of health as an absolute end-in-itself, an absolute good by which to determine what to do. On the contrary, he forms his general idea of health as an end and a good (value) for the patient on the ground of what his techniques of examination have shown to be the troubles from which patients suffer and the means by which they are overcome. There is no need to deny that a general and abstract conception of health finally develops. But it is the outcome of a great number of definite, empirical inquiries, not an a priori preconditioning "standard" for carrying on inquiries.

The other illustration is more general. In all inquiry, even the most completely scientific, what is proposed as a conclusion (the end-in-view in that inquiry) is evaluated as to its worth on the ground of its ability to resolve the *problem* presented by the conditions under investigation. There is no a priori standard for determining the value of a proposed solution in concrete cases. A hypothetical possible solution, as an end-in-view, is used as a methodological means to direct further observations and experiments. Either it performs the function of resolution of a problem for the sake of which it is adopted and tried or it does not. Experience has shown that problems for the most part fall into certain recurrent kinds so that there are general principles which, it is believed, proposed solutions must satisfy in a particular case. There thus develops a sort of framework of conditions to be satisfied—a framework of reference which operates in an *empirically* regulative way in given cases. We may even say that it operates as an "a priori" principle, but in exactly the same sense in which rules for the conduct of a technological art are both empirically antecedent and controlling in a given case of the art. While there is no a priori standard of health with which the actual state of human beings can be compared so as to determine whether they are well or ill, or in what respect they are ill, there have developed, out of past experience, certain criteria which are operatively applicable in new cases as they arise. Ends-in-view are appraised or valued as *good* or *bad* on the ground of their serviceability in the direction of behavior dealing with states of affairs found to be objectionable because of some lack or conflict in them. They are appraised as fit or unfit, proper or improper, *right* or *wrong,* on the ground of their *requiredness* in accomplishing this end.

Considering the all but omnipresence of troubles and "evils" in human experience (evils in the sense of deficiencies, failures, and frustrations), and considering the amount of time that has been spent explaining them away, theories of human activity have been strangely oblivious of the concrete function troubles are capable of exercising when they are taken as *problems* whose conditions and consequences are explored with a view to finding methods of solution. The two instances just cited, the progress of medical art and of scientific inquiry, are most instructive on this point. As long as actual events were supposed to be judged by comparison with some absolute end-value as a standard and norm, no sure progress was made. When standards of health and of satisfaction of conditions of knowledge were conceived in terms of analytic observation of existing conditions, disclosing a trouble statable in a problem, criteria of judging were progressively self-corrective through the very process of use in observation to locate the source of the trouble and to indicate the effective means of dealing with it. These means form the content of the specific end-in-view, not some abstract standard or ideal.

This emphasis upon the function of needs and conflicts as the controlling factor in institution of ends and values does not signify that the latter are themselves negative in content and import. While they are framed with reference to a negative factor, deficit, want, privation, and conflict, their function is positive, and the resolution effected by performance of their function is positive. To attempt to gain an end *directly* is to put into operation the very conditions that are the source of the experienced trouble, thereby strengthening them and at most changing the outward form in which they manifest themselves. Ends-in-view framed with a negative *reference* (i.e., to some trouble or problem) are means which inhibit the operation of conditions producing the obnoxious result; they enable positive conditions to operate as resources and thereby to effect a result which is, in the highest possible sense, positive in content. The content of the end as an object *held in view* is intellectual or methodological; the content of the attained outcome or the end *as consequence* is existential. It is positive in the degree in which it marks the doing-away of the need and conflict that evoked the *end-in-view*. The negative factor operates as a condition of forming the appropriate *idea* of an end; the idea when acted upon determines a positive outcome.

The attained end or consequence is always an organization of activities, where organization is a coordination of all activities which enter as factors. The *end-in-view* is that particular activity which operates as a coordinating factor of all other subactivities involved. Recognition of the end as a coordination or unified organization of activities, and of the end-in-view as the special activity which is the means of effecting this coordination, does away with any appearance of paradox that seems to be attached to the idea of a temporal continuum of activities in which each successive stage is equally end and means. The *form* of an attained end or consequence is always the same: that of adequate coordination. The content or involved matter of each successive result differs from that of its predecessors; for, while it is a *reinstatement* of a unified ongoing action, after a period of interruption through conflict and need, it is also an *enactment* of a new state of affairs. It has the qualities and properties appropriate to its being the consummatory resolution of a previous state of activity in which there was a peculiar need, desire, and end-in-view. In the continuous temporal process of organizing activities into a coordinated and coordinating unity, a constituent activity is both an end and a means: an end, in so far as it is temporally and relatively a close; a means, in so far as it provides a condition to be taken into account in further activity.

Instead of there being anything strange or paradoxical in the existence of situations in which means are constituents of the very end-objects they have helped to bring into existence, such situations occur whenever behavior succeeds in intelligent projection of ends-in-view that direct activity to resolution of the antecedent trouble. The cases in which ends and means fall apart are the abnormal ones, the ones which deviate from activity which is intelligently conducted. Wherever, for example, there is sheer drudgery, there is separation of the required and necessary means from both the end-in-view and the end attained. Wherever, on the other side, there is a so-called "ideal" which is utopian and a matter of fantasy, the same separation occurs, now from the side of the so-called *end*. Means that do not become constituent elements of the very ends or consequences they produce form what are called "necessary evils," their "necessity" being relative to the existing state of knowledge and art. They are comparable to scaffoldings that had to be later torn down, but which were necessary in erection of buildings until elevators were introduced. The latter remained for use in the building erected and were employed as means of transporting materials that in turn became an integral part of the building. Results or consequences which at one time were necessarily waste products in the production of the particular thing desired were utilized in the light of the development of human experience and intelligence as means for further desired consequences. The generalized ideal and standard of economy-efficiency which operates in every advanced art and technology is equivalent, upon analysis, to the conception of means that are constituents of ends attained and of ends that are usable as means to further ends.

It must also be noted that *activity* and *activities,* as these words are employed in the foregoing account, involve, like any actual behavior, existential materials, as breathing involves air; walking, the earth; buying and selling, commodities; inquiry, things investigated, etc. No human activity operates in a vacuum; it acts in the world and has materials upon which and through which it produces results. On the other hand, no material—air, water, metal, wood, etc.—is *means* save as it is employed in some human activity to accomplish something. When "organization of activities" is mentioned, it always includes within itself organization of the materials existing in the world in which we live. That organization which is the "final" value for each concrete situation of valuation thus forms part of the existential conditions that have to be taken into account in further formation of desires and interests or valuations. In the degree in which a particular valuation is invalid because of inconsiderate shortsighted investigation of things in their relation of means-end, difficulties are put in the way of subsequent reasonable valuations. To the degree in which desires and interests are formed after critical survey of the conditions which as means determine the actual outcome, the more smoothly continuous become subsequent activities, for consequences attained are then such as are evaluated more readily as means in the continuum of action.

VII. Theory of Valuation as Outline of a Program

Because of the confusion which affects current discussion of the problem of valuation, the analysis undertaken in the present study has been obliged to concern itself to a considerable extent with tracking the confusion to its source. This is necessary in order that empirical inquiry into facts which are taken for granted by common sense may be freed from irrelevant and confusing associations. The more important conclusions may be summarized as follows.

1. Even if "value-expressions" were ejaculatory and such as to influence the conduct of other persons, genuine propositions about such expressions would be possible. We could investigate whether or not they had the effect intended; and further examination would be able to discover the differential conditions of the cases that were successful in obtaining the intended outcome and those that were not. It is useful to discriminate between linguistic expressions which are "emotive" and those which are "scientific." Nevertheless, even if the former said nothing whatever, they would, like other natural events, be capable of becoming the subject matter of "scientific" propositions as a result of an examination of their conditions and effects.

2. Another view connects valuation and value-expressions with desires and interests. Since desire and interest are behavioral phenomena (involving at the very least a "motor" aspect), the valuations they produce are capable of being investigated as to *their* respective conditions and results. Valuations are empirically observable patterns of behavior and may be studied as such. The propositions that result are *about* valuations but are not of themselves value-propositions in any sense marking them off from other matter-of-fact propositions.

3. Value-propositions of the distinctive sort exist whenever things are appraised as to their suitability and serviceability as means, for such propositions are not about things or events that have occurred or that already exist (although they cannot be validly instituted apart from propositions of the kind mentioned in the previous sentence), but are about things *to be* brought into existence. Moreover, while they are logically conditioned upon matter-of-fact predictions, they are more than simple predictions, for the things in question are such as will *not* take place, under the given circumstances, except through the intervention of some personal act. The difference is similar to that between a proposition predicting that in *any* case a certain eclipse will take place and a proposition that the eclipse will be seen or experienced by certain human beings in case the latter intervene to perform certain actions. While valuation-propositions as appraisals of means occur in all arts and technologies and are grounded in strictly physical propositions (as in advanced engineering technologies), nevertheless they are distinct from the latter in that they inherently involve the means-end relationship.

4. Wherever there are desires, there are *ends-in-view*, not simply effects produced as in the case of sheer impulse, appetite, and routine habit. Ends-in-view as anticipated results reacting upon a given desire are *ideational* by definition or tautologically. The involved foresight, forecast or anticipation is warranted, like any other intellectual inferent factor, in the degree in which it is based upon propositions that are conclusions of adequate observational activities. Any given desire is what it is in its actual content or "object" *because* of its ideational constituents. Sheer impulse or appetite may be described as affective-motor; but any theory that connects valuation with desire and interest by that very fact connects valuation with behavior which is affective-

ideational-motor. This fact proves the *possibility* of the existence of distinctive valuation-propositions. In view of the role played by ends-in-view in directing the activities that contribute either to the realization or to the frustration of desire, the *necessity* for valuation-propositions is proved if desires are to be intelligent, and purposes are to be other than shortsighted and irrational.

5. The required appraisal of desires and ends-in-view, as means of the activities by which actual results are produced, is dependent upon observation of consequences attained when they are compared and contrasted with the content of ends-in-view. Careless, inconsiderate action is that which foregoes the inquiry that determines the points of agreement and disagreement between the desire actually formed (and hence the valuation actually made) and the things brought into existence by acting upon it. Since desire and valuation of objects proposed as ends are inherently connected, and since desire and ends-in-view need to be appraised as means to ends (an appraisal made on the basis of warranted physical generalizations) the valuation of ends-in-view is tested by consequences that actually ensue. It is verified to the degree in which there is agreement upon results. Failure to agree, in case deviations are carefully observed, is not mere failure but provides the means for improving the formation of later desires and ends-in-view.

The net outcome is (i) that the problem of valuation in general as well as in particular cases concerns things that sustain to one another the relation of means-ends; that (ii) ends are determinable only on the ground of the means that are involved in bringing them about; and that (iii) desires and interests must themselves be evaluated as means in their interaction with external or environing conditions. Ends-in-view, as distinct from ends as accomplished results, themselves function as directive means; or, in ordinary language, as *plans*. Desires, interests, and environing conditions as means are modes of action, and hence are to be conceived in terms of energies which are capable of reduction to homogeneous and comparable terms. Coordination or organizations of energies, proceeding from the two sources of the organism and the environment, are thus both means and attained result or "end" in all cases of valuation, the two kinds of energy being theoretically (if not as yet completely so in practice) capable of statement in terms of physical units.

The conclusions stated do not constitute a complete theory of valuation. They do, however, state the conditions which such a theory must satisfy. An actual theory can be completed only when inquiries into things sustaining the relation of ends-means have been systematically conducted and their results brought to bear upon the formation of desires and ends. For the theory of valuation is itself an intellectual or methodological means and as such can be developed and perfected only in and by use. Since that use does not now exist in any adequate way, the theoretical consideration advanced and conclusions reached outline a program to be undertaken, rather than a complete theory. The undertaking can be carried out only by regulated guidance of the formation of interests and purposes in the concrete. The prime condition of this undertaking (in contrast with the current theory of the relation of valuation to desire and interest) is recognition that desire and interest are not given ready-made at the outset, and a fortiori are not, as they may at first appear, starting-points, original data, or premises of any theory of valuation, for desire always emerges within a prior system of activities or interrelated energies. It arises within a *field* when the field is disrupted or is menaced with disruption, when conflict introduces the tension of need or threatens to introduce it. An interest represents not just a desire but a set of interrelated desires which have been found in experience to produce, because of their connection with one another, a definite order in the processes of continuing behavior.

The test of the existence of a valuation and the nature of the latter is actual behavior as that is subject to observation. Is the existing field of activities (including environing conditions) *accepted*, where "acceptance" consists in effort to maintain it against adverse conditions? Or is it *rejected*, where "rejection" consists of effort to get rid of it and to produce another behavioral field? And in the latter case, what is the actual field to which, as an end, desire-efforts (or the organization of desire-efforts constituting an interest) are directed? Determination of this field as an objective of behavior determines *what* is valued. Until there is actual or threatened shock and disturbance of a situation, there is a green light to go ahead in immediate act— overt action. There is no need, no desire, and no valuation, just as where there is no doubt, there is no cause of inquiry. Just as the problem which evokes inquiry is related to an empirical situation in which the problem presents itself, so desire and the projection of ends as consequences to be reached are relative to a concrete situation and to its need for transformation. The burden of proof lies, so to speak, on occurrence of conditions that are impeding, obstructive, and that introduce conflict and need. Examination of the situation in respect to the conditions that constitute lack and need and thus serve as positive means for formation of an attainable end or outcome, is the method by which warranted (required and effective) desires and ends-in-view are formed: by which, in short, valuation takes place.

The confusions and mistakes in existing theories, which have produced the need for the previous prolonged analysis, arise very largely from taking desire and interest as original instead of in the contextual situations in which they arise. When they are so taken, they become ultimate in relation to valuation. Being taken, so to speak, at large, there is nothing by which we can empirically check or test them. If desire were of this original nature, if it were independent of the structure and requirements of some concrete empirical situation and hence had no function to perform with reference to an existential situation, then insistence upon the necessity of an ideational or intellectual factor in every desire and the consequent necessity for fulfilment of the empirical conditions of its validity would be as superfluous and irrelevant as critics have said it is. The insistence might then be, what it has been called, a "moral" bias springing from an interest in the "reform" of individuals and society. But since in empirical fact there are no desires and interests apart from some field of activities in which they occur and in which they function, either as poor or as good means, the insistence in question is simply and wholly in the interest of a correct empirical account of what actually exists as over against what turns out to be, when examined, a dialectical manipulation of *concepts* of desire and interest at large, a procedure which is all that is possible when desire is taken in isolation from its existential context.

It is a common occurrence in the history of theories that an error at one extreme calls out a complementary error at the other extreme. The type of theory just considered isolates desires as sources of valuation from any existential context and hence from any possibility of intellectual control of their contents and objectives. It thereby renders valuation an arbitrary matter. It says in effect that any desire is just as "good" as any other in respect to the value it institutes. Since desires—and their organization into interests—are the sources of human action, this view, if it were systematically acted upon, would produce disordered behavior to the point of complete chaos. The fact that in spite of conflicts, and unnecessary conflicts, there is not complete disorder is proof that actually some degree of intellectual respect for existing conditions and consequences does operate as a control factor in formation of desires and valuations. However, the implications of the theory in the direction of intellectual and practical disorder are such as to evoke a contrary theory, one, however, which has the same fundamental postulate of the isolation of valuation from concrete empirical situations, their potentialities, and their requirements. This is the theory of "ends-in-themselves" as ultimate standards of all valuation—a theory which denies implicitly or explicitly that desires have anything to do with "final values" unless and until they are subjected to the external control of a priori absolute ends as standards and ideals for their valuation. This theory, in its endeavor to escape from the frying pan of disordered valuations, jumps into the fire of absolutism. It confers the simulation of final and complete rational authority upon certain interests of certain persons or groups at the expense of all others: a view which, in turn, because of the consequences it entails, strengthens the notion that no intellectual and empirically reasonable control of desires, and hence of valuations and value-properties, is possible. The seesaw between theories which by definition are not empirically testable (since they are a priori) and professed empirical theories that unwittingly substitute conclusions derived from the bare *concept* of desire for the results of observation of desires in the concrete is thus kept up. The astonishing thing about the a priori theory (astonishing if the history of philosophical thought be omitted from the survey) is its complete neglect of the fact that valuations are constant phenomena of human behavior, personal and associated, and are capable of rectification and development by use of the resources provided by knowledge of physical relations.

VIII. Valuation and the Conditions of Social Theory

We are thus brought to the problem which, as was shown in the opening section of this study, is back of the present interest in the problem of valuation and values, namely, the possibility of genuine and grounded propositions about the purposes, plans, measures, and policies which influence human activity whenever the latter is other than merely impulsive or routine. A theory of valuation *as* theory can only set forth the conditions which a method of formation of desires and interests must observe in concrete situations. The problem of the existence of such a method is all one with the problem of the possibility of genuine propositions which have as their subject matter the intelligent conduct of human activities, whether personal or associated. The view that value in the sense of *good* is inherently connected with that which promotes, furthers, assists, a course of activity, and that value in the sense of *right* is inherently connected with that which is needed, required, in the maintenance of a course of activity, is not in itself novel. Indeed, it is suggested by the very etymology of the word *value*, associated as it is with the words 'avail,' 'valor,' 'valid,' and 'invalid.' What the foregoing discussion has added to the idea is proof that if, and *only* if, valuation is taken in this sense, are empirically grounded propositions about desires and interests as sources of valuations possible— such propositions being grounded in the degree in which they employ scientific physical generalizations as means of forming propositions about activities which are correlated as ends-means. The resulting general propositions provide rules for valuation of the aims, purposes, plans, and policies that direct intelligent human activity. They are not rules in the sense that they enable us to tell directly, or upon bare inspection, the values of given particular ends (a foolish quest that underlies the belief in a priori values as ideals and standards); they are rules of methodic procedure in the conduct of the investigations that determine the respective conditions and consequences of various modes of behavior. It does not purport to solve the problems of valuation in and of itself; it does claim to state conditions that inquiry must satisfy if these problems are to be resolved, and to serve in this way as a leading principle in conduct of such inquiries.

I. Valuations exist in fact and are capable of empirical observation so that propositions about them are empirically verifiable. What individuals and groups hold dear or prize and the grounds upon which they prize them are capable, in principle, of ascertainment, no matter how great the *practical* difficulties in the way. But, upon the whole, in the past values have been determined by customs, which are then commended because they favor some special interest, the commendation being attended with coercion or exhortation or with a mixture of both. The practical difficulties in the way of scientific inquiry into valuations are great, so great that they are readily mistaken for inherent theoretical obstacles. Moreover, such knowledge as does exist about valuations is far from organized, to say nothing about its being adequate. The notion that valuations do not exist in empirical fact and that therefore value-conceptions have to be imported from a source outside experience is one of the most curious beliefs the mind of man has ever entertained. Human beings are continuously engaged in valuations. The latter supply the primary material for operations of further valuations and for the general theory of valuation.

Knowledge of these valuations does not of itself, as we have seen, provide valuation-propositions; it is rather of the nature of historical and cultural-anthropological knowledge. But such factual knowledge is a *sine qua non* of ability to formulate valuation-propositions. This statement only involves recognition that past experience, when properly analyzed and ordered, is the sole guide we have in future experience. An individual within the limits of his personal experience revises his desires and purposes as he becomes aware of the consequences they have produced in the past. This knowledge is what enables him to foresee probable consequences of his prospective activities and to direct his conduct accordingly. The ability to form valid propositions about the relation of present desires and purposes to future consequences depends in turn upon ability to analyze these present desires and purposes into their constituent elements. When they are taken in gross, foresight is correspondingly coarse and indefinite. The history of science shows that power of prediction has increased *pari passu* with analysis of gross qualitative events into elementary constituents. Now, in the absence of adequate and organized knowledge of human valuations as occurrences that have taken place, it is a fortiori impossible that there be valid propositions formulating new valuations in terms of consequences of specified causal conditions. On account of the continuity of human activities, personal and associated, the import of present valuations cannot be validly stated until they are placed in the perspective of the past valuation-events with which they are continuous. Without this perception, the future perspective, i.e., the consequences of present and new valuations, is indefinite. In the degree in which existing desires and interests (and hence valuations) can be judged in their connection with past conditions, they are seen in a context which enables them to be revaluated on the ground of evidence capable of observation and empirical test.

Suppose, for example, that it be ascertained that a particular set of current valuations have, as their antecedent historical conditions, the interest of a small group or special class in maintaining certain exclusive privileges and advantages, and that this maintenance has the effect of limiting both the range of the desires of others and their capacity to actualize them. Is it not obvious that this knowledge of conditions and consequences would surely lead to revaluation of the desires and ends that had been assumed to be authoritative sources of valuation? Not that such revaluation would of necessity take effect immediately. But, when valuations that exist at a given time are found to lack the support they have previously been supposed to have, they exist in a context that is highly adverse to their continued maintenance. In the long run the effect is similar to a warier attitude that develops toward certain bodies of water as the result of knowledge that these bodies of water contain disease germs. If, on the other hand, investigation shows that a given set of existing valuations, including the rules for their enforcement, be such as to release individual potentialities of desire and interest, and does so in a way that contributes to mutual reinforcement of the desires and interests of all members of a group, it is impossible for this knowledge not to serve as a bulwark of the particular set of valuations in question, and to induce intensified effort to sustain them in existence.

II. These considerations lead to the central question: What are the conditions that have to be met so that knowledge of past and existing valuations becomes an instrumentality of valuation in formation of new desires and interests—of desires and interests that the test of experience show to be best worth fostering? It is clear upon our view that no abstract theory of valuation can be put side by side, so to speak, with existing valuations as the standard for judging them.

The answer is that improved valuation must grow out of existing valuations, subjected to critical methods of investigation that bring them into systematic relations with one another. Admitting that these valuations are largely and probably, in the main, defective, it might at first sight seem as if the idea that improvement would spring from bringing them into connection with one another is like recommending that one lift himself by his bootstraps. But such an impression arises only because of failure to consider how they actually may be brought into relation with one another, namely, by examination of their respective conditions and consequences. Only by following this path will they be reduced to such homogeneous terms that they are comparable with one another.

This method, in fact, simply carries over to human or social phenomena the methods that have proved successful in dealing with the subject matter of physics and chemistry. In these fields before the rise of modern science there was a mass of facts which were isolated and seemingly independent of one another. Systematic advance dates from the time when conceptions that formed the content of theory were derived from the phenomena themselves and were then employed as hypotheses for relating together the otherwise separate matters-of-fact. When, for example, ordinary drinking water is operatively regarded as H_2O what has happened is that water is related to an immense number of other phenomena so that inferences and predictions are indefinitely expanded and, at the same time, made subject to empirical tests. In the field of human activities there are at present an immense number of facts of desires and purposes existing in rather complete isolation from one another. But there are no hypotheses of the same empirical order which are capable of relating them to one another so that the resulting propositions will serve as methodic controls of the formation of future desires and purposes, and, thereby, of new valuations. The material is ample. But the means for bringing its constituents into such connections that fruit is borne are lacking. This lack of means for bringing actual valuations into relation with one another is partly the cause and partly the effect of belief in standards and ideals of value that lie outside ("above" is the usual term) actual valuations. It is cause in so far as some method of control of desires and purposes is such an important desideratum that in the absence of an empirical method, *any* conception that seems to satisfy the need is grasped at. It is the effect in that a priori theories, once they are formed and have obtained prestige, serve to conceal the necessity for concrete methods of relating valuations and, by so doing, provide intellectual instruments for placing impulses and desires in a context where the very place they occupy affects their evaluation.

However, the difficulties that stand in the way are, in the main, practical. They are supplied by traditions, customs, and institutions which persist without being subjected to a systematic empirical investigation and which constitute the most influential source of further desires and ends. This is supplemented by a priori theories serving, upon the whole, to "rationalize" these desires and ends so as to give them apparent intellectual status and prestige. Hence it is worth while to note that the same obstacles once existed in the subject matters now ruled by scientific methods. Take, as an outstanding example, the difficulties experienced in getting a hearing for the Copernican astronomy a few centuries ago. Traditional and customary beliefs which were sanctioned and maintained by powerful institutions regarded the new scientific ideas as a menace. Nevertheless, the methods which yielded propositions verifiable in terms of actual observations and experimental evidence maintained themselves, widened their range, and gained continually in influence.

The propositions which have resulted and which now form the substantial content of physics, of chemistry, and, to a growing extent, of biology, provide the very means by which the change which is required can be introduced into beliefs and ideas purporting to deal with human and social phenomena. Until natural science had attained to something approaching its present estate, a grounded empirical theory of valuation, capable of serving in turn as a method of regulating the production of new valuations, was out of the question. Desires and interests produce consequences only when the activities in which they are expressed take effect in the environment by interacting with physical conditions. As long as there was no adequate knowledge of physical conditions and no well-grounded propositions regarding their relations to one another (no known "laws"), the kind of forecast of the consequences of alternative desires and purposes involved in their evaluation was impossible. When we note how recently—in comparison with the length of time man has existed on earth—the arts and technologies employed in strictly physical affairs have had scientific support, the backward condition of the arts connected with the social and political affairs of men provides no ground for surprise.

Psychological science is now in much the same state in which astronomy, physics, and chemistry were when they first emerged as genuinely experimental sciences, yet without such a science systematic theoretical control of valuation is impossible; for without competent psychological knowledge the force of the human factors which interact with environing nonhuman conditions to produce consequences cannot be estimated. This statement is purely truistic, since knowledge of the human conditions *is* psychological science. For over a century, moreover, the ideas central to what passed for psychological knowledge were such as actually obstructed that foresight of consequences which is required to control the formation of ends-in-view. For when psychological subject matter was taken to form a psychical or mentalistic realm set over against the physical environment, inquiry, such as it was, was deflected into the metaphysical problem of the possibility of interaction between the mental and the physical and away from the problem central in evaluation, namely, that of discovering the concrete interactions between human behavior and environing conditions which determine the actual consequences of desires and purposes. A grounded theory of the phenomena of human behavior is as much a prerequisite of a theory of valuation as is a theory of the behavior of physical (in the sense of nonhuman) things. The development of a science of the phenomena of living creatures was an unqualified prerequisite of the development of a sound psychology. Until biology supplied the material facts which lie between the nonhuman and the human, the apparent traits of the latter were so different from those of the former that the doctrine of a complete gulf between the two seemed to be the only plausible one. The missing link in the chain of knowledge that terminates in grounded valuation propositions is the biological. As that link is in process of forging, we may expect the time soon to arrive in which the obstacles to development of an empirical theory of valuation will be those of habits and traditions that flow from institutional and class interests rather than from intellectual deficiencies.

Need for a theory of human relations in terms of a sociology which might perhaps instructively be named cultural anthropology is a further condition of the development of a theory of valuation as an effective instrumentality, for human organisms live in a cultural environment. There is no desire and no interest which, in its distinction from raw impulse and strictly organic appetite, is not what it is because of transformation effected in the latter by their interaction with the cultural environment. When current theories are examined which, quite properly, relate valuation with desires and interests, nothing is more striking than their neglect—so extensive as to be systematic—of the role of cultural conditions and institutions in the shaping of desires and ends and thereby of valuations. This neglect is perhaps the most convincing evidence that can be had of the substitution of dialectical manipulation of the concept of desire for investigation of desires and valuations as concretely existent facts. Furthermore, the notion that an adequate theory of human behavior—including particularly the phenomena of desire and purpose—can be formed by considering individuals apart from the cultural setting in which they live, move, and have their being—a theory which may justly be called metaphysical individualism— has united with the metaphysical belief in a mentalistic realm to keep valuation-phenomena in subjection to unexamined traditions, conventions, and institutionalized customs.[2] The separa-

2. The statement, sometimes made, that metaphysical sentences are "meaningless" usually fails to take account of the fact that culturally speaking they are very far from being devoid of meaning, in the sense of having significant cultural effects. Indeed, they are so far from being meaningless in this respect that there is no short dialectic cut to their elimination, since the latter can be accomplished only by concrete applications of scientific method which modify cultural conditions. The view that sentences having a nonempirical reference are meaningless, is sound in the sense that what they purport or pretend to mean cannot be given intelligibility, and this fact is presumably what is intended by those who hold this view. Interpreted as symptoms or signs of actually existent conditions, they may be and usually are highly significant, and the most effective criticism of them is disclosure of the conditions of which they are evidential.

tion alleged to exist between the "world of facts" and the "realm of values" will disappear from human beliefs only as valuation-phenomena are seen to have their immediate source in biological modes of behavior and to owe their concrete content to the influence of cultural conditions.

The hard-and-fast impassable line which is supposed by some to exist between "emotive" and "scientific" language is a reflex of the gap which now exists between the intellectual and the emotional in human relations and activities. The split which exists in present social life between ideas and emotions, especially between ideas that have *scientific* warrant and uncontrolled emotions that dominate practice, the split between the affectional and the cognitive, is probably one of the chief sources of the maladjustments and unendurable strains from which the world is suffering. I doubt if an adequate explanation upon the psychological side of the rise of dictatorships can be found which does not take account of the fact that the strain produced by separation of the intellectual and the emotional is so intolerable that human beings are willing to pay almost any price for the semblance of even its temporary annihilation. We are living in a period in which emotional loyalties and attachments are centered on objects that no longer command that intellectual loyalty which has the sanction of the methods which attain valid conclusions in scientific inquiry, while ideas that have their origin in the rationale of inquiry have not as yet succeeded in acquiring the force that only emotional ardor provides. The *practical* problem that has to be faced is the establishment of cultural conditions that will support the kinds of behavior in which emotions and ideas, desires and appraisals, are integrated.

If, then, discussion in the earlier sections of this study seems to have placed chief emphasis upon the importance of valid *ideas* in formation of the desires and interests which are the sources of valuation, and to have centered attention chiefly upon the possibility and the necessity of control of this ideational factor by empirically warranted matters-of-fact, it is because the *empirical* (as distinct from a priori) theory of valuation is currently stated in terms of desire as emotional in isolation from the ideational. In fact and in net outcome, the previous discussion does not point in the least to supersession of the emotive by the intellectual. Its only and complete import is the need for their integration in behavior—behavior in which, according to common speech, the head and the heart work together, in which, to use more technical language, prizing and appraising unite in direction of action. That growth of knowledge of the physical—in the sense of the nonpersonal—has limited the range of freedom of human action in relation to such things as light, heat, electricity, etc., is so absurd in view of what has actually taken place that no one holds it. The operation of desire in producing the valuations that influence human action will also be liberated when they, too, are ordered by verifiable propositions regarding matters-of-fact.

The chief *practical* problem with which the present *Encyclopedia* is concerned, the unification of science, may justly be said to centre here, for at the present time the widest gap in knowledge is that which exists between humanistic and nonhumanistic subjects. The breach will disappear, the gap be filled, and science be manifest as an operating unity in fact and not merely in idea when the conclusions of impersonal nonhumanistic science are employed in guiding the course of distinctively human behavior, that, namely, which is influenced by emotion and desire in the framing of means and ends; for desire, having ends-in-view, and hence involving valuations, is the characteristic that marks off human from nonhuman behavior. On the other side, the science that is put to distinctively human use is that in which warranted ideas about the nonhuman world are integrated with emotion as human traits. In this integration not only is science itself *a* value (since it is the expression and the fulfilment of a special human desire and interest) but it is the supreme means of the valid determination of all valuations in all aspects of human and social life.

Selected Bibliography

Ayer, A. J. *Language, Truth and Logic*. New York, 1936.

Dewey, John. *Essays in Experimental Logic*. Pp. 349–89. Chicago, 1916.

————. *Experience and Nature*. "Lectures upon the Paul Carus Foundation, First Series." 1st ed., Chicago, 1925; 2d ed., New York, 1929.

————. *Human Nature and Conduct*. New York, 1922.

————. *Logical Conditions of a Scientific Treatment of Morality*. Chicago, 1903. Reprinted from *The Decennial Publications of the University of Chicago, First Series*, III, 115–39.

————. *The Quest for Certainty.* New York, 1929.

————. *Art as Experience.* New York, 1934.

Dewey, John, and Tufts, J. H. *Ethics.* Rev. ed. New York, 1932.

Dewey, John, *et al. Creative Intelligence.* New York, 1917.

Joergensen, J. "Imperatives and Logic," *Erkenntnis,* VII (1938), 288–96.

Kallen, H. "Value and Existence in Philosophy, Art, and Religion," in *Creative Intelligence,* John Dewey *et al.* New York, 1917.

Köhler, W. *The Place of Value in a World of Facts.* New York, 1938.

Kraft, Viktor. *Die Grundlagen einer wissenschaftlichen Wertlehre.* Vienna, 1937.

Laird, John. *The Idea of Value.* Cambridge, 1929.

Mead, G. H. "Scientific Method and the Moral Sciences," *International Journal of Ethics,* XXXIII (1923), 229–47.

Moore, G. E. *Principia Ethica.* London, 1903.

Neurath, Otto. *Empirische Soziologie; der wissenschaftliche Gehalt der Geschichte und Nationalökonomie.* Vienna, 1931.

Pell, O. A. H. *Value-Theory and Criticism.* New York, 1930.

Perry, Ralph Barton. *General Theory of Value.* New York, 1926. Also articles in the *International Journal of Ethics* (1931), *Journal of Philosophy* (1931), and *Philosophical Review* (1932).

Prall, David W. "A Study in the Theory of Value," *University of California Publications in Philosophy,* III, No. 2 (1918), 179–290.

————. "In Defense of a 'Worthless' Theory of Value," *Journal of Philosophy,* XX (1923), 128–37.

Reid, John. *A Theory of Value.* New York, 1938.

Russell, B. *Philosophical Essays.* New York, 1910.

Schlick, Moritz. *Fragen der Ethik.* Vienna, 1930. English trans., *Problems of Ethics.* New York, 1939.

Stuart, Henry Waldgrave. "Valuation as a Logical Process," in *Studies in Logical Theory,* ed. John Dewey *et al. The Decennial Publications of the University of Chicago,* Vol. XI. Chicago, 1903.

Essays

The Determination of Ultimate Values or Aims through Antecedent or A Priori Speculation or through Pragmatic or Empirical Inquiry

I. Alternative Conceptions of Philosophy

Philosophy is frequently presented as the systematic endeavor to obtain knowledge of what is called Ultimate and Eternal Reality. Many thinkers have defended this conception of its task and aim on the ground that human life can derive stable guidance only by means of ideals and standards that have their source in Ultimate Reality. On the other hand, scepticism about the worth of philosophy usually rests upon denial of the possibility of attaining such knowledge. When the business of philosophy is conceived in this manner, philosophical oppositions and controversies are believed to spring from conflicting conceptions of the nature of Ultimate and Perfect Reality. One school holds that it is spiritual; another that it is material. One school of thought holds that the particulars of the Universe are held together only externally by mechanical bonds; another school holds that they are organically united because of common subordination to a final controlling end and purpose that they all serve. Such divisions are inevitable as long as philosophy is defined as knowledge of supreme reality supposed to be beyond and beneath the things of experience.

But there is an alternative conception of philosophy, and the deepest philosophic divisions do not have their origin in a different conception of ultimate reality, but in the conflict between two opposed conceptions of what philosophy is about, its aim and task. According to this alternative view, the work of philosophy is confined to the things of actual experience. Its business is criti-

[First published as chapter 38 in *Thirty-Seventh Yearbook of the National Society for the Study of Education,* ed. Guy Montrose Whipple, pt. 2, *The Scientific Movement in Education* (Bloomington, Ill.: Public School Publishing Co., 1938), pp. 471–85.]

cism of experience as it exists at a given time and constructive projection of values, which, when acted upon, will render experience more unified, stable, and progressive. Defects and conflicts in experience as it exists demand thoroughgoing criticism of its contents and procedures. This phase of inquiry is not, however, final; criticism does not end with mere intellectual discrimination. It provides the basis for projection of values as yet unrealized, values that are to be translated into ends that move men to action. Philosophy thus conceived does not involve a flight and escape to that which is beyond experience. It is concerned with making the most possible out of experience, personal and social. Everyday homely objects and occupations of everyday life are possessed of potentialities that, under the guidance of deliberate and systematic intelligence, will make life fuller, richer, and more unified.

There are defects and conflicts in abundance in experience as it exists at any time. But they are to be dealt with in terms of experience, not by running away from it. They are a challenge to project, through systematic reflection, a better ordered and more inclusive experience. Systematic endeavor to meet this challenge constitutes the reality of genuine philosophy. The first-mentioned idea of the work of philosophy rests upon distrust of the capacity of experience to generate fundamental values and to direct deliberate effort in behalf of their realization. This distrust involves lack of loyalty to practical intelligence, substituting in its place dependence upon so-called *a priori* intuitions and upon an alleged faculty of pure Reason that grasps absolute non-empirical truth.

Hence, there is a further fundamental difference between the two ideas of the business of philosophy. According to the first-mentioned view, knowledge, provided that it is knowledge of ultimate reality, is the final goal, complete in independence of practical activity. According to the other view, thought and knowledge cannot themselves resolve the discords of existence and life. Even if there were a Reality beyond and behind the things of the experienced world and even if knowledge of it were possible, knowledge would leave the defects and inconsistencies of the world in which we live just what they were before. Only action can change things in the direction of unity and stability. To accomplish this result, action must be directed by leading principles, and such action, as the fruit of reflection upon actual experience, reveals new and as yet unrealized possibilities. The systematic critical work that is philosophy has its constructive phase in projection of values and ends that, by their very constitution, demand application in action and guide the active operations they project.

There is a practical effect of absolute philosophies. But it is that of promoting conflicts and strengthening appeal to external authority as the sole agency for establishing order and unity in experience. Every absolute philosophy must claim to be in exclusive possession of *the* ultimate truth or else go back on its own pretensions. Absolute philosophies cannot tolerate rivals or learn from opposed philosophies. History shows that such philosophies have met with general acknowledgment only when they have had the support of powerful institutions, political and ecclesiastical. Their practical logic calls for external authority to enforce submission and punish heretical deviations. Absolute truth exacts absolute obedience. Recognition of the relation of philosophic ideas to the conditions set by experience furthers, on the contrary, intercommunication, exchange, and interaction. Through these processes differences of belief are modified in the direction of consensus. They are negotiable.

II. The Bearing of the Two Conceptions upon the Relation of Philosophy and Science

The most important practical difference that follows from the two opposed conceptions of the aim of philosophy (especially with respect to the philosophy of education) concerns the relationship of philosophy and science. Since natural and humane sciences are based upon experience, and since, according to the first view of philosophy, the subject matter of experience is intrinsically inferior to that of Ultimate Reality, philosophy and science are, according to it, necessarily rivals unless science is willing to accept the dictates of metaphysics as a servant obeys his master. Adherents of this philosophy speak with lofty disdain of science as being "merely empirical."

From the standpoint of the other view, there is no competition between science and philosophy. They exist, so to speak, in distinct, although connected, dimensions. As far as knowledge is concerned, the primacy and ultimacy of science is admitted. For what "science" means is simply the most authentic knowledge of nature, man, and society that is possible at any given time by means of the methods and techniques then and there available. The work of philosophy as critical and constructive does not attempt to furnish additional knowledge beyond the reach of science. Its concern is rather with the values and ends that known facts and principles should subserve. This concern is manifested in ideas whose claim is to have authority over *action* in effecting realization of the ends and values in question, not to be authoritative in presenting any kind of superior "reality" and knowledge.

This is the sense and the only sense in which philosophy can claim to be more comprehensive than science. This greater comprehensiveness exists because every intelligent systematic attempt to determine the values and uses to which ascertained knowledge should be put is philosophical as far as it goes, not because of any prerogatives inherent in a separate domain labelled "philosophy." Man is more than a knowing being. He is primarily a being who acts and makes and who must do and make in order to live. His activity is first of all an expression of emotion; of love and aversion, hope, and fear; of curiosities that lead him to explore and perils that make him draw back; a manifestation of impulse, desire, and habit. His behavior ranges from actions dictated by stupid callousness, by bare routine, and momentary caprice to an ordered behavior unified by planned purpose. The difference that exists between the former and the latter modes of conduct is due to an intelligence informed by known facts and principles. Purpose is vain and utopian unless based upon knowledge of existing conditions, which constitute both obstacles to overcome and means by which ends must be executed. Science is a name for the most exact and inclusive knowledge of these conditions that is attainable at a given time. But knowledge by itself, no matter how comprehensive and precise, does not tell what shall be done with what is known. "Pure knowledge," if called by its right name, would be termed "knowledge isolated from connection with activity." Upon the physiological side this isolation is equivalent to an impossible separation of the cortical cells of the brain from the muscles and the autonomic nervous system. Philosophy, once more, is a deliberate critical survey of the linkages that exist, in collective associated life and in individual life, between knowledge and values that determine man's fundamental purposes and desires.

It is often said that every person has *some* philosophy. This is true in the sense that everyone who does not float on the surface of the stream of life has some general scheme of values that joins what he believes with what he does. Artisan and architect, physician and engineer, artist and statesman, in as far as they live up to the demands and possibilities of their callings, exemplify a working connection of ideas and activities. Some degree and quality of philosophy is necessary to give articulation and design to the multitude of details and circumstances that constitute living. Such philosophies, as a rule, are partial, because formed uncritically. "Philosophy," in the more technical sense of the word, grows out of these more limited philosophies by placing them in a wider context and a more extended horizon of values and ends. Even when perceived ends are fairly adequate in giving unity to the activities of a particular individual, they fail to meet the needs of ordered and progressive activity in behalf of relations.

The chief rival of philosophy, then, is not science but routine; beliefs that have grown up and taken on strong emotional and emotive force, no one knows how; the pressure of immediate circumstances; the influence of uncriticized example and precept; submissive accommodation to the demands of existing institutions and traditions. It is with respect to such forces that philosophy is systematic criticism. The criticism exercises a liberating power; it tends to free human activity from the grip of custom by opening up new possibilities. Through comparison of the very customs and habits that are in conflict with one another, intelligence is enabled to project new values, which, when acted upon, will create new customs.

III. The Philosophy of Education

I. ITS OUTSTANDING IMPORTANCE

The philosophy of education is one phase of philosophy in general. It may be seriously questioned whether it is not the most important single phase of general philosophy. For education, when it is genuinely educational, brings about not only acquisition of knowledge and skills, but it forms also attitudes and dispositions that direct the uses to which acquired information and skill are put. While not as yet the most powerful existing agency in the formation of the disposition of individuals in its active relation to social needs and values, it is the one agency that deals deliberately and intentionally with the practical solution of the basic relations of the individual and the social. Moreover, it has to do with perpetuation of the positive values of inherited culture by embodying them in the dispositions of individuals who are to transmit culture into the future, and also with the creation of attitudes, understanding, and desire that will produce a better future culture. It performs its work in the medium of learning. Hence, the whole philosophic problem of the origin, nature, and function of knowledge is a live issue in education, not just a problem for exercise of intellectual dialectical gymnastics. Indeed, it would be difficult to find a single important problem of general philosophic inquiry that does not come to a burning focus in matters of the determination of the proper subject matter of studies, the choice of methods of teaching, and the problem of the social organization and administration of the schools.

2. A TYPICAL PROBLEM: THE RELATION OF SCIENTIFIC KNOWLEDGE TO PRACTICAL ACTIVITY

Consequently, the ground is too extensive to be adequately covered in this chapter. It is necessary to select a few typical aspects for discussion. The fact that the fundamental division between different philosophies is set by two opposed conceptions of the aim and business of philosophy suggests that the problem of knowledge, especially scientific knowledge, in its relation to practical activity be chosen for special consideration. The question of which type of philosophy shall control the philosophy of education is one of practical import. With respect to the organization and conduct of education, the issue is virtually whether traditions established in the past, in a pre-scientific age—traditions that have long endured, that have found expression in institutions that affect life most deeply, and that have gathered about themselves intense emotional attachments—or whether science and the scientific method in connection with experience shall exercise fundamental control.

As a force in the conduct of human affairs, scientific method is extremely new; as a force in education, it is even newer. In the latter, as in life generally, it is still a comparatively superficial coating over a thick layer of deposits from ancient customs, social institutions, and habitual outlooks. Science is endured and even highly approved as long as it is confined to providing more effective means for accomplishing results that are in harmony with the inherited scheme of cultural values. It is distrusted and feared when it threatens to influence and to alter the old system of ends, instead of limiting itself to supplying better means for realizing them. The application of science is welcomed, for example, in industrial life as far as new inventions and new technologies for production and distribution of commodities are concerned. But any endeavor to apply science to the reconstruction of human relations in the existing framework of economic and political institutions, any attempt to alter the values, positive and negative, that the existing system produces, is met with suspicion and active hostility. It is even sometimes treated as an effort to undermine the very foundations of social order.

Something of the same sort exists in the field of education. The application of the results of scientific study to change the methods of teaching subjects that have the sanction of scholastic tradition encounters the resistance of inertia. But upon the whole they are gladly adopted as far as they give increased efficiency in the teaching of reading, writing, arithmetic, geography, etc. Attempt to use the newer knowledge of man and of social relations to give changed social direction to all the subjects of school teaching might be condemned as subversive of the established constitution of human relationships.

At this point what has been said about the general relation of science and philosophy applies to the special field of education. Science can examine the relation of cause and effect between established procedures in teaching and the results that follow in the learning by students of these particular subjects. Knowledge of this relation enables techniques to be developed that accomplish better results with less waste of energy, exactly as knowledge of cause and effect in physical and chemical fields is readily convertible into improved techniques for production of material commodities. But critical survey of the value of the consequences to which even the most improved techniques contribute would place the subjects in a wider context of their relationship to present social needs and issues. Improvement of old procedures is a gain. But it does not decide the nature of the ends to which education should contribute nor the right of the studies, even when taught more efficiently, to a place in the course of study. That question can be settled only by consideration of possibilities inherent in the science of social and cultural life—possibilities not adequately represented in the scheme of education that has come to us from traditions that have not been subjected to thoroughgoing criticism.

What has just been said does not imply, however, that there is a sharp separation, a hard-and-fast line of division, between science and philosophy in education. Existing conditions and their effects can be examined scientifically in a sense that unrealized possibilities cannot be. Yet there is a necessary connection between existing conditions and the values and ends that as yet are possible rather than actual. It is true, for example, that while science can determine the most effective ways of producing explosives, it cannot within this limited physical and chemical field determine the ends for which they shall be used; whether for destruction of life and property in war, or for blasting away obstructions to easy communication and providing materials for the better housing of human beings. But an examination of the human consequences of warlike and peaceful pursuits is also possible, and this examination should be carried on in the objective spirit of science. The institution of war is capable of being subjected to critical survey, and critical survey will be intelligent only as it adopts the method of tracing relations of cause and effect that have proved to be effective in attaining knowledge in physical matters. When the effects taken into account are consequences upon human welfare, inquiry has passed into a field that, by comparison, is philosophical, since it has to do with values.

The narrower the field of inquiry, the more strictly scientific will it be, because conditions are then capable of more strict control. The wider the context, the more difficult becomes exact control of causal conditions. When the field is so broad as to include human weal and woe, and when it raises the problem of how existing social conditions can be modified to contribute more effectively to the values judged to be fundamental, inquiry is openly philosophy. But there is no fixed line at which it can be said that science ends and philosophy begins. The distinction between the two is relative to two things that vary with changes in historical and social condition. It is not absolute. One of the variables is the scope of the hypotheses that are involved in inquiry. It should not be necessary to insist upon the indispensability of ideas that function as hypotheses in scientific inquiry. But in the progress of science two kinds of hypotheses occur. While in any case a hypothesis goes beyond what has been definitely ascertained and is a venture into the unknown, in some instances a scientific hypothesis falls within the scope of a more comprehensive theory that has already been tested and experimentally confirmed. In some other instances, the hypothesis requires taking a new point of view, one so new that it contains what may justifiably be called a speculative element when it is judged from the standpoint of the established science of the time. Such hypotheses as the indestructibility of matter, the equivalent transformation of different forms of energy into one another, and the ideas of evolution and relativity, were philosophical at the outset. Only after long and arduous detailed observation and reflective elaboration did they take on strictly scientific character. The progress of science from one horizon to another depends upon willingness to entertain hypotheses that, when first advanced, outrun the possibility of scientific confirmation. The function of hypothesis is thus at once a link between science and philosophy and a basis of distinguishing between them on the ground of the breadth of the hypothesis as it first presented itself.

There is another variable involved, that of reference to unrealized possibilities. The possibilities represented by hypotheses in the physical field are possibilities with respect to the knowledge of the time in which they originate. When they are established by subsequent inquiry, we believe that they were there all the time as part of the order of nature. The case is not the same with those possibilities of human value with which philosophy is occupied. They have existed in some obscure and partial form or else our thought of them has no justifying basis. They must at least be suggested by what exists. But as directive principles of activity they present values that *should* be realized rather than things we discover to have existed all the time. What is implied in the constructive ideas of philosophy is that they have authority over activity to impel it to bring possible values into existence, not, as in the case of science, that they have authoritative claim to acknowledgment because they are already part of the order of nature.

It is not, then, an accidental matter that the present-day adherents of absolutistic, super-empirical philosophies base their criticisms of existing education and their proposals of reform upon appeal to Greek and Medieval tradition. For it was in ancient Greece that a philosophy of super-empirical Reality, and of truths about it that are identical under all conditions of experience, was formulated; and it was in the Middle Ages that, because of the sanction and support of a powerful social institution, philosophy actually flourished in the organized constitution of society. The conflict of the two philosophies of education is, therefore, a conflict between the intellectual and moral attitudes of a prescientific past and those consonant with the potentialities of the living present. Insistence upon the necessity of making a sharp separation between liberal and vocational education, upon the importance of literary classics in contrast with scientific subjects (with the exception of mathematics treated as an examplar of a system of absolute truths instead of as an ordered system of deductions from freely chosen postulates), and lack of faith in anything approaching first-hand experience in the schools, all flow logically from the philosophy that rests upon return to the past. The function of a philosophy of education based upon experience is, on the contrary, constructive exploration of the possibilities of experience directed by scientific method.

For the only way out of existing educational confusion and conflict is just the critical and constructive exploration of the potentialities of existing experience as that experience is brought under the fuller control of intelligence represented by scientific method. The existing school system presents, like existing life and culture, an incoherent mixture of values and standards derived from the old and the new. The school has neither the benefit of values inherent in a culture that existed centuries ago nor yet of the values inherent in those possibilities of present experience that can be realized by a more thoroughgoing use of scientific method. On the one hand, schools are so peculiarly subject to the power of tradition and of uncriticized custom that they embody the subjects and ends of the past. On the other hand, pressure of demands arising from existing conditions, especially those arising from contemporary industrial and economic institutions, has compelled the introduction of new subjects and new courses of study. The educational response in the latter case has been, however, almost as uncritical as the response that is exhibited in the adoption of values and ends having the sanction of tradition. Science and the applications of science that ushered in first the machine age and now the age of power have forced by their sheer social pressure the introduction into the educational system of scientific subjects and of occupational training. But to a large extent these new subjects overlay the older ones as a recent geological stratum overlays, with "faults" and distortions, older deposits.

3. THE PLACE OF SCIENCE AND SCIENTIFIC METHOD IN THE SCHOOLS

Consider first the place now given to science in the educational scheme. As far as form is concerned, the battle waged two and three generations ago to secure a place in the schools for the natural sciences has been won. Not so with respect to the substance of science. For the heart of science lies not in conclusions reached but in the method of observation, experimentation, and mathematical reasoning by which conclusions are established. Yet in large measure, it is the conclusions that are taught in schools, with a modicum of attention to the methods of controlled observation and testing, upon which the conclusions depend. So taught, "science" (1) becomes a body of ready-made truth about facts and principles, and (2) is divorced from the everyday experiences out of which science grows and into which it returns. In other words, with respect to its educational status, science was to a large extent brought under the control of just those old standards and aims that scientific method was, by right, undermining. It became an additional subject added to those previously existing, instead of being a method employed to reconstruct those subjects in the interest of a new, unified system of values. Moreover, when science is treated as a special and isolated body of facts and principles, it is adapted only to the capacity of comparatively mature intelligence, since it involves a special technical language and special skill in execution of technical procedures. The formation of the intellectual attitudes and habits of the young is thus left to the mercy of forces devoid of the controlling influence of scientific method.

In effect, the new scientific subjects were in considerable measure assimilated to the values, aims, and standards embodied in the subjects that expressed the intellectual habits of a prescientific age. Science as method, on the contrary, would permeate all school subjects. As method, it is the living spirit that actuates the formation and testing of beliefs in all subjects. As method, it is undeviating respect for the authority of evidence obtained from first-hand experience, is constant attention to the need of experimental activity to institute the observations that have the force of evidence, and is high valuation of ideas as means of interpreting and organizing the facts authenticated by controlled observation. Only as the living spirit of dealing with all subjects, engrained in all the procedures of learning, can science create the values inherent in it as method. There is a radical difference between a body of facts and principles, no matter how well established by the inquiries of others that are given and are accepted ready-made and the facts and principles that are developed through living experience under the direction of scientific method. The first constitutes a load of information. The second informs, in the sense of being the fundamental form of all intellectual response in all subjects.

4. THE RELATION OF KNOWLEDGE
TO EXPERIENCE

The issue of the relation of knowledge to experience is strikingly raised by the two opposed philosophies of education. According to one of them, knowledge is a final end in itself and nothing has a right to the name of "knowledge" (in its full sense) unless it is attained by a faculty of reason and rational intuition supposed to be independent of experience. To treat knowledge as an end in itself is equivalent to isolating it from activity. Hence, the conviction of those who hold this philosophy that education is "intellectual" only as knowledge is pursued apart from connection with practical experience. The other philosophy demands with equal insistence that education be made to nurture and develop intelligence. But intelligence is not supposed to be that separate faculty to which classic traditional philosophy gave the name "intellect"; it is trained power of judgment in choosing and forming means and ends in all the situations that life presents. The alternatives to formation of the fundamental attitudes and habits of life experience and of values and ends that give life whatever ordered articulation it possesses through the use of science are convention, prejudice, custom, and desire to believe that which it is agreeable to believe, either because of its harmony with personal wishes or its conformity with the expectations and requirements of the particular group of which one is a member.

The philosophy that holds knowledge to be inherently related to experience, when experience is informed by scientific method, requires that the schools provide a place for first-hand experience. It is not enough, as is sometimes assumed by so-called "progressive" schools, that any kind of experience, as long as it is first-hand, will do. Nor is it enough to assume, as schools under the influence of routine tradition are given to assuming, that the function of experience is to produce forms of automatic skill. First-hand experience must be such as to evoke reflective observation and suggest ideas to be tested in appropriate forms of action. There must be continuity, not a stab at one thing one day and a jab at another thing the next day. Experience had outside school walls provides many opportunities for introduction within the school of activities under conditions that will utilize familiar everyday experiences for ends and values not subserved in the experiences had outside, values such as intellectual habits that are in harmony with the demands of scientific method and ability to understand social conditions and relations.

Science through its applications has already profoundly affected ordinary experience and the customary relations of human beings to one another. Modern industry in production and distribution of goods is the direct product of science. Machine and power technologies in creation of modern industrial methods have modified the family, the church, and state, as well as industry. The intimate connection between every present social and political issue with conditions that grow out of the consequences of industry and finance is sufficient evidence of the deep effect that applications of the new science have had upon human relationships. It is commonplace to call attention to the social consequences of stationary and internal combustion engines, the steam locomotive, the dynamo, the telegraph and telephone, the automobile, radio, and airplane, and the revolution going on in many industries because of the application of chemical processes. These consequences permeate every nook and corner of life: nothing in the domain of human relations remains what it was. But the bearing of all these changes upon the work of the schools in promoting understanding of scientific method and of the forces, problems, and needs of social life has received comparatively little attention. Here lies the opportunity to which the philosophy of experience is peculiarly relevant.

There has been a tremendous increase of pre-industrial, industrial, vocational, and professional education. But upon the whole these subjects have been introduced to serve comparatively narrow practical ends. They have been treated as means of furnishing the information and skill demanded by industry and finance, as means of getting jobs and making money under existing social conditions. Their wider practical value as means of understanding the nature of scientific method and the social consequences of applied science, as means of insight into agencies by which a more humane and just social order may be created, has been, comparatively speaking, slighted.

Those who still adhere to the philosophy of Aristotle and St. Thomas are logical in their demand that there be even a greater separation between occupational and "liberal and cultural" education than now exists. This demand is predicated upon the common practice of treating occupational education as rule-of-thumb procedures and a body of information about occupations, involving in both cases no reflective thinking. Hence the only way in which their criticisms and proposals can be fundamentally met is to avoid this common practice and to use the rich store of scientific and social values contained in the so-called "practical" studies and activities. It is not the actual structure and processes of experience, even in its practical factors, that produce the consequences that are objected to but certain preconceptions about it and about education. The *a priori* philosophy confirms these preconceptions, since it holds that experience is incapable of generating significant ideas, while the older empiristic philosophy, by reducing ideas to copies of prior experiences, tended in the same direction.

In the third count, the older empirical philosophy was intensely individualistic. It had no room for any processes save those going on between what was supposed to be a strictly individual consciousness and the physical environment. It did not recognize how intimately relations with other human beings enter into the very constitution of experience. Its tendency, accordingly, was to pulverize society into a number of atomic constituents having only external relations with one another. It lacked power to explain existing social institutions and still more to provide ideas by which social relations could be bettered. It served a useful purpose as far as institutions repressed and suppressed individuals; it proclaimed the inherent right of individuals to a freedom denied them. But it was impotent with respect to indication of new social syntheses to replace those it criticized. In educational application it strengthened introduction of forms of information and skill that would further individualistic success, but, so far as its influence went, it was weak in cultivating attitudes of cooperative and unified effort. Its gaps and defects called out a reaction in favor of absolutistic philosophy as the only ground upon which the interests of social unity could be maintained.

The fact that adherents of *a priori,* non-empirical, and anti-scientific philosophy still base their criticisms of the philosophy of experience in itself and in its educational import upon conceptions of experience formulated in the earlier empirical philosophy gives additional point to the importance of a philosophy that recognizes the inherent place and function in experience of practical constructive intelligence, the union of knowledge with action, and the permeation of experience with social values. It makes clear the fact that the sole effective way of combating reactionary tendencies, with their appeal to external authority, is deliberate development of a philosophy of experience based upon recognition of the liberating and directive force of intelligence. It takes full advantage of the intimate connection of science with changes in social institutions and in human relationships. It is superstition to suppose that experience is not capable of developing values of the most precious sort. It is disloyalty to intelligence to suppose that it is not capable of apprehending these values and giving them the form in which they are capable of directing organized and ordered collective endeavor. It is a defeatist libel upon human nature to suppose that it is incapable of responding actively to the claims of these values and the power of intelligence to work for their realization.

The trouble with education does not proceed from introduction of scientific subjects and vocational activities. It proceeds from the inconsistent mixture of the values inherent in these subjects with those derived from traditions and customs that originated in the prescientific and predemocratic age but that still endure in the educational system. Systematic development of the values potentially present in personal and social experience, as that moves under control by scientifically informed intelligence, provides the road out. The immediate task of a philosophy of education is to clarify the meaning of such a movement in terms of subject matter and methods of school activities and studies from the very beginning through the university. This task is negative as far as criticism is concerned with the materials, methods, and aims that hold over from the traditions and customs of a prescientific age. It is positive in that it discloses values inherent in experience as that is transformed through the efforts of those who are actuated by practical and collective intelligence. The promises of education and of social life are identical in this respect. A philosophy of education faithful to the possibilities of experience and scientific method will not of itself accomplish the needed change. But it will contribute by making clear the road to be followed and the goal to which it leads.

Unity of Science as a Social Problem

I. The Scientific Attitude

Anyone who attempts to promote the unity of science must ask himself at least two basic questions: "What is meant by that whose unity is to be promoted, namely, science?" and "What sort of unity is feasible or desirable?" The following pages represent the conclusions the present writer has reached in reflecting upon these two themes.

With respect to the question as to the meaning of science, a distinction needs to be made between science as attitude and method and science as a body of subject matter. I do not mean that the two can be separated, for a method is a way of dealing with subject matter and science as a body of knowledge is a product of a method. Each exists only in connection with the other. An attitude becomes psychopathic when it is not directed to objects beyond itself. What is meant is, first, that attitude and method come before the material which is found in books, journals, and the proceedings of scientific organizations; and, second, that the attitude is manifested primarily toward the objects and events of the ordinary world and only secondarily toward that which is already scientific subject matter.

Stated in other words, the scientific method is not confined to those who are called scientists. The body of knowledge and ideas which is the product of the work of the latter is the fruit of a method which is followed by the wider body of persons who deal intelligently and openly with the objects and energies of the common environment. In its specialized sense, science is an elabora-

[First published in *International Encyclopedia of Unified Science,* vol. 1, no. 1, *Encyclopedia and Unified Science* (Chicago: University of Chicago Press, 1938), pp. 29–38.]

tion, often a highly technical one, of everyday operations. In spite of the technicality of its language and procedures, its genuine meaning can be understood only if its connection with attitudes and procedures which are capable of being used by all persons who act intelligently is borne in mind.

On the level of common sense there are attitudes which are like those of science in its more specialized sense, while there are attitudes which are thoroughly unscientific. There are those who work by routine, by casual cut-and-try methods, those who are enslaved to dogma and directed by prejudice, just as there are those who use their hands, eyes, and ears to gain knowledge of whatever comes their way and use whatever brains they have to extract meaning from what they observe. Few would rule engineers from out the scientific domain, and those few would rest their case upon a highly dubious distinction between something called "pure" science and something else called "applied" science. As Dr. Karl Darrow has said in his *Renaissance of Physics:*

> Many of the things which modern science has to tell us are fantastic and inconceivable indeed, but they have been attested by the same sort of man with the same sort of training and using the same sort of reasoning as those who have made it possible to speak over a wire with San Francisco and over the ether of space to London, to cross the Atlantic in four days by steamer and in twenty-four hours by aeroplane, to operate a railroad with power transmitted invisibly through rails, and to photograph the bones inside the body with a light no eye can see and no fire can send forth.

When the achievements of the engineer are disparaged under the name "applied" science, it is forgotten that the inquiries and the calculations required to produce these achievements are as exacting as those which generate the science called "pure." Pure science does not apply itself automatically; application takes place through use of methods which it is arbitrary to distinguish from those employed in the laboratory or observatory. And if the engineer is mentioned, it is because, once he is admitted, we cannot exclude the farmer, the mechanic, and the chauffeur, as far as these men do what they have to do with intelligent choice of means and with intelligent adaptation of means to ends, instead of in dependence upon routine and guesswork. On the other hand, it is quite possible for the scientist to be quite unscientific in forming his beliefs outside his special subject, as he does whenever he permits such beliefs to be dictated by unexamined premisses accepted traditionally or caught up out of the surrounding social atmosphere.

In short, the scientific attitude as here conceived is a quality that is manifested in any walk of life. What, then, is it? On its negative side, it is freedom from control by routine, prejudice, dogma, unexamined tradition, sheer self-interest. Positively, it is the will to inquire, to examine, to discriminate, to draw conclusions only on the basis of evidence after taking pains to gather all available evidence. It is the intention to reach beliefs, and to test those that are entertained, on the basis of observed fact, recognizing also that facts are without meaning save as they point to ideas. It is, in turn, the experimental attitude which recognizes that while ideas are necessary to deal with facts, yet they are working hypotheses to be tested by the consequences they produce.

Above all, it is the attitude which is rooted in the problems that are set and questions that are raised by the conditions of actuality. The unscientific attitude is that which shuns such problems, which runs away from them, or covers them up instead of facing them. And experience shows that this evasion is the counterpart of concern with artificial problems and alleged ready-made solutions. For all problems are artificial which do not grow, even if indirectly, out of the conditions under which life, including associated living, is carried on. Life is a process which goes on in connection with an environment which is complex, physically and culturally. There is no form of interaction with the physical environment and the human environment that does not generate problems that can be coped with only by an objective attitude and an intelligent method. The home, the school, the shop, the bedside and hospital, present such problems as truly as does the laboratory. They usually present the problems in a more direct and urgent fashion. This fact is so obvious that it would be trite to mention it were it not that it shows the potential universality of the scientific attitude.

The existence of artificial problems is also an undeniable fact in human history. The existence of such problems and the expenditure of energy upon the solution of them are the chief reasons why the potentiality of scientific method is so often unrealized and frustrated. The word 'metaphysics' has many meanings, all of which are generally supposed to be so highly technical as to be of no interest to the man in the street. But in the sense that 'metaphysical' means that which is outside of experience, over and beyond it, all human beings are metaphysical when they occupy themselves with problems which do not rise out of experience and for which solutions are sought outside experience. Men are metaphysical not only in technical philosophy but in many of their beliefs and habits of thought in religion, morals, and politics. The waste of energy that results is serious enough. But this is slight compared with that which is wrought by artificial problems and solutions in preventing, deflecting, and distorting the development of the scientific attitude which is the proper career of intelligence.

II. The Social Unity of Science

When we turn from the question of what is meant by science to the question of what is meant by its unity, we seem, at first sight, to have shifted ground and to be in another field. The unity of science is usually referred to in connection with unification of the attained results of science. In this field the problem of attaining the unity of science is that of coordinating the scattered and immense body of specialized findings into a systematic whole. This problem is a real one and cannot be neglected. But there is also a human, a cultural, meaning of the unity of science. There is, for instance, the question of unifying the efforts of all those who exercise in their own affairs the scientific method so that these efforts may gain the force which comes from united effort. Even when an individual is or tries to be intelligent in the conduct of his own life-affairs, his efforts are hampered, oftentimes defeated, by obstructions due not merely to ignorance but to active opposition to the scientific attitude on the part of those influenced by prejudice, dogma, class interest, external authority, nationalistic and racial sentiment, and similar powerful agencies. Viewed in this light, the problem of the unity of science constitutes a fundamentally important social problem.

At the present time the enemies of the scientific attitude are

numerous and organized—much more so than appears at superficial glance. The prestige of science is indeed great, especially in
the field of its external application to industry and war. In the
abstract, few would come out openly and say that they were opposed to science. But this small number is no measure of the influence of those who borrow the results of science to advance by
thoroughly unscientific and antiscientific methods private, class,
and national interests. Men may admire science, for example, because it gives them the radio to use, and then employ the radio to
create conditions that prevent the development of the scientific
attitude in the most important fields of human activity—fields
which suffer terribly because of failure to use scientific method.
In particular, science is not welcomed but rather opposed when it
"invades" (a word often used) the field now pre-empted by religion, morals, and political and economic institutions.

To bring about unity of the scientific attitude is, then, to bring
those who accept it and who act upon it into active cooperation
with one another. This problem transcends in importance the
more technical problem of unification of the results of the special
sciences. It takes precedence over the latter issue. For it is not too
much to say that science, even in its more specialized sense, now
stands at a critical juncture. It must move forward in order to
maintain its achievements. If it stands still, it will be confined to
the field in which it has already won victories and will see the
fruits of its victories appropriated by those who will use them by
antiscientific methods for nonhumane ends.

Accordingly, the great need is for those who are actuated by
the scientific spirit to take counsel regarding the place and function of science in the total scene of life. It follows that a movement in behalf of the unity of science need not and should not lay
down in advance a platform to be accepted. It is essentially a cooperative movement, so that detailed specific common standpoints and ideas must emerge out of the very processes of cooperation. To try to formulate them in advance and insist upon
their acceptance by all is both to obstruct cooperation and to be
false to the scientific spirit. The only thing necessary in the form
of agreement is faith in the scientific attitude and faith in the human and social importance of its maintenance and expansion.

What has been said does not minimize the difficulties that arise
from the great degree of isolated specialization that now charac-

terizes science or the importance of overcoming these difficulties. To a great extent those who now pursue the different branches of science speak different languages and are not readily understood by one another. Translation from one branch to another is not easy. In consequence, workers tend to be deprived of the useful intellectual instruments that would be available in their own special work if there were a freer give and take.

But the needed work of coordination cannot be done mechanically or from without. It, too, can be the fruit only of cooperation among those animated by the scientific spirit. Convergence to a common centre will be effected most readily and most vitally through the reciprocal exchange which attends genuine cooperative effort. The attempt to secure unity by defining the terms of all the sciences in terms of some one science is doomed in advance to defeat. In the house which science might build there are many mansions. The first task, to change the metaphor, is to build bridges from one science to another. There are many gaps to be spanned. It seems to me, however, that the great need is the linkage of the physico-chemical sciences with psychological and social fields of science through the intermediary of biology. I should probably be expressing my own view or that of a particular and perhaps small group if I said that convergence can best be attained by considering how various sciences may be brought together in common attack upon practical social problems. But it is wholly within the scope of the present theme to say that the cooperative endeavor held in view by the present movement for the unity of science is bound gradually to disclose the causes of present gaps and to indicate where and how bridges may be built across the gulfs that still separate workers in different fields.

A very short history has been enjoyed by free scientific method in comparison with the long history enjoyed by forces which have never felt the influence of science. Ideas that descend from the prescientific epoch are still with us and are crystallized in institutions. They are not to be exorcised by reiteration of the word 'science.' Every scientific worker is still subject to their influence, certainly outside his special field and sometimes even within it. Only constant critical care, exercised in the spirit of the scientific attitude, can bring about their gradual elimination. Ultimately, this criticism must be self-criticism. But the agencies and instrumentalities of self-criticism can be had only by means of as full and free cooperation with others as it is possible to secure.

The advance of scientific method has brought with it, where the influence of the method has been felt, a great increase in toleration. We are now in a world where there is an accelerated development of intolerance. Part of the cause for this growth can be found, I think, in the fact that tolerance so far has been largely a passive thing. We need a shift from acceptance of responsibility for passive toleration to active responsibility for promoting the extension of scientific method. The first step is to recognize the responsibility for furthering mutual understanding and free communication.

III. Education and the Unity of Science

It is perhaps within the scope of my theme to say something about the connection of the movement for the unity of science with education. I have already mentioned the fact that scientific method has reached a crisis in its history, due, in final analysis, to the fact that the ultra-reactionary and the ultra-radical combine, even while acclaiming the prestige of science in certain fields, to use the techniques of science to destroy the scientific attitude. The short history of science in comparison with the history of institutions that resist its application by the mere fact of their inertia has also been mentioned. These two influences combine to render the agencies of education the crucial point in any movement to bring about a greater and more progressive unity of the scientific spirit.

After a struggle, the various sciences have found a place for themselves in the educational institutions. But to a large extent they exist merely side by side with other subjects which have hardly felt the touch of science. This, however, is far from being the most depressing feature of the educational situation as respects the place of science. For it is also true that the spirit in which the sciences are often taught, and the methods of instruction employed in teaching them, have been in large measure taken over from traditional nonscientific subjects.

I mention certain things which confirm this statement. In the first place, science has barely affected elementary education. With a very few exceptions it has not touched the early years of the elementary school. Yet this is the time when curiosity is most awake, the interest in observation the least dulled, and desire for new experiences most active. It is also the period in which the fundamental attitudes are formed which control, subconsciously if not consciously, later attitudes and methods.

In the second place, scientific subjects are taught very largely as bodies of subject matter rather than as a method of universal attack and approach. There may be laboratories and laboratory exercises and yet this statement remain true. For they may be employed primarily in order that pupils acquire a certain body of information. The resulting body of information about facts and laws has a different content from that provided in other studies. But as long as the ideal is information, the sciences taught are still under the dominion of ideas and practices that have a pre-scientific origin and history. Laboratory exercises and class demonstrations may be a part of a regular routine of instruction, and yet accomplish little in developing the scientific habit of mind. Indeed, except in a chosen few the mere weight of information may be a load carried in the memory, not a resource for further observation and thought.

In the third place, apart from some institutions of research and graduate departments of universities which attract relatively a small number, most money and energy go into institutions in which persons are prepared for special professional pursuits. This fact is not itself objectionable, as I have already indicated in speaking of "applied" and "pure" science. But this technical education, as it is at present conducted, is directed to narrow ends rather than to the wide and liberal end of developing interest and ability to use the scientific method in all fields of human betterment. It is quite possible, unfortunately, for a person to have the advantage of this special training and yet remain indifferent to the application of the scientific attitude in fields that lie outside his own specialized calling.

The final point is a corollary. Something called by the name of "science" gets shut off in a segregated territory of its own. There are powerful special interests which strive in any case to keep science isolated so that the common life may be immune from its influence. Those who have these special interests fear the impact of scientific method upon social issues.

They fear this impact even if they have not formulated the nature and ground of their fear. But there are influences within the status of science itself in the educational system which promote its isolation. If the schools are used for the purpose of instilling belief in certain dogmas—a use in which something called "education" becomes simply an organ of propaganda—and this use continues to grow, it will be in some measure because science has not been conceived and practiced as the sole universal method of dealing intellectually with all problems. The movement to unify workers in different fields of science is itself an educative movement for those who take part in it. It is also a precondition of effort to give the scientific attitude that place in educational institutions which will create an ever increasing number of persons who habitually adopt the scientific attitude in meeting the problems that confront them.

I said that I thought that reference to education belonged within the scope of the present theme. On the one hand, the future of the scientific attitude as a socially unified force depends more upon the education of children and youth than upon any other single force. On the other hand, the teaching of science can hardly take the place which belongs to it, as an attitude of universal application, unless those who are already animated by the scientific attitude and concerned for its expansion actively cooperate. The first condition to be satisfied is that such persons bestir themselves to become aware of what the scientific attitude is and what it is about so as to become diligently militant in demonstrating its rightful claims.

The import of what has been said is that the scientific attitude and method are at bottom but the method of free and effective intelligence. The special sciences reveal what this method is and means, and what it is capable of. It is neither feasible nor desirable that all human beings should become practitioners of a special science. But it is intensely desirable and under certain conditions practicable that all human beings become scientific in their attitudes: genuinely intelligent in their ways of thinking and acting. It is practicable because all normal persons have the potential germs which make this result possible. It is desirable because this attitude forms the sole ultimate alternative to prejudice, dogma, authority, and coercive force exercised in behalf of some special interest. Those who are concerned with science in its more technical meaning are obviously those who should take the lead by cooperation with one another in bringing home to all the inherent universality of scientific method.

The Relation of Science and Philosophy as the Basis of Education [1]

Empirical and experimental philosophy has no quarrel with science, either in itself or in its application to education. On the contrary, scientific conclusions and methods are the chief ally of an empirical philosophy of education. For according to empirical philosophy, science provides the only means we have for learning about man and the world in which he lives. Some have thought that this fact makes philosophy unnecessary. They have supposed that the admission that science is supreme in the field of knowledge covers the whole ground of human experience. The elimination does rule out *one* kind of philosophy, namely, that which held that philosophy is a higher form of knowledge than the scientific kind, one which furnishes knowledge of ultimate higher reality. But it does not follow from the elimination of this particular type of philosophy that philosophy itself must go.

It would follow if man were simply and only a knowing being. But he is not. He is also an acting being, a creature with desires, hopes, fears, purposes and habits. To the average person knowledge itself is of importance because of its bearing upon what he needs to do and to make. It helps him in clarifying his wants, in constructing his ends and in finding means for realizing them. There exist, in other words, values as well as known facts and principles and philosophy is concerned primarily with values— with the ends for the sake of which man acts. Given the most extensive and accurate system of knowledge, and man is still faced with the question of what he is going to do about it and what he is going to do with the knowledge in his possession.

In this matter of the connection of what is known with values,

1. Read before the National Society for the Study of Education, on the evening of February 26, at the Atlantic City meeting of the American Association of School Administrators.

[First published in *School and Society* 47 (9 April 1938): 470–73.]

science is an ally of an empirical philosophy against absolute philosophies which pretend that fixed and eternal truths are known by means of organs and methods that are independent of science. The objection to this position is not merely theoretical. The practical objections to it are that it strengthens appeal to authority and promotes controversies which can not be settled by the use of the methods of inquiry and proof that have been worked out in the sciences. The only remaining alternative is the use of coercion and force, either openly or covertly through falling back on customs and institutions as they happen to exist. There is no great danger that the present-day revival in some quarters of Greek and medieval philosophies of eternal first principles will make much headway as a theoretical philosophy. There is always danger that such philosophies will have practical influence in reinforcing established social authority that is exercised in behalf of maintenance of the *status quo*. Against this danger, an experimental philosophy stands in firm alliance with the methods by which the natural sciences arrive at warranted truths.

The philosophy of education is not a poor relation of general philosophy even though it is often so treated even by philosophers. It is ultimately the most significant phase of philosophy. For it is through the processes of education that knowledge is obtained, while these educational processes do not terminate in mere acquisition of knowledge and related forms of skill. They attempt to integrate the knowledge gained into enduring dispositions and attitudes. It is not too much to say that education is *the* outstanding means by which union of knowledge and the values that actually work in actual conduct is brought about. The difference between educational practices that are influenced by a well-thought-out philosophy, and practices that are not so influenced is that between education conducted with some clear idea of the ends in the way of ruling attitudes of desire and purpose that are to be created, and an education that is conducted blindly, under the control of customs and traditions that have not been examined, or in response to immediate social pressures. This difference does not come about because of any inherent sacredness in what is called philosophy, but because any effort to clarify the ends to be attained is, as far as it goes, philosophical.

The need for such systematic clarification is especially urgent at the present time. Applications of natural science have made an

enormous difference in human relations. They have revolutionized the means of production and distribution of commodities
and services. They have effected an equally great change in communication and all the means for influencing the public opinion
upon which political action depends. These applications decide,
more than any other force or set of forces, the conditions under
which human beings live together and under which they act, enjoy and suffer. Moreover, they have produced communities that
are in a state of rapid change. Wherever the effect of the applications of science has been felt, human relations have ceased to be
static. Old forms have been invaded and often undermined, in the
family, in politics and even in moral and religious habits as well
as in the narrower field of economic arrangements. Almost all
current social problems have their source here. Finally, ends and
values that were formed in the pre-scientific period and the institutions of great power that were formed in the same period retain their influence. Human life, both individually and collec-
tively, is disturbed, confused and conflicting.

Either the instrumentalities of education will ignore this state
of affairs and the schools will go their own way, confining themselves for the most part to providing standardized knowledge
and forms of skill as ends in themselves, modified only by conces-
sions to temporary social pressures, or they will face the question of the relation of school-education to the needs and possibilities of the social situation. If the latter problem is faced, then there
arise problems of the re-adaptation of materials of the curriculum,
methods of instruction and the social organization of the school.
A philosophy of education can not settle once for all how these
problems shall be resolved. But it can enforce perception of the
nature of these problems, and can give suggestions of value as to
the only ways in which they can satisfactorily be dealt with. Administrators and teachers who are imbued with the ideas can test
and develop them in their actual work so that, through union of
theory and practice, the philosophy of education will be a living,
growing thing.

I come back, then, to the question of the alliance of empirical
pragmatic philosophy with science against both a philosophy of
truths and principles that are alleged to be superior to any that
can be ascertained by empirical methods of science, and also
against dogmatic authority, custom, routine and the pressure of
immediate circumstances. Science used in the educational field

can ascertain the actual facts, and can generalize them on the basis of relations of cause and effect. It can not itself settle the value of the consequences that result from even the best use of more economical and effective methods as causes of effects produced. The consequences have to be evaluated in the light of what is known about social problems, evils and needs. But without the knowledge of actual conditions and of relations of cause and effect, any values that are set up as ends are bare ideals in the sense in which "ideal" means utopian, without means for its realization.

I shall mention two or three matters in which the need for cooperation between philosophy and science is especially intimate. Since scientific method depends upon first-hand experimentally controlled experiences, any philosophic application of the scientific point of view will emphasize the need of such experiences in the school, as over against mere acquisition of ready-made information that is supplied in isolation from the students' own experience. So far, it will be in line with what is called the "progressive" movement in education. But it will be an influence in counteracting any tendencies that may exist in progressive education to slur the importance of continuity in the experiences that are had, and the importance of organization. Unless the science of education on its own ground and behalf emphasizes *subject-matters* which contain within themselves the promise and power of continuous growth in the direction of organization, it is false to its own position as scientific. In cooperation with a philosophy of education, it can lend invaluable aid in seeing to it that the chosen subject-matters are also such that they progressively develop toward formation of attitudes of understanding the world in which students and teachers live and towards forming the attitudes of purpose, desire and action which will make pupils effective in dealing with social conditions.

Another point of common interest concerns the place in the schools of the sciences, especially the place of the habits which form scientific attitude and method. The sciences had to battle against entrenched foes to obtain recognition in the curriculum. In a formal sense, the battle has been won, but not yet in a substantial sense. For scientific subject-matter is still more or less segregated as a special body of facts and truths. The full victory will not be won until every subject and lesson is taught in connection with its bearing upon creation and growth of the kind of power of observation, inquiry, reflection and testing that are the heart of scientific intelligence. Experimental philosophy is at one with the genuine spirit of a scientific attitude in the endeavor to obtain for scientific method this central place in education.

Finally, the science and philosophy of education can and should work together in overcoming the split between knowledge and action, between theory and practice, which now affects both education and society so seriously and harmfully. Indeed, it is not too much to say that institution of a happy marriage between theory and practice is in the end the chief meaning of a science and a philosophy of education that work together for common ends.

Does Human Nature Change?

I have come to the conclusion that those who give different answers to the question I have asked in the title of this article
are talking about different things. This statement in itself, however, is too easy a way out of the problem to be satisfactory. For
there is a real problem, and so far as the question is a practical
one instead of an academic one, I think the proper answer is that
human nature *does* change.

By the practical side of the question, I mean the question
whether or not important, almost fundamental, changes in the
ways of human belief and action have taken place and are capable of still taking place. But to put this question in its proper
perspective, we have first to recognize the sense in which human
nature does not change. I do not think it can be shown that the
innate needs of men have changed since man became man or that
there is any evidence that they will change as long as man is on
the earth.

By "needs" I mean the inherent demands that men make because of their constitution. Needs for food and drink and for
moving about, for example, are so much a part of our being that
we cannot imagine any condition under which they would cease
to be. There are other things not so directly physical that seem to
me equally engrained in human nature. I would mention as examples the need for some kind of companionship; the need for
exhibiting energy, for bringing one's powers to bear upon surrounding conditions; the need for both cooperation with and
emulation of one's fellows for mutual aid and combat alike; the
need for some sort of aesthetic expression and satisfaction; the
need to lead and to follow; etc.

[First published in *Rotarian* 52 (February 1938): 8–11, 58–59.]

Whether my particular examples are well chosen or not does not matter so much as does recognition of the fact that there are some tendencies so integral a part of human nature that the latter would not be human nature if they changed. These tendencies used to be called instincts. Psychologists are now more chary of using that word than they used to be. But the word by which the tendencies are called does not matter much in comparison to the fact that human nature has its own constitution.

Where we are likely to go wrong after the fact is recognized that there is something unchangeable in the structure of human nature is the inference we draw from it. We suppose that the manifestation of these needs is also unalterable. We suppose that the manifestations we have got used to are as natural and as unalterable as are the needs from which they spring.

The need for food is so imperative that we call the persons insane who persistently refuse to take nourishment. But what kinds of food are wanted and used are a matter of acquired habit influenced by both physical environment and social custom. To civilized people today, eating human flesh is an entirely unnatural thing. Yet there have been peoples to whom it seemed natural because it was socially authorized and even highly esteemed. There are well-accredited stories of persons needing support from others who have refused palatable and nourishing foods because they were not accustomed to them; the alien foods were so "unnatural" they preferred to starve rather than eat them.

Aristotle spoke for an entire social order as well as for himself when he said that slavery existed by nature. He would have regarded efforts to abolish slavery from society as an idle and utopian effort to change human nature where it was unchangeable. For according to him it was not simply the desire to be a master that was engrained in human nature. There were persons who were born with such an inherently slavish nature that it did violence to human nature to set them free.

The assertion that human nature cannot be changed is heard when social changes are urged as reforms and improvements of existing conditions. It is always heard when the proposed changes in institutions or conditions stand in sharp opposition to what exists. If the conservative were wiser, he would rest his objections in most cases, not upon the unchangeability of human nature, but upon the inertia of custom; upon the resistance that acquired habits offer to change after they are once acquired. It is hard to teach an old dog new tricks and it is harder yet to teach society to adopt customs which are contrary to those which have long prevailed. Conservatism of this type would be intelligent and it would compel those wanting change not only to moderate their pace, but also to ask how the changes they desire could be introduced with a minimum of shock and dislocation.

Nevertheless, there are few social changes that can be opposed on the ground that they are contrary to human nature itself. A proposal to have a society get along without food and drink is one of the few that are of this kind. Proposals to form communities in which there is no cohabitation have been made and the communities have endured for a time. But they are so nearly contrary to human nature that they have not endured long. These cases are almost the only ones in which social change can be opposed simply on the ground that human nature cannot be changed.

Take the institution of war, one of the oldest, most socially reputable of all human institutions. Efforts for stable peace are often opposed on the ground that man is by nature a fighting animal and that this phase of his nature is unalterable. The failure of peace movements in the past can be cited in support of this view. In fact, however, war is as much a social pattern as is the domestic slavery which the ancients thought to be an immutable fact.

I have already said that, in my opinion, combativeness is a constituent part of human nature. But I have also said that the manifestations of these native elements are subject to change because they are affected by custom and tradition. War does not exist because man has combative instincts, but because social conditions and forces have led, almost forced, these "instincts" into this channel.

There are a large number of other channels in which the need for combat has been satisfied, and there are other channels not yet discovered or explored into which it could be led with equal satisfaction. There is war against disease, against poverty, against insecurity, against injustice, in which multitudes of persons have found full opportunity for the exercise of their combative tendencies.

The time may be far off when men will cease to fulfill their need for combat by destroying each other and when they will manifest it in common and combined efforts against the forces that are enemies of all men equally. But the difficulties in the way are found in the persistence of certain acquired social customs and not in the unchangeability of the demand for combat.

Pugnacity and fear are native elements of human nature. But so are pity and sympathy. We send nurses and physicians to the battlefield and provide hospital facilities as "naturally" as we change bayonets and discharge machine guns. In early times there was a close connection between pugnacity and fighting, for the latter was done largely with the fists. Pugnacity plays a small part in generating wars today. Citizens of one country do not hate those of another nation by instinct. When they attack or are attacked, they do not use their fists in close combat, but throw shells from a great distance at persons whom they have never seen. In modern wars, anger and hatred come after the war has started; they are effects of war, not the cause of it.

It is a tough job sustaining a modern war; all the emotional reactions have to be excited. Propaganda and atrocity stories are enlisted. Aside from such extreme measures there has to be definite organization, as we saw in the World War, to keep up the morale of even non-combatants. And morale is largely a matter of keeping emotions at a certain pitch; and unfortunately fear, hatred, suspicion, are among the emotions most easily aroused.

I shall not attempt to dogmatize about the causes of modern wars. But I do not think that anyone will deny that they are social rather than psychological, though psychological appeal is highly important in working up a people to the point where they want to fight and in keeping them at it. I do not think, moreover, that anyone will deny that economic conditions are powerful among the social causes of war. The main point, however, is that whatever the sociological causes, they are affairs of tradition, custom, and institutional organization, and these factors belong among the changeable manifestations of human nature, not among the unchangeable elements.

I have used the case of war as a typical instance of what is changeable and what is unchangeable in human nature, in their relation to schemes of social change. I have selected the case because it is an extremely difficult one in which to effect durable changes, not because it is an easy one. The point is that the obstacles in the way are put there by social forces which do change from time to time, not by fixed elements of human nature. This fact is also illustrated in the failures of pacifists to achieve their ends by appeal simply to sympathy and pity. For while, as I have said, the kindly emotions are also a fixed constituent of human nature, the channel they take is dependent upon social conditions.

There is always a great outburst of these kindly emotions in time of war. Fellow feeling and the desire to help those in need are intense during war, as they are at every period of great disaster that comes home to observation or imagination. But they are canalized in their expression; they are confined to those upon our side. They occur simultaneously with manifestation of rage and fear against the other side, if not always in the same person, at least in the community generally. Hence the ultimate failure of pacifist appeals to the kindly elements of native human nature when they are separated from intelligent consideration of the social and economic forces at work.

William James made a great contribution in the title of one of his essays, "The Moral Equivalent of War." The very title conveys the point I am making. Certain basic needs and emotions are permanent. But they are capable of finding expression in ways that are radically different from the ways in which they now currently operate.

An even more burning issue emerges when any fundamental change in economic institutions and relations is proposed. Proposals for such sweeping change are among the commonplaces of our time. On the other hand, the proposals are met by the statement that the changes are impossible because they involve an impossible change in human nature. To this statement, advocates of the desired changes are only too likely to reply that the present system or some phase of it is contrary to human nature. The argument *pro* and *con* then gets put on the wrong ground.

As a matter of fact, economic institutions and relations are among the manifestations of human nature that are most susceptible of change. History is living evidence of the scope of these changes. Aristotle, for example, held that paying interest is unnatural, and the Middle Ages reechoed the doctrine. All interest was usury, and it was only after economic conditions had so changed that payment of interest was a customary and in that sense a "natural" thing, that usury got its present meaning.

There have been times and places in which land was held in common and in which private ownership of land would have been regarded as the most monstrous of unnatural things. There have been other times and places when all wealth was possessed by an overlord and his subjects held wealth, if any, subject to his pleasure. The entire system of credit so fundamental in contemporary financial and industrial life is a modern invention. The invention of the joint stock company with limited liability of individuals has brought about a great change from earlier facts and conceptions of property. I think the need of owning something is one of the native elements of human nature. But it takes either ignorance or a very lively fancy to suppose that the system of ownership that exists in the United States in 1938, with all its complex relations and its interweaving with legal and political supports, is a necessary and unchangeable product of an inherent tendency to appropriate and possess.

Law is one of the most conservative of human institutions; yet through the cumulative effect of legislation and judicial decisions it changes, sometimes at a slow rate, sometimes rapidly. The changes in human relations that are brought about by changes in industrial and legal institutions then react to modify the ways in which human nature manifests itself, and this brings about still further changes in institutions, and so on indefinitely.

It is for these reasons that I say that those who hold that proposals for social change, even of rather a profound character, are impossible and utopian because of the fixity of human nature, confuse the resistance to change that comes from acquired habits with that which comes from original human nature. The savage, living in a primitive society, comes nearer to being a purely "natural" human being than does civilized man. Civilization itself is the product of altered human nature. But even the savage is bound by a mass of tribal customs and transmitted beliefs that modify his original nature, and it is these acquired habits that make it so difficult to transform him into a civilized human being.

The revolutionary radical, on the other hand, overlooks the force of engrained habits. He is right, in my opinion, about the indefinite plasticity of human nature. But he is wrong in thinking that patterns of desire, belief, and purpose do not have a force comparable to the momentum of physical objects once they are set in motion, and comparable to the inertia, the resistance to movement, possessed by these same objects when they are at rest. Habit, not original human nature, keeps things moving most of the time, about as they have moved in the past.

If human nature is unchangeable, then there is no such thing as education and all our efforts to educate are doomed to failure. For the very meaning of education is modification of native human nature in formation of those new ways of thinking, of feeling, of desiring, and of believing that are foreign to raw human nature. If the latter were unalterable, we might have training but not education. For training, as distinct from education, means simply the acquisition of certain skills. Native gifts can be trained to a point of higher efficiency without that development of new attitudes and dispositions which is the goal of education. But the result is mechanical. It is like supposing that while a musician may acquire by practice greater technical ability, he cannot rise from one plane of musical appreciation and creation to another.

The theory that human nature is unchangeable is thus the most depressing and pessimistic of all possible doctrines. If it were carried out logically, it would mean a doctrine of predestination from birth that would outdo the most rigid of theological doctrines. For according to it, persons are what they are at birth and nothing can be done about it, beyond the kind of training that an acrobat might give to the muscular system with which he is originally endowed. If a person is born with criminal tendencies, a criminal he will become and remain. If a person is born with an excessive amount of greed, he will become a person living by predatory activities at the expense of others; and so on. I do not doubt at all the existence of differences in natural endowment. But what I am questioning is the notion that they doom individuals to a fixed channel of expression. It is difficult indeed to make a silk purse out of a sow's ear. But the particular form which, say, a natural musical endowment will take depends upon the social influences to which he is subjected. Beethoven in a savage tribe would doubtless have been outstanding as a musician, but he would not have been the Beethoven who composed symphonies.

The existence of almost every conceivable kind of social institution at some time and place in the history of the world is evidence of the plasticity of human nature. This fact does not prove that all these different social systems are of equal value, ma-terially, morally, and culturally. The slightest observation shows that such is not the case. But the fact in proving the changeability of human nature indicates the attitude that should be taken to-ward proposals for social changes. The question is primarily whether they, in special cases, are desirable or not. And the way to answer that question is to try to discover what their conse-quences would be if they were adopted. Then if the conclusion is that they are desirable, the further question is how they can be accomplished with a minimum of waste, destruction, and need-less dislocation.

In finding the answer to this question, we have to take into ac-count the force of existing traditions and customs; of the pat-terns of action and belief that already exist. We have to find out what forces already at work can be reinforced so that they move toward the desired change and how the conditions that oppose change can be gradually weakened. Such questions as these can be considered on the basis of fact and reason.

The assertion that a proposed change is impossible because of the fixed constitution of human nature diverts attention from the question of whether or not a change is desirable and from the other question of how it shall be brought about. It throws the question into the arena of blind emotion and brute force. In the end, it encourages those who think that great changes can be produced offhand and by the use of sheer violence.

When our sciences of human nature and human relations are anything like as developed as are our sciences of physical nature, their chief concern will be with the problem of how human nature is most effectively modified. The question will not be whether it is capable of change, but of how it is to be changed under given conditions. This problem is ultimately that of education in its widest sense. Consequently, whatever represses and distorts the processes of education that might bring about a change in human dispositions with the minimum of waste puts a premium upon the forces that bring society to a state of deadlock, and thereby encourages the use of violence as a means of social change.

Democracy and Education in the World of Today

It is obvious that the relation between democracy and education is a reciprocal one, a mutual one, and vitally so. Democracy is itself an educational principle, an educational measure and policy. There is nothing novel in saying that even an election campaign has a greater value in educating the citizens of the country who take any part in it than it has in its immediate external results. Our campaigns are certainly not always as educational as they might be, but by and large they certainly do serve the purpose of making the citizens of the country aware of what is going on in society, what the problems are and the various measures and policies that are proposed to deal with the issues of the day.

Mussolini remarked that democracy was passé, done with, because people are tired of liberty. There is a certain truth in that remark, not about the democracy being done with, at least we hope not, but in the fact that human beings do get tired of liberty, of political liberty and of the responsibilities, the duties, the burden that the acceptance of political liberty involves. There is an educational principle and policy in a deeper sense than that which I have just mentioned in that it proposes in effect, if not in words, to every member of society just that question: do you want to be a free human being standing on your own feet, accepting the responsibilities, the duties that go with that position as an effective member of society?

The meaning of democracy, especially of political democracy which, of course, is far from covering the whole scope of democracy, as over against every aristocratic form of social control and political authority, was expressed by Abraham Lincoln when he said that no man was good enough or wise enough to govern

[First published as a pamphlet by the Society for Ethical Culture, New York, 1938, 15 pp.]

others without their consent; that is, without some expression on their part of their own needs, their own desires and their own conception of how social affairs should go on and social problems be handled.

A woman told me once that she asked a very well known American statesman what he would do for the people of this country if he were God. He said, "Well, that is quite a question. I should look people over and decide what it was that they needed and then try and give it to them."

She said, "Well, you know, I expected that to be the answer that you would give. There are people that would *ask* other people what they wanted before they tried to give it to them."

That asking other people what they would like, what they need, what their ideas are, is an essential part of the democratic idea. We are so familiar with it as a matter of democratic political practice that perhaps we don't always think about it even when we exercise the privilege of giving an answer. That practice is an educational matter because it puts upon us as individual members of a democracy the responsibility of considering what it is that we as individuals want, what our needs and troubles are.

Dr. Felix Adler expressed very much the same idea. I am not quoting his words, but this was what he said, that "no matter how ignorant any person is there is one thing that he knows better than anybody else and that is where the shoes pinch on his own feet"; and because it is the individual that knows his own troubles, even if he is not literate or sophisticated in other respects, the idea of democracy as opposed to any conception of aristocracy is that every individual must be consulted in such a way, actively not passively, that he himself becomes a part of the process of authority, of the process of social control; that his needs and wants have a chance to be registered in a way where they count in determining social policy. Along with that goes, of course, the other feature which is necessary for the realization of democracy—mutual conference and mutual consultation and arriving ultimately at social control by pooling, by putting together all of these individual expressions of ideas and wants.

The ballot box and majority rule are external and very largely mechanical symbols and expressions of this. They are expedients, the best devices that at a certain time have been found, but beneath them there are the two ideas: first, the opportunity, the right and the duty of every individual to form some conviction and to express some conviction regarding his own place in the social order, and the relations of that social order to his own welfare; second, the fact that each individual counts as one and one only on an equality with others, so that the final social will comes about as the cooperative expression of the ideas of many people. And I think it is perhaps only recently that we are realizing that that idea is the essence of all sound education.

Even in the classroom we are beginning to learn that learning which develops intelligence and character does not come about when only the textbook and the teacher have a say; that every individual becomes educated only as he has an opportunity to contribute something from his own experience, no matter how meagre or slender that background of experience may be at a given time; and finally that enlightenment comes from the give and take, from the exchange of experiences and ideas.

The realization of that principle in the schoolroom, it seems to me, is an expression of the significance of democracy as the educational process without which individuals cannot come into the full possession of themselves nor make a contribution, if they have it in them to make, to the social well-being of others.

I said that democracy and education bear a reciprocal relation, for it is not merely that democracy is itself an educational principle, but that democracy cannot endure, much less develop, without education in that narrower sense in which we ordinarily think of it, the education that is given in the family, and especially as we think of it in the school. The school is the essential distributing agency for whatever values and purposes any social group cherishes. It is not the only means, but it is the first means, the primary means and the most deliberate means by which the values that any social group cherishes, the purposes that it wishes to realize, are distributed and brought home to the thought, the observation, judgment and choice of the individual.

What would a powerful dynamo in a big power-house amount to if there were no line of distribution leading into shops and factories to give power, leading into the home to give light? No matter what fine ideals or fine resources, the products of past experience, past human culture, exist somewhere at the centre, they become significant only as they are carried out, or are distributed. That is true of any society, not simply of a democratic society; but what is true of a democratic society is, of course, that its special values and its special purposes and aims must receive such distribution that they become part of the mind and the will of the members of society. So that the school in a democracy is contributing, if it is true to itself as an educational agency, to the democratic idea of making knowledge and understanding, in short the power of action, a part of the intrinsic intelligence and character of the individual.

I think we have one thing to learn from the anti-democratic states of Europe, and that is that we should take as seriously the preparation of the members of our society for the duties and responsibilities of democracy, as they take seriously the formation of the thoughts and minds and characters of their population for their aims and ideals.

This does not mean that we should imitate their universal propaganda, that we should prostitute the schools, the radio and the press to the inculcation of one single point of view and the suppression of everything else; it means that we should take seriously, energetically and vigorously the use of democratic schools and democratic methods in the schools; that we should educate the young and the youth of the country in freedom for participation in a free society. It may be that with the advantage of great distance from these troubled scenes in Europe we may learn something from the terrible tragedies that are occurring there, so as to take the idea of democracy more seriously, asking ourselves what it means, and taking steps to make our schools more completely the agents for preparation of free individuals for intelligent participation in a free society.

I don't need to tell these readers that our free public school system was founded, promoted, just about 100 years ago, because of the realization of men like Horace Mann and Henry Barnard that citizens need to participate in what they called a republican form of government; that they need enlightenment which could come about only through a system of free education.

If you have read the writings of men of those times, you know how few schools existed, how poor they were, how short their terms were, how poorly most of the teachers were prepared, and, judging from what Horace Mann said, how general was the indifference of the average well-to-do citizen to the education of anybody except his own children.

You may recall the terrible indictment that he drew of the well-to-do classes because of their indifference to the education of the masses, and the vigor with which he pointed out that they were pursuing a dangerous course; that, no matter how much they educated their own children, if they left the masses ignorant they would be corrupted and that they themselves and their children would be the sufferers in the end. As he said, "We did not mean to exchange a single tyrant across the sea for a hydra-headed tyrant here at home"; yet that is what we will get unless we educate our citizens.

I refer to him particularly because to such a very large extent the ideas, the ideals which Horace Mann and the others held have been so largely realized. I think even Horace Mann could hardly have anticipated a finer, more magnificent school plan, school building and school equipment than we have in some parts of our country. On the side of the mechanical and the external, the things that these educational statesmen 100 years ago strove for have been to a considerable extent realized. I should have to qualify that. We know how poor many of the rural schools are, especially in backward states of the country, how poorly they are equipped, how short their school years are; but, in a certain sense, taking what has been done at the best, the immediate ideals of Horace Mann and the others have been realized. Yet the problem we have today of the relation of education and democracy is as acute and as serious a problem as the problem of providing school buildings, school equipment, school teachers and school monies was a hundred years ago.

If, as we all know, democracy is in a more or less precarious position throughout the world, and has even in our own country enemies of growing strength, we cannot take it for granted as something that is sure to endure. If this is the actual case, one reason for it is that we have been so complacent about the idea of democracy that we have more or less unconsciously assumed that the work of establishing a democracy was completed by the founding fathers or when the Civil War abolished slavery. We tend to think of it as something that has been established and that it remains for us simply to enjoy.

We have had, without formulating it, a conception of democracy as something static, as something that is like an inheritance that can be bequeathed, a kind of lump sum that we could live off and upon. The crisis that we are undergoing will turn out, I think, to be worthwhile if we learn through it that every generation has to accomplish democracy over again for itself; that its very nature, its essence, is something that cannot be handed on from one person or one generation to another, but has to be worked out in terms of needs, problems and conditions of the social life of which, as the years go by, we are a part, a social life that is changing with extreme rapidity from year to year.

I find myself resentful and really feeling sad when, in relation to present social, economic and political problems, people point simply backward as if somewhere in the past there were a model for what we should do today. I hope I yield to none in appreciation of the great American tradition, for tradition is something that is capable of being transmitted as an emotion and as an idea from generation to generation. We have a great and precious heritage from the past, but to be realized, to be translated from an idea and an emotion, this tradition has to be embodied by active effort in the social relations which we as human beings bear to each other under present conditions. It is because the conditions of life change, that the problem of maintaining a democracy becomes new, and the burden that is put upon the school, upon the educational system is not that of stating merely the ideas of the men who made this country, their hopes and their intentions, but of teaching what a democratic society means under existing conditions.

The other day I read a statement to the effect that more than half of the working people in shops and factories in this country today are working in industries that didn't even exist forty years ago. It would seem to mean that, as far as the working population is concerned, half of the old industries have gone into obsolescence and been replaced by new ones. The man who made that statement, a working scientist, pointed out that every worker in every industry today is doing what he is doing either directly or indirectly because of the progress that has been made in the last half century in the physical sciences. In other words, in the material world, in the world of production, of material commodities and material entities, the progress of knowledge, of science, has revolutionized activity (revolutionized is not too strong a word) in the last fifty years.

How can we under these circumstances think that we can live from an inheritance, noble and fine as it is, that was formed in earlier days—one might as well say pre-scientific and pre-industrial days—except as we deliberately translate that tradition and that inheritance into the terms of the realities of present society which means simply our relations to one another.

Horace Mann and other educators 100 years ago worked when the United States was essentially agricultural. The things with which we are most familiar that enter into the formation of a material part of our life didn't exist. Railways were just beginning, but all the other great inventions that we take for granted were hidden in the darkness of future time. Even then in those earlier days, Thomas Jefferson predicted evils that might come to man with the too-rapid development of manufacturing industries, because, as he saw it, the backbone of any democratic society was the farmer who owned and cultivated his own land. He saw the farmer as a man who could control his own economic destiny, a man who, therefore, could stand on his own feet and be really a free citizen of a free country. What he feared was what might happen when men lost the security of economic independence and became dependent upon others.

Even Alexander Hamilton, who belonged to the other school of thought, when speaking of judges, maintained that those who controlled a man's subsistence controlled his will. If that is true of judges on the bench it is certainly true to a considerable extent of all people; and now we have economic conditions, because of the rapid change in industry and in finance, where there are thousands and millions of people who have the minimum of control over the conditions of their own subsistence. That is a problem, of course, that will need public and private consideration, but it is a deeper problem than that; it is a problem of the future of democracy, of how political democracy can be made secure if there is economic insecurity and economic dependence of great sections of the population if not upon the direct will of others, at least upon the conditions under which the employing sections of society operate.

I mention this simply as one of the respects in which the relation of education and democracy assumes a very different form than it did in the time when these men supposed that "If we can only have schools enough, only have school buildings and good school equipment and prepared teachers, the necessary enlightenment to take care of republican institutions will follow almost as a matter of course."

The educational problem today is deeper, it is more acute, it is infinitely more difficult because it has to face all of the problems of the modern world. Recently we have been reading in some quarters about the necessity of coalition, whether in arms or not, at least some kind of a coalition of democratic nations, formed to oppose and resist the advance of Fascist, totalitarian, authoritarian states. I am not going to discuss that issue, but I do want to ask a few questions. What do we mean when we assume that we, in common with certain other nations, are really democratic, that we have already so accomplished the ends and purposes of democracy that all we have to do is to stand up and resist the encroachments of non-democratic states?

We are unfortunately familiar with the tragic racial intolerance of Germany and now of Italy. Are we entirely free from that racial intolerance, so that we can pride ourselves upon having achieved a complete democracy? Our treatment of the Negroes, anti-Semitism, the growing (at least I fear it is growing) serious opposition to the alien immigrant within our gates, is, I think, a sufficient answer to that question. Here, in relation to education, we have a problem; what are our schools doing to cultivate not merely passive toleration that will put up with people of different racial birth or different colored skin, but what are our schools doing positively and aggressively and constructively to cultivate understanding and goodwill which are essential to democratic society?

We object, and object very properly, to the constant stream of false propaganda that is put forth in the states for the suppression of all free inquiry and freedom, but again how do we stand in those respects? I know we have in many schools a wonderful school pledge where the children six years old and up probably arise and pledge allegiance to a flag and to what that stands for—one indivisible nation, justice and liberty. How far are we permitting a symbol to become a substitute for the reality? How far are our citizens, legislators and educators salving their conscience with the idea that genuine patriotism is being instilled in these children because they recite the words of that pledge? Do they know what allegiance and loyalty mean? What do they mean by an indivisible nation when we have a nation that is still more or less torn by factional strife and class division? Is that an indivisible nation and is the reciting of a verbal pledge any educational guarantee of the existence of an indivisible nation?

And so I might go on about liberty and justice. What are we doing to translate those great ideas of liberty and justice out of a formal ceremonial ritual into the realities of the understanding, the insight and the genuine loyalty of the boys and girls in our schools?

We say we object, and rightly so, to this exaggerated, one-sided nationalism inculcated under the name of devotion to country, but until our schools have themselves become clear upon what public spirit and good citizenship mean in all the relations of life, youth cannot meet the great responsibilities that rest upon them.

We deplore, also, and deplore rightly, the dependence of these authoritarian states in Europe upon the use of force. What are we doing to cultivate the idea of the supremacy of the method of intelligence, of understanding, the method of goodwill and of mutual sympathy over and above force? I know that in many respects our public schools have and deserve a good reputation for what they have done in breaking down class division, creating a feeling of greater humanity and of membership in a single family, but I do not believe that we have as yet done what can be done and what needs to be done in breaking down even the ordinary snobbishness and prejudices that divide people from each other, and that our schools have done what they can and should do in this respect.

And when it comes to this matter of force as a method of settling social issues, we have unfortunately only to look at our own scene, both domestic and international. In the present state of the world apparently a great and increasing number of people feel that the only way we can make ourselves secure is by increasing our army and navy and making our factories ready to manufacture munitions. In other words, somehow we too have a belief that force, physical and brute force, after all is the best final reliance.

With our fortunate position in the world I think that if we used our resources, including our financial resources, to build up among ourselves a genuine, true and effective democratic society, we would find that we have a surer, a more enduring and a more powerful defense of democratic institutions both within ourselves and with relation to the rest of the world than the surrender to the belief in force, violence and war can ever give. I know that our schools are doing a great deal to inculcate ideas of peace, but I sometimes wonder how far this goes beyond a certain sentimental attachment to a realization of what peace would actually mean in the world in the way of cooperation, goodwill and mutual understanding.

I have endeavored to call your attention first to the inherent, the vital and organic relation that there is between democracy and education from both sides, from the side of education, the schools, and from the side of the very meaning of democracy. I have simply tried to give a certain number of more or less random illustrations of what the problems of the schools are today with reference to preparing the youth of the country for active, intelligent participation in the building and the rebuilding and the eternal rebuilding—because, as I have said, it never can be done once for all—of a genuinely democratic society, and, I wish to close (as I began) with saying, that after all the cause of democracy is the moral cause of the dignity and the worth of the individual. Through mutual respect, mutual toleration, give and take, the pooling of experiences, it is ultimately the only method by which human beings can succeed in carrying on this experiment in which we are all engaged, whether we want to be or not, the greatest experiment of humanity—that of living together in ways in which the life of each of us is at once profitable in the deepest sense of the word, profitable to himself and helpful in the building up of the individuality of others.

Education, Democracy, and Socialized Economy

The editor of the *Social Frontier* has asked me to say something upon the topic represented by the above caption, taking at least my text and point of departure from the articles of Drs. Bode and Childs in the November number of this periodical. I consented before I had seen and read the two articles. After reading them I am wondering whether my promise was not somewhat rash. Both writers quote from my own writings with approval in support of their views, so I am forced to wonder whether I have been unsure as to my own ground and have taken different positions at different times—which might well be the case. But my chief embarrassment comes from the fact that the two writers, after agreeing about 100 percent on what seems to be the main issue, then proceed to differ radically about its application. A witty former colleague used to speak of philosophic disputants charging furiously at one another down parallel lines. Since I cannot suppose this is the case with Drs. Childs and Bode, I am moved to try and discriminate basic issues from secondary and derived ones.

The articles agree on the fundamental points that *all education takes its direction from a social aim,* and that in this country *the social aim is set by the democratic principle.* We then find that Dr. Bode believes that Dr. Childs is so devoted to a certain scheme of economic reform that he would make the schools an instrument for accomplishing "a specific program for social reform," a course which is said to commit educators to trying to promote democracy by conditioning its movement in a certain direction fixed in advance of, and independently of, conclusions reached by democratic procedures. On the other hand, we find

[First published in *Social Frontier* 5 (December 1938): 71–72. For Boyd H. Bode's and John L. Childs's articles to which Dewey refers, see Appendixes 2 and 3.]

that Dr. Childs believes that Dr. Bode's refusal to consider the relation of the economic order of society to realization of the democratic principles leaves him in a kind of educational vacuum,
since teachers are to study economic and social problems but are
to refuse to reach and adopt definite conclusions about them.

As far as I can see, two questions are raised in this clash of
views. One of them is: "What in fact is the relation between *realization* of the ideas and principles of democracy and the economic, industrial, and financial order of society?" The other
question concerns the further issue: "What sort of *methods* of
teaching are consonant with and required by acceptance of the
democratic orientation and frame of reference?" This second
question is involved because it is clear that Dr. Bode believes that
Dr. Childs's position entails something close to, or identical
with, a method of antidemocratic inculcation, while Dr. Childs
believes that the position of Dr. Bode involves commitment to
methods of instruction so colorless, so indifferent to concrete
conclusions on important social issues, that profession of democratic ends tends to become empty, almost verbal.

Independently, then, of what these writers say about positions
taken by the other, two issues emerge: (1) *What relation, if any,
exists between the actual or effective realization of democracy
and the economic structure of society?* (2) What does the democratic end involve as to methods to be adopted in instruction, so
as to avoid, especially, undemocratic inculcation of ready-made
conclusions on one hand and aimless vagueness on the other
hand?

If the relation between the economic organization of society
and the realization of the democratic principle is simply a matter
of adoption of "a specific reform," then insistence, if it should
exist, that educators should use the schools to promote this reform conflicts with the professed democratic aim. But the "if"
covers a good deal of ground. The belief that there is an *inherent*
connection between the *realities* of a democratic society, under
present conditions, and a change in economic affairs in the direction of greater control and planning exercised in the social interest does not seem to be correctly described as a "specific social
and economic reform." Doubtless there are those who think of it
as an end in itself and hence something to be attained independently of the effect upon democracy; there is a political party

which, until recently, has held that it can be effected only by a period of a class dictatorship in which democracy is abrogated. But all this is quite different from the position that the democratic end and ideal demands for its *own* adequate realization a pretty thoroughgoing change in the economic structure of society, one to be brought about by democratic methods and not by means of suppression of democracy.

Now, quite apart from the solution this problem may receive, it should be clear that *the question at issue is one of fact, not one that can be settled by an analysis of the concept of democracy*— even though it must be settled in accordance with conclusions reached in analysis of that conception. I am not going to argue here for the thesis that under conditions as they now exist it is democracy itself which demands basic reconstruction of economic institutions. But when the issue is looked at as one of fact, *it is a question of the bearings of the existing economic order upon the liberty, equality, and, possibly, fraternity that are so intrinsic to the democratic idea that without them democracy becomes a farce.* Furthermore, the problem of the existence of opportunity to work and of the obligation to render useful service in work is, in the minds of many, an economic question which has moral implications that are fundamentally important for the realization of democracy.

Now, whatever may be the actual conclusion reached in discussion of these questions, it ought to be clear that the issue cannot be assumed in advance to be one of the relation of merely external mechanical devices to democracy as an intrinsic moral end. This position, if it be taken, begs the exact question at issue, namely, *whether or not the economic structure of society bears, under present conditions, an inherent relation to the realization of the democratic idea.* Were this issue discussed, and discussed on the ground of social facts and forces rather than as one of the implications of the abstract concept of democracy, it seems to me discussion would be fruitful in enlightenment and in progress toward agreement. If disagreement resulted, we should at least know where it is located and why it came about.

I come now to the issue regarding method. If it is asserted that educators should take a position upon the issue just stated without careful reflection, involving cooperative discussion, and should then proceed in teaching to attempt to make their students swallow the idea whole, it seems clear enough that the procedure would be wholly antidemocratic. Although there are persons to whom socialism and communism are dogmatic, unquestionable creeds, I have difficulty in supposing that their attitude describes a point that is at issue between Dr. Bode and Dr. Childs. *If teachers who hold that there is an intrinsic relation between actualization of democracy and social planning of economic institutions and relations hope to bring others to the same conclusions by use of the method of investigation and free cooperative discussion, I see nothing undemocratic in the procedure.* It looks to me like an educational procedure, and, moreover, to be of the same sort that teachers who have been led to accept the conclusion might then use with their own students.

That there are those who would impose a socialistic or communistic point of view upon others, that there is even a political party, having presumably some representatives among teachers, who hold that a socialist order is so supremely important that it should be attained by a period of class dictatorship in which democracy is suppressed, is doubtless a fact. But I can hardly believe that Dr. Bode imagines that this position is necessarily involved in the position taken by Dr. Childs. Or, stating the issue of method in less extreme terms, while there is always danger of the use of methods of inculcation and indoctrination that *are* foreign and hostile to democracy, why should it be assumed that this must be the case? *Why not consider a concrete problem: What methods, in fact, are fitted to bring about democratic orientation and devotion to social ends and values? I cannot see that in principle the question is any different in the case of democracy itself than in that of other social ends.* How can our schools accomplish a genuine democratic orientation in students? Does accomplishment of this result involve, as far as methods are concerned, a nondemocratic conditioning? The question is not a rhetorical one. *I can think of no question that is more vitally and practically important than just this question of how the schools today are to render the idea of democracy a living and effective reality in the minds of the youth who form the future citizenship of the country.* Were the problem discussed as one of concrete, practical fact and factors, we should, perhaps, get out of the region of abstract generalities in which head-on intellectual conflicts flourish.

Doubtless my own predilections regarding solution of the particular problem raised in the debate between Drs. Childs and Bode show through in what I have written. But my intention is not to argue for one solution rather than another. My intention is to indicate the need of clarifying the issues involved and freeing them from irrelevant accretions. For the present it seems to me that perhaps this can best be accomplished by stating a number of principles in hypothetical form and exploring the consequences that follow from them as hypotheses. *If* democracy as a moral principle is *independent* of economic institutions, we shall be directed to a different solution than *if* the two are closely connected. Discussion of the alternative "ifs" or hypotheses will take us, it seems to me, out of cloudy generalities. The same thing can be said of alternative hypotheses about the methods by which, in accord with democratic principles, students will be brought to understanding of the concrete significance of democracy and to practical devotion to its cause.

The Economic Basis of the New Society

The imminence of the "next world war" has caused the last World War to recede from thought, discussion and imagination except in negative ways. During the progress of the World War positive attitudes and hopes were generated and positive plans and objectives put forward for the creation of a better human society. The fact that these hopes were betrayed and objectives failed to be realized is evidence of our failure to take advantage of the opportunity that was unquestionably there. It is not a condemnation of those hopes and objectives.

The constructive thought of that period centered about two comprehensive objectives: the establishment of a system of international law that would ensure peaceful relations between nations; and the reorganization of the social and economic relations within nations. Passing over the former objective, let us consider the latter.

I quote the statement I made then concerning the objectives for internal social reorganization then afoot, plans and programs, it may be pointed out, which claimed the attention not only of progressive individuals but of political parties. Unfortunately, I need make no apology for quoting from an article written nearly twenty years ago. The evils existing then still exist now, the things needing to be done then still need to be done now.

"The first of the deficiencies which will have to be cared for in any effective reorganization which may take place after the war is the failure of our social order in the past to secure to its members steady and useful employment. It would be difficult to bring any more severe indictment against anything that calls itself a civilization, than the fact that it is not able to utilize the energy,

[First published in *Intelligence in the Modern World*, ed. Joseph Ratner (New York: Modern Library, 1939), pp. 416–38.]

physical, intellectual and moral, of the members who are desir-
ous and anxious of rendering some kind of service, of producing
some kind of needed and useful commodity; that it has not been
able systematically to give all of its members a chance to do
something. The evil, and the unnecessary character of the evil of
unemployment is, then, the thing which I would put first, because it represents, in anything that professes to be civilization,
the most obvious and definite point of weakness.

"Now, this is serious, not merely from the standpoint of the
enormous poverty and misery which insecure and precarious
employment entails upon a large part of the population, but, if
possible, even more serious because of the undermining of morale, of character, which comes with such a situation as this. We
all know how demoralizing charity is. Every society of organized
charity is teaching and constantly preaching the evils of indis-
criminate charity, how it destroys the character of those who become its recipients. Cannot we generalize this lesson and apply it
to the whole industrial situation? What is the effect upon the
self-respect of the large classes of men and women who periodi-
cally, once in so often, find themselves in large numbers thrown
out of employment, and find that they have to beg, not for
charity, but for even a chance to do work in turning out commodities or in rendering services which society actually needs?
The undermining of confidence in oneself, of respect for oneself,
the undermining of faith or belief in the world and in others that
comes because of precarious and insecure tenure of employment
is I think impossible to overestimate. When people find that they
cannot do things that they are capable of doing, the attitude that
comes toward the world is either one of impotence and enfeeble-
ment, or else one of bitterness and hostility. Now, these things
are, perhaps, sufficiently obvious. They are not new. There was
plenty of discussion of the problem of unemployment and the
remedies for it, before the war, but the war in its conduct has
made the consciousness of it more acute and more general, and it
has shown that the problem is not inevitable, that it is capable of
human administration and handling. It has proved that it is possible for men, pooling and organizing their intelligence and experience, and having the authority of the government behind them,
to take hold of the industrial and economic processes and see to
it, even in a period of such great stress as during the war, that no

man or woman who is capable of work shall lack useful, steady, and reasonably remunerative employment.

"The second evil is the degraded and inhuman standard, or scale, of living which is found on the part of so many of the industrial population—of course, partly as a consequence of chronic unemployment or, at least, insecure employment, but partly because of the low rate of return for employment. We are accustomed, of course, to connect low wages and lack of work with poverty and suffering, but we too often fail to translate poverty and the misery that goes with it into terms of the general vitiation, the general deterioration of the scale of life on the part of a large element of the population. We fail to note what an unhuman lowering it means of the standard of physical health—though here again was a point that was being agitated more and more, even before the war, involving a consideration of the question of the socially unnecessary deaths, illnesses, accidents and incapacitations that come from the bad economic conditions under which so much of modern industry is carried on. We need only to think of the conditions under which masses of our populations live, not merely in the slums, but wherever there is a congested industrial population, to realize how low, as compared with the attained standards of the well-to-do element of the population, their plane of living really is.

"In the third place, the war has revealed the serious weaknesses and defects which exist with respect to efficiency of production and distribution. Now, this is the particular phase of the matter upon which our existing old social order most prided itself. It might have admitted that it had not done so well with the human side of the problem, but it has been contended that, so far as efficiency in the invention, organization and utilization of the machinery of production and distribution is concerned, the present age is almost infinitely in advance of any that has preceded. Of course, in a certain sense, as compared with older civilizations—those that came before the great industrial revolution—this is true enough; for these mechanical inventions are, of course, the product of scientific discovery. They are the product of the release of men's minds in the study of nature and the mystery of natural forces. It is a great mistake to suppose that our mechanical inventions of machines and implements—the steam engine, the telegraph, the telephone, the motor car, and the other agencies of production and distribution—are the actual fruit of the present industrial order. On the contrary, they are the fruit of the discoveries of a comparatively small number of scientific men who have not labored for recognition and who have never got it, very much—at least, in the way of pecuniary recognition. It simply happened that conditions were such that the men of means, men possessed of the financial and pecuniary resources, could utilize these fruits of natural science.

"Furthermore, efficiency is not an absolute thing; but, of course, as every engineer tells us, it is a matter of ratio. Efficiency is a matter of the ratio which the actual output bears to the available resources; and looked at from that standpoint, not in comparison with the output of past ages, but as a matter of ratio which exists now between the present output and the resources now available, we cannot pride ourselves on having attained any great amount of even industrial efficiency in production. I need hardly remind you of the fact that when greater efficiency was required in England and in this country, the government had to take charge of the distributing agencies, the railroads. I need not remind you of the breakdown in the production and distribution of coal, from which we suffered; and however much or however little the blame for that is to be laid at the doors of any particular individuals, the real difficulty, of course, goes much further back. It goes back to the fact that we have had production and distribution organized on a non-social basis—a basis of pecuniary profit. And when they suddenly had to be switched over to the basis of public need and public service, they naturally broke down. The great inefficiency here is, however, the failure to utilize human power. The great advance has, of course, been in the utilizing of natural power—steam and electricity, the machines, implements, and so on; but we have not succeeded in engaging, enlisting and releasing available human energy.

"The first great demand of a better social order, I should say, then, is the guarantee of the right, to every individual who is capable of it, to work—not the mere legal right, but a right which is enforceable so that the individual will always have the opportunity to engage in some form of useful activity; and if the ordinary economic machinery breaks down through a crisis of some sort, then it is the duty of the state to come to the rescue and see that individuals have something to do that is worth while—

not breaking stone in a stone yard, or something else to get a soup ticket with, but some kind of productive work which a self-respecting person may engage in with interest and with more than mere pecuniary profit. Whatever may be said about the fortunes of what has technically been called socialism, it would seem to be simply the part of ordinary common sense that society should reorganize itself to make sure that individuals can make a living and be kept going, not by charity, but by having productive work to do.

"In the second place, war has revealed the *possibilities* of intelligent administration—administration which *could* be used to raise and maintain on a higher level the general standard and scale of living. The minimum wage is not one of the visions of the nations that have been longer in the war than we have; it is not, with them, a dream, an uplift notion: it is an accomplished fact. Great Britain is already spending an immense amount of money for the housing of its laborers, and, as we have found out in connection with our shipping program, we can not do what we have got to do, unless we first see to it that there are decent, comfortable and sanitary housing facilities for the population. One of the demands which has already been made in England, which would help, also, to take care of the unemployment problem after the war, is that this great work of housing, conducted under national social auspices, shall go on until the slums, with their bad sanitary, moral, and bad aesthetic influence, have disappeared and every individual has a home to live in and surroundings to live in which observe the ordinary amenities of human life. The movements for insurance against accident, insurance against illness, insurance against the contingencies of old age, which were already active before the war, have also, of course, been given a tremendous acceleration.

"The third phase that I mention is the need of securing greater industrial autonomy, that is to say, greater ability on the part of the workers in any particular trade or occupation to control that industry, instead of working under these conditions of external control where they have no interest, no insight into what they are doing, and no social outlook upon the consequences and meaning of what they are doing. This means an increasing share given to the laborer, to the wage earner, in controlling the conditions of his own activity. It is so common to point out the absurdity of conducting a war for political democracy which leaves industrial and economic autocracy practically untouched, that I think we are absolutely bound to see, after the war, either a period of very great unrest, disorder, drifting, strife—I would not say actual civil war, but all kinds of irregular strife and disorder, or a movement to install the principle of self-government within industries.

"These three things, then, seem to me the essential minimum elements of an intelligent program of social reorganization."

The idea of reconstruction was at the time the foregoing was written something to conjure with. In retrospect, we may come to the conclusion, widely prevalent today, that the whole idea of social reorganization was an illusion bred of the excited state of mind of the war. If that idea seems an illusion today, it is because we failed to *learn* the lesson, which could be truly learned only by carrying it out into practice. If we fail to learn the lessons of the present day—in fundamental respects identical with those of twenty years ago—then we may be sure that twenty years hence our present most ardent hopes and inspired programs will also be dismissed as illusions.

To quote again:

"Now, in such a situation as this, we are not, I think, entitled to unthinking optimism about the certainty of great progress or about the particular direction which social reorganization will take after the war. There is going to be, of course, a very great demand and a very great pressure, especially from the side of labor, but there will also be a very great inertia, very great obstacles and difficulties to contend with. We are not entitled to assume that automatically there is going to be a desirable reorganization and reconstruction after the war. We may, possibly—it is conceivable—go through a long period of social drifting and social unrest. The question is whether society, because of the experience of the war, will learn to utilize the intelligence, the insight and foresight which are available, in order to take hold of the problem and to go at it, step by step, on the basis of an intelligent program—a program which is not too rigid, which is not a program in the sense of having every item definitely scheduled in advance, but which represents an outlook upon the future of the things which most immediately require doing, trusting to the experience which is got in doing them to reveal the next things needed and the next steps to be taken. Now, the one great thing that the war has accomplished, it seems to me, of a permanent sort, is the enforcement of a psychological and educational lesson. Before the war, most persons would have said, who recognized these evils: Well, they are very great. We all recognize them. We deplore them, but the whole situation is so big and so complicated that it is not possible to do anything about it. We have got to wait for the slow process of evolution. We have got to wait for the working out of unconscious, natural law to accomplish anything serious and important in the way of reorganization. Well, I think the war has absolutely put an end to the right to the claim of anybody to say things of that sort. It is proved now that it is possible for human beings to take hold of human affairs and manage them, to see an end which has to be gained, a purpose which must be fulfilled, and deliberately and intelligently to go to work to organize the means, the resources and the methods of accomplishing those results.

"It seems to me that we cannot in any good conscience return, after the war, to the old period of drifting, so-called evolution, as a necessary method of procedure. The real question with us will be one of effectively discerning whether intelligent men of the community really want to bring about a better reorganized social order. If the desire, the will and the purpose are strong enough, it has been demonstrated that, under conditions of very great strain—abnormal strain and pressure—human beings can get together cooperatively and bring their physical resources and their intellectual resources to bear upon the problem of managing society, instead of letting society drift along more or less at the mercy of accident."[1]

Events after the war in this country seemed to give the lie to the hopes then entertained. "Return to Normalcy" was not only the slogan but the practice, "normalcy" meaning the old social-economic regime. Attempts at radical social change were defeated in Europe in every country save Russia. Italy and Germany moved into Fascist dictatorships and other European and South American countries in that direction. Social reorganization did take place but in a direction opposite to that of the hopes entertained by liberals and radicals in the earlier period. Nevertheless,

---

1. All quotations from an article entitled "Internal Social Reorganization after the War," first printed in the *Journal of Race Development*, April 1918; reprinted in *Characters and Events*, vol. II, pp. 745 ff. [*Middle Works* 11:73 ff.]

the forecast of "serious internal disorder and unrest" has been fulfilled.

After the world depression of 1929, the earlier idea of reconstruction revived, not under that name but in this country under the slogan of the New Deal. It has become increasingly evident that the conditions which caused the World War remain in full force, intensified indeed by the growth of exacerbated Nationalism—which is the direction in which "internal social reorganization" has in fact mainly moved. Failure of the world communities to "meet and forestall" needed change with "sympathy and intelligence" has left us with the old problems unsolved and new ones added.

The change is not, however, a matter of mere addition. Regrouping of forces has crystallized forces which were more or less in solution and has given a new face, theoretically and practically, to the whole set of social problems that is involved. The urgent and central question at the present time is whether the needed economic-social changes (with which legal and political changes are bound up) can be effected in ways which preserve and develop what was fundamental in earlier liberalism, or whether social control is to be instituted by means of coercive governmental control from above in ways which destroy for a time (a time whose length cannot now be measured) all that was best worth conserving in older democratic ideas and ideals: Intellectual and moral freedom; freedom of inquiry and expression; freedom of association in work, recreation and for religious purposes; the freedom of intercourse among nations, which, always hampered by tariff-walls and fear of war, is now deliberately suppressed in many countries by a multitude of new technical devices.

This new face of the problem is far from being exhibited solely in Fascist nations, although in them the suppression of liberties of thought, expression, and teaching; the dissolution of voluntary groupings, such as trade unions; the threat to voluntary association for worship; and the prevention of free intercourse with other nations have their most marked expression. Nor is the problem confined to the one country in which reconstruction in the line of collectivist control, during the early period after the World War, made the most headway; for, contrary to the earlier belief in the "withering away of the State," governmental restriction of the essential liberties for which democracy stood has reached, through control of thought, expression, propaganda and direct coercion, a point in which there is little difference discernible between the U.S.S.R. and Fascist countries.

The fundamental problem is also acute in the countries that remain democratic in form and that so far have maintained, though with many violations, the ancient democratic liberties of free inquiry, free assembly, and freedom of voluntary association. For in these countries we have to a very large extent a continuation of the older policy of social drifting plus an amount of social tinkering accompanied by social unrest and uncertainty. Experience has proved that this policy is attended by economic collapse and breakdowns of ever increasing severity. As long as the alternatives set before us are rigid governmental control on the one hand, whether of the Fascist or the Russian type, and "democracy" of the drifting type on the other hand, the question to which I referred in the article quoted, "whether society will learn to utilize the intelligence, the insight and foresight which are available to go at the problem" of economic-social readjustment remains and is even more urgent today in this country than it was when the words were first written.

How much progress has been made in the intervening years? How does the situation now stand? We have a recognition which did not exist before of social responsibility for the care of the unemployed whose resources are exhausted in consequence of unemployment. But at best, the method we employ is palliative; it comes after the event. The positive problem of instituting a social-economic order in which all those capable of productive work will do the work for which they are fitted remains practically untouched. As a result, the conduct of relief and charitable care is almost never at what was termed "at the best." The personal deterioration that results from enforced idleness is a coercion which excludes the idle from the factors that contribute most effectively to decent self-respect and to personal development. While the mass of unemployed have met the situation with patience and even dignity, there can be no question that the corroding influence of living without work, upon the charity of others, private and public, is operating. In the long run, it would be difficult to find anything more destructive of the best elements of human nature than a continued prospect of living, at least of subsisting, in more or less parasitical dependence upon charity, even if it is public.

In saying these things, I am expressing no sympathy for those who complain about the growing amount of money spent upon taking care of those thrown out of productive work and the consequent increase in taxation. Much less am I expressing sympathy with the reckless charges brought against the unemployed, of loving idleness and wishing to live at the expense of society. Such complaints and charges are the product of refusal to look at the causes which produce the situation and of desire to find an alibi for their refusal to do anything to remove the causes, causes which are inherent in the existing social-economic regime. The problem of establishing social conditions which will make it possible for all who are capable to do socially productive work is not an easy one. I am not engaging in criticism because it has not been solved. I am pointing out that the problem is not even being thought much about, not to speak of being systematically faced. The reason for the great refusal is clear. To face it would involve the problem of remaking a profit system into a system conducted not just, as is sometimes said, in the interest of consumption, important as that is, but also in the interest of positive and enduring opportunity for productive and creative activity and all that that signifies for the development of the potentialities of human nature.

What gain has been made in the matter of establishing conditions that give the mass of workers not only what is called "security" but also constructive interest in the work they do? What gain has been made in giving individuals, the great mass of individuals, an opportunity to find themselves and then to educate themselves for what they can best do in work which is socially useful and such as to give free play in development of themselves? The managers of industries here and there have learned that it pays to have conditions such that those who are employed know enough about what they are doing so as to take an interest in it. Educators here and there are awake to the need of discovering vocational and occupational abilities and to the need of readjusting the school system to build upon what is discovered. But the basic trouble is not the scantiness of efforts in these directions, serious as is their paucity. It is again that the whole existing industrial system tends to nullify in large measure the effects of these efforts even when they are made. The problem of the adjustment of individual capacities and their development to actual occupations is not a one-sided or unilateral one. It is bilateral and reciprocal. It is a matter of the state of existing occupations, of the whole set-up of productive work;—of the structure of the industrial system. Even if there were a much more widespread and searching concern with the capacities of individuals and much more preparation of them along the lines of their inherent fitness and needs than now exists, what assurance is there in the existing system that there will be opportunity to use their gifts and the education they have obtained? As far as the mass is concerned, we are now putting the social cart before the social horse.

If we take the question of production, what do we find? I pass by the basic fact that real production is completed only through distribution and consumption, so that mere improvement in the mechanical means of mass production may—and does—intensify the problem instead of solving it. I pass it over here because recurring crises and depressions, with the paradox of want amid plenty, has forced the fact upon the attention of every thoughtful person. The outcome is sufficient proof that the problem of production cannot be solved in isolation from distribution and consumption. I want here to call attention rather to the fact that the present method of dealing with the problem is *restriction* of productive capacity. For scarcity of materials and surplus of those who want to work is the ideal situation for profit on the part of those situated to take advantage of it. *Restriction of production* at the very time when *expansion* of production is most needed has long been the rule of *industrialists*. Now the Government is adopting the same policy for agriculturalists. Those who practice restriction of production in their own businesses cry out loudly when the Government, following their example, intervenes to kill pigs, plow under cotton, and reduce the crop of cereals, and does it moreover when there is the most urgent need for food. Here again, as in the case of public relief, critics prefer to complain about symptoms rather than to face the cause:—The inherent exigencies of the existing social-economic system. Anyone can wax eloquent about the high social function of those who farm, mine and quarry, providing the raw materials not only of food, clothing and shelter but also of all later forms of production of both capital and consumer goods. Anyone can wax pathetic over the plight of agriculture. But under present conditions, the former course is to put the burden of carrying society upon the class now least competent to bear it and the latter course is to engage in idle sentiment.

The ultimate problem of production is the production of human beings. To this end, the production of goods is intermediate and auxiliary. It is by this standard that the present system stands condemned. "Security" is a means, and although an indispensable social means it is not the end. Machinery and technological improvement are means, but again are not the end. Discovery of individual needs and capacities is a means to the end, but only a means. The means have to be implemented by a social-economic system that establishes and uses the means for the production of free human beings associating with one another on terms of equality. Then and then only will these means be an integral part of the end, not frustrated and self-defeating, bringing new evils and generating new problems.

The problem today remains one of using available intelligence; of employing the immense resources science has put at our disposal:—A pooled and coordinated social intelligence, not the mere scattered individualized intelligences of persons here and there, however high their I.Qs. may be. Mere individual intellectual capacities are as ineffective as are mere personal good intentions. The existence of social objective intelligence brings us back to the point where we started. Social control effected through organized application of social intelligence is the sole form of social control that can and will get rid of existing evils without landing us finally in some form of coercive control from above and outside.

A great tragedy of the present situation may turn out to be that those most conscious of present evils and of the need of thoroughgoing change in the social-economic system will trust to some short-cut way out, like the method of civil war and violence. Instead of relying upon the constant application of all socially available resources of knowledge and continuous inquiry they may rely upon the frozen intelligence of some past thinker, sect and party cult: frozen because arrested into a dogma.

That "intelligence," when frozen in dogmatic social philosophies, themselves the fruit of arrested philosophies of history,

generates a vicious circle of blind oscillation is tragically exemplified in the present state of the world. What *claims* to be social
planning is now found in Communist and Fascist countries. The
social consequence is complete suppression of freedom of inquiry, communication and voluntary association, by means of a
combination of personal violence, culminating in extirpation,
and systematic partisan propaganda. The results are such that in
the minds of many persons the very idea of social planning and of
violation of the integrity of the individual are becoming intimately bound together. But an immense difference divides the
plann*ed* society from a *continuously* plann*ing* society. The former requires fixed blue-prints imposed from above and therefore
involving reliance upon physical and psychological force to secure conformity to them. The latter means the release of intelligence through the widest form of cooperative give-and-take. The
attempt to *plan* social organization and association without the
freest possible play of intelligence contradicts the very idea in *social* plann*ing*. For the latter is an operative method of activity,
not a predetermined set of final "truths."

When social "planning" is predicated on a set of "*final*"
truths, the social end is fixed once for all, and the "end" is then
used to justify whatever means are deemed necessary to attain it.
"Planning" then takes place only with respect to means of the
latter sort, not with respect to ends, so that planning with respect to even means is constrained and coercive. The social result
is that the means used have quite other consequences than the
end originally set up in idea and afterwards progressively reduced
to mere words. As the events of the past twenty years have shown,
the seizure of political power by force signifies the continued
maintenance of power by force with its continued suppression of
the most precious freedoms of the individual spirit. Maintenance
of power in order to use force becomes the actual end. Means
used determine the end actually reached. The end justifies the
means only when the means used are such as actually bring
about the desired and desirable end.

Only when reflection upon means and choice of ends are free
can there be actual social planning. Every arrest of intelligence
(and every form of social dogma is an arrest) obstructs and finally suppresses free consideration and choice of means. The
method of social intelligence is primarily concerned with free

determination of means to be employed. Until that method of social action is adopted we shall remain in a period of drift and unrest whose final outcome is likely to be force and counter force, with temporary victory to the side possessed of the most machine guns.

The Unity of the Human Being

We have no words that are prepared in advance to be fit for framing and expressing sound and tested ideas about the unity of the human being, the wholeness of the self. If we ask an economist, "What is money?" the proper official reply is, that it is a medium of exchange. The answer does not stand in the way of a great deal of money being accumulated by using it to obstruct the processes of exchange. Similarly we say that words are a means of communicating ideas. But upon some subjects,—and the present one falls in this class—the words at our disposal are largely such as to *prevent* the communication of ideas. The words are so loaded with associations derived from a long past, that instead of being tools for thought, our thoughts become subservient tools of words.

The meanings of such words as soul, mind, self, unity, even body, are hardly more than condensed epitomes of mankind's age-long efforts at interpretation of its experience. These efforts began when man first emerged from the state of the anthropoid ape. The interpretations which are embodied in the words that have come down to us are the products of desire and hope, of chance circumstance and ignorance, of the authority exercised by medicine men and priests as well as of acute observation and sound judgment.

Physicists had in the beginning a like problem. They are solving it by the invention of technical terms and a technical language. Symbols have, in principle, only the meanings that are put upon them because of special inquiries engaged in. It will be a long time before anything of this sort will be accomplished for human beings. To expel traditional meanings and replace them

[First published in *Intelligence in the Modern World*, ed. Joseph Ratner (New York: Modern Library, 1939), pp. 817–35, from an address to the American College of Physicians, St. Louis, 21 April 1937.]

by ideas that are products of controlled inquiries is a slow and painful process.

Doubtless advance is possible, and will be made, by invention of words that are not charged with the debris of man's past experience. But it is also possible that this process cannot be carried with safety as far as it can be with physical things. Our technical terms might easily represent such artificial constructions that they would fail to help us in dealings with human beings—with the John Smiths and Susan Joneses with whom we rub elbows in daily life.

The words in which I try to communicate ideas to you are, then, at best, but means of stimulating personal observation and reflection. This statement holds even of the phrase "the unity of the human being." At first, the words have only a meaning derived from a contrast-effect. The idea of man as an integral whole is projected against a background of beliefs about man which are chiefly of emotional origin and force; against belief in a dualism that was the expression of religious and moral institutions and traditions.

The phrase "unity of man" has at first, accordingly, a negative meaning. It expresses a way of *not* talking about soul *and* body, body *and* mind. The word "unity" is a protest against the canonized dualism expressed in the presence of the word "and." Nevertheless, the split expressed in this word is so engrained in our emotional and intellectual habits, that no sooner have we consciously rejected it in one form than it recurs in another. The dualism is found today even among those who have abandoned its earlier manifestations. It is shown in separations made between the structural and the functional; between the brain and the rest of the body; between the central nervous system and the vegetative nervous system and viscera; and, most fundamentally, between the organism and the environment. For the first of each of these pairs of terms—structure, brain, organism—retains something of the isolation and alleged independence that used to belong to the "soul and the mind," and later to "consciousness."

While it is necessary to advance from the negative meaning of the phrase "the unity of man," the idea of unity also has its perils. For it has taken on associations during centuries of philosophic discussion that make it a dangerous word. It has become almost an invitation to set an abstraction in place of concrete phenomena. You and I can easily think of comprehensive systems—psychiatric, therapeutic, philosophical and psychological—suggested in the first place by undoubted facts, which under the protecting shield of the idea of unity, have been built up so as to force the facts, disguising and distorting them. At the present time there is a revulsion against the endless splitting up of human beings into bits. It is going on with respect to cells, structures and organs, sensations, ideas, reflexes; and with respect to atoms and electrons. The phrase "unity of man" is a protest against analysis of man into separate ultimate elements, as well as against the traditional split into body and soul. But it is easier, much easier, to set up the idea of unity in a vague way, than it is to translate it into definite facts.

"Unity of the human being" only indicates, at best, a point of view, and the point of view has no meaning save as it is used as a vantage point from which to observe and interpret actual phenomena.

We often hear such phrases as the unity of a family, the unity of a nation. These phrases stand for something. Yet in the history of social and political speculation, men have allowed the words to take the bit in their teeth and run away from inquiry into the actual facts to which they refer. These instances of the use of "unity" may, however, provide a suggestion from which it is safe to set out. Whatever else the unity is or is not, it at least means the way in which a number of different persons and things work together toward a common end. This *working together* exists in action, in operation, not as a static object or collection of objects. It is this kind of unity that seems to me to give the clew to understanding the unity of the human being.

We can recognize and identify a man as a single object, a numerical unit, by observation which marks out boundaries, as we note that the bounded object moves as a whole. In that way you recognize me as a single object standing here on the stage before you. That is the way in which we recognize a rock, tree, or house as a single object, as a unity and whole. But that which makes a rock a single whole is the interaction of swarms of molecules, atoms and electrons; its unity is an affair of the way elements work together. The boundaries by which we mark off a human being as a unit are very different from the energies and organization of energies that make *him* a *unified human being*. We can observe the boundaries at a single moment. We can grasp the unity only, so to speak, longitudinally—only as something that goes on in a stretch of time. It is not found in any number of cross-sectional views.

Nevertheless, if we could look into the minds of our neighbors, I think we should not be much surprised to find in them quite frequently the notion that a man exists within the boundaries which are visible, tangible, and observable. In a word, the man is identified with what is underneath his skin. We incline to suppose that we would know all about him if we could find out everything that is happening in his brain and other parts of his nervous system: in his glands, muscles, viscera, heart and lungs and so on.

Now up to a certain point we are on the right track, provided we emphasize sufficiently the interaction, the working together, of all these diverse processes. We can get a better idea of the unity of the human being as we know more about all these processes and the way they work together, as they check and stimulate one another and bring about a balance. But the one positive point I wish to present is that while this is necessary it is not enough. We must observe and understand these internal processes and their interactions from the standpoint of their interaction with what is going on outside the skin—with that which is called the *environment*—if we are to obtain a genuine conception of the unity of the human being.

Our attitude with respect to this matter is a strange mixture. In special points we take for granted the inclusion of the conditions and energies that are outside the boundaries set by the skin. No one supposes for a moment that there can be respiration without the surrounding air; or that the lungs are anything more than organs of interaction with what is outside the body. No one thinks of separating the processes of digestion from connection with foodstuffs derived by means of other organs from the environment. We know that eye, ear and hand, and somatic musculature, are concerned with objects and events outside the boundaries of the body. These things we take for granted so regularly and unconsciously that it seems foolish to mention them. Physiologists at least recognize that what is true of breathing and digestion holds also of the circulation of fluids that goes on entirely within the body, although the connection of these processes with environing conditions is a stage more indirect. The structure and processes of the central nervous system do not have that immediate connection with the outside world that the peripheral neural structures have.

Yet an authority upon the anatomy and physiology of the nervous system recently used these words: "Every movement is the result of the messages which pass from the central mass of nerve cells to the muscles, and the outgoing messages are varied according to the reports submitted by the sense organs. These show what is happening in the world outside, and the nervous system must evolve a plan of action appropriate to the occasion." [1]

That movements affected by the muscles have to do, directly and indirectly, with activities of seeking, defense, and taking possession of energies of the outside world, is obvious. The central nervous system has the function of evolving the plans and procedures that take effect in dealing with outside conditions as they are reported through sense organs—and I suppose it would be admitted that these reports vary, depending upon what the body was doing previously in connection with outside conditions.

In other words, with respect to every special set of organic structures and processes, we take it for granted that things beyond the body are involved in interaction with those inside the body, and that we cannot understand the latter in isolation. This states a fact so generally recognized as to be a commonplace. The strangeness of the mixture of which I spoke consists in the fact that while we recognize the involvement of conditions external to the body in all organic processes, when they are taken one by one, we often fail to recognize and act upon the idea as an inclusive principle by which to understand the unity of man and the disorders which result from disruption of this unity.

Whole philosophical systems have been built up, for example, by treating thinking, especially in so-called abstract ideas, as having no connection with the activities the body executes in the environment in use and enjoyment of the conditions it presents. There is many a mathematician who would be shocked if he were told that his constructions had anything to do with activities carried on in the environment. Yet we know that neural structures and processes developed in control and use of the environment

1. E. Adrian, *Harvard Tercentenary Publications,* Vol. I, p. 4.

are the organs of all thinking. Even some who call themselves behaviorists, who pride themselves on their strictly scientific attitude, have identified the behavior about which they talk with the behavior of the nervous system in and by itself. Having for example identified thought with language—a position for which much may be said—they go on to locate language in the vocal cords, ignoring the transaction of communication in which, directly and indirectly, other human beings take part. It may even be that on occasion physicians think of diseases, and even psychical disorders, as something that goes on wholly inside the body, so that they treat what goes on outside as, at most, an external cause rather than a constituent and interacting factor in the disease.

At all events, there is a good deal of description and interpretation in many fields in which the structural and static lord it over the active and functioning. Whenever we find this to be the case we may be sure that some structure of the body has been described and interpreted in isolation from its connection with an activity in which an environment plays an integral part.

On the other hand, when physicians proceed to regulate the diet, sleep and exercise of patients, when they inquire into and give advice about their habits, they are dealing with the "use of the self" in its active functional connection with the outside world. What then I am urging is simply the systematic and constant projection of what is here involved into all our observations, judgments and generalizations about the unity and the breakdowns of unity of human beings. For its implications are that all beliefs and practices which gratuitously split up the unity of man have their final root in the separation of what goes on inside the body from integrated interaction with what goes on outside.

This abstract principle becomes concrete as soon as one thinks not of environment in general, but of the human environment; that which is formed by contacts and relations with our human fellows. Psychiatrists have made us familiar with disturbances labelled "withdrawal from reality." They have pointed out the role of this withdrawal in many pathological occurrences. What are these withdrawals but cases of the interruption or cessation of "the active operative presence of environing conditions in the activities of a human being"? What are the resulting pathological phenomena but evidences that the self loses its integrity *within itself* when it loses integration with the medium in which it lives?

It is only necessary to think of those mild instances of withdrawal, forming ordinary day-dreaming and fantasy building, to appreciate that the environment which is involved is human or social. When a person builds up not only a systematized delusion of wealth but engages in a day-dream in which he has come into possession of a large sum of money, it is not the physical money he is thinking of but the prestige and power it gives him over his fellows. If a fantasy becomes habitual and controlling, it brings about, sooner or later, retraction from even the physical environment. But these withdrawals from physical surroundings originate in disturbances of relationship with the human environment. They go back to such things as pettings and coddlings, personal rejections, failure to win recognition and approvals, fear of those in authority, frustration of hope and desire by social conditions.

We may, then, anticipate a time when our entire traditional psychology will be looked upon as extraordinarily one-sided in its exclusive concern with actions and reactions of human beings with their physical surroundings to the neglect of interpersonal relationships. We have, to be sure, reached a point where we have chapters and books entitled "social psychology." But we are far from having reached the point in which it is seen that the whole difference between animal and human psychology is constituted by the transforming effect exercised upon the latter by intercourse and association with other persons and groups of persons. For apart from unconditioned reflexes, like the knee-jerk, it may be questioned whether there is a single human activity or experience which is not profoundly affected by the social and cultural environment. Would we have any intellectual operations without the language which is a social product? As for our emotional life, permit me to cite two passages written by a physician: "Contact with human beings is the stimulus that elicits emotional and visceral reactions. It is not the clutter of railways and motors, this 'fast hurrying age in which we live' so often spoken of; it is rather the pride, the envy, the ambition, the rage, the disappointment, the defeat that develop in purely human relations that stir the viscera"; and again: "There is an immense amount of hokum uttered about the psychological tensions caused by our swiftly moving era, as though the telephone, the radio, and the electric refrigerator were instruments that could swerve the viscera. The emotional life does not actually hinge on machinery but on the type of response to living situations, situations that for the most part are created by human contacts."[2]

I do not believe I am going beyond the implications of these passages when I say that the operation of "living situations created by human contacts" is the only intelligible ground upon which we can distinguish between what we call the *higher* and the *lower* (the physical on one side and the ideal and "spiritual" on the other) in human experience. The occurrence of a sensation, for example, may be described as an interaction between certain neural processes and certain vibrations. The principle involved here is the same in animals and in man. But the *significance* of a quality of red depends upon the part it plays in the customary uses and enjoyments of the social group of which a person is a member. To a bull, its presence is a purely physiological stimulus. For a child, it may be that a dress worn perhaps only on a festal occasion or a ribbon worn for adornment in the presence of others is that which fixes the significance of red. When we wait in an automobile for a traffic light to turn, red is still a physiological stimulus. But it has its *significance* in terms of adaptation of the behavior of individuals to one another. The emotional import of red in a red, white and blue flag to a patriotic American citizen is surely not native in physiological structure.

Examples do not *prove* the principle laid down. But I do believe that reflection upon these and similar cases will show that the only verifiable basis we have for marking off the experiences that have practical, emotional and intellectual significance from those which do not is the influence of cultural and social forces upon internal physiological processes.

At least what I have said is a challenge to produce any instance of an experience having so-called ideal or even "spiritual" meaning that cannot be accounted for on this ground. Otherwise, we must have recourse to the old division between soul and body. Take the case of those who revolt against the old dualism and who because of their revolt imagine they must throw away and

2. Houston, *The Art of Treatment*, pp. 348–9, and p. 450.

deny the existence of all phenomena that go by the names of *higher,* intellectual and moral. Such persons exist. They suppose they are not scientific unless they reduce everything to the exclusively somatic and physiological. This procedure is a conspicuous instance of what must happen when observation, description and interpretation of human events are confined to what goes on under the skin to the exclusion of their integrated interaction with environmental conditions, particularly the environment formed by other human beings. Knowledge of strictly somatic organs and processes is certainly necessary for scientific understanding of "higher" phenomena. But only half-way science neglects and rules out the other factor.

We may reject the traditional dualism. In my conviction we should reject it. We cannot be scientific save as we seek for the physiological, the physical, factor in every emotional, intellectual and volitional experience. As more is known of this factor, more intellectual capital and more resources of control are at our command. In the case of the physician especially is it so true as to be a truism, that the more anatomical, chemical and immunological information he has, the better prepared is he for his work. And it is also true that our knowledge of social relations and their effects upon native and original physiological processes is scanty and unorganized in comparison with the physical knowledge at command.

But in view of the role played by human contacts and relations in developing and sustaining the emotional and intellectual quality of human experience on one side, and in bringing disturbance and disorder into it on the other, this fact is all the more reason for devoting constant attention to the as yet relatively unknown factor in the case of every human being who comes under observation. This need cannot be met by knowledge of even the most up-to-date scientific psychology which now exists. For, unfortunately, this psychology suffers for the most part from exactly the one-sided concern in question: the failure to take into account the operations and effects of relationships between human beings.

To me, a layman, it appears that physicians have a unique opportunity for building up just the kind of knowledge that is now so largely lacking. Physicians are the persons who have the most direct, intimate and continued contact with the living situations in which the problem is most acutely present. Since the decline of the influence of priest and pastor, no other professional body is in a position to make such a contribution and render such a service; though it should be acknowledged that the group of teachers also has an opportunity of which it fails to take adequate advantage. I am impressed, as every one else naturally is, with the now oft-made statement that at least one-half of those who consult physicians are suffering from ailments having a strictly neural basis and that show psychopathological traits. Indeed, this statement seems to me to be actually a great under-statement of the seriousness of the situation.

For the conception of good health is so vague that most persons do not go to see a physician until their ailments have become rather extreme. No one knows how many who do not come suffer loss of energy, efficiency and happiness because of difficulties that have a psychic aspect. A fair guess would be, I take it, that this group includes in some degree everybody. If the factor of human relationships is as fundamental in production of these disorders, slight and intense, as we now have reason to believe is the case, it is impossible to over-state the extent or the importance of the concrete body of knowledge physicians can build up.

At this point, I must invite your attention again to the dubious and controversial state in which the whole matter of so-called higher mental states finds itself, and the disastrous consequences that ensue. In saying this, I am not referring to controversies between philosophers and psychologists about the relations of the mental and physical—controversies that pass under the names of interactionism, parallelism, materialism, etc. I think these are of no great practical importance save as they reflect certain divisions of a more practical kind that are rife. There are some who are so impressed with the influence of mind upon body, and with opportunities for exploiting those whose troubles have a marked psychic phase, that they form special cults, while there are others who react to the opposite extreme. They will have as little to do with anything that cannot be located and described in some specific lesion or specific somatic process. The respective views and practices of the two groups supply ammunition the one to the other. It is this situation which gives practical point to the search for the unity of the human being and that justifies presentation of the view that unity and its breakdowns must be sought for in the interactions between individual organisms and their environment, especially that of human associations.

In this connection may be cited some rather simple facts which indicate that there is nothing mystical or metaphysical in acknowledgment of the "higher" functions when they are interpreted by the view that has been set forth. When one of us steps on the toes of his neighbor in a crowded place, we offer regrets, since otherwise we are likely to subject ourselves to sour looks, irritation and resentment. A strictly physical event has taken place, but even from an ordinary common sense point of view the physical is not the whole of the matter. The presence of a personal relation introduces a qualifying factor.

If I stub my toe on an object left lying on a public street my response is quite different from that which happens if I stub it on the root of a tree in climbing a mountain. In the first case, I feel the object has no business there; that somebody has been careless; that something ought to be done about such things. A personal element has modified an otherwise purely physical reaction. In the second case, I may suffer equal or greater pain, but if the pain should be partly that of irritation, the irritation is directed at my own awkwardness. Again, I can hardly imagine anyone thinking that the pain a child suffers from colic is of the same quality as the agony of torture a sensitive child suffers from an act of injustice or unkindness at the hands of some one from whom he expects different treatment.

Sentimentalists put the pain a dog suffers in undergoing an act of vivisection on the same level with what a parent suffers who has lost a child. To other people, this attitude seems to display rather extraordinary callousness towards distinctively human pain—a pain that is what it is because the processes of the human organism have been profoundly affected by relations with another human being.

The point illustrated by these simple instances is that the whole ground for the difference between a sensation and an emotion seems to lie in the absence or presence of a response coming from another human being. Persons acquire likes and dislikes for physical objects and physical scenes. But upon the strictly physical level—meaning by that, one in which a human relation plays no part—a dislike is expressed by simple rejection,—as say, one "doesn't like olives or castor oil." When the rejection is accompanied by emotion, even a layman suspects there is something back of it. When such cases are studied it is found, practically without exception, that the object rejected is of a kind that has been socially "conditioned," as the term goes. The strong stirring of emotional interest that most people experience when revisiting, after a lapse of years, the scenes of their childhood is called out by the fact that these scenes were not merely the theatrical stage and properties of early activities, but have entered so intimately into personal relations with father and mother, brother and sisters, and playmates, that it is impossible to draw a line and say the influence of the physical ends *here* and that of the social begins *there*.

It may be assumed, I suppose, that all students of biology and physiology now take it for granted that there is no recollection apart from a modification of neural structure undergone in consequence of an earlier experience. But would any one attempt to read off from even the most minute and thorough study of the structure of the modified neural cells and the chemical processes going on in them, what the nature of the earlier experience was? I imagine not; I also imagine that there are few indeed who think any possible future development of knowledge will enable this result to come to pass, making it possible to reconstitute a past experience on the basis of what can be observed about an organic structure. What is relied upon is personal contact and communication; while personal attitudes, going deeper than the mere asking of questions, are needed in order to establish the confidence which is a condition for the patient's telling the story of his past. The organic modification is there—it is indispensable. Without it the patient would not be able to recall past incidents. But this is not enough. The physical fact has to be taken up into the context of personal relations between human being and human being before it becomes a fact of the living present.

Intellectual operations are discriminative. They bring things to a focus, to a point, down as we say to brass tacks. But when we are angry or depressed we are mad or sad all over. A *physical* pain may be more or less definitely and accurately localized. But while we may feel severe local burnings and constrictions in the case of severe grief, there is also a *total* experienced response which occurs. It operates through organic structures, especially the viscera. But if it were referred exclusively to them to the exclusion of a relation to another human being, it would not *be* grief.

I remember as a child trying to reinstate on a hot summer's day, the experience of a day in winter—not just to recall intellectually that it was cold, but to recover the actual feeling. Naturally, I never succeeded, and I was not aware that if I had succeeded it would have been an hallucination. What I was attempting was, however, hardly more difficult than it is when we are experiencing an intense emotion to procure or permit the introduction of ideas associated with another mood. Elation and strong hope take such possession of us that we cannot entertain ideas that suggest the possibility of failure as long as the emotions last. The person depressed with melancholy has no room for any idea connected with success or vital hope.

Now, it may be doubted whether there is any idea, no matter how intellectual and abstract, that is not tinged, if not dyed, with the emotion that arises from the total response of the whole organism to its surroundings. The cases, then, of the influence of emotions upon somatic conditions, even to the extent of producing neuroses in some cases and creating astonishing recoveries in other cases, have nothing mystical or metaphysical about them. They are expressions of the regulative force exercised over partial organic processes by the whole of which they are part.

I have given a number of illustrations which by themselves are commonplace rather than weighty. The principle they are intended to illustrate is, however, of the utmost importance. For, as I have suggested, disruption of the unity of the self is not limited to the cases that come to physicians and institutions for treatment. They accompany every disturbance of normal relations of husband and wife, parent and child, group and group, class and class, nation and nation. Emotional responses are so total as compared with the partial nature of intellectual responses, of ideas and abstract conceptions, that their consequences are more pervasive and more enduring. I can, accordingly, think of nothing of greater practical importance than that the psychic effects of human relationships, normal and abnormal, should be the object of continued study, including among the consequences the indirect somatic effects.

We cannot understand the conditions that produce unity in the

human being and conditions that generate disruptions of this
unity until the study of the relations of human beings to one another is as alert, as unremitting and as systematic as the study of
strictly physiological and anatomical processes and structures
has been in the past. The plea is not for any remission on the side
of the latter. But we need to recover from the impression, now
wide-spread, that the essential problem is solved when chemical,
immunological, physiological and anatomical knowledge is sufficiently obtained. We cannot understand and employ this knowledge until it is placed integrally in the context of what human
beings do to one another in the vast variety of their contacts and
associations. Until the study is undertaken in this spirit, neglect
will continue to breed and so support belief in the soul, and in
mental processes supposed to be wholly independent of the organism and of somatic conditions. The consequences produced by
this belief will not be confined to errors of theory. The practical
outcome is division and conflict in action where unity and cooperation of social effort are urgently required.

I may rephrase what I have said by saying that the fine old saying "A sound mind in a sound body" can and should be extended
to read, "A sound human being in a sound human environment."
The mere change in wording is nothing. A change in aims and
methods of working in that direction, would mean more than
any of us can estimate. Is there anything in the whole business of
politics, economics, morals, education, indeed in any profession,
save the construction of a proper human environment that will
serve by its very existence to produce sound and whole human
beings, who in turn will maintain a sound and healthy human
environment?

This is the universal and all-embracing human task. Its first
phase cannot be turned over to politicians alone, and the second
phase cannot be turned over to parents, preachers and teachers
alone. It is not the peculiar business of any special calling. Yet
perhaps there is none who is more intimately concerned with
aiding production of sound individual human beings than the
physician. There is none who has as much opportunity as he has
to observe the effects of disturbed and disordered human relations, in production of warped and divided personalities. The
situations with which physicians deal are not artificially produced in laboratories. They are nevertheless sufficiently extensive

and varied to provide conditions of control like those of the laboratory.

I cannot help thinking that the idea of preventive medicine and of public health policies have bearing and application upon the point made. Because of the unity of the human being, because of the inextricable intertwining of the physical and psychical in his make-up, the work of preventing disease and disorders is not completely done when the physical conditions of sanitation, pure water, and milk supply, sewage disposal, and healthy homes have been attended to. The social conditions that make for the production of unified, effective, reasonably happy human beings and their opposites, come into the picture also. We may solve the problems of dualism and monism satisfactorily in theory, and yet not have touched the sore spots in society and in individuals, and this is the place where they have to be resolved practically.

What Is Social Study?

In the new proper emphasis upon social studies, the primary problem, it seems to me, is to determine the scope and range of the subject-matter designated by "social." More definitely, the question is: how far that which is social can be separated and treated by itself, and how far the social is a limiting function of the subject-matter of all studies—what philosophers might call a category by which all materials of learning are to be interpreted. There is of course a restricted sense in which it is correct enough to isolate social materials. Questions of family life, of politics and economics, of war and peace, are obviously social questions. The problem I am raising is how far such materials can be understood and be educative in the full sense without a background of study of matters which lie outside of the social as thus limited.

No one would deny, I suppose, that many political questions at the present time have economic roots. Issues of the relation of capital and labor, of concentration and distribution of wealth, of economic security and unemployment, occupy the attention of our legislative bodies. They are primarily economic questions but they find their way into political action because their impact upon human relations and their public consequences are intense and widespread. Can the student stop when he has traced these political themes to their economic sources? Or does understanding of the economic situation demand going further?

It would probably be admitted on all hands that the present economic situation is a historical development, and that while present facts may be amassed in quantities, the information thus gained needs to be placed in an historic setting if it is to be intelligently grasped and used. Many, perhaps all, of the economic

[First published in *Progressive Education* 15 (May 1938): 367–69.]

questions have also definitely geographical aspects. The problem of the farmer comes to mind, for example, and that of the railways as means of distribution of products. So does that of soil conservation and reforestation. The question of the distribution of population, of congestion in industrial and commercial centres, is another aspect of the same general question. Careful studies show that in recent years there have been a number of great regional migrations which have left certain large regions in a state of relative desolation while the burdens of relief, hospitalization, etc., have been greatly increased in the areas to which they have gone. That miners live and work where there are mines and lumbermen work where there are still forests, as well as that farmers live on farms, and that certain centres are what they are because of facilities of transportation and need for reshipment of products, are obvious facts. But they raise the question how far are social studies to be conducted in the light of fundamental geographic and physiographic knowledge?

The reference that was made in an earlier paragraph to the historic context of economic questions suggests in turn the scientific background. The industrial and commercial change which has taken place in the world in the last century, in the past forty years, is the product of the great change which has taken place in physical, chemical and, more recently, biological science. The prime factor in the economic and political history of this period is what is known as the industrial revolution. The story of that revolution is the story of new technologies in the production and distribution of goods, which are themselves the result of a scientific revolution. Any vital comprehension of existing economic and political issues demands insight into processes and operations that can be grasped only through understanding of fundamental physical and chemical operations and laws. I will not press the point further, though it might be extended into the subjects of literature, the fine arts and mathematics. The obvious objection that may be made to what has been said is that if it is accepted it swells the social studies beyond all limits; that they have so many ramifications and absorb so much of other studies that teacher and student alike are confronted with an unwieldy, unmanageable mass. The objection, when it is analyzed, brings us to the other aspect of the educational question.

When I asked how far the social is from an educational point of view the limiting function of all the studies, the question I had in mind was whether such subjects as, for example, the history, geography and natural science already mentioned can be isolated, so as to be treated as independent subjects; or whether from the beginning and constantly they should be treated in their social bearings and consequences—consequences in the way, on one side, of problems and on the other side of opportunities. The human and cultural is after all the embracing limit to which all other things tend. In the higher reaches of school education there must, of course, be provision for training of experts and specialists. In them, a certain amount of relative separation of subjects from their social context and function is legitimate. But it is a fair question whether society is not suffering even here because the expert specialists have not the educational background which would enable them to view their special skills and knowledge in connection with social conditions, movements and problems.

But the particular point I would make is that in any case we have carried the isolation of subjects from their social effects and possibilities too far down the educational scale. From the psychological and moral standpoint it may be urged that for most boys and girls the material of studies loses vitality, becomes relatively dead, because it is separated from situations, and that much of the need which is felt at the present time for resorting to extraneous devices to make subjects interesting or else to coerce attention is a necessary effect of this isolation. Natural docility leads to acceptance. But underneath, there is the subconscious questioning, "What does all this mean? What is it for? What do the studies signify outside of the schoolroom or do they belong only there?"

The problem of congestion of studies and diversion of aims with resulting superficiality is a pressing one today. The progressive and the reactionary agree in this one thing on the negative side. Both insist that there is lack of unity of aim, that there is dispersion and confusion. As far as I can see, the one hope of obtaining the desired unification is that which has been suggested. The natural focus, the assembling point, of the various studies is their social origin and function. Any other scheme of unification and correlation seems to me artificial and doomed to only transitory success. Progressive education has reached a point where it is looking for a lead which will give coherence and direction to its efforts. I believe it will find it here and that in the end emphasis upon social studies as a separate line of study may only add to the confusion and dispersion that now exist! Not because they are not important, but precisely because they are so important that they should give direction and organization to all branches of study.

In conclusion, I want to say that in my judgment what has been said has a definite bearing upon what is called indoctrination, or, if one prefer, teaching, with respect to preparation for a different social order. Social studies as an isolated affair are likely to become either accumulations of bodies of special factual information or, in the hands of zealous teachers, to be organs of indoctrination in the sense of propaganda for a special social end, accepted enthusiastically, perhaps, but still dogmatically. Young people who have been trained in all subjects to look for social bearings will also be educated to see the causes of present evils. They will be equipped from the sheer force of what they have learned to see new possibilities and the means of actualizing them. They will be indoctrinated in its deeper sense without having had doctrines forced upon them.

To Those Who Aspire to the Profession of Teaching

There are three questions which I should want answered if I were a young man or woman thinking of choosing an occupation. I should want to know first what opportunities the vocation offers, opportunities for cultural development, intellectual, moral, social, and its material rewards along with its opportunities for usefulness and for personal growth. In the second place I should want to know what special demands it makes so that I could measure my personal qualifications against those which are required for genuine success in that calling. And thirdly, I should want to know something of the discouragements and "outs," the difficulties connected with the vocation I had in mind.

It does not require any long argument to show that teaching is pre-eminent among the callings in its opportunities for moral and spiritual service. It has always ranked with the ministry in that respect. Without drawing any invidious comparisons there are certain traits in the profession of education that are especially appealing at the present time. In the first place, it deals with the young, with those whose minds are plastic and whose characters are forming. Horace Mann said, "Where anything is growing one former is worth a thousand reformers." One who deals with the young does not have the obstacles to overcome that one has to meet who is dealing with adults. Educational work is moreover free from sectarian divisions and other divisions which depend upon dogma. The teacher can meet all pupils on a common ground. This fact adds to the ready approach afforded by the youthful mind. Again all modern psychology increasingly emphasizes the formative character of the earlier years of life. In very many cases, the adjustments which are made *then* are those

[First published in *My Vocation, By Eminent Americans: Or What Eminent Americans Think of Their Callings*, comp. Earl Granger Lockhart (New York: H. W. Wilson Co., 1938), pp. 325–34.]

which control the activities of adult life, normal adjustments to others being the foundation of a normal life in the later years, and failures in sane and wise social and personal adaptations being the chief source of later unhappiness and morbid states. The teacher shares with the parent the opportunity to have a direct part in promoting the mental and moral life which is healthy and balanced. The teacher has not only the advantage of dealing with a greater number of children, but also is in a condition to judge more wisely and impartially because of not being involved in emotional ways as the parent is.

The opportunities for intellectual development are so obvious that they hardly need extended exposition. All of the so-called learned professions bring those who pursue them in intimate contact with books, studies, ideas. They stimulate the desire for increased knowledge and wider intellectual contacts. No one can be really successful in performing the duties and meeting these demands who does not retain his intellectual curiosity intact throughout his entire career. It would not, therefore, be just to claim that there is anything unique in the opportunities for intellectual growth furnished by the vocation of teaching. But there are opportunities in it sufficiently great and varied so as to furnish something for every taste. Since literature and science and the arts are taught in the schools, the continued pursuit of learning in some or all of these fields is made desirable. This further study is not a side line but something which fits directly into the demands and opportunities of the vocation.

The social opportunities of teaching, in the narrower sense of the word "social" differ widely in different sections and places, so that no unqualified statement can be made. It is said, and probably with a great deal of truth, that in the large cities teachers are not as much looked up to as they once were; that in some places they are classed almost as household servants. These conditions, however, are exceptional. In general, the profession ranks high in the esteem of the public, and teachers are welcomed because of their calling as well as for their own sake.

The material or pecuniary rewards of the calling are not the chief reason for going into it. There are no financial prizes equalling those to be obtained in business, the law, or even, if we take the exceptional physician as the measure, in medicine. On the other hand, there are not the great disparities and risks which exist in most other callings. The rewards, if not great, are reasonably sure. Until the depression they were, moreover, pretty steadily increasing. If we include vacation periods as part of the material reward of teaching, the profession ranks high. There is no other calling which allows such a prolonged period for travel, for study, and recreation as does the educational. To many temperaments, this phase of teaching counterbalances all the material drawbacks.

The personal qualifications which are needed are indicated in a general way by the opportunities which the vocation presents, since from the standpoint of the individual who is thinking of going into the profession, these are demands made upon him. Good health is, under usual conditions, a prerequisite for success in all callings. One special feature of it may, however, be emphasized in connection with teaching. Those persons who are peculiarly subject to nervous strain and worry should not go into teaching. It is not good for them nor for the pupils who come under their charge. One of the most depressing phases of the vocation is the number of care-worn teachers one sees, with anxiety depicted on the lines of their faces, reflected in their strained high pitched voices and sharp manners. While contact with the young is a privilege for some temperaments, it is a tax on others, and a tax which they do not bear up under very well. And in some schools, there are too many pupils to a teacher, too many subjects to teach, and adjustments to pupils are made in a mechanical rather than a human way. Human nature reacts against such unnatural conditions.

This point of nervous balance and all-round health connects slowly with the next point. Those who go into teaching ought to have a natural love of contact with the young. There are those who are bored by contact with children and even with youth. They can be more useful in other professions. Their contacts soon become perfunctory and mechanical, and children even if they are not able to express the matter in words, are conscious of the lack of spontaneous response, and no amount of learning or even of acquired pedagogical skill makes up for the deficiency. Only those who have it in themselves to stay young indefinitely and to retain a lively sympathy with the spirit of youth should remain long in the teaching profession.

The point which I would emphasize next is a natural love of

communicating knowledge along with a love of knowledge itself. There are scholars who have the latter in a marked degree but who lack enthusiasm for imparting it. To the "natural-born" teacher learning is incomplete unless it is shared. He or she is not contented with it in and for its own sake. He or she wants to use it to stir up the minds of others. Nothing is so satisfactory as to see another mind get the spark of an idea and kindle into a glow because of it. One of the finest teachers I have ever known said to me, "I have never known a first-class teacher who did not have something of the preacher about him"—or her. And he went on to explain that what he meant was the love of arousing in others the same intellectual interests and enthusiasms which the teacher himself experienced.

Finally, the teacher should combine an active and keen interest in some one branch of knowledge with interest and skill in following the reactions of the minds of others. I would not say that a teacher ought to strive to be a high-class scholar in all the subjects he or she has to teach. But I would say that a teacher ought to have an unusual love and aptitude in some one subject; history, mathematics, literature, science, a fine art, or whatever. The teacher will then have the *feel* for genuine information and insight in all subjects; will not sink down to the level of the conventional and perfunctory teacher who merely "hears" recitations, and will communicate by unconscious contagion love of learning to others.

The teacher is distinguished from the scholar, no matter how good the latter, by interest in watching the movements of the minds of others, by being sensitive to all the signs of response they exhibit; their quality of response or lack of it, to subject-matter presented. A personal sympathy is a great thing in a teacher. It does its best work, however, when it is in sympathy with the *mental* movements of others, is alive to perplexities and problems, discerning of their causes, having the mental tact to put the finger on the cause of failure, quick to see every sign of promise and to nourish it to maturity. I have often been asked how it was that some teachers who have never studied the art of teaching are still extraordinarily good teachers. The explanation is simple. They have a quick, sure and unflagging sympathy with the operations and process of the minds they are in contact with. Their own minds move in harmony with those of others, appreciating their difficulties, entering into their problems, sharing their intellectual victories.

I am not interested in putting any obstacles in the way of those who think of becoming teachers by dwelling on the obstacles it presents. To an active and energetic character, these will prove only stimuli to greater effort. But few things are more disastrous than the round peg in the square hole, than a person in a work to which he or she is not suited. Those who go into the profession of teaching should then realize in advance that for some temperaments it is too safe, too protected, a calling. There is not enough stimulus from competition with their equals to call out their best energies. There are those to whom the young are inferiors; they tend to teach down to them from above, and to acquire a manner which is either tyrannical or patronizing. Such persons should refrain from teaching. There are communities in which political influences operate with great strength. Would-be teachers should ask themselves whether they have the strength of character to sustain their integrity against these influences; whether they can play their part with others without becoming timeservers, chair-warmers, place-holders. The so-called educator who is little more than a cheap politician looking out for his own interests is a sorry spectacle. In fact, every one can call up in his own experience the hard places he is likely to run into and ask whether he has the force to meet and overcome the difficulties which arise.

For those who are fitted for the work, the calling of the teacher combines three rewards, each intense and unique. Love of knowledge; sympathy with growth, intellectual and moral; interest in the improvement of society through improving the individuals who compose it.

In Defense of the Mexican Hearings

Since I agree with the main finding of Mr. Rodman's article, which I take to be that American radicals (and I would add the American people generally) must resort to quite other tactics and philosophy than that of violent Marxist-Leninist class struggle, and must also study what has gone on and is still going on in the U.S.S.R., in connection with that philosophy, I shall confine my comments to some statements which Mr. Rodman makes incidentally and it seems to me quite unguardedly.

As to the Mexican hearings. It is not true, as alleged, that two members of the sub-commission were or ever had been "partisans" of Trotsky. This statement was made, when the sub-commission of inquiry was formed, in order to discredit any opportunity on the part of Trotsky to present whatever evidence he possessed bearing on the charges made against him in the Moscow trials. There was no truth in it. Further, the member who resigned made false statements as to the reasons for his resignation, namely, that he had been prevented from asking questions—a statement which inverted the truth. He had been given every opportunity to ask them, and was told by me, at the close of the meeting before his resignation (sent in the next morning), that he would have full opportunity at the next session to continue his questioning.

In the third place, the most important point, he says the "Commission could prove nothing finally." The reason for making this statement is, in his own words, "That the case will never be proved, because if One True Church cannot be wrong, neither can Two." In addition, he refers to the fact that one member of the Commission (whom he gives credit for being a liberal) was "hesitant to identify the common philosophy that leads to only

[First published in *Common Sense* 7 (January 1938): 20–21. For Selden Rodman's article to which this is a reply, see Appendix 4.]

apparently different actions." The only possible implication of these passages is that the Commission's business was, or should have been, to examine the respective philosophies of the existing regime in Russia and of Trotsky and to reach some conclusion about their respective merits or common demerits.

This is an entire misconception of what the function of the Commission was, should, or could have been. We were in Mexico for a definite purpose, to hear whatever evidence Trotsky had to present bearing on the charges brought against him in the Moscow trials, and to examine and weigh that evidence, oral and especially documentary, in connection with similar evidence gathered by a European sub-commission in France. Mr. Rodman, either by his own unaided efforts or with some help from the Mexican hearings, has reached the conclusion that Trotsky was not guilty of these charges. To arrive at a conclusion on the point of guilt was the entire and sole purpose of the investigation which the full Commission of Inquiry has conducted. The question is one of fact, based, on one side on the testimony of the Moscow trials and on the other side upon the evidence, oral, written and documentary, which the Commission itself gathered.

It is an interesting question whether, as Mr. Rodman says, "Trotsky and the Oppositionists would have acted in the same way, given the opportunity." But, in the first place, it is a question of argument not of fact, and in the second a question entirely outside the scope of the Commission.

That the Commission in the course of its hearings elicited some material bearing on the question how far the Marxist-Leninist theory of seizing political power by force, exercised by a special class, tends to produce an epoch of terrorism and falsification, is, in my personal judgment, all to the good, provided the material leads radicals to consider more fully than they have done in the past the alternative philosophies of social change which underlie different strategies and tactics.

Means and Ends

Their Interdependence, and Leon Trotsky's Essay on "Their Morals and Ours"

The relation of means and ends has long been an outstanding issue in morals. It has also been a burning issue in political theory and practise. Of late the discussion has centered about the later developments of Marxism in the U.S.S.R. The course of the Stalinists has been defended by many of his adherents in other countries on the ground that the purges and prosecutions, perhaps even with a certain amount of falsification, were necessary to maintain the alleged socialistic régime of that country. Others have used the measures of the Stalinist bureaucracy to condemn the Marxist policy on the ground that the latter leads to such excesses as have occurred in the U.S.S.R. precisely because Marxism holds that the end justifies the means. Some of these critics have held that since Trotsky is also a Marxian he is committed to the same policy and consequently if he had been in power would also have felt bound to use any means whatever that seemed necessary to achieve the end involved in dictatorship by the proletariat.

The discussion has had at least one useful theoretical result. It has brought out into the open for the first time, as far as I am aware, an explicit discussion by a consistent Marxian of the relation of means and ends in social action.[1] At the courteous invitation of one of the editors of this review, I propose to discuss this issue in the light of Mr. Trotsky's discussion of the interdependence of means and ends. Much of the earlier part of his essay does not, accordingly, enter into my discussion, though I may say that on the ground of *tu quoque* argument (suggested by the title) Trotsky has had no great difficulty in showing that some of his critics have acted in much the same way they attribute to him.

1. "Their Morals and Ours," by Leon Trotsky, the *New International*, June 1938, pp. 163–173.

[First published in *New International* 4 (August 1938): 232–33.]

Since Mr. Trotsky also indicates that the only alternative position to the idea that the end justifies the means is some form of absolutistic ethics based on the alleged deliverances of conscience, or a moral sense, or some brand of eternal truths, I wish to say that I write from a standpoint that rejects all such doctrines as definitely as does Mr. Trotsky himself, and that I hold that the end in the sense of consequences provides the only basis for moral ideas and action, and therefore provides the only justification that can be found for means employed.

The point I propose to consider is that brought up toward the end of Mr. Trotsky's discussion in the section headed "Dialectic Interdependence of Means and Ends." The following statement is basic: "A means can be justified only by its end. But the end in turn needs to be justified. From the Marxian point of view, which expresses the historic interests of the proletariat, the end is justified if it leads to increasing the power of man over nature and to the abolition of the power of man over man." (P. 172.) This increase of the power of man over nature, accompanying the abolition of the power of man over man, seems accordingly to be *the* end—that is, an end which does not need itself to be justified but which is the justification of the ends that are in turn means to it. It may also be added that others than Marxians might accept this formulation of *the* end and hold that it expresses the moral interest of society—if not the historic interest—and not merely and exclusively that of the proletariat.

But for my present purpose, it is important to note that the word "*end*" is here used to cover two things—the final justifying end and ends that are themselves means to this final end. For while it is not said in so many words that some ends are but means, that proposition is certainly implied in the statement that some ends "*lead to* increasing the power of man over nature," etc. Mr. Trotsky goes on to explain that the principle that the end justifies the means does not mean that every means is permissible. "That is permissible, we answer, which really leads to the liberation of mankind."

Were the latter statement consistently adhered to and followed through it would be consistent with the sound principle of interdependence of means and end. Being in accord with it, it would lead to scrupulous examination of the means that are used, to ascertain what their actual objective consequences will be as far as it is humanly possible to tell—to show that they do "really" lead to the liberation of mankind. It is at this point that the double significance of *end* becomes important. As far as it means consequences actually reached, it is clearly dependent upon means used, while measures in their capacity of means are dependent upon the end in the sense that they have to be viewed and judged on the ground of their actual objective results. On this basis, an *end-in-view* represents or is an *idea* of the final consequences, in case the idea is formed *on the ground of the means that are judged to be most likely to produce the end*. The end-in-view is thus itself a means for directing action—just as a man's *idea* of health to be attained or a house to be built is not identical with end in the sense of actual outcome but is a means for directing action to achieve that end.

Now what has given the maxim (and the practise it formulates) that the end justifies the means a bad name is that the end-in-view, the end professed and entertained (perhaps quite sincerely) justifies the use of certain means, and so justifies the latter that it is not necessary to examine what the actual consequences of the use of chosen means will be. An individual may hold, and quite sincerely as far as his personal opinion is concerned that certain means will "really" lead to a professed and desired end. But the real question is not one of personal belief but of the objective grounds upon which it is held: namely, the consequences that will actually be produced by them. So when Mr. Trotsky says that "dialectical materialism knows no dualism between means and end," the natural interpretation is that he will recommend the use of means that can be shown by their own nature to lead to the liberation of mankind as an objective consequence.

One would expect, then, that with the idea of the liberation of mankind as the end-in-view, there would be an examination of *all* means that are likely to attain this end without any fixed preconception as to what they *must* be, and that every suggested means would be weighed and judged on the express ground of the consequences it is likely to produce.

But this is *not* the course adopted in Mr. Trotsky's further discussion. He says: "The liberating morality of the proletariat is of a revolutionary character. . . . It *deduces* a rule of conduct from the laws of the development of society, thus primarily from the class struggle, the law of all laws." (Italics are mine.) As if to leave no doubt of his meaning he says: "The end flows from the his-torical movement"—that of the class struggle. The principle of interdependence of means and end has thus disappeared or at least been submerged. For the choice of means is not decided upon on the ground of an independent examination of measures and policies with respect to their actual objective consequences. On the contrary, means are "*deduced*" from an independent source, an alleged law of history which is *the* law of all laws of social development. Nor does the logic of the case change if the word "alleged" is stricken out. For even so, it follows that means to be used are not derived from consideration of the end, the lib-eration of mankind, but from another outside source. The pro-fessed end—the end-in-view—the liberation of mankind, is thus subordinated to the class struggle as the means by which it is to be attained. Instead of *inter*dependence of means and end, the end is dependent upon the means but the means are not derived from the end. Since the class struggle is regarded as the *only* means that will reach the end, and since the view that it is the only means is reached deductively and not by an inductive ex-amination of the means-consequences in their interdependence, the means, the class struggle, does not need to be critically exam-ined with respect to its actual objective consequences. It is auto-matically absolved from all need for critical examination. If we are not back in the position that the *end-in-view* (as distinct from objective consequences) justifies the use of any means in line with the class struggle and that it justifies the neglect of all other means, I fail to understand the logic of Mr. Trotsky's position.

The position that I have indicated as that of genuine inter-dependence of means and ends does not automatically rule out class struggle as one means for attaining the end. But it does rule out the deductive method of arriving at it as a means, to say noth-ing of its being the *only* means. The selection of class struggle as a means has to be justified, on the ground of the interdependence of means and end, by an examination of actual consequences of its use, not deductively. Historical considerations are certainly relevant to this examination. But the assumption of a *fixed law* of social development is not relevant. It is as if a biologist or a phy-sician were to assert that a certain law of biology which he ac-cepts is so related to the end of health that the means of arriving at health—and the only means—can be deduced from it, so that no further examination of biological phenomena is needed. The whole case is prejudged.

It is one thing to say that class struggle is a means of attaining the end of the liberation of mankind. It is a radically different thing to say that there is an absolute *law* of class struggle which determines the means to be used. For if it determines the means, it also determines the end—the actual consequences, and upon the principle of genuine interdependence of means and end it is arbitrary and subjective to say that that consequence will be the liberation of mankind. The liberation of mankind is the end to be striven for. In any legitimate sense of "moral," it is a moral end. No scientific law can determine a moral end save by deserting the principle of interdependence of means and end. A Marxian may sincerely believe that class struggle is *the* law of social development. But quite aside from the fact that the belief closes the doors to further examination of history—just as an assertion that the Newtonian laws are the final laws of physics would preclude further search for physical laws—it would not follow, even if it were *the* scientific law of history, that it is the means to the moral goal of the liberation of mankind. That it is such a means has to be shown not by "deduction" from a law but by examination of the actual relations of means and consequences; an examination in which given the liberation of mankind as end, there is free and unprejudiced search for the means by which it can be attained.

One more consideration may be added about class struggle as a means. There are presumably several, perhaps many, different ways by means of which the class struggle may be carried on. How can a choice be made among these different ways except by examining their consequences in relation to the goal of liberation of mankind? The belief that a law of history determines the particular way in which the struggle is to be carried on certainly seems to tend toward a fanatical and even mystical devotion to use of certain ways of conducting the class struggle to the exclusion of all other ways of conducting it. I have no wish to go outside the theoretical question of the interdependence of means and ends but it is conceivable that the course actually taken by the revolution in the U.S.S.R. becomes more explicable when it is noted that means were deduced from a supposed scientific law instead of being searched for and adopted on the ground of their relation to the moral end of the liberation of mankind.

The only conclusion I am able to reach is that in avoiding one kind of absolutism Mr. Trotsky has plunged into another kind of absolutism. There appears to be a curious transfer among orthodox Marxists of allegiance from the ideals of socialism and scientific *methods* of attaining them (scientific in the sense of being based on the objective relations of means and consequences) to the class struggle as the law of historical change. Deduction of ends set up, of means and attitudes, from this law as the primary thing makes all moral questions, that is, all questions of the end to be finally attained, meaningless. To be scientific about ends does not mean to read them out of laws, whether the laws are natural or social. Orthodox Marxism shares with orthodox religionism and with traditional idealism the belief that human ends are interwoven into the very texture and structure of existence— a conception inherited presumably from its Hegelian origin.

Miscellany

The Philosophy of the Arts

Ladies and Gentlemen, especially members of the Dance Association and their friends, I am really sorry that I am not competent to give a talk upon the dance as an art, considering the particular auspices under which I am speaking to you here this afternoon. I might just say I am not competent to speak upon that art and let it go at that, but without perhaps forcing matters or being too arbitrary, I can hook up my inability to speak on that subject with an historical matter which is of considerably more importance than my own competency or incompetency, and that is the history of the arts.

As an historical fact it is, I suppose, known to most students of the arts that the dance in its connection with music, song, pantomime and at least some form of plastic art in the scenic decorations is the source of all of the arts. But children are often ungrateful. If not deliberately so, they grow to maturity and independence and carve out their own careers and become oblivious of their parentage. And so it is with the drama, with poetry, with instrumental music, and plastic designs and representations. All of these were originally closely associated with the dance, but as they grew to maturity they naturally asserted their independence. They had to develop each of its own accord, and certainly the scene of the arts would be much more limited and impoverished if each of them had not developed, grown to maturity on its own account and in its own way.

The result was that for a long time the dance was hardly recognized to be an art. In fact, one may doubt whether it deserved to be acknowledged as an art for a long period. In part it was relegated to the position of part of the social entertainment of the

[Not previously published. From a transcript of a lecture delivered 13 November 1938 to the Washington Dance Association at the Phillips Memorial Gallery, Washington, D.C. Transcript in Fletcher Free Library, Burlington, Vt.]

courtly classes, an exhibition of certain graces, an ornament of the ball room (a sort of sharp light, again upon the opera) or a form of exercise which could be recommended by some as very helpful, to be deplored and condemned by others on moral grounds. Only in our own day, practically in our own day, can it be said that the art of the dance has come again to be recognized as one of the genuinely fine arts. When it arrived at that condition I was too old to re-educate myself.

In other words the dance is at once the oldest and the youngest of the fine arts and as the youngest I suppose that perhaps in a somewhat peculiar sense in an unusual degree it is the art best understood as best enacted by the youngest generation. So much by way of general introduction and if it at all needed an apology to the members of the Dance Association for my not speaking on their particular subject.

What I am going to try to talk to you about this afternoon are the traits, the characteristics of the human experiences that have the quality that for lack of any other name we call esthetic. What are some of the traits, the characteristics, that mark off those movements of our experience that we have from time to time that are peculiar and manifestly esthetic in their nature? Perhaps what I mean by this can best be indicated by saying that I am not going to talk about art in terms of what we call works of art, but rather of what a human being undergoes and enjoys when he is in the presence of one of these works of art, in its presence not merely physically but with his make-up, with his full mind and feeling. Of course, it is quite possible for those who are competent to discuss the arts from the standpoint of the works of art—the great paintings, statues, symphonies, novels, dramas, poems, etc., the great buildings. One could approach the matter from the side of the Parthenon in architecture, Shakespeare in drama, the great symphonies of Beethoven and Wagner, the poets of the race, epics or the poems by Robert Burns, great novels, etc. I am going to try to tell you what it is that they have in common, in spite of their great differences in make-up, with all works of art.

Instead of doing that, as I have already said, I want to approach the matter with you from the other side, asking what it is that you and I and anybody that has any kind of esthetic appreciation goes through which, for him at least, makes any one of these works of art a real esthetic object instead of something which he has learned from others is the sort of thing that conventionally one ought to admire in order to have the reputation of being esthetically cultivated.

Unfortunately, there is a tendency when we think of works of art primarily to associate them with the art museums, the art galleries, or the music hall or opera house, places where we can go and see or hear those objects which have become recognized as works of art. If we approach the matter from our end we get a more flexible approach and one that is more inclusive, one that is more tolerant. It recognizes that we may have this experience in the presence of all kinds of things—the graciousness of a person in approach and intercourse in relation to other people—that great deeds of people not merely of those who are recognized as heroes, but humble people, may then have the grace or nobility because of the way that they strike us. If we approach from this side it seems to me that it tends to enlarge us. If we become more on the lookout for the moments of this kind of experience we do not think of them as experiences we have to have by going to certain places, but that we may have at any time of day in connection with any, not everyone, but with contacts with objects, scenes, persons that are not in any way labeled to be works of fine art.

I suppose that to the scientist even a mathematical equation may have a certain esthetic quality. The story, you know, is often told of Charles Darwin that he said to somebody that when he was young he enjoyed music and poetry but owing to his exclusive devotion to scientific investigation he thought that those powers of his as he grew older had become somewhat atrophied. Doubtless they had for certain forms of art that he might have gone out and enjoyed, but I should hesitate to say that that power in him was atrophied. It may have been in these particular local directions, but I think no one can contemplate his scientific career without being convinced that in the presence of nature (the same for plant and animal life to him) that he had experiences that were very genuinely esthetic. I suppose anyone who knows Mr. Einstein at present would say that he had quite as genuine and esthetic an experience from his mathematical calculations and their results that would mean nothing to us as he does from playing on his violin. Indeed, I have heard people who have heard him play say that probably he was a better performer in the other sphere than he is with the violin, although he gets great pleasure out of it.

I mention these things simply to suggest that we must not be overawed by the idea of works of art. It is quite true, of course, that there is a great difference in the quality of different esthetic experiences, in their range and depth, etc. But I think the fact is significant that museums, often calling themselves museums or galleries of fine art, often have in them utensils like rugs, carpets, vases, weapons, etc., that at the time of their origin were things of daily use, put out by the people who used them as utensils and appliances and yet now they are deemed worthy to be found in these museums. We cannot say, of course, that their quality and their depth is as high as plastic works of art, but they have the power of exciting an experience which, so far as it goes, has the quality which the great works of art have.

There is one other respect in which it seems to me this mode of approach is freer, frees us and helps us drop off some of the undue timidity or awe with which many people feel that works of art ought to be approached. I think that when speaking of the Fine Arts, spelling both words with a capital letter, there is a tendency to associate Beauty, also spelled with a capital B. People feel that in the presence of beauty they ought to have some peculiar kind of thrill or rapture, and they try to work themselves up to it in an unreal way. I doubt if artists, those engaged in actual production, are as conscious of any single thing that is spelled with a capital B or any capital letter as these people who allow themselves to be, as I have already suggested, rather intimidated by the setting apart of the works of fine art.

I want to read a few sentences from a great artist in poetry. He said, "As to the poetical character, it is every thing and nothing. It enjoys light and shade. It lives in gusto, be it high or low, rich or poor, mean or elevated. It does no harm from its relish of the dark side of things any more than from its taste for the bright one." And so he goes on and speaks of his own personal tendencies to identify himself with people in a room or with the object with which he comes in contact. It is the universality of the esthetic experience that he is speaking of. It is a potential thing. We all know as a matter of fact that many artists have made foremost works of art out of things that are ugly. Ugliness properly treated is capable of giving rise to a genuine esthetic experience.

People who are too much under the influence of what I called the works of art end of this experience—of course, there is a genuine limit on their own personal experiences—almost always are unable to recognize the dawn of any new esthetic form. Those interested in literature know how universal it was when Ibsen's plays first appeared to call them sordid and low and ugly because they were not in the lines of the works they already knew. I still remember very well the first exhibit of modern art, post-impressionistic art, at the exhibit in New York City twenty-five or more years ago, and how one writer spoke of the obvious eagerness and enjoyment and curiosity and enlightenment that the audience got as they went through those things that were very new. But one art critic, one of the best traditional art critics of New York, rebuked one man for admiring the works of Cézanne and Renoir and the others who are now having their recognized position practically as classics. I think the reason was that this art critic approached the thing simply from the standpoint of conventions that he had formed through his acquaintance with the works of art with which he was familiar and of which, because of his familiarity, he was a good judge but which actually stood in his way of recognizing as works of art those objects when they were outside of his accustomed vein of appreciation.

I think, again, that if we look at the whole matter more from the standpoint of what we do or what we feel and undergo we are less likely to get petrified by the old forms. Thus, as I imagine, there is an incidental application here in the case of the modern and contemporary dance that some people just cannot see very much in it because it is different from the associations they have had with the accustomed forms, while, if they took the matter from the other standpoint and were willing to take it in the way of an experience which the dance artists might give them, they would have a genuinely new experience.

This is perhaps too long an introduction. What is it that does mark the experience that gives it the characteristic of being esthetic? Here again I first approach it negatively. Certain kinds of experiences that we know pretty well are not esthetic. No one has ever been tempted, I think, to confuse a purely routine experience, especially with an element of drudgery in it, for an esthetic experience. There is something about sheer routine, a mechanical habit, doing the same thing over and over that certainly rules it out of the world of esthetic experience. We may get a certain elementary rudimentary esthetic experience from watching a squirrel go around in a wheel in his cage, but we do not get it when we feel that we are moving in anything that approaches a treadmill. Now, there are many things that are routine that we do not label as such. Our experiences become conventionalized when they are not automatically routine. You have heard of the people undoubtedly who thought they were thinking when they were only trying to think what other people think they ought to think and what applies there in their ideas and beliefs about things in general may come in and make experience so conventional that it loses its esthetic quality even when the person tries to deceive himself or does unconsciously deceive himself in thinking that he has a genuine experience.

Anything that hardens an experience in certain lines as if they were the proper lines in which it should run becomes a burial to a genuine esthetic experience. Now, a great deal of our experience is too over-intellectualized on the other hand. It isn't routine. We are thinking, but we are thinking to try and solve a problem, maybe a very simple one. One who is driving a car on the road looks at a sign to get his direction or to get his distances from the other towns. He doesn't take the object for what it is in and of itself as an experience that he can get out of it. He takes it simply as something that points to something else. That is what I mean by a one-sided experience in our intellectual life. We don't allow ourselves to see and feel and appreciate things for what they are directly, for what they in their own qualities have to say to us. We try to have it teach us a lesson of some kind. This very simple example that I gave is simply an example of what direction they move the car in, how far they go.

It might be well to take the experience for what it is and the object for what true appeal it makes, not because we think it should teach a moral lesson, or that we should be edified in some way. A book has been written on the English criticism of the novel during a large part of the last century, the period we call the Victorian period. As we see it now it is striking; it seems peculiar and strange that so little of that criticism had anything to do with the esthetic qualities. It was satisfactory if it could bring a blush to the cheek of any person. That seemed to be the chief consideration in the minds of the critics and that must have meant that it was that way in the minds of many people regarding the literary arts, particularly. This is also true in a great deal of the nineteenth century painting. One might also say that the great movement of the main stream of painting in the nineteenth century up to the impressionistic movement had this blight upon it, in that it must teach a moral lesson. The picture must represent something, something literary like an illustration of a poem or a story, or illustrate some great historic movement or incident. At least one great merit of the impressionistic movement in painting was that it broke away from that. The word impressionistic was used first at a time of diverse criticism, that nature landscapes had something to give us immediately and directly. There was a play of lights and of color without trying to tell us anything over and beyond itself.

Now, as I have already suggested, while no experience is esthetic unless our emotions are involved, unless we are in some way excited by whatever calls out the experience, there are experiences that fail to be esthetic because they are not much else but feelings and they tend to be sentimental. Those of you who have read recently James' *Psychology* may recall this illustration, my second point as well, the story of being in the gallery and some English ladies looking at Titian's *Assumption,* and they had a certain rapt look on their faces, and one of them was saying about the virgin, "What a look of abnegation; how unworthy she is feeling." They wanted the picture to tell something; they also felt it was necessary to work up some peculiar feeling in the presence of the work of art. When people begin to enjoy their own feelings instead of enjoying the scene or the material of their experience, then I say they are becoming sentimental and they are getting at best imitations to those esthetic experiences.

Now, the lesson, the conclusion rather, that I would draw from these negative illustrations is that a genuine esthetic experience is a total experience. It isn't one-sided. It isn't split up. That is the reason it is so hard to talk about any genuine esthetic experience. You may remember that the author of certainly one of the great English novels of recent years, *Of Human Bondage,* in his book called *The Summing Up,* says that the best critic in the world in relation to a beautiful painting which he thinks has the quality of beauty to perhaps an unrivalled degree, if he wants to talk about it, if he has intelligence, all he can tell to the people is to go and look at it and get the experience themselves.

If the esthetic experience were one-sided, if it were predominantly an active motor doing things, or if it were emotional or intellectual, then we would have some line to talk about, but being as it is. a fusion of all of these things it is just the complete and total vital experience that it is. The only way to have it is by having it. In that sense the significance of esthetic experience is that the very idea of it is a sort of direction to us to make our experiences as complete, as full, as total in their vitality as we can. Why is it that there is so much idealization of early childhood? Why is it that people so almost spontaneously turn to early childhood to get illustrations of experiences that they regard as peculiarly pure, peculiarly delightful and worthwhile? I think it is just for the reason that the young child who has had normal healthy parents in his happy life has a whole life. It hasn't begun to be split up into "Now I have to do something," and then having to think out certain problems and having certain feelings or emotions attached only to a few experiences. All of these things fuse together, and I don't think I am wrong in believing that we turn so naturally and spontaneously to the childish experience as having an ideal quality that we would be glad to recover if we only could because it stands to us without our knowing it as a symbol of what a really vital esthetic experience is.

You know, painters talk about recovering the innocence of the eye, especially when students are learning to paint or draw. As adults we have all learned to see things as signs of something else. I know there is a corner up there where things meet at right angles, but my eye alone doesn't tell me that. The one who is going to reproduce it in a drawing has again to get away from what that stands for.

As there is this innocence of the eye, so there is a kind of innocence of the totality of experience. That is one reason why the life activities of the happy child and the wholesome surroundings appeal to us. It is so difficult to describe. We can describe it only by analyzing it, and so all of those elements which I have spoken of when they become one-sided or exaggerated come to stand in the way of esthetic experience. Yet I need hardly call your attention to the fact that there is movement involved in every art. It is obviously almost the substance of the dance. Obviously, no art can be produced without movement—in sculpture, in poetry; even the poet has to do something. The artists who portray on the stage are all in action, and psychologists have proved that when we look at things and see things we are just taking in things somewhat passively with the eye that there is a certain muscular motor attitude throughout the whole body, and if that motor response, even in observation, were taken away from us, we would not have an esthetic observation. We would not have even a perception that would mean anything to us. We have to make distinctions, to draw lines so to speak, and to relate things together. There is a motor acting mechanism involved in doing this. So, when it becomes, this element of action becomes routine, the esthetic element is gone, but it has to be there.

Now, there is, of course, a great difference between the people who are capable of creative effort and the people who can only enjoy and appreciate it. I don't think fundamentally the gulf is as great as it sometimes is supposed to be. The artist, that is, the honest producer or creator, has a certain balance, largely physiological as well as psychological, between his motor side and his feelings, so that if he is a painter it tends to go out in the creation of the picture. So with those other things. We think when we get a genuine appreciation we ourselves tend to become artists of a secondary sort, but that after all we do not need to repeat the same experiences the artist had by any means, but we need to have an experience that has some of the same relations in it that the artist had in producing it. Our motor attitude and abilities are a very large element in this re-creation.

I think words just as words sometimes have a great deal to tell us. We talk about re-creation. Now if we pronounce it a little differently and call it recreation, we get, I think, the theory that art is a form of play. It isn't the whole truth, but there is a ratio of truth in it, and it means that the one who appreciates the work of art must mingle with his seriousness and intentness of observation and of freedom of all of his mental powers in which he reproduces or re-creates to some extent the mood and the attitude of the artist in the original creation.

There is one thing so obvious and so complex in the esthetic experience that we perhaps don't attach the meaning to it that it deserves and that is that all of the arts appeal to our senses, to our eyes, to our ears, to our sense of body movement which the psychologist calls the kinesthetic sense, and even indirectly to the sense of touch, what are called the tactile values in many of the arts. Why is it that the qualities of the senses of the eyes and the ears, the tone, color, motion, as directly observed are so important? I think perhaps an adequate answer, a full answer, is beyond the power of anybody, but certainly one thing is that it is through our senses that we get a direct, first hand, an original communication with the world about us. Moralists have treated the senses rather harshly. They regard them as the sources of temptation—the lusts of the eye, and professional moralists have tended to look with fear and suspicion upon the arts just because of this sensuous element which they deprecate by calling it sensual. It is extraordinary how much we lose our powers of direct observation, more than observation I mean our sensitiveness, our responsiveness, to the world of persons and objects and natural events about us because we fall into certain routines or because of our occupations we have certain ends more or less remote that control our thought and attention, and we become oblivious to a great deal of the human scene around us.

One great function, speaking now for a moment from the standpoint of the works of art, of the work of art is that it can break down these barriers to sensitivity or responsivity that we have allowed our habits of life, our special callings and vocations to build walls up around us, and give our senses, our eyes and ears, the sense of movement, a fresh baptism that makes them more aware of things, more acutely aware of them. I have an idea that a large part of our appreciation of beauty in nature is, without our knowing it, a result of the education that we have had through various forms of the plastic arts. I have an idea that a great deal of our ability to respond and know character in people, to interpret their movements and gestures is the production of an education that some of us have got more directly, but a large part of us have got through the great literary artists.

There is a very peculiar union of passivity, of receptivity, and of activity involved in this sensitivity of the eye and the ear and the body to the scene around us. When we say sensitivity we are thinking of the receptive side. When we call it responsiveness we bring in the active side. There is no genuine sensitivity without

some active response, just as there can be no active response without some sensitivity. It is the balance between receptiveness and
activity in the way of responsiveness that seems to me to charac-
terize very large elements in the experience of things that make
them for us, while we are having the experience, works of art.

I just want to say a word about the intellectual element. As I
have said, if any intellectual element becomes so predominant
that it shuts out other things and we look at things simply as
signs of something beyond themselves instead of for what they
are, if we sense them and preserve them, they cease to be esthetic.
On the other hand, a very large part of the difference in the
world of works of art from jazz to symphony, or from a cheap
spectacle to a noble dramatic exhibit, depends upon the wealth
of background originally of an intellectual sort that stirred it up.

I want to quote something that William James said. He said
it about religious experience, but I think he might have said it
about esthetic experience. "Man's conscious wit and will are aiming at something only dimly and inaccurately imagined as yet, all
the while the forces of organic ripening within him are going on.
His conscious strainings are letting loose subconscious allies
behind the scenes, which work towards rearrangement; and the
rearrangement towards which all these deeper forces tend is definitely different from what he consciously conceives and determines. When the new centre of energy has been incubated so
long as to be brought into flower, 'hands off' is the only word
for us."

I would apply that in a slightly different manner than what
James meant. Our conscious experiences of a more intellectual kind become capitalized. They become unconscious back-
grounds. We are as unconscious of them as we were when we first
had them. Certainly, a large part of the power of the work of art,
or the measure of the power of the work of art, is its ability to let
loose, as it were, this background that has become unconscious
in a way. It focuses it and orders it in a single experience, which
we might say is self-intellectual, not in any sense mystical, but
just because so many elements which perhaps we couldn't consciously recall if we tried to are brought to a head and focused
and brought into proper relations to each other, that we have a
genuinely esthetic experience. It is because the esthetic experience brings together in a balanced ordered way things that in our

daily life tend to get separated from each other and opposed to each other that the esthetic experience is what it is and has the value that it has.

There is tranquility of emotion and at the same time there is excitement. Now in ordinary life tranquility and excitement don't hang together. They more or less fight each other, just as the receptivity to things about us and our outgoing activity tend to be separated together. It is this fullness, this totality or wholeness of esthetic experience which exists because these things get separated and divided from each other in our daily living and are brought back into the unity where they belong, the unity which I said little children have before they get more or less spoiled or sophisticated or intimidated by the struggles of existence.

I might conclude by stating that, after all, what we call an esthetic experience, if we only had it often enough and if it were only normal enough, we should leave off the adjective esthetic. We should know it for what it is—simply experience itself, having experiences at their best and at their fullest.

Foreword to David Lindsay Watson's *Scientists Are Human*

"Great is Science"—much greater, judging by popular acclaim, than ever was Diana of Ephesus even among the Ephesians. But great in what? Great in actuality or great in prestige? Certainly great in actuality, in its practical applications, in the physical and chemical technologies that control industrial productivity, and great in many of the phases of medicine and public health. The community at large is without doubt tremendously influenced by the results, the external products of science. It is a commonplace that our ways of external behavior and external association have been revolutionized by "science." But when this is said, is it not also true that "science" takes on a significance as external as are the changes in behavior which make up this revolution? Until the transformation is one in the ways of human feeling and thinking, is it not possible that science itself will be conceived of as a specialized technique directed upon special problems, which are special just because they are not linked with the fundamental and inescapable issues of personal and associated living?

Science has certainly affected deeply the beliefs of large numbers of human beings. But beliefs themselves may be external. They *are* external when they are associated with special matters, while all matters are special and specialized as far as they are not intimately connected with basic human impulses and the needs rooted in organic life. That science is a way of thinking—of thinking not just inside the head, but in active operations with and upon things—is obvious. But "thinking" is itself a specialized affair as long as it is not integrated with feeling, with emotions, desires, impulses that are at once deeply personal and

[First published in David Lindsay Watson, *Scientists Are Human* (London: Watts and Co., 1938), pp. vii–xi.]

deeply communal. For they are communal, and not just personal, because they are shared by every human being, and because their equitable cultivation and harmonious expression by all persons are the ultimate problem of free cooperative human living.

The relatively external and specialized character of science is, it may be assumed, a function of its very short historical career. It is young, and human life on earth is old, encompassed in old traditions, customs, institutions, and symbols. The contrast is so great that it would be unreasonable to expect that science could, in the short time it has had at its disposal, make its way very far *in*. It has, however, now reached such a relative state of maturity and has overcome sufficiently a number of its earlier open antagonists, so that here and there individuals and groups are beginning to ask what it is all about anyway. In Great Britain there is a group of scientific men, more active if not more numerous than any similar group in America, who are asking what the role of science is, actually and potentially, in the modern world. They point out the extent to which, actually, science is frustrated and even prostituted by subordination to nationalistic aims, centring about war, and to industry conducted for private profit. They urge that scientific men accept responsibility for the human consequences of their efforts. They point out that, unless scientific workers actively recognize this responsibility, political control will remain in the hands of those who are ignorant of the forces which are in fact shaping the modern world.

Dr. Watson's book approaches the problem from a different angle. He is concerned to show that the pursuit of science and the products of science are relative to the mental world of the scientist, to the organization of his personality in all its phases, and that this in turn is relative to the social organization that subsists. The angle of approach is different from that just mentioned. But the problem and the ultimate appeal are the same. Indeed, the two modes of approach are polar and complementary. We have to know both what science is doing to make our world what it is and what it could do to make a different and human world. We have to know also what the conditions of present social life are doing to the scientist, and what, in consequence, the scientist does to and with science. Dr. Watson accomplishes a much-needed work, admirable in form and content, showing how science itself is limited, arrested, deflected, distorted, by the "mental world" which reflects our social organization. He shows by direct demonstration, rather than by demonstration through argument, that the prevalence of mechanical modes of social organization has produced not merely mechanistic philosophies of science—a relatively minor matter—but a mechanism in the mind of the inquirer which stands in the way of the manifestation of his whole personality in the scientific work he does—a major matter. The exclusion of the full personality from the work of the scientist takes its toll in what is scientifically accomplished—in the methods of science and the body of knowledge which is their fruit.

I am not called upon to summarize awkwardly what Dr. Watson has stated vividly in the pages which follow. But I cannot refrain from calling particular attention to the chapter "On the Similarity of Forms . . .". It is somewhat more technical in content, although not in style, than the other chapters, because it constructs their intellectual base. It is in effect a well-grounded plea for a recognition of the inherent likeness of aesthetic response and of artistic creativity with genuine scientific procedure. A few years ago a scientist, whose work in his own field has won international recognition, said to me that it often took two or three years before his assistants in the laboratory, well trained through graduate work, were able to see what was before their eyes. The reason he gave was that certain conceptions fixed in a certain framework had been so built into their mental organization that they could see only what conformed to the framework. So far there is confirmation of the point which Dr. Watson makes about similarity of forms. He added that education had deprived these men of their native spontaneous sensitivities; of those immediate responses which are the heart of aesthetic experience. Dr. Watson does not make light of the importance of guiding conception and an orderly framework of conceptions. But his book is a powerful and, as I have said, urgently needed presentation of the fact that the framework of conceptions becomes a restriction of scientific inquiry unless it unites intimately and thoroughly with that vital sensitivity of impulse and response which is the property of unspoiled common sense, and which finds its effective expression in the work of the creative artist.

When Dr. Watson's exposition of this point is accepted in conjunction with his exposition of the forms of social organization which bring about hardening of the arteries through which flows the life-blood of scientific inquiry, the reader finds himself in the presence of a work in which criticism is raised to the plane of creative construction.

Appendixes

Appendix 1
Editorial Foreword to *Experience and Education*

Experience and Education completes the first ten-year cycle of the Kappa Delta Pi Lecture Series. The present volume therefore is, in part, an anniversary publication honoring Dr. Dewey as the Society's first and tenth lecturer. Although brief, as compared with the author's other works, *Experience and Education* is a major contribution to educational philosophy. Appearing in the midst of widespread confusion, which regrettably has scattered the forces of American education and exalted labels of conflicting loyalties, this little volume offers clear and certain guidance toward a united educational front. Inasmuch as teachers of the "new" education have avowedly applied the teachings of Dr. Dewey and emphasized experience, experiment, purposeful learning, freedom, and other well-known concepts of "progressive education," it is well to learn how Dr. Dewey himself reacts to current educational practices. In the interest of clear understanding and a union of effort the Executive Council of Kappa Delta Pi requested Dr. Dewey to discuss some of the moot questions that now divide American education into two camps and thereby weaken it at a time when its full strength is needed in guiding a bewildered nation through the hazards of social change.

Experience and Education is a lucid analysis of both "traditional" and "progressive" education. The fundamental defects of each are here described. Where the traditional school relied upon subjects or the cultural heritage for its content, the "new" school has exalted the learner's impulse and interest and the current problems of a changing society. Neither of these sets of values is sufficient unto itself. *Both* are essential. Sound educational experience involves, above all, continuity and interaction between the learner and what is learned. The traditional curriculum undoubt-

[First published in Dewey's *Experience and Education* (New York: Macmillan Co., 1938), pp. ix–xii.]

edly entailed rigid regimentation and a discipline that ignored the capacities and interests of child nature. Today, however, the reaction to this type of schooling often fosters the other extreme—inchoate curriculum, excessive individualism, and a spontaneity which is a deceptive index of freedom. Dr. Dewey insists that neither the old nor the new education is adequate. Each is mis-educative because neither of them applies the principles of a carefully developed philosophy of experience. Many pages of the present volume illustrate the meaning of experience and its relation to education.

Frowning upon labels that express and prolong schism, Dr. Dewey interprets education as the scientific method by means of which man studies the world, acquires cumulatively knowledge of meanings and values, these outcomes, however, being data for critical study and intelligent living. The tendency of scientific inquiry is toward a body of knowledge which needs to be understood as the means whereby further inquiry may be directed. Hence the scientist, instead of confining his investigation to problems as they are discovered, proceeds to study the nature of problems, their age, conditions, significance. To this end he may need to review related stores of knowledge. Consequently, education must employ progressive organization of subject-matter in order that the understanding of this subject-matter may illumine the meaning and significance of the problems. Scientific study leads to and enlarges experience, but this experience is educative only to the degree that it rests upon a continuity of significant knowledge and to the degree that this knowledge modifies or "modulates" the learner's outlook, attitude, and skill. The true learning situation, then, has longitudinal and lateral dimensions. It is both historical and social. It is orderly and dynamic.

Arresting pages here await the many educators and teachers who are earnestly seeking reliable guidance at this time. *Experience and Education* provides a firm foundation upon which they may unitedly promote an American educational system which respects all sources of experience and rests upon a positive—not a negative—philosophy of experience and education. Directed by such a positive philosophy, American educators will erase their contentious labels and in solid ranks labor in behalf of a better tomorrow.

Alfred L. Hall-Quest
Editor of Kappa Delta Pi Publications

Appendix 2
Dr. Childs and Education for Democracy
By Boyd H. Bode

No thoughtful observer of American education can have failed to notice that a significant change is taking place in the progressive movement. This movement started as a protest against regimentation and the "imposition" of adult standards and adult needs. The sinfulness of such imposition has long been a favorite theme wherever the faithful were gathered together. As in the case of the Mother Goose rhymes, endless repetition, curiously enough, seemed to enhance the charm.

During recent years, however, a new note has been introduced. There is a growing realization that *the social implications of education must receive more serious consideration than has been given to them in the past.* As Dr. Kilpatrick puts it: "We must—so I believe and hope—hold to essential democracy and educate accordingly." [1]

Thesis of Professor Childs

This view obviously makes it necessary to determine what is meant by "essential democracy" and how we are to "educate accordingly." With respect to the former, Dr. Childs has argued forcibly that education in general, and progressive education in particular, must assume "definite responsibility for sharing in the development of certain new ideological patterns." [2] These new patterns, moreover, must be definitely aimed at a thoroughgoing revision of our present industrial system. "Under present socio-economic conditions it seems to me that the only adequate social point of view for education is one which includes as an

1. *School and Society*, April 20, 1935, p. 526.
2. The *Social Frontier*, March, 1935, p. 23.

[First published in *Social Frontier* 5 (November 1938): 38–40. For Dewey's comments on this article, see this volume, pp. 304–8.]

essential part the conception of the class struggle." [3] It is futile to assume that "our present problems can be solved by perpetuating indefinitely the two classes of 'employers' and 'workers.'" [4]

With respect to the question how we are to "educate accordingly," Dr. Childs insists that we should aim frankly to win recruits for democracy as thus conceived. On no other terms, as he contends, can we make a social philosophy meaningful.

How consistent is it to assert that progressive education lacks a social philosophy and a scheme of values which should contribute essential criteria for the determination of the needs of children, and then proceed to affirm that it is contrary to the very nature of democratic education to seek adherents for any particular social outlook, or way of life? Again is it consistent to hold that mind is built of actual experiencing, and is not an inborn faculty which develops by a process of unfolding from within, and, at the same time, to deplore deliberate selection and weighting of experience by the school which seeks to cultivate desirable emotional and intellectual dispositions? Can we, on the one hand, condemn progressive education for failing to give the child definite views about what he is *for* and what he is *against* in a civilization rocked to its foundations, and then consistently go on to limit the function of education to the intellectual analysis of issues, characterizing all attempts to educate on the basis of a considered social and economic program a form of indoctrination? [5]

The argument has the merit of recognizing that education must be pointed consciously towards a social ideal. It also insists that we should make no bones about conceiving this ideal in terms of class struggle, and that the attempt should be made to put it across in the classroom. Here is something for progressive education to think about. Does this pronunciamento from a leader in progressive education mean that the machinery of the movement has gone into reverse? Apparently *we are being told that "imposition" is not really a crime but a high moral obligation, provided, of course, that it is of the right kind and done in*

3. *Ibid.*, June, 1936, p. 278.
4. *Ibid.*, March, 1935, p. 24.
5. *Ibid.*, May, 1938, p. 267.

the right way. Or, to put it differently, the mission of progressive education, so it would seem, is not to substitute child worship for ancestor worship, but to provide the child with a different set of ancestors.

The Perils of "Conditioning"

The real issue raised by Dr. Childs, however, is not so simple. The moment we give up the notion that education is a process of "unfolding from within" we are committed to a program of selecting and weighting the experiences of pupils. Pretenses of neutrality are just pretenses. But, on the other hand, "essential democracy"—not to speak of progressive education—is incompatible with a program of cold-blooded and calculating "conditioning." Dr. Childs contends that there is a middle course, and this view is essentially sound. This middle course is what we need to explore.

Essential democracy includes both a certain quality of attitude and an intellectualized outlook or standard of value. The attitude is an attitude of generous give-and-take, of reciprocity and sharing. The intellectual outlook is a clear recognition that *common* interests have the right of way over *special* interests, and that *the continuous expansion of our common life is the final test of progress.* Social organization of every kind is just machinery for this end. Democracy is committed to the principle of what Dr. Childs calls "shared control."

Education in a democracy is duty bound to cultivate both this attitude and this outlook, which is to say that democracy must be both practiced and understood. Democracy is an empty name unless one gets the "feel" of the sentiment, "Blest Be the Tie That Binds." Kindliness, consideration for others, satisfaction in promoting understandings, and voluntary coöperation have a quality of their own, which is realized in and through appropriate modes of conduct. The school, then, becomes a place where a certain way of living is maintained. Within varying limits we all believe in democracy. So far, then, such an organization of the school is not a form of indoctrination, if we define indoctrination, with Dewey, as "the systematic use of every possible means to impress upon the minds of pupils a particular set of political and economic views to the exclusion of every other."[6] Perhaps the scientific attitude offers a fair analogy. Affording an opportunity to conduct investigations in the spirit of science opens the way to a first-hand experience of the scientific attitude. *Doing this betrays partisanship as against the possible view that such experiences are dangerous and to be avoided.* To provide these experiences, however, cannot be called indoctrination in any useful sense of the term.

The plot thickens when we formulate this democratic attitude into a supreme principle for conduct. This at once precipitates a series of collisions in every major field of human interest. A formulation of this kind can be handled in either of two ways: (*a*) as a standard for the way in which the pupil is to be "conditioned," or (*b*) as a competing principle for the organization of life and conduct. In analogous fashion the assumption of science that every event is reducible to a "naturalistic" interpretation may be made explicit and be used either to cultivate an attitude of intolerance toward supernaturalism and superstition, or to stimulate an endeavor to see whether the assumption of naturalism can be stretched so as to go the whole way. In the case of science there is plainly but one road to travel. Conditioning in scientific education means that the pupil substitutes the experiences and the conclusions of the teacher for his own. This conclusion applies equally to the democratic outlook. Conditioning in education is the negation of democracy. So, once more, the term indoctrination seems inappropriate. The middle way is to encourage and assist the pupil in the reconstruction, undertaken independently, of his personal experience, with reference to the principle of democracy.

Democracy as a Social Ideal and as Method

Our concern at the moment, however, is not with a definition of indoctrination, but with the meaning of "essential democracy." Unless democracy has a distinctive spirit and a distinctive approach to contribute, it inevitably becomes merely another tyranny masquerading under a fine name. As I have already indicated, I find myself in extensive agreement with Dr. Childs's

6. *Ibid.*, May, 1937, p. 238 [*Later Works* 11:415].

position. We must aim at a democratic social order and we must avoid indoctrination. This is entirely sound. What troubles me is the fear that Dr. Childs, in an excess of zeal, sacrifices both the ideal and the method of democracy. His demand for a more genuinely social type of education springs from indignation at the disgraceful shortcomings of our present industrial and economic organization—an indignation which every right-minded person is bound to respect. Under the impetus of indignation, however, he shows a disposition to identify democracy with a campaign for a specific scheme of ownership and distribution. Hand in hand with this goes a bold demand for "inculcation" and for a crusade to win adherents. It is true that Dr. Childs attempts to distinguish this from ordinary indoctrination. He calls it "a process of emotional conditioning," when it is done by the other fellow, as against a process by which beliefs are "communicated in such a manner that an individual can make creative use of them,"[7] when it is done by himself. As a literary feat this distinction has merit, but it must not be permitted to obscure the fact that this proposed scheme of education is deliberately aimed at fostering a disposition which will make the pupil intolerant and "sore" with respect to the contrast between employers and workers.

There is plenty of room for doubt whether teachers, as a group, have either the qualifications or the mission to provide blueprints for the social order of the future. In any case, *when means are mistaken for ends, "essential democracy" fades out of the picture.* All we have left is the fact that another dog has entered the fight for the same bone. The rules, or lack of rules, governing the fight remain the same. What, for example, would be a sound labor policy, in terms of a democratic philosophy? Is progress to be measured solely in terms of higher wages, shorter hours, and improved conditions of labor? To put it more bluntly, are we automatically moving toward democracy to the extent that employers are pushed out of the picture and every worker becomes a sleek, stall-fed, vice-president of the firm? If the substitution of one form of selfishness for another constitutes progress, we are bound to conclude, with the poet, that God moves in mysterious ways his wonders to perform.

The moment we neglect to deal with industrial reform as an

7. *Ibid.*, May, 1938, p. 268.

expression of a moral and philosophical point of view, we lose our way. The desire to abolish the worker-employer relationship may have a variety of origins, ranging all the way from a feeling of abstract "right" to a disposition to engage in high-jacking the employer whenever there is an opportunity. If we permit the "new ideological patterns" for which Dr. Childs contends to simmer down to a particular scheme for ownership and distribution, then "essential democracy" becomes a name for an armed camp which uses precisely the same weapons as its opponents in fighting for its ends.

Education as an Outlining of Consequences

We are living in an interdependent social order, which requires continuous extension of governmental regulation. This is admitted even by the spokesmen of the Republican party, which presumably makes it unanimous. Eventually the schools will doubtless hear about it too. When that happens, what are they to do about it? It is undoubtedly true that as long as teachers shun economic issues and retire to an ivory tower for abstract discussions of sweetness and light, there is something seriously wrong. As Dr. Childs says: "Only as we come to grips with definite conditions and institutions can we avoid this form of barren formalism."[8] But there is a possibility that the schools will be just as seriously wrong if they become agencies for promoting a specific type of reform. *The remaining alternative is to center our program on the meaning or implications of democracy in a modern world.* Unfortunately, this is too revolutionary a proposition to make it likely that it will be adopted very widely, but there seems to be no other choice. The refusal to predetermine conclusions by a process of conditioning may be designated, according to taste, as "respect for personality" or as a hard-headed realization that it is stupid to get into one's own way, or as an abiding faith in the common man. A program to promote democracy by a process of conditioning is licked before it starts.

In sum, my disagreement with Dr. Childs relates less to the broad outlines of his position than to the specific application

8. *Ibid.,* May, 1938, p. 267.

which he gives to it. His general philosophy offers a conception of democracy which is an invaluable interpretation of the spirit or meaning of the progressive movement. In my judgment progressive education must move in the general direction indicated by that philosophy or cease before long to be a significant movement in American education. The special application, however, of this philosophy which is suggested by Dr. Childs would, if taken seriously, constitute not a development of progressive education but a repudiation of it. *What is required of progressive education is not a choice between academic detachment and adoption of a specific program for social reform, but a renewed loyalty to the principle of democracy.*

Appendix 3
Dr. Bode on "Authentic" Democracy
By John L. Childs

Dr. Bode's response to my review of his book on progressive education raises questions about the meaning of democracy and of the functions of American education which merit further discussion.[1] On the whole, his article tends to bring our positions somewhat closer together. In my reply I shall state what I understand to be our agreements, and what I think are still the most important issues between us.

Points of Agreement

1. Deliberate education of the young, by its very nature, cannot be a neutral undertaking. We educate because we desire to make of the young something which, if left to their own unguided interactions with the culture, they would not become. Dr. Bode's article removes all ambiguity from his position on this important issue. Progressive education will be better equipped to deal with the vital problems of our time when all of its leaders recognize with him that "pretenses of neutrality are just pretenses."

2. Educational objectives are not to be derived by an inspection of the individual child taken in isolation from the society of which he is a member. The distinctive meaning of American society is found in its democratic tradition and purpose. Hence this democratic conception, which contains a theory of social relationships, should provide the criteria for that "selecting and

1. Boyd H. Bode, *Progressive Education at the Crossroads*, reviewed by J. L. Childs in the *Social Frontier*, May, 1938.

[First published in *Social Frontier* 5 (November 1938): 40–43. For Dewey's comments on this article, see this volume, pp. 304–8.]

weighting of the experience of pupils" which is inherent in our educational activity.

3. The democratic principle demands that "common interests have the right of way over special interests." Call it "imposition," "conditioning," "growth," "learning through experience," or what you will, the fact remains that our public schools have been designed, as Dr. Bode states, to cultivate in the young "a certain quality of attitude and an intellectualized outlook or standard of value" which are the correlatives of our democratic way of life. Subtract this purpose from their program, and our schools lose one of their essential reasons for existence. To be sure, from the standpoint of the wholesome development of children, certain educational methods for the achievement of these objectives are far superior to others. Progressive education has made important contributions by its study of these matters of method. But in so far as it has assumed that concern about *method* can substitute for concern about *objectives*, it has confused and diverted educational thought and practice.

4. Respect for human personality is the cornerstone of democracy. Democracy demands that in all of the relationships of life each person be treated as an end, and never merely as a means. This conception has its educational implications; it signifies that education for democracy must seek to help each child develop a mind of his own. Mind, among other things, denotes capacity of the individual to evaluate group modes of life and thought in terms of changing conditions and experienced consequences. According to democratic theory such ability to judge of values is an essential trait of a mature person. Any educator, therefore, who believes in the democratic conception, is bound to be more interested in the liberation of the intelligence of his pupils than he is in making them adherents to some specific program of social reform which he has come to favor. Thus, in a democracy, the distinction between education and indoctrination is irreducible.

I am in emphatic agreement with Dr. Bode on this issue. I have never been able to follow the logic which maintains that all types of educational program are equally forms of arbitrary imposition on the child, since all alike involve a manifestation of preference for some definite mode of group life. This conclusion would follow only if we are prepared to admit that, from the standpoint of the individual they desire to nurture, the differences represented by the fascist, communist, and social-democratic patterns of group life are ethically insignificant.

5. Questions of economic and industrial reform are not merely economic and engineering questions; they are also questions of the kind of civilization we want. Hence they have fundamental moral and educational implications and should be approached in terms of some considered philosophy of the good life. Man cannot live without bread, but it is equally true that he does not live by bread alone. Our problem is to make the processes by which he earns his bread also processes for the enrichment of personality. It is just because I agree with Dr. Bode that these so-called economic affairs are also moral matters, that I believe they are a proper part of the educator's interest and function.

On all the foregoing I think Dr. Bode and I are in essential accord. I welcomed his book on progressive education because of its pointed and powerful analysis of these and related issues. I find so much of worth in his discussion, that I am the more concerned about what seem to me to be inadequacies in his interpretation of both the meaning of democracy and the rôle of education in the present transitional period in American life. If we are to have a democratic and peaceful resolution of our present difficulties, I believe that the schools, colleges, universities, and other educational agencies will have to undertake more than is sanctioned by Dr. Bode's version of "authentic democracy." This brings us to the disagreements.

Points of Difference

1. Essential democracy, according to Dr. Bode, includes three things: (*a*) "an attitude of generous give-and-take, of reciprocity and sharing," (*b*) "a clear recognition that common interests have the right of way over special interests," and (*c*) "recognition that the continuous expansion of our common life is the final test of progress." These principles define the end of democracy, and "social organization of every kind is just machinery for this end." Thus questions about "the scheme of ownership and distribution" pertain to the *means,* not the *end* of democracy. Teachers, as a group, moreover, are probably not qualified to

pass judgment on these difficult problems of means. This is not a serious limitation because the "mission" of teachers is with the ends of democracy, not with the design "for the social order of the future." "When means are mistaken for ends," Dr. Bode avers, "essential democracy fades out of the picture." My own hypothesis that the interests of both American democracy and liberal education are now bound in with the program for the realization of a workers' society is a flagrant example of this confusion of ends and means. "If taken seriously," Dr. Bode asserts, "it would constitute, not a development of progressive education, but a repudiation of it."

These are strange doctrines from an experimentalist in philosophy and education. They raise fundamental questions. To what extent can "ends" be divorced from "means" and still retain significant intellectual and moral meaning? More specifically, can a statement of the ends of American democracy contain meaning sufficiently definite to guide educational activity unless it gives some indication of the direction in which social reconstruction is now to move? Confronted with the actual context of American life in 1938, how adequate is it to allow our interpretation of democracy to simmer down to a generalized formula of "reciprocity" and "the continuous expansion of the common life"? Can education measure up to its present democratic responsibilities if it assumes that the kind of economic and social organization we are to achieve is a mere detail of machinery?

The difference here is crucial. I agree with Dr. Kilpatrick when he asserts: "the economic situation defines the moral obligation of today. We cannot avoid it."[2] For me, no statement of the meaning of democracy can be considered adequate which fails to recognize that the reconstruction of our economic system is now such an important *means* that it necessarily becomes one of the controlling *ends* of democratic effort for our generation.

Neither do I consider the emphasis on the need for economic reorganization to be a repudiation of the purpose of authentic democratic education. On the contrary, I see no escape from Dr. Dewey's conclusion that social conceptions of education "must be translated into descriptions and interpretations of the life which actually goes on in the United States for the purpose of

2. William H. Kilpatrick, *Education and the Social Crisis,* p. 30.

dealing with the forces which influence and shape it" unless we are "to be content with formal generalities, which are of value only as an introduction of a new point of view."[3] I find no attempt to give such realistic description and interpretation of American life in Dr. Bode's article.

2. In his discussion of the ends of democracy, Dr. Bode says nothing explicitly about equality of opportunity. Nevertheless, I believe he would agree that it is an authentic element in the American democratic tradition. The exploration of the implications of this principle of equality under changing life conditions seems to me to constitute an essential part of the present task of American education.

Historically, our ideal of equality has been associated, in the economic realm, with the open-market system of free competition for private gain. But the practice of laissez-faire in our highly interdependent industrial society now tends toward anarchy, widespread unemployment and insecurity, and restriction of production. There is growing recognition that some form of socioeconomic planning, coördination, and control is required. The crucial issue is what form this planning is to assume.

I do not pretend to have the blueprints for the new social order. Its means of control and administration will have to be experimentally developed. But if a planning society is to continue essential American democratic principles and ideals, it must have the following characteristics:

a) It will seek to utilize our material, technological, and human resources, and not to waste them.

b) It will regard socially useful work, in all of its forms, not as a necessary evil, not as a sordid, materialistic means for personal aggrandizement, but as a positive social resource for the development of personality and the enrichment of life.

c) It will be designed to serve the interests of all rather than to perpetuate the privileges of a favored minority. It will require appropriate instrumentalities of control so that all can share effectually in the formulation, criticism, and evaluation of policies.

In sum, it is my hypothesis that democracy is no longer compatible with our historic laissez-faire profit system, and that the present supreme technological, political, and educational task is

3. See *The Educational Frontier*, p. 34 [*Later Works* 8:44–45].

the construction of a planning society that can provide the means for the continued development of our democratic values. It is within this definite frame of reference that I undertake my educational activity.

3. Although Dr. Bode has affirmed repeatedly that there can be no neutrals in education, he is shocked at the thought of associating democratic education with a definite conception of socioeconomic planning. His attitude is the more puzzling in view of his hearty endorsement of my statement that teachers can avoid barren formalities only as they "come to grips with definite conditions and institutions." Apparently he wants educators to study social and economic problems, but at the same time to exercise due care to see that they never reach any conclusions concerning them. For educational purposes, study must be pure, unending, and unapplied. Once a teacher reaches a conclusion on any subject, he is disqualified, on Dr. Bode's basis, from acting as a true educator in that area.

Thus he assumes that, since I believe in a workers' society, I must become a blatant propagandist, necessarily transforming my educational activity into a mere crusade for adherents to my point of view. This seems to me to be a complete *non sequitur*.

Take the field of natural science, for example. Do we teach science as a bare method of inquiry, or as a controlled method of inquiry plus the tested findings which have been achieved through its use? Is introduction of the young to the knowledge already discovered in a given field considered antithetical to the development of the student's own intelligence in that field? Is a teacher barred from serving as an educator because researches in his field have already led to important discoveries? To ask these questions is to answer them. Obviously, in the field of natural science, the utilization of knowledge and principles of interpretation already attained is not opposed to growth of creative independent thought on the part of the individual.

Is the situation completely transformed when we move from the natural to the social realm? Demonstrable knowledge is indeed more difficult to attain, but I see nothing in the social world which would justify the assumption that teachers who have no hypotheses and principles of interpretation are necessarily the best educators. As the Commission on the Teaching of the Social Studies so ably stated, all education necessarily moves within some framework of things deemed necessary, possible, and desirable. Unless Dr. Bode is willing to retract all that he has said about the nature of education as a manifestation of preference for a preferred social order, he must accept this proposition. For my part, I know many sincere teachers who believe that democratic values can be conserved within the framework of a reconstructed capitalist system. I have never supposed that this disqualified them from serving as true educators or that it made them mere propagandists for their particular position. Why cannot the same hold for the teacher who has concluded that a more promising road out of our difficulties is offered by the conception of a coöperative, workers' society? Is the nature of this hypothesis such as to dispose those who entertain it to curb free inquiry, to restrict the study of rival hypotheses, to insinuate conclusions without giving the young a chance to evaluate the processes by which those conclusions are reached?

I find nothing in the record which indicates that the foes of academic freedom in the United States are those who believe in a socialized economy. It is not the workers who are the crusaders for loyalty oaths and other repressive legislation.

I hope, therefore, that Dr. Bode will reconsider his premises and decide that it is possible for a teacher to believe in a socialized economy and still be considered a worthy member of progressive education. In spite of his effort to read us out of the movement of authentic democratic education, we shall continue to maintain that an interpretation of "progressive" and "democratic" which leads to such an illiberal conclusion is itself not an authentic version of American democracy.

Appendix 4
Trotsky in the Kremlin: An Interview
What the Exiled Bolshevik Leader Might Have Done in Stalin's Place
By Selden Rodman

Late in September the Editor of *Common Sense* spent several hours interviewing Leon Trotsky at his house in Coyoacán, Mexico City. But the material on which this article is based is not merely the interview and the prepared statements which were handed to its author. These materials have been used to illustrate the thesis that Trotskyism and Stalinism stem from the same absolutist philosophy and the same development of undemocratic tactics, and this thesis has been arrived at through a study of the Moscow trials and the Mexican hearings, as well as the evidence of the Bolshevik revolution and recently published material relating thereto.

It is a curious fact that Trotsky, whose personality has been one of the most stimulating and disturbing of our epoch, wishes to be judged by his ideas alone. The editor of sectarian emigré newspapers, who lifted himself from the Bronx to the Kremlin in a few months by the sheer force of his ability to inspire confidence, order and enthusiasm where there had been doubt and confusion and apathy—the orator who breathed fire into one revolution and inspired the armies of another on ten fronts with enough zeal to make up for what they lacked in equipment—this man distrusts everything but the intellect.

When the author of this article presented his credentials one afternoon late in September and asked for an interview, the former Bolshevik leader looked at him coldly over the heavy horn rims of his spectacles and asked what questions could possibly not be answered on paper. It was suggested that a story confined to the analysis of ideas would be as dry as a cactus spine. Nonsense! Ideas are never dry . . . But, Comrade Trotsky, I know

[First published in *Common Sense* 6 (December 1937): 17–21. For Dewey's reply, see this volume, pp. 347–48.]

what you think—who doesn't? I want to get some inkling of why you think so, and what you are—if that is possible; surely there is a give and take in argument that is different from the cold letters on a white sheet. And I am not interested in ideas exclusively; rightly or wrongly I think that psychology and emotions play a large part in determining *anybody's* ideas.

He consented—but not graciously. Grace and an interest in human beings as human beings are not qualities in the Trotskyan personality. Whether he was suspicious of this interest in nonintellectual things, he was certainly suspicious of *Common Sense,* and particularly its title.

"Why 'common sense'? Your countrymen have too much of that already—that excuse for disorganized thinking . . . You say you took the title from Thomas Paine? I remember it now; but that was the contribution of English empiricism and had its place in the 18th Century; before Hegel and Marx these sceptical attitudes had a progressive character; but no longer. I have hesitated to write for a certain American publication, though in many respects it appears very promising. Why? Because its prospectus announces that it will 'steer clear of dogmas.' You have not enough dogmas, not enough doctrine, not enough respect for theory in your 'common sense' country! But enough. You will return to your hotel and put your questions into writing. You will mail them to my secretary. For the answers to those I have already dealt with you will come an hour before the interview and study the documents. Then I will see you."

The study, a long, cool-white chamber lined with low bookcases opened onto a sunny patio. Suspended from the ceiling by threads were several ornamental glass globes. The big desk with its modern chromium lamp was littered several inches deep with clippings from the world press: prominent was the New York *Socialist Call* heavily scored with a red pencil. The man behind the desk in his blue wind-breaker had iron-gray hair; his face was deeply lined and the glass in his spectacles was very thick. But the energy in that wiry body, the crackle of those eyes, the foxlike rapidity with which every idea was grasped, the rasping wit that turned the phrases—these would have been almost embarrassing to a mind and body thirty-five years younger were it not for the strange sense of two different and disparate worlds.

It was clear instantly how this personality had inspired confidence in millions under the tension of war. Clear equally how there was no place for it in peace-time. Trotsky can command supremely. It would be difficult to imagine him negotiating.

II

For the moment we will take his advice and return to what authority we can squeeze from the printed word. If we make as good a case as we can for both Stalin and Trotsky and then watch Trotsky at the Mexican hearings,[1] we will be in a better position to ask more questions and come to some conclusions.

One of the things that seems to make Trotsky and the Trotsky-ists most indignant about Stalin is the fact that he ousted the former War Lord for demanding ultra-leftist agricultural and industrial programs and then blandly proceeded to put those very programs into effect. To be sure Trotsky criticizes the tempo and the methods used in the "liquidation of the kulaks as a class" and the 5-Year Plan, but it is the fact that Stalin proved to be just as radical that rankles.

Both men detested each other thoroughly. The slow Stalin detested the spectacular qualities of his quick-witted rival; he distrusted his intellectualism, the culture he had acquired in a long life of exile during which Stalin had done the dirty work in Tsarist Russia. Trotsky for opposite reasons hated the immense Georgian with his long, crafty memory.

But unfortunately for Trotsky, Stalin was the politician of the two and his friends were less mercurial than those wobbling spirits who now worshipped and now hated the ruthless ex-War Lord. Furthermore Stalin had a veritable arsenal at his disposal when Lenin died, and it had to be one or the other of them. Trotsky had only joined the Bolsheviks in 1917. The files of the exile press were full of Lenin's disparaging invective and (what was worse in a Marxist atmosphere where heresy-hunting was already becoming habitual) of Trotsky's acid rejoinders. "That professional exploiter of every backwardness in the Russian labor movement," he had called Lenin, adding, "The whole edifice of

1. *The Case of Leon Trotsky,* just published by Harpers, is reviewed in *Common Sense* 6 (December 1937): 26.

Leninism at the present time is based on lies and falsifications and contains within itself the poisonous beginnings of its own disintegration." However prophetically this last sentence may sound to some today, it was an historical fact that Lenin and Trotsky were reconciled in 1917. But that made no difference. For Stalin controlled the Party and the Party controlled the press. Trotsky took the only remaining avenue, underground organization and propaganda. But infraction of Party discipline is the unforgiveable sin in Russia. Trotsky's doom had struck.

Following the period of exile, however, a more serious charge has been levelled against Trotsky. It is said that his fiery temperament and agitational talents are essentially destructive; that Stalin has wisely subordinated international insurrections to construction on the home front; and that Trotsky, wittingly or unwittingly, has played into the hands of reactionary enemies of the regime. Leaving the last till we come to the hearings, it is probably true that the average worker in Soviet Russia today is behind Stalin's purges. It is easy to answer that he has to be; but it is nevertheless true that he feels that Stalin is removing incompetent and plotting superiors: the purges do not affect the rank and file directly. How long the worker will continue to reason this way depends upon how long Stalin can continue to increase production without translating that increase into consumer-goods and a higher living standard.

The case for Stalin has never been put more persuasively if less orthodoxly than by Harold Loeb in his "Science and Faith at the Moscow Trials."[2] A copy of this article lay on Trotsky's desk in Coyoacán the afternoon this writer returned, and it must be said that his eye fell upon the familiar cover with some uneasiness!

"So this is the 'common sense' judgment of Stalinism!"

"Economically, yes; but we make a distinction between Soviet economics and politics; in the box accompanying the article you will find our reservations, including our comments on the concept of justice behind the Moscow Trials."

Trotsky has a way of cocking his head to one side and chuckling humorlessly like a schoolmaster when he disagrees with you. This time he hardly chuckled, but his face grew red. He shook his finger.

"Did you ever hear of Pontius Pilate?"

2. *Common Sense*, March, 1937.

I had heard of him—in fact I expected to hear of him.

"Well, this is no difference, your box! It is worse than the article. You cannot be for Stalin and against him. You must be one or the other."

Why "must," I wondered. Is there no relativity in politics? Have the absolutes driven out by science come back to roost in the barren branches of political theory? What are the roots of this absolutism in the Marxist world that make it so alien not only to the scientific mind which insists upon discarding a theory or even a part of a theory the minute it fails to check against new facts, but equally to the pragmatic American?

III

The hearings of the Preliminary Commission of Inquiry were held in this same house in Coyoacán in April. As everybody knows, the Chairman of this committee was the great American philosopher, John Dewey, inheritor of James' pragmatic mantle, and the Commissioners were Otto Ruehle, Benjamin Stolberg, Carleton Beals and Suzanne La Follette.

This writer, having talked to the "defendant" as well as to several of the Commissioners and others present, and having studied the verbatim account of both this "trial" and the ones held in Moscow, has come to the following convictions about the Mexican hearings and the issues behind them:

That Trotsky certainly, and the Moscow defendants probably, were guilty neither of terrorism nor of plotting with foreign powers;

That the Moscow trials, call them frame-ups if you will, are not primarily manifestations of some sinister latter-day sorcery known as Stalinism, but are a direct result of the Marxist-Leninist philosophy in which the end is made to justify the means (more of this later);

That similarly it can be argued fairly that Trotsky and the Oppositionists would have acted in the same way, given the opportunity;

That the Commission itself being composed of two ardent admirers of Trotsky, two liberals and one inaudible Herr Doktor, could prove nothing finally;

That one of the liberals became so irritated with the partisans and with Trotsky's innate inability to answer a simple question without making a speech, that he asked unfair questions and precipitated his own resignation, thereby striking (whether deliberately or not) a serious blow at the Commission's impartiality, but not proving himself thereby a "Stalinist";

That the other liberal was right and courageous in demanding a hearing for Trotsky but hesitant to identify the common philosophy that led to only apparently different actions;

That the case will never be proved because if One True Church cannot be wrong, neither can Two.

The most interesting features of the published testimony, at least to this writer, are the examples of amazing *a priori* Marxist reasoning on the part of the defendant.

Trotsky: "A strike—what is a strike? A strike is an embryo revolution."

Trotsky: "For the working class of all countries, an international evaluation is totally natural."

What does it matter to Trotsky that no International has ever engineered a successful revolution anywhere, least of all in Russia? He upholds the latest, his own 4th International, on the *a priori* grounds that a working class revolution *must* be guided by an International. When Dr. Dewey asks him whether it is not true that since the War the proletariat everywhere has been more nationally than internationally minded, he blandly replies: "Capitalism pushes the workers to revolution . . . In Europe the nations are more connected with each other . . . I can predict that the revolution in France would immediately, if it moves on in any way, exercise or provoke a revolution in Hitler Germany." And conversely. Evidence? Proof? Did the revolution in Russia provide more than abortive ones anywhere else? No matter. It is in the Book. The working class has a "historic mission." Q.E.D.

IV

There are kinds of great minds. The broad, deep intelligence of the philosopher and the sharp, activist intelligence of the egotist. The minds of a Goethe, a Thomas Mann, a Dewey. The minds of a Calvin, a Robespierre, a Clemenceau. Lenin had a measure of both, but not Trotsky. Yet who will deny the courage, the indomitable will and even the grandeur of the activist when his back is against the wall?

Trotsky in exile, cut off from the people he would like to reach in every country, would be a tragic figure were he not bristling with the same rebellious zeal and truculent self-confidence that made him the captain of October. There is little of the futility and sputtering despair of most exiles here. Certainly he is bitter and as certainly his point of view is warped by his isolation from reality and the perpetual company of twittering disciples. But he works 17 hours a day. He keeps up with every fluctuation of world politics that seeps through the press and he is filled with no sense of frustration.

"Thinking," he told me, "gives man full satisfaction. Mental work depends comparatively little on external circumstances. If one has at hand books, paper and pen, it is sufficient for formulating conclusions about one's life-experience and the experience of others, and with that participate in the preparation for the future. It would be incorrect, therefore, to say that I have abstained from politics; I am *not* participating in current politics . . . But my literary activity, whether it is devoted to theory or history, always has in view the further destiny of humanity and tries to assist the movement for the liberation of the workers in whatever manner possible . . . During my forty years of revolutionary struggle I had power for almost eight years. I did not feel any happier during that period. In similar manner I do not see any reason for considering my exile a personal misfortune. The exile was conditioned by the revolutionary struggle and, in that sense, was a natural, logical link in my life. My present life is little different from that which I led in the Kremlin: it is devoted to work. I am fully satisfied with my stay in Mexico. True, the agents of Stalin (there is no reason for my naming them) do what they can here to spoil my sojourn. But long experience has taught me to disregard them with indifference, to which is added a grain of contemptuousness . . . Conviction in the correctness of one's position and the struggle for the triumph of truth over lies and falsification brings the very highest satisfaction possible to a human being."

It is clear that there is no reason to pity a man in such a frame of mind.

All of the old zeal, all of the old watchfulness for heresy is here.

Once in the course of a heated argument on the nature of fascism, when this writer exposed his unorthodox views to the extent of suggesting that the German capitalists were having a hard time of it under Hitler, the old Marxist leaped to his feet and thundered: "The interview is terminated!" Strange conduct for one accused by Vyshinsky of being "a leader of one of the storm detachments of fascism."

Nor has time blunted his mind. Trotsky must master language as he mastered military tactics and the organization of rolling stock. "These ideas have already been seeped up"—he said, and then hesitated. "What is that word?" "Absorbed?" "Ah, yes, absorbed," and he continued as rapidly as before.

We parted amicably, he insisting half-seriously that my political friends if in office would never allow him to enter the United States, I assuring him most sincerely that they would find him no more of a menace and liability than the Mexicans do.

V

At the hearings already referred to, Trotsky was asked to make a more serious prediction. What would he have done to Stalin and his friends if *he* and not Stalin had won out? Would he have eliminated them?

Trotsky: "You know the first thing I would do? It is to expel from the Party all the demoralized people such as Vyshinsky, Yagoda and others who are the enemies of the working class and who are working now only for their personal, material interest. Not persons with different opinions from mine. That is a different thing. Not I myself would expel them. I would convoke a conference of workers: 'You may select between honest and dishonest people in the Party.' I mean workers from the factories without ambitions for a career. I am sure they would make a good selection."

This answer is extraordinarily revealing. Trotsky knows *a priori* who are the "enemies of the working class"—just as Stalin does. Stalin did not execute his enemies in his own name either. He executed them in the name of the workers. And is there the slightest reason to suppose that Trotsky's supposed selection of workers to judge his enemies would be any more unprejudiced a tribunal than the Party press of Soviet Russia which unanimously demanded the heads of the Trotskyites even before they had come to the dock? Like every religious fanatic since the dawn of history, Trotsky's opponents are not people whose *opinions* differ—oh no! They are people who "are working for their material, personal interests" only. The accuser is always "disinterested," "honest," "incapable of intrigue"; the opponent is invariably "self-seeking," "mercenary" and a "confirmed plotter." Every one of Leon Trotsky's enemies is characterized not merely as wrong but as *cynical!* Stalin's description of Trotskyists is not only "cynical" but "rotten."

From the moment the Bolsheviks seized power in 1917—indeed earlier—the philosophy of Marxism was modified to justify not only the dictatorship of a minority party but the *use of terror.* Trotsky himself said in his statement for this interview that "the Bolshevik party in the years of civil war looked upon terror as an unavoidable temporary weapon, attendant, as history shows, upon each revolution. The aim of this terror was to free the nation from old coercive chains and to clear the way for the development of a socialist society." But when he comes to the use of terror in the Moscow trials, Trotsky makes the dual function of this weapon only too apparent. "The present terror of the Soviet bureaucracy has a reactionary, not revolutionary character." Just who is to make these distinctions? Hitler too justified the use of terror, and so did Mussolini in 1922—on the grounds that the Bolsheviks had used it and would use it again.

Clearly it is the duty of every group desiring social change to investigate the origins of this philosophy and decide just how far, after all, the end justifies the means.

Suffice it to say here that the disregard of democratic methods should be traced to the very beginnings of Bolshevik power in 1917, when the Bolsheviks, defeated in an election by the Social Revolutionaries, attacked parliamentary forms in favor of "class politics." Later, the duly elected members of the Constituent Assembly were ousted from the Tauride Palace by Bolshevik bayonets. Trotsky, who agitated for years against the death penalty, promptly reintroduced it in the Red Army. Political power was transferred from the comparatively democratic Central Executive Committee and the Soviet of People's Commissars to a Bureau of nine members within the Executive Committee of the Communist Party itself. The uprising of the Social Revolutionaries was answered with firing squads. The demands of the rebellious Kronstadt sailors—in 1921, at the height of Trotsky's power— for freely elected Soviets chosen by secret ballot, for free speech, assembly and organization were not only rejected; the sailors were massacred for "counter-revolution."[3] A year later, in a letter to the then-Commissar of Justice, Lenin wrote that "In my opinion it is necessary to extend the application of execution by shooting (with the substitution of exile abroad, see Art. 1 below) to all phases covering the activities of Mensheviks, Social Revolutionaries and the like; *a formula must be found that would place these activities in connection with the international bourgeoisie and its struggles against us* . . ." This letter was published in Moscow just before the Radek trial—and small wonder. Even if spurious, its concepts can be duplicated a hundred times in the published writings and historical records of the Russian Revolution. "History," says Lenin again (in his famous letter of November 6, 1917, to the members of the Central Executive Committee of the Party) "will not forgive delay by revolutionists who could surely be victorious today (and will surely be victorious today) while they risk losing much tomorrow, they risk losing all. If we seize power today, we seize it *not against the Soviets but for them*. Seizure of power is the point of the uprising; its political task will be clarified after the seizure. *It would be a disaster or formalism to wait for the uncertain voting of November 7.* The people have a right and a duty to decide such questions not by voting but by force." (My italics.)

It is true that most revolutions have been accompanied by terror and few have escaped dictatorship, but the time has come for American radicals to stop juggling with the comparative merits of Trotskyism and Stalinism and to determine the consequences of the philosophy and tactics that underlie both.

3. See review of article from *International Review* in "What's Left," *Common Sense* 6 (December 1937): 23.

Notes

The following notes, keyed to the page and line numbers of the present edition, explain references to matters not found in standard sources.

67.8   one of his letters] Jefferson to Adams, 22 January 1821.

72.39–40   "History . . . history."] This motto, attributed to Edward A. Freeman on the title page of every issue of *Johns Hopkins University Studies in Historical and Political Science* through volume 19 (1901), the last volume edited by H. B. Adams, was dropped in volume 20 when J. M. Vincent, J. H. Hollander, and W. W. Willoughby assumed joint editorship. Various versions of the quotation were used by Freeman throughout his writings.

110.27   President Eliot] Charles W. Eliot, president-emeritus of Harvard University. See his *The Future of Trades-Unionism and Capitalism in a Democracy* (New York and London: G. P. Putnam's Sons, 1910).

119.37–38   stood Hegel on his head.] In his Preface to the Second Edition of *Capital: A Critique of Political Economy,* Marx states about Hegelian dialectic that "with him it is standing on its head."

139.9   Plato's statement] This statement can be found in *The Republic,* Book II, sec. 368. See Checklist of Dewey's References.

141.13   "brutish and nasty,"] Dewey chose these two qualities from Hobbes's "solitary, poor, nasty, brutish, and short." (*Leviathan,* Part I, chapter 13, p. 64.) See Checklist of Dewey's References.

143.7   "Love of power,"] The most likely source for Dewey's use of this phrase is Bertrand Russell's

Power: A New Social Analysis, since Dewey quoted from this book in the succeeding chapter of *Freedom and Culture.* See this volume, p. 160, and Checklist of Dewey's References.

166.37–38   Baconian . . . den] in Aphorism XXXIX of his *The New Organon,* Bacon identifies four classes of Idols: Idols of the Tribe, Idols of the Cave, Idols of the Market-place, and Idols of the Theatre. See Checklist of Dewey's References.

170.20   "Public . . . trust."] This motto was used by the Grover Cleveland administration, but other statesmen such as Thomas Jefferson and John C. Calhoun used similar phrases.

173.14–15   "the definitions . . . government,"] In a 6 April 1859 letter to H. L. Pierce and others, Lincoln wrote that "The principles of Jefferson are the definitions and axioms of a free society." This quotation was selected as the headnote to Appendix 1 in Jefferson's *Democracy,* in Dewey's personal library (John Dewey Papers, Special Collections, Morris Library, Southern Illinois University at Carbondale). See Checklist of Dewey's References.

196.27–197.22   "If . . . do"] The quotations on these two pages are from Alfred J. Ayer, *Language, Truth and Logic* (New York: Oxford University Press, 1936). In a 24 March 1939 letter to Charles W. Morris, Dewey incorrectly referred to Ayer as "Ayres."

294.1–2   Democracy . . . Today] Two paragraphs of tribute to Felix Adler that introduced Dewey's address were omitted for publication.

294.15–16   democracy . . . liberty.] In his "Forza e Consenso" ("Force and Consent"), first published in *Gerachia,* March 1923, pp. 801–3, Mussolini states: "The plain truth that must stare into the eyes of anyone not blinded by dogmatism, is that men are perhaps tired by liberty." See Herbert W. Schneider, *Making the Fascist State* (New York: Oxford University Press, 1928), p. 342. In the foreword, Schneider acknowledges his indebtedness to Dewey for his "encouragement, advice and criticism."

294.31–295.1   no man . . . consent] Lincoln's discussion of political democracy can be found in his 16 October 1854 speech at Peoria, Illinois, in reply to Senator Douglas.

300.13–21   evils . . . others.] Jefferson's attitude concerning agriculture and manufacturing is expressed in Query XIX of his *Notes on Virginia,* "The Present State of Manufactures, Commerce, Interior and Exterior Trade?"

300.23–24   those . . . will.] Hamilton states that "*a power over a man's subsistence amounts to a power over his will.*" See his *The Federalist* (Washington, D.C.: National Home Library Foundation, 1938), p. 512, in Dewey's personal library (John Dewey Papers, Special Collections, Morris Library, Southern Illinois University at Carbondale).

305.40   political party] An editorial footnote at this point in *Social Frontier* identified this as "The Communist or official Stalinist party in the United States."

308.2   written.] An editorial footnote at this point in *Social Frontier* explained: "Professor Dewey supported Norman Thomas in the presidential campaigns of 1932 and 1936 as well as in the recent New York gubernatorial contest."

309.1   Society] In an editorial footnote in *Intelligence in the Modern World,* Joseph Ratner indicated that this article was "written specially for this volume." It appeared as part 2 of chapter 6, "The Individual in the New Society."

309.15   former objective] Ratner explained in an editorial footnote in *Intelligence in the Modern World* that "'The former objective' is the subject of Chapter Nine," entitled "International Law and the Security of Nations."

317.17–19   "whether . . . problem"] Although quotation marks appear, this is not a direct quotation from *Journal of Race Development* but a paraphrase.

347.1   In . . . Hearings] This symposium in which Dewey's
                     comments appeared opened with the following
                     headnote: "In the opinion of the Editors this collec-
                     tion of opinions from a group of celebrated writers
                     is a valuable contribution to thought on this basic
                     moral and social problem, and in view of the inclu-
                     sion of comments from two members of the Mexico
                     City Trotsky Commission [Dewey and Benjamin
                     Stolberg], it is of historical significance as well."

347.10–12   two members . . . "partisans"] Benjamin Stolberg
                     and Suzanne La Follette were frequently identified as
                     Trotskyites.

347.12–13   sub-commission of inquiry] The five sub-commis-
                     sion members were Dewey; Benjamin Stolberg, edi-
                     tor of labor and literary journals; Suzanne La Fol-
                     lette, editor of New Freeman; Otto Ruehle, leading
                     German Socialist and biographer of Karl Marx; and
                     Carleton Beals, authority on Latin-American affairs.

347.16   the member] Dewey is referring to Carleton Beals,
                     who, on 17 April 1937, resigned from the sub-
                     commission of inquiry investigating the charges
                     against Leon Trotsky. For information on the Trot-
                     sky inquiry, see Later Works 11:301–36, 598–99,
                     and 636–52.

347.28–29   one member of the Commission] This member was
                     probably Otto Ruehle, who was sometimes referred
                     to as "anti-Bolshevist."

357.6   afternoon] As reported in the Washington Post, 6
                     and 14 November 1938, it was at the request of his
                     friend Evelyn Davis, president of the Washington
                     Dance Association, that Dewey spoke to an audi-
                     ence of two hundred on Sunday afternoon, 13 No-
                     vember 1938.

361.8   first exhibit] The exhibit referred to is the 1913 Ar-
                     mory exhibition in New York City. For Royal Cor-
                     tissoz's discussion of the exhibit, see "A Memorable
                     Exhibition," in his Art and Common Sense (New
                     York: Charles Scribner's Sons, 1913), pp. 139–59.

369.4   Diana of Ephesus] See Acts 19:28.

Checklist of Dewey's References

This section gives full publication information for each work cited by Dewey. Books in Dewey's personal library (John Dewey Papers, Special Collections, Morris Library, Southern Illinois University at Carbondale) have been listed whenever possible. When Dewey gave page numbers for a reference, the edition has been identified by locating the citation; for other references, the edition listed here is his most likely source by reason of place or date of publication, general accessibility during the period, or evidence from correspondence and other materials.

Adrian, Edgar Douglas. "The Nervous System." In *Factors Determining Human Behavior*, vol. 1, Harvard Tercentenary Publications, pp. 3–11. Cambridge: Harvard University Press, 1937.

Angell, Norman. *The Defence of the Empire*. New York: D. Appleton-Century Co., 1937.

Ayer, Alfred J. *Language, Truth and Logic*. New York: Oxford University Press, 1936.

Bacon, Francis. *The New Organon*. In *Translations of the Philosophical Works*, vol. 4 of *The Works of Francis Bacon*, pp. 39–248. London: Longmans and Co., 1875.

Darrow, Karl K. *The Renaissance of Physics*. New York: Macmillan Co., 1936.

Dewey, John. *The Public and Its Problems*. New York: Henry Holt and Co., 1927. [*The Later Works of John Dewey, 1925–1953*, edited by Jo Ann Boydston. Carbondale and Edwardsville: Southern Illinois University Press, 1984, 2:235–372.]

———. "Internal Social Reorganization after the War." *Journal of Race Development* 8 (April 1918): 385–400. [*The Middle Works of John Dewey, 1899–1924*, edited by Jo Ann Boydston. Carbondale and Edwardsville: Southern Illinois University Press, 1982, 11:73–86.]

Hobbes, Thomas. *Leviathan; or, The Matter, Form and Power of a Commonwealth, Ecclesiastical and Civil*. 4th ed. London: George Routledge and Sons, 1894.

Hogben, Lancelot. *Mathematics for the Million*. New York: W. W. Norton and Co., 1937.

Houston, William R. *The Art of Treatment*. New York: Macmillan Co., 1937.

James, William. *The Varieties of Religious Experience: A Study in Human Nature*. New York: Longmans, Green and Co., 1928.

———. "The Moral Equivalent of War." In *Memories and Studies*, pp. 265–96. London: Longmans, Green, and Co., 1911.

Jefferson, Thomas. *Democracy*. Edited by Saul K. Padover. New York and London: D. Appleton-Century Co., 1939.

———. *The Writings of Thomas Jefferson*. Edited by H. A. Washington. Vol. 7. Washington, D.C.: Taylor and Maury, 1854.

Jörgensen, Jörgen. "Imperatives and Logic." *Erkenntnis* 7 (1937–38): 288–96.

Kallen, Horace M. "Value and Existence in Philosophy, Art, and Religion." In *Creative Intelligence: Essays in the Pragmatic Attitude*, pp. 409–67. New York: Henry Holt and Co., 1917.

Keats, John. *The Complete Works of John Keats*. Edited by H. Buxton Forman. Vol. 4. Glasgow: Gowars and Gray, 1901.

Kohler, Wolfgang. *The Place of Value in a World of Facts*. New York: Liveright Publishing Corp., 1938.

Kraft, Viktor. *Die Grundlagen einer wissenschaftlichen Wertlehre*. Vienna: Verlag von Julius Springer, 1937.

Laird, John. *The Idea of Value*. Cambridge: At the University Press, 1929.

Maugham, W. Somerset. *Of Human Bondage*. New York: Grosset and Dunlap, 1915.

———. *The Summing Up*. Garden City, N.Y.: Doubleday, Doran and Co., 1938.

Mead, George H. "Scientific Method and the Moral Sciences." *International Journal of Ethics* 33 (1923): 229–47.

Mill, John Stuart. *A System of Logic, Ratiocinative and Inductive: Being a Connected View of the Principles and Evidence and the Methods of Scientific Investigation*. New York: Harper and Brothers, 1850.

Moore, George Edward. *Principia Ethica*. Cambridge: At the University Press, 1903.

Neurath, Otto. *Empirische Soziologie; der wissenschaftliche Gehalt der Geschichte und Nationalökonomie*. Vienna: Julius Springer, 1931.

Oppenheimer, Franz. *The State: Its History and Development Viewed Sociologically*. Authorized translation by John M. Gitterman. New York: Vanguard Press, 1926.

Pell, Orlie A. H. *Value-Theory and Criticism*. Ph.D. diss., Columbia University, 1930.

Perry, Ralph Barton. *General Theory of Value: Its Meaning and Basic*

Principles Construed in Terms of Interest. New York: Longmans, Green and Co., 1926.

————. "A Theory of Value Defended." *Journal of Philosophy* 28 (1931): 449–60.

————. "Value and Its Moving Appeal." *Philosophical Review* 41 (1932): 337–50.

————. "Value as an Objective Predicate." *Journal of Philosophy* 28 (1931): 447–84.

————. "Value as Simply Value." *Journal of Philosophy* 28 (1931): 519–26.

Plato. *The Republic.* In *The Dialogues of Plato,* translated by Benjamin Jowett, 2:1–452. Boston: Jefferson Press, 1871.

Prall, David Wight. "In Defense of a *Worthless* Theory of Value." *Journal of Philosophy* 20 (1923): 128–37. [*Middle Works* 15:338–48.]

————. "A Study in the Theory of Value." *University of California Publications in Philosophy* 3 (1918–21): 179–290.

Reid, John R. *A Theory of Value.* New York: Charles Scribner's Sons, 1938.

Rodman, Selden. "Trotsky in the Kremlin: An Interview. What the Exiled Bolshevik Leader Might Have Done in Stalin's Place." *Common Sense* 6 (December 1937): 17–21.

Russell, Bertrand. *Philosophical Essays.* New York and London: Longmans, Green, and Co., 1910.

————. *Power: A New Social Analysis.* New York: W. W. Norton and Co., 1938.

Santayana, George. *The Sense of Beauty.* New York: Charles Scribner's Sons, 1896.

Schlick, Moritz. *Fragen der Ethik.* Vienna: Verlag von Julius Springer, 1930. [*Problems of Ethics.* Translated by David Rynin. New York: Prentice-Hall, 1939.]

Soddy, Frederick. *Science and Life.* London: John Murray, 1920.

Strachey, John. *What Are We to Do?* New York: Random House, 1938.

Stuart, Henry Waldgrave. "Valuation as a Logical Process." In *Studies in Logical Theory.* University of Chicago, The Decennial Publications, second series, 11:227–340. Chicago: University of Chicago Press, 1903.

Tennyson, Alfred. *The Poetical Works of Alfred Tennyson.* Boston: Houghton, Osgood and Co., 1880.

Trotsky, Leon. "Their Morals and Ours." *New International* 4 (June 1938): 163–73.

Index

Improvisation: value of, 52
Impulse: and desire, 43, 45–46, 217, 220–21; formation of, 218; in human nature, 140, 141; inhibition of, 41; *inner*, 70; as start of purpose, 42, 43–45; vital, 206, 221, 222, 225. *See also* Desire; Habits
Individual: adapting to the, 27; in democracy, 295; development of, 319; freedom and, 80–81, 85, 102; vs. group, 33–34, 108; Mill on, 138
Individualism, 138; bad name of, 78, 179; laissez-faire, 114, 125, 157, 182; metaphysical, 248; vs. socialism, 114, 146, 260
Individuality: culture affects, 77–78; freedom connected with, 80, 102, 149, 180–81
Indoctrination, 341, 381, 385; definition of, 379–80
Industrialists: rule of, 319
Industry, 147; consequences of, 129, 311; depends on nature, 69; development of, 112, 126; division of labor in, 180; processes of, 113; as product of science, 267–68; social control of, 114
Inherency, 215
Inhibition: externally vs. internally imposed, 41
Initiative, 147
Inquiry, 86, 232, 320; hypotheses in, 263; importance of, 222; in science, 135, 144, 166, 262–63, 285, 371; in valuation, 221, 242–43
Insincerities: frequency of, 97
Instinct, 87, 211, 287–88
Institutions: formation of new, 186; history of, 51; political, 150; reform of, 147; schools as,

5–6; self-governing, 155
Instruction: aims and methods of, xiii, 6; beginning of, 49
Insurance, 313
Intelligence: exercise of, 53, 54, 256, 320–21; in experience, 269; freedom of, 39; impulses ordered by, 42, 45; work of, 43, 266–67
Intelligence in the Modern World, 403
Interaction: analytic observation of, 86–87, 91; and continuity, 25–26, 31; effects of, 68, 89–90; of human nature and culture, 79, 86, 117, 142, 184, 246–48, 273; of objective and internal, 24, 137, 325–26; principles of, 25–26, 27, 31, 86, 325–27; problems in, 273; significance of, 115
Interdependence: physical vs. moral, 180
Interests: common and special, 111, 379, 385; conflict of, 100, 101, 115, 124–25, 133; in contexts, 207; of groups, 205–6; objects in, 207; scientific, 165; subject to defeat, 217. *See also* Desire
"Internal Social Reorganization after the War," 315*n*
Intolerance: essence of, 152–53, 277; in Germany and Italy, 301
Intrinsic: meaning of, 327
Intrinsicalness, 216
Intuiting: vs. valuing, 194
Intuitionism, xii
Intuitions: a priori, 256
Inventions: as products of science, 311–12; social effect of, 253
Investigation: of valuations, 245
Irresponsibility, 128, 158

Pagination Keys

Pagination Key to the First Edition of
Experience and Education

Scholarly studies in the past have referred to the 1938 Macmillan Company publication of *Experience and Education*. The list below relates that pagination to the pagination of the present edition. Before the colon appear the 1938 edition page numbers; after the colon appear the corresponding page numbers from the present edition.

v:3	25:17−18	52:30	79:43−44
vi:3−4	26:18	53:31	80:44
vii:4	27:18−19	54:31	81:44−45
1:5	28:19	55:31−32	82:45
2:5−6	29:19−20	56:32	83:45−46
3:6	30:20	57:32−33	84:46
4:6	31:20−21	58:33	85:46−47
5:6−7	32:21	59:33−34	86:48
6:7	33:21−22	60:34	87:48
7:7−8	34:22	61:34−35	88:48−49
8:8	35:22	62:35	89:49
9:8−9	36:22−23	63:35−36	90:49−50
10:9	37:23	64:36	91:50
11:9−10	38:23−24	65:36	92:50−51
12:11	39:24	66:36−37	93:51
13:11	40:24−25	67:37	94:51−52
14:11−12	41:25	68:37−38	95:52
15:12	42:25−26	69:39	96:52−53
16:12−13	43:26	70:39	97:53
17:13	44:26−27	71:39−40	98:53
18:13−14	45:27	72:40	99:53−54
19:14	46:27	73:40−41	100:54
20:14−15	47:27−28	74:41	101:54−55
21:15	48:28	75:41−42	102:55
22:15−16	49:28−29	76:42	103:55−56
23:17	50:29	77:43	104:56
24:17	51:29−30	78:43	105:56−57

106:57	109:58	112:59–60	115:61–62
107:57–58	110:58–59	113:61	116:62
108:58	111:59	114:61	

Pagination Key to the First Edition of *Freedom and Culture*

Scholarly studies in the past have referred to the 1939 G. P. Putnam's Sons publication of *Freedom and Culture*. The list below relates that pagination to the pagination of the present edition. Before the colon appear the 1939 edition page numbers; after the colon appear the corresponding page numbers from the present edition.

3:65	35:87–88	67:110–11	99:133–34
4:65–66	36:88–89	68:111–12	100:134
5:66–67	37:89	69:112–13	101:134–35
6:67	38:89–90	70:113	102:135
7:67–68	39:90–91	71:113–14	103:136
8:68–69	40:91	72:114–15	104:136–37
9:69	41:91–92	73:115	105:137–38
10:69–70	42:92–93	74:116	106:138
11:70–71	43:93–94	75:116–17	107:138–39
12:71–72	44:94	76:117–18	108:139–40
13:72	45:94–95	77:118	109:140
14:72–73	46:95–96	78:118–19	110:140–41
15:73–74	47:96	79:119–20	111:141–42
16:74	48:96–97	80:120	112:142–43
17:74–75	49:97–98	81:120–21	113:143
18:75–76	50:99	82:121–22	114:143–44
19:76	51:99–100	83:122	115:144–45
20:76–77	52:100–101	84:122–23	116:145
21:77–78	53:101	85:123–24	117:145–46
22:78–79	54:101–2	86:124–25	118:146–47
23:79	55:102–3	87:125	119:147
24:80	56:103	88:125–26	120:147–48
25:80–81	57:103–4	89:126–27	121:148–49
26:81–82	58:104–5	90:127	122:149–50
27:82	59:105	91:127–28	123:150
28:82–83	60:105–6	92:128–29	124:150–51
29:83–84	61:106–7	93:129	125:151–52
30:84	62:107–8	94:129–30	126:152
31:84–85	63:108	95:130–31	127:152–53
32:85–86	64:108–9	96:131–32	128:153–54
33:86–87	65:109–10	97:132	129:154
34:87	66:110	98:132–33	130:154–55

131:156	143:164	155:173	167:181–82
132:156–57	144:165	156:173–74	168:182
133:157–58	145:165–66	157:174–75	169:182–83
134:158	146:166–67	158:175	170:183–84
135:158–59	147:167	159:175–76	171:184
136:159–60	148:167–68	160:176–77	172:184–85
137:160	149:168–69	161:177	173:185–86
138:160–61	150:169	162:177–78	174:186
139:161–62	151:169–70	163:178–79	175:186–87
140:162	152:170–71	164:179	176:187–88
141:162–63	153:171	165:179–80	
142:163–64	154:171–72	166:180–81	

Pagination Key to the First Edition of
Theory of Valuation

Scholarly studies in the past have referred to the 1939 University of Chicago publication of *Theory of Valuation*. The list below relates that pagination to the pagination of the present edition. Before the colon appear the 1939 edition page numbers; after the colon appear the corresponding page numbers from the present edition.

1:191–92	18:206–7	35:221–22	52:237–38
2:192	19:207–8	36:222–23	53:238–39
3:192–93	20:208–9	37:223–24	54:239–40
4:193–94	21:209–10	38:224–25	55:240
5:194–95	22:210–11	39:225–26	56:240–41
6:195–96	23:211–12	40:226–27	57:241–42
7:196–97	24:212	41:227–28	58:242–43
8:197–98	25:212–13	42:228–29	59:243–44
9:198–99	26:213–14	43:229–30	60:244–45
10:199–200	27:214–15	44:230–31	61:245–46
11:200–201	28:215–16	45:231	62:246–47
12:201–2	29:216–17	46:231–32	63:247–48
13:202	30:217–18	47:232–33	64:248–49
14:202–3	31:218–19	48:233–34	65:249–50
15:203–4	32:219–20	49:234–35	66:250
16:204–5	33:220–21	50:235–36	67:250–51
17:205–6	34:221	51:236–37